PUBLICATION

NTA UGC NET

Geography (Paper-II)

Latest Edition
Practice Kit

10 Tests
10 Mock Test

Based On Real Exam Pattern

✓ Thoroughly Revised and Updated

✓ Detailed Analysis of all MCQs

Title	: NTA UGC NET Geography (Paper-II)
Author Name	: Mr. Rohit Manglik
Published By	: EduGorilla Community Pvt. Ltd.
Publishers Address	: 12/651, First Floor Opp. Arvindo Park, Near Jama Masjid, Indira Nagar, Lucknow, Uttar Pradesh-226016, India

Copyright EduGorilla

Disclaimer EduGorilla

ROHIT MANGLIK
CEO, EduGorilla

Dear Applicants,

People say *"Success comes to those who work hard."* But I've seen people working hard for their exams day in and day out for marginal success. While others succeed in their examinations by putting in just half the work. So are they God Gifted? No! I believe that it's because they work *smart* and not just *hard*. Similarly, for your exams, you should strategize your preparation so as to increase the likelihood of success. Well with EduGorilla get ready to increase your *chances of selection* in your exam by *16x*.

EduGorilla helps you in not only working *hard* but also working in a *smart and strategic* manner. With EduGorilla's preparation package, you get a chance to make your exam preparation easy, and a fun learning path towards selection. Finding the right path to your preparations can be difficult if you don't know in which direction to head. Don't worry, we have you covered! EduGorilla will be your guide to success in your journey. With our Preparation Package, you can prepare strategically and beat the exam in just one attempt.

EduGorilla's Preparation Package includes-

• **Test Series**   • **Books**

Our preparation package is handcrafted as per the latest changes, expert opinions, and students' discretion. Thus, enabling you to get through each stage of the selection process for your exam.

Our Books are designed by the teachers and experts of the respective exam with a combined 150+ years of experience; to provide you with easy, efficient, and effective learning. Our books are smart, in the sense that not only do they give you the answers to the questions but also provide similar questions for practice.

EduGorilla's competent Test Series gives you real-time experience and confidence through which you can clear your offline or online exam in just one attempt. We currently host 83,000+ mock tests for 1,440+ competitive and academic exams.

Thus, EduGorilla misses no chance to assist you in your preparation and covers all stages of the exam, so that you don't have to look anywhere else.

We provide complete preparation packages for defense, banking, teaching, and other National & State-Level exams. Hence, it doesn't matter which exam you aspire to because you will reach your success.

ALL THE BEST !
Let EduGorilla be your Guide to Success.

Rohit Manglik,
Founder and CEO, EduGorilla

INTRODUCTION

EduGorilla focuses on guiding students to succeed in their examinations. With that in mind, our book, titled "NTA UGC NET : Geography (Paper-II)", has been drafted through the collective efforts of our distinguished experts with 150+ years of combined experience. This book consists of questions that are created following the latest changes in the syllabus and exam pattern. We compiled the book on the basis of questions that are most likely to appear in the UGC NET Geography. Through EduGorilla's "NTA UGC NET : Geography (Paper-II)" your chances of success will increase 16x.

EduGorilla does this through our Complete Preparation Package. This package consists of well-conceptualized and structured content in the form of questions that are tailor-made according to your needs and will help you practice for exams in a smart way by pinpointing all the necessary information. It also provides hints and solutions, along with a smart answer sheet for your self-evaluation. You can assess your shortcomings and work accordingly on areas that may require more of your attention.

EduGorilla promises to help you succeed in your examination and accomplish your dream goals. We believe in our aspirants and see them at the top of the merit list. And the first step towards the top is to start preparing with us. EduGorilla's "NTA UGC NET : Geography (Paper-II)" includes the following attributes.

➤ Well-Researched Content

➤ Top-Notch Quality

➤ Detailed Answers and Analysis

➤ Smart Answer Sheet

➤ Exam Relevant Questions

Therefore, EduGorilla fortifies your preparation and makes it durable enough to help you stand tall and beat the examination.

UGC NET Geography
Scan QR code for Eligibility, Exam Pattern, Syllabus and more.

Book ID: 0210

TABLE OF CONTENTS

Q.1 Consider the following statements-

a) The term plate was first used by the Canadian Geophysicist J. Tuzo Wilson.

b) The process of breaking and bending of the rocks of the entire lithosphere including the crust is known as plate tectonics.

c) There are 5 major plates on the Earth's surface today.

d) The Thermal convection currents are responsible for the movement of plates.

Which of the following statements are correct?

A. a and b **B.** c and d

C. b, c and d **D.** a and d

Q.2 The Peru-Chile Trench has been formed due to

A. Convergence of the plates

B. Divergence of plates

C. Parallel movement of plates

D. Transform faults

Q.3 Consider the following statements-

a) Diastrophism processes include two forces which are epeirogenetic forces and Denudational forces

b) Folding and Faulting is a part of the Epeirogenetic forces.

c) The overthrust limb of the fold is referred to as Nappe.

d) The processes of degradation, aggradation and gradation are closely interlinked.

Which of the following statements are correct?

A. a and b **B.** b and d

C. a, b and c **D.** c and d

Q.4 Given below are two statements- one is labelled as Assertion (A) and the other is labelled as Reason (R):

Assertion(A)- Exogenous processes are responsible for gradation.

Reason(R)- Weathering and erosion is often described as the essential phase in the denudation process of landscapes.

Choose the correct option:

A. Both A and R are true and R is the correct explanation of A

B. Both A and R are true but R is not the correct explanation of A

C. A is true but R is false

D. A is false but R is true.

Q.5 Which of the following statement is correct in the case of weathering?

A. Talus and scree are formed by granular disintegration.

B. Erosion is a mobile process unlike the static process of weathering.

C. Mechanical weathering involves breaking up of the rocks by crystal-growth, pressure release and thermal tension.

D. All of the above

Q.6 Consider the following statements:-

a) L.C . King's theory is based on the arid topography as well as the semi-arid regions of South Africa.

b) He mentioned that the profile of an ideal hillslope must consist of summit, scarp, slope and pediments.

c) According to King, the African landscape consisted of scarps which have steep slopes and varied in angle from 15-30 degree.

d) He also did explain the presence of Yardangs and Zuegen as prime features of the African Landscape.

Which of the following options are correct?

A. a and b **B.** b and d

C. a, b and c **D.** c and d

Q.7 Match List I with List II

List I (Volcanic Landforms)	List II(Examples)
a. Ash or Cinder cones	1. Mayen of Philippines
b. Acid Lava cone	2. Mauna Loa of Hawaiian Island
c. Basic Lava cone	3. Lessen Peak in California
d. Composite cones	4. Cones of Krakatoa

A. a-1 b-2 c-4 d-3 **B.** a-3 b-4 c-2 d-1

C. a-4 b-3 c-2 d-1 **D.** a-2 b-3 c-1 d-4

Q.8 Which of the following is NOT a characteristic of Absteigende Entwickelung or waning rate of development in the geomorphic cycle of Penck?

A. Absence of upliftment

B. Progressive decline of landforms

C. Lateral erosion

D. Vertical erosion

Q.9 Which of the following is an erosional landform?

A. Loess **B.** Coastal Dunes

C. Yardangs **D.** Meanders

Q.10 Read the following statements and select the correct answer using the code given below:

a) The closed folds are formed due to mild compressive action.

b) Joints are fractures, where a significant amount of rocks are displaced.

c) Asymmetrical folds have irregular and unequal limbs.

d) The Isoclinal folds are formed when a compressive force is strong on both sides leading to parallel limbs in a fold.

A. Only (d) is correct

B. (a) and (d) are correct

C. (a), (b) and (c) are correct

D. (b) and (d) are correct

Q.11 Which among the following state of India is best known for Saffron Cultivation?

A. Sikkim **B.** Assam

C. Jammu & Kashmir **D.** Meghalaya

Q.12 For cotton cultivation which among the following soils is considered most suitable?

| A. Red Soil | B. Black Soil |
| C. Laterite Soil | D. Alluvial Soil |

Q.13 Which of the following states is sole producer of agate, chalk, and perlite in India?

| A. Rajasthan | B. Karnataka |
| C. Gujarat | D. Tamil Nadu |

Q.14 Polavaram Project is located in which state?

| A. Madhya Pradesh | B. Gujarat |
| C. Andhra Pradesh | D. Karnataka |

Q.15 Which among the following state produces maximum raw silk in India?

| A. Bihar | B. Assam |
| C. West Bengal | D. Karnataka |

Q.16 Match List-I with List-II

List-I(Date)	List-II(significance)
(a) 21st March	(i) Arrival of Monsoon in India
(b) 1st June	(ii) Winter Solstice
(c) 22nd Dec	(iii) Summer Solstice
(d) 21st June	(iv) Equinox

Code:

A. (a)-(iv),(b)-(i), (c)-(ii), (d)-(iii)
B. (a)-(iii),(b)-(i), (c)-(ii), (d)-(iv)
C. (a)-(iv),(b)-(iii), (c)-(ii), (d)-(i)
D. (a)-(iii),(b)-(iv), (c)-(ii), (d)-(i)

Q.17 Given below are two statements. One is labelled as Assertion (A) and the other is labelled as Reason (R).

Assertion (A): Anti-cyclone leads to violent thunderstorms.

Reason (R): Anti-cyclones have high pressure at its centre.

Select the correct answer from options given below:

A. Both (A) and (R) are true and (R) is the correct explanation of (A)
B. Both (A) and (R) are true, but (R) is not the correct explanation of (A)
C. (A) is true, but (R) is false
D. (A) is false, but (R) is true

Q.18 El Nino originates in

| A. Atlantic Ocean | B. Pacific Ocean |
| C. Arctic Ocean | D. Indian Ocean |

Q.19 Which of the following is a cause of Global warming?

A. Heavy Rainfall
B. Melting of Glaciers
C. Lack of snowfall in Alps
D. Deforestation

Q.20 Consider the following statements and choose which amongst them is true:

i. Sunspots are features on the solar surface which appears as dark spot

ii. Sunspots are huge magnetic storms that occur on sun's surface.

Choose the correct options:

| A. Only (i) | B. Only (ii) |
| C. Both (i) and (ii) | D. Neither (i) nor (ii) |

Q.21 Which types of weather is mainly witnessed in the case of anticyclones?

| A. sunny weather | B. rainy weather |
| C. Moist weather | D. Hot weather |

Q.22 In the quaternary age what was the evidence of climate change?

| A. Glacial spread | B. Smog formation |
| C. Rainfall | D. Drought |

Q.23 Match the following according to Thornthwaite's climatic classification.

List- I (Types)	List – II (Vegetation)
a. A(wet)	i) Forest
b. B(humid)	ii) Steppe
c. C(sub humid)	iii) Rainforest
d. D(semiarid)	iv) Grassland

Choose the correct answer:

A. a –iii b –ii c –i d –iv
B. a –i b –iv c –ii d –iii
C. a –iii b –iv c –ii d –i
D. a –iii b –i c –iv d –ii

Q.24 Consider the following statements-

i. T.C Chamberlin advanced the carbon dioxide theory.

ii. Carbon dioxide and water vapour produces greenhouse effect.

Choose the correct answer:

A. Only (i) is true
B. Only (ii) is true
C. Both (i) and (ii) are true
D. Neither (i) nor (ii) is true

Q.25 Which one of the following instrument is used for determination of degree of stability or instability of an air parcel?

| A. Viscometer | B. Radiosondes |
| C. SONAR | D. pH meter |

Q.26 Read the following passage and answer the question given below:

Ocean currents are generated due to variation of the temperature, density, salinity of water at the ocean surface and the wind. An ocean current is a flow of sizable body of water (like a river) from one region of ocean to another. The equatorial waters are warm and, therefore, in North Atlantic a warm North Equatorial current flow from west coast of Africa towards east coast of South America, under the influence of trade winds. Before reaching the east coast of South America, this warm current is deflected north towards to higher latitudes as Gulf Stream along Western North Atlantic. The warm current ameliorates the temperatures and increases the rainfall along the east coast of North America. Around latitude 40° N, under the influence of zonal westerly wind flow, the comparatively warmer waters of Gulf Stream start drifting eastwards as North Atlantic Drift.

Which of the following is NOT a reason for generation of ocean currents?

A. Temperature
C. Density
B. Rock structure
D. Salinity of water

Q.27 Read the following passage and answer the question given below:

Ocean currents are generated due to variation of the temperature, density, salinity of water at the ocean surface and the wind. An ocean current is a flow of sizable body of water (like a river) from one region of ocean to another. The equatorial waters are warm and, therefore, in North Atlantic a warm North Equatorial current flow from west coast of Africa towards east coast of South America, under the influence of trade winds. Before reaching the east coast of South America, this warm current is deflected north towards to higher latitudes as Gulf Stream along Western North Atlantic. The warm current ameliorates the temperatures and increases the rainfall along the east coast of North America. Around latitude 40^0 N, under the influence of zonal westerly wind flow, the comparatively warmer waters of Gulf Stream start drifting eastwards as North Atlantic Drift.

The North Equatorial current flows from

A. West coast of Africa to east coast of South America
B. East Coast of Africa to west coast of South America
C. West coast of Africa to west coast of South America
D. East Coast of South America to West coast of Africa

Q.28 Read the following passage and answer the question given below:

Ocean currents are generated due to variation of the temperature, density, salinity of water at the ocean surface and the wind. An ocean current is a flow of sizable body of water (like a river) from one region of ocean to another. The equatorial waters are warm and, therefore, in North Atlantic a warm North Equatorial current flow from west coast of Africa towards east coast of South America, under the influence of trade winds. Before reaching the east coast of South America, this warm current is deflected north towards to higher latitudes as Gulf Stream along Western North Atlantic. The warm current ameliorates the temperatures and increases the rainfall along the east coast of North America. Around latitude 40^0 N, under the influence of zonal westerly wind flow, the comparatively warmer waters of Gulf Stream start drifting eastwards as North Atlantic Drift.

Near 40^0 N latitude, the Gulf stream is called as

A. Peru Current
C. Norwegian Current
B. Labrador Current
D. North Atlantic Drift

Q.29 Direction: Read the following passage and answer the question given below:

Ocean currents are generated due to variation in the temperature, density, salinity of the water at the ocean surface and the wind. An ocean current is a flow of a sizable body of water (like a river) from one region of the ocean to another. The equatorial waters are warm and, therefore, in North Atlantic a warm North Equatorial current flow from the west coast of Africa towards the east coast of South America, under the influence of trade winds. Before reaching the east coast of South America, this warm current is deflected north towards higher latitudes as Gulf Stream along Western North Atlantic. The warm current ameliorates the temperatures and increases

the rainfall along the east coast of North America. Around latitude 40^0 N, under the influence of zonal westerly wind flow, the comparatively warmer waters of the Gulf Stream start drifting eastwards as North Atlantic Drift.

Which of the following is a warm ocean current?

A. North Equatorial Current
B. Gulf Stream
C. Peru Current
D. North Atlantic Drift

Q.30 Read the following passage and answer the question given below:

Ocean currents are generated due to variation of the temperature, density, salinity of water at the ocean surface and the wind. An ocean current is a flow of sizable body of water (like a river) from one region of ocean to another. The equatorial waters are warm and, therefore, in North Atlantic a warm North Equatorial current flow from west coast of Africa towards east coast of South America, under the influence of trade winds. Before reaching the east coast of South America, this warm current is deflected north towards to higher latitudes as Gulf Stream along Western North Atlantic. The warm current ameliorates the temperatures and increases the rainfall along the east coast of North America. Around latitude 40^0 N, under the influence of zonal westerly wind flow, the comparatively warmer waters of Gulf Stream start drifting eastwards as North Atlantic Drift.

The Gulf Stream drift westwards in 40^0 North latitude due to

A. Zonal Westerly winds
B. Trade winds
C. Polar easterly winds
D. Brick fielder winds

Q.31 In the UN's sustainable development goals are intended to be achieved by the year
A. 2020 **B.** 2022 **C.** 2025 **D.** 2030

Q.32 Match the List - I with List - II and select the correct answer from the code given below:

List - I(Process)	List - II(Outcome)
a. Decomposition	(i) CO_2
b. Transpiration	(ii) O_2
c. Respiration	(iii) CH_4
d. Photosynthesis	(iv) Water vapour

A. a-(i) b-(iv) c-(ii) d-(iii)
B. a-(iv) b-(iii) c-(i) d-(ii)
C. a-(iii) b-(iv) c-(i) d-(ii)
D. a-(iii) b-(iv) c-(ii) d-(i)

Q.33 When was National environment planning and coordination (NEPC) established?
A. 1972 **B.** 1973 **C.** 1974 **D.** 1975

Q.34 Consider the following statements about Ocean acidification :

i. Ocean acidification is occurred due to climate change.

ii. Sea water absorbs 30% to 40% of carbon dioxide.

iii. The chemical gets absorbed in water making its composition acidic.

Choose the correct options:

A. Only (i) **B.** Only (ii)
C. (i) and (iii) **D.** All of the above

Q.35 Given below are the two statements, one labelled as Assertion (A) and the other labelled as Reason (R). Select your answer from the code given below:

Assertion (A)- All living things have intrinsic value.

Reason (R) - Diversity of life forms contribute to the realization of these values .

A. Both A and R are true, and R correctly explains A
B. Both A and R are true but R does not explains A
C. A is true and R is false.
D. Both A and R are false

Q.36 According to the Central Place Theory, the Transport Principle can express as

A. K=2 **B.** K=4 **C.** K=7 **D.** K=3

Q.37 Read the following statements and select the correct answer from the code given below:

(a) The satellite towns are a part of the main city's municipal corporation.

(b) The satellite towns develop beyond city's green belt.

(c) The satellite towns are totally dependent upon the main city area.

(d) The satellite towns are separated from the main city physically by a geographical barrier like river.

Code:

A. Only (a) is true
B. (a) and (c) are true
C. (b) and (d) are true
D. (a), (b) and (d) are true

Q.38 Read the following statements and select the correct answer from the code given below:

a) The land in the rural urban fringe is cheaper than the land in the central city.

b) Urbanization at a rapid rate takes place in the rural urban fringe as compared to the city.

c) The traffic in the rural urban fringe is high and dense in comparison to the central city.

d) There is ample space for development in the rural urban fringe.

Code:

A. Only (a) is true
B. (a), (b) and (c) are true
C. (a) and (c) are true
D. (a) and (d) are true

Q.39 Match the List I with List II

List I (Name of settlement)		List II (Image)
(a) Star-shaped pattern	(i)	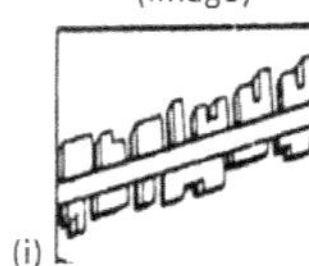
(b) Circular pattern	(ii)	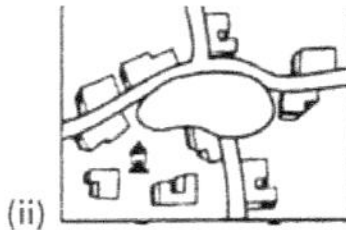
(c) Linear pattern	(iii)	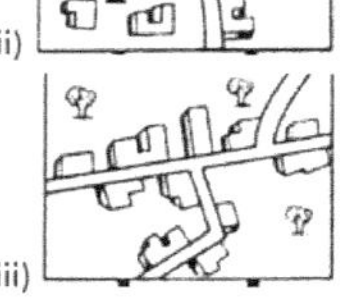
(d) T-shaped pattern	(iv)	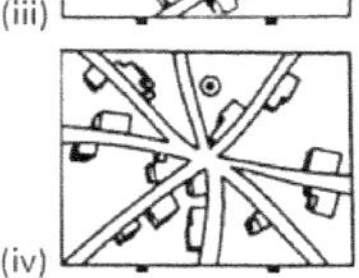

Code:

A. (a)-(iii), (b)-(ii), (c)-(iv),d-(i)
B. (a)-(i),b-(iii),(c)-(iv),(d)-(ii)
C. (a)-(iv),b-(ii),(c)-(i),(d)-(iii)
D. (a)-(ii),b-(ii),(c)-(iv),(d)-(iii)

Q.40 Match the List-I with List-II

List-I State	List-II Sex ratio
(a) Maharashtra	(i) 879
(b) Haryana	(ii) 918
(c) Uttar Pradesh	(iii) 929
(d) Bihar	(iv) 912

Choose the correct option:

A. (a)-(iii), (b)-(i), c-(iv), d-(ii)
B. (a)-(iii), (b)-(iv), c-(i), d-(ii)
C. (a)-(iv), (b)-(iii), c-(ii), d-(i)
D. (a)-(iv), (b)-(ii), c-(i), d-(iii)

Q.41 Given below are two statements. One is labelled as Assertion (A) and the other is labelled as Reason (R).

Assertion (A): World Trade Organization has taken steps to fight climate change.

Reason (R) : The lack of clean technology in underdeveloped nations is a major hindrance in fight against climate change.

Select the correct answer from options given below:

A. Both (A) and (R) are true and (R) is the correct explanation of (A)
B. Both (A) and (R) are true, but (R) is not the correct explanation of (A)
C. (A) is true, but (R) is false
D. (A) is false, but (R) is true

Q.42 The model that is associated with the statement 'The attraction between two objects is proportional to their mass and inversely proportional to their respective distance' is

A. Spatial analysis model
B. Urban Mobility model
C. Industrial location model
D. Gravity Model

Q.43 Calculate the Beta index of the following figure

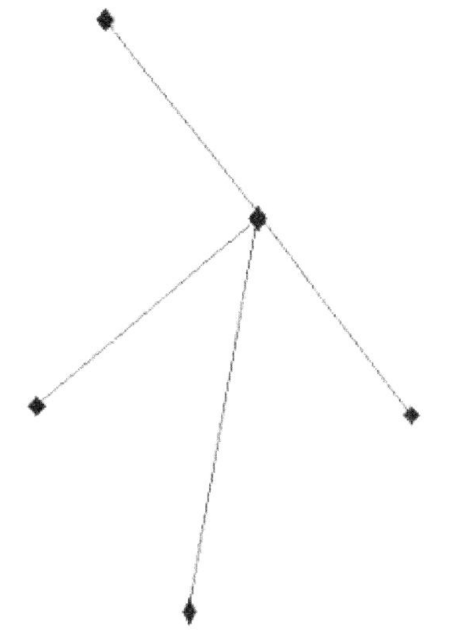

A. 0.8 **B.** 0.9 **C.** 0.3 **D.** 0.5

Q.44 Match the List - I with List - II and select the correct answer from the code given below :

List - I	List – II
(Activity)	(Type of economic activity)
(a) Mining	(i) Tertiary
(b) Tourism	(ii) Primary
(c) Metal factory	(iii) Quaternary
(d) Business Consultancy	(iv) Secondary

A. (a)- (ii) ,(b)- (i) ,(c)- (iv) ,(d)- (iii)
B. (a)- (iv) ,(b)- (iii) ,(c)- (i) ,(d)- (ii)
C. (a)- (i) ,(b)- (ii) ,(c)- (iv) ,(d)- (iii)
D. (a)- (ii) ,(b)- (iii) ,(c)- (i) ,(d)- (iv)

Q.45 'The structure of movement and household travel behavior' was given by

A. Edward Ullman **B.** Alfred Weber
C. Kevin Lynch **D.** M.E . Hurst

Q.46 Which country holds the top position in the ICT Development Index (IDI) ranking?

A. Switzerland
B. Iceland
C. United States of America
D. United Kingdom

Q.47 The following model of industrial location was given by

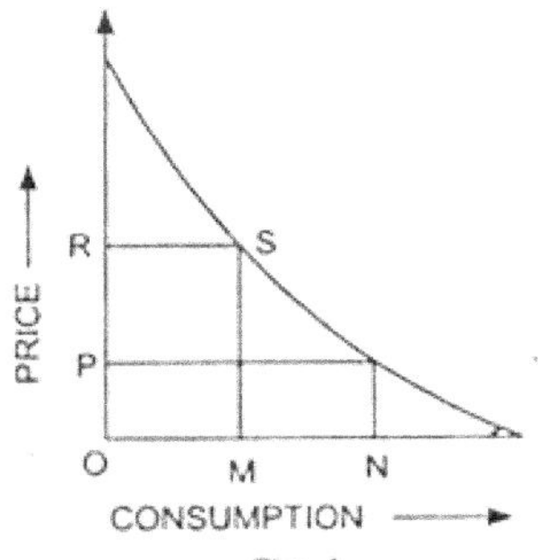

A. August Losch **B.** Alfred Weber
C. Allen Pred **D.** D . M. Smith

Q.48 Which of the following statements are true about Von Thunen's model of regional land use?

(a) Raw materials are available at one fixed point.

(b) There is perfect competitive pricing

(c) The demand for the product is not constant.

(d) Transport rated may vary according to climatic and socio-economic conditions.

A. Only (a) is true **B.** (a) and (c) are true
C. (a) and (b) are true **D.** Only (d) is true

Q.49 Who gave a behavioral matrix for industrial location?

A. Alfred Weber **B.** Allen Pred
C. Tord Pallander **D.** Augsut Losch

Q.50 Which of the following statements are true about Von Thunen's model of regional land use?

(a) It is assumed that the land near the market is flat and has uniform fertility.

(b) Livestock farming is done in areas nearest to the marketplace.

(c) There are multiple markets available for sale of local produce.

(d) The cost of the land increases as its distance from the marketplace increases.

Code:

A. (a) and (b) are true.
B. (a), (b), and (d) are true
C. Only (a) is true.
D. Only (d) is true.

Q.51 The ratio of agricultural inputs to agricultural outputs is the measurement for _______.

A. Agricultural intensity
B. Agricultural productivity
C. Cropping intensity
D. Agricultural ratio

Q.52 The formula for crop combination mentioned below was given by

$$D = \frac{\Sigma D^2 p - D^2 n}{N^2}$$

A. Rafiullah **B.** Doi

C. Weaver   **D.** Von Thunen

Q.53 Which of the following statements are true about John Friedmann's Matter of the Centre Vs. Periphery?

(a) The theory is similar to Growth Pole Theory by Francis Perroux.

(b) Development poles are urban centers with many economic activities which are diversified in nature.

(c) The central town is the supplier of commodities for consumption.

(d) The central district provides raw material to the peripheral towns.

Select the correct answer from the codes given below:

A. (a) ,(b) and (c)   **B.** (a) and (b)
C. (a) and (c)   **D.** Only (d)

Q.54 Given below are two statements. One is labelled as Assertion (A) and the other is labelled as Reason (R):

Assertion (A): Investment in SOC increases investment in Direct Productive Activities, providing cheap energy and power supply.

Reason (R) : Albert Hirschmann suggests investment in Social Overhead Capital(SOC).

Select the correct answer from options given below:

A. Both (A) and (R) are true and (R) is the correct explanation of (A)
B. Both (A) and (R) are true, but (R) is not the correct explanation of (A)
C. (A) is true, but (R) is false
D. (A) is false, but (R) is true

Q.55 Which one of the following in the correct sequence of economic integration between countries?

A. Preferential Trade Area- Customs Union-Free trade- Economic Union
B. Economic Union- Free Trade Area- Customs Union- Preferential Trade Area
C. Preferential Trade Area- Free Trade Area- Customs Union- Economic Union
D. Customs Union-Free Trade Rae- Preferential Trade Area

Q.56 Whose work is "the study of social geography"?

A. George Wilson Hoke
B. Marcel Mauss
C. Patrik Geddes
D. Carl Ritte

Q.57 According to the Global Climate Risk Index of 2020 India is at which place ?

A. 3rd   **B.** 5th   **C.** 10th   **D.** 15th

Q.58 Who called his real-world theory, the functional theory of mineral resources?

A. Zimmerman   **B.** Philips
C. Veranius   **D.** Carl OSauer

Q.59 The statistical methods for the study of distribution and pattern of settlement is known as:

A. Settlement

B. Quantitative method
C. Nearest neighbor analysis
D. None of these

Q.60 Who is known as the father of cultural geography?

A. Carl O Sauer   **B.** Strabo
C. Ptolemy   **D.** Semple

Q.61 Consider the following statements about Demangeon:

i. Demangeon was the pupil of Vidal de la Blache

ii. "La Picardie et les regions veisines" is his monograph

ii. He wrote L'Lomme el la Terre

iv. He was of the view that man destroyed natural flora and fauna.

Choose the correct option from below.

A. Only (i)   **B.** (i), (ii) and (iii)
C. (i) and (ii)   **D.** (i), (ii), (iii) and (iv)

Q.62 Given below are two statements. One is labelled as Assertion (A) and the other is labelled as Reason (R).

Assertion- Richard Hartshorne attempts to capture difference between systematic geography and regional geography.

Reasoning- Regional geography is study of any two-dimensional area of interest.

Select the correct answer from options given below :

A. Both A and R are true, and R correctly explains A
B. Both A and R are true, but R does not explain A
C. A is true and R is false.
D. Both A and R are false

Q.63 Match the list one with list two.

List-I (Geographer)	List-II (works)
a. Homer	i) Syntaxis
b. Ptolemy	ii) odyssey
c. Al Masudi	iii) Qi Sheng
d. Yu Qin	iv) Kitab-Muraj-al-Dhahab

Choose the correct option from below :

A. a-iii b-ii c-i d-iv   **B.** a-ii b-i c-iv d-iii
C. a-i b-ii c-iii d-iv   **D.** a-iii b-i c-iv d-ii

Q.64 Given below are two statements. One is labelled as Assertion (A) and the other is labelled as Reason (R).

Assertion(A)- Aerial differentiation is about the unique regions reveal the co variance of a phenomena that can be understood through identifying regions.

Reasoning(R)- The surface of earth may be divided into regions.

Select the correct answer from options given below:

A. Both A and R are true, and R correctly explains A
B. Both A and R are true, but R does not explain A
C. A is true and R is false.
D. Both A and R are false

Q.65 Match List-I with List-II and select the correct answer from the codes given below :

List-I	List-II
a. Buffon	i) Rivers formed vallies
b. Leonardo da Vinci	ii) Rivers lead erosion

| c. Targioni Tozetti | iii) Food plains |
| d. Guttenberg | iv) Irregular course of river |

Choose the correct option from below:

A. a-iii b-ii c-i d-iv **B.** a-ii b-i c-iv d-iii
C. a-iii b-iv c-ii d-i **D.** a-iii b-i c-iv d-ii

Q.66 Who questioned the philosophy of exceptionalism?

A. Schaefer **B.** Hettener **C.** Ritter **D.** Humbolt

Q.67 Which of the following philosophy is also called hypothetic deductive explanation:-

A. Possibilism **B.** Positivism
C. Behaviouralism **D.** Structuralism

Q.68 Given below are two statements. One is labelled as Assertion (A) and the other is labelled as Reason (R).

Assertion(A)- According to Anthony Giddens human agency and social structure are not two separate concepts.

Reason(R)- Structure is a continuous process which is carried out in a flow.

Select the correct answer from options given below:

A. Both A and R are true, and R correctly explains A
B. Both A and R are true, but R does not explain A
C. A is true and R is false.
D. Both A and R are false

Q.69 Given below are two statements. One is labelled as Assertion (A) and the other is labelled as Reason (R).

Assertion: Humanism in geography developed for the understanding of man environment relationship.

Reasoning: Humanistic geography focuses on products of human activity.

Select the correct answer from options given below:

A. Both A and R are true, and R correctly explains A
B. Both A and R are true, but R does not explain A
C. A is true and R is false.
D. Both A and R are false

Q.70 Match the list one with list two.

List-I(Works)	List-II (Geographers)
a. Planning atlas of Andhra Pradesh	i) A Ramesh
b. Resource atlas of Tamil Nadu	ii) SM Alam
c. Planning Atlas of Uttar Pradesh	iii) BK Roy
d. Census atlas of India	iv) LR Singh

Choose the correct option from below:

A. a-iii b-ii c-i d-iv **B.** a-ii b-i c-iv d-iii
C. a-i b-ii c-iii d-iv **D.** a-iii b-i c-iv d-ii

Q.71 Match List I with List II:-

List I (Maps)	List II (Examples)
a. Cartogram	i. Settlement maps
b. Choropleth	ii. Political Maps
c. Qualitative Dot	iii. World Distribution Maps
d. Choroschematic	iv. Population Density Maps

A. a - i b – ii c - iv d - iii
B. a - iv b – iii c - ii d - i
C. a - iii b – iv c - i d - ii

D. a - ii b – iii c - i d - iv

Q.72 Consider the following statements:

a. Flow maps tell us what is flowing or being migrated

b. It tells us about the direction of the movement

c. Flow maps give a general information about what is flowing and how it is flowing

d. Flow maps also tell us about the speed at which the flow occurs.

Which of the above statements are correct?

A. a and c **B.** b and d
C. a, b, and c **D.** All of the above

Q.73 Atlas and wall maps fall under which category of maps?

A. Large-scale maps **B.** Cartograms
C. Medium scale maps **D.** Small scale maps

Q.74 The Photograph that is obtained if the camera's optical axis deviates more than a few degree than vertical and the horizon is visible is known as

A. Vertical Aerial Photograph
B. Convergent Aerial Photograph
C. High Oblique Photograph
D. Narrow angle Photograph

Q.75 Given below are two statements. One is labelled as Assertion (A) and the other is labelled as Reason (R).

Assertion(A) : Unsupervised Classification normally requires only a minimal amount of input from the analyst.

Reason(R) : A priori knowledge of the scene or training sites are required to run this classification.
Select the correct answer from options given below :

A. Both A and R are true and R is the correct explanation of
B. Both A and R are true but R is not the correct explanation of A.
C. A is true but R is false.
D. A is false but R is true.

Q.76 How many satellites in orbit are required for the functioning for the NavIC system and provide accurate real-time positioning service?

A. 7 **B.** 8 **C.** 4 **D.** 3

Q.77 One of the purposes of this sampling technique is to ensure that all sections of the population are adequately represented. Identify the Sampling technique:-

A. Systematic Sampling
B. Stratified Sampling
C. Simple random sampling
D. Multi-Stage Sampling

Q.78 Brahmaputra River when it flows out of India into Bangladesh is called as _______?

A. Bangshi River **B.** Mahananda River
C. Jamuna River **D.** Yamuna River

Q.79 Whose stream ordering technique is most often considered in drainage basin studies?

A. Strahler **B.** Horton

C. Gravelius   **D.** Schumm

Q.80 Consider the following statements about rectangular drainage pattern:

a. Generally results from the presence of joints and fractures

b. The arrangement of the channels is such that the principal tributary streams are parallel and very long.

c. Common in areas with parallel fractures or faults.

d. Characterised by right-angle bends.

Which of the above statements are correct?

A. a and b   **B.** a and d   **C.** b and c   **D.** c and a

Q.81 Which state has the largest tribal population according to the census of 2011?

A. Meghalaya   **B.** Maharashtra

C. Madhya Pradesh   **D.** Mizoram

Q.82 Given below are two statements. One is labelled as Assertion (A) and the other is labelled as Reason (R).

Assertion (A): The River Ganga has a deep but narrow channel at Rishikesh.

Reason (R) : Lateral cutting occurs at the youthful stage in rivers.

Select the correct answer from options given below:

A. Both (A) and (R) are true and (R) is the correct explanation of (A)

B. Both (A) and (R) are true, but (R) is not the correct explanation of (A)

C. (A) is true, but (R) is false

D. (A) is false, but (R) is true

Q.83 When was the Integrated Rural Development Programme launched?

A. 1950   **B.** 1991   **C.** 1980   **D.** 1978

Q.84 Which of the following statements are true? Choose your answer from the code given below:

(a) The industrial region of Mumbai-Pune flourished due to the development of cotton textile industry.

(b) The Kollam-Thiruvanathapuram industrial region has agricultural processing and market-oriented light industries.

(c) Chotanagpur industrial region is called Ruhr of India.

(d) The Gurgaon-Delhi-Meerut industrial region is famous from heavy industries.

A. (a), (b) and (c) are true.

B. (a) and (b) are true

C. Only (d) is true

D. Only (a) is true

Q.85 The classical theory of Indian Monsoon was explained by

A. John Flohn   **B.** Edmund Halley

C. Frost   **D.** Thompson

Q.86 The intersection of high and low pressure over the Pacific and the Indian Ocean is called as

A. El Nino Effect

B. La Nina Effect

C. Southern Oscillation

D. Walker Circulation

Q.87 Given below are two statements. One is labelled as Assertion (A) and the other is labelled as Reason (R).

Assertion (A): The hilly topography of Jammu and Kashmir is most favorable for development of ground water resources.

Reason (R) : Groundwater level is falling rapidly all over the country.

Select the correct answer from options given below:

A. Both (A) and (R) are true and (R) is the correct explanation of (A)

B. Both (A) and (R) are true, but (R) is not the correct explanation of (A)

C. (A) is true, but (R) is false

D. (A) is false, but (R) is true

Q.88 Which Union Territory has the highest sex ratio in India as per census of 2011?

A. Lakshadweep

B. Puducherry

C. Andaman and Nicobar

D. Daman and Diu

Q.89 India is the leading producer of which of the following crop?

A. Rice   **B.** Wheat

C. Sesamum   **D.** Cotton

Q.90 Given below are two statements- one is labelled as Assertion (A) and the other is labelled as Reason (R):

Assertion:- The Himalayas are still rising, and the process of uplift has not yet completed.

Reason:- The Himalayas are tectonic mountains and the rivers are torrential.

Choose the correct option:

A. Both A and R are true, and R is the correct explanation of A

B. Both A and R are true, but R is not the correct explanation of A

C. A is true, but R is false

D. A is false, but R is true

Q.91 Consider the following statements about the Lateritic soils:

1) It is of little use in crop production

2) It is highly retentive of moisture

3) It cover an area of about 2.48 lakh sq. km.

4) It is rich in potash and lime.

Which of the following options are correct?

A. 1 and 4   **B.** 1 and 3

C. 2 and 4   **D.** 1, 2, and 3

Q.92 The major geographical factor for which the Great plain of North India is an area of intensive agriculture.

A. Relief   **B.** Soil

C. Rainfall   **D.** Temperature

Q.93 Which of the following is a major reason for the rising development of the cotton textile industry of Mumbai?

A. Humid Climate

B. Skilled Labour

C. Cheap Land price

D. Cheap Cost of living

Q.94 Consider the following statement about Pradhan Mantri Awas Yojana (Urban):

a) It was launched on 25th June 2015.

b) It aims to provide housing for all in urban areas by year 2024.

c) It has mandatory provision for the female head of the family to be the owner or co-owner of the house under this Mission.

Choose the correct options:

A. only b   **B.** a and c

C. only c   **D.** a, b and c

Q.95 Which zone is referred to as the Zone of Comparative intensity depending on the intensity and frequency of earthquakes?

A. The Indo-Gangetic Zone

B. The Peninsular Zone

C. The Himalayan Zone

D. None of the above

Q.96 Which of the following are the main Objectives of the Agro-climatic zones?

a) To optimise agricultural production

b) To increase farm income

c) To generate more employment

Choose the correct option:

A. Only a   **B.** b and c

C. a and c   **D.** a, b and c

Q.97 Which of the following factors are required for the cultivation of wheat?

A. Sandy soil with poor drainage

B. Grown in areas more than 150 cm of rainfall.

C. Mean monthly temperature of 30-35 degree Celsius.

D. Cool climate with moderate rainfall.

Q.98 Which period in demographic history of India is known as the 'demographic divide'?

A. Period of rapid growth rate

B. Period of declining growth rate

C. Period of steady growth rate

D. Period of stagnant growth rate

Q.99 Match List I with List II

List I (Health Indicators)	List II (Definition)
a. Infant mortality rate	1. number of children born to a woman during her reproductive age
b. Life expectancy at birth	2. Simplest measure of mortality
c. Crude death rate	3. Number of years a person would live
d. Total fertility rate	4. used for indicating mortality among children

A. a-4 b-3 c-2 d-1   **B.** a-4 b-2 c-3 d-1

C. a-1 b-3 c-4 d-2   **D.** a-3 b-2 c-4 d-1

Q.100 Which of the following is NOT a component of Green Revolution? Choose your answer from the code given below:

a) Guaranteed employment

b) High Yielding Variety(HYI) of seeds

c) Rural electrification

d) No Poverty

e) Agricultural Universities

f) Land Reforms

A. (a) and (b)   **B.** (d) and (e)

C. (a) and (d)   **D.** (a),(b) and (f)

// Smart Answer Sheet //

Correct   Percentage of students who answered correctly.   **Skipped**   Percentage of students who skipped.

Q.	Ans.	Correct / Skipped	Q.	Ans.	Correct / Skipped	Q.	Ans.	Correct / Skipped	Q.	Ans.	Correct / Skipped	Q.	Ans.	Correct / Skipped
1	D	49.19 % / 8.69 %	17	D	31.37 % / 24.45 %	33	A	41.97 % / 9.87 %	49	B	30.34 % / 24.15 %	65	B	21.8 % / 24.74 %
2	A	43.89 % / 19.44 %	18	B	59.35 % / 22.54 %	34	D	37.7 % / 22.68 %	50	C	16.05 % / 20.33 %	66	A	44.04 % / 19.73 %
3	D	26.22 % / 15.16 %	19	D	70.1 % / 6.19 %	35	A	53.76 % / 16.49 %	51	B	52.28 % / 14.14 %	67	B	26.66 % / 23.56 %
4	A	35.05 % / 24.3 %	20	C	49.04 % / 13.26 %	36	B	52.72 % / 16.79 %	52	A	35.94 % / 13.84 %	68	A	31.52 % / 24.0 %
5	D	51.55 % / 23.56 %	21	A	38.73 % / 12.96 %	37	C	16.49 % / 24.01 %	53	A	42.27 % / 23.86 %	69	B	19.88 % / 23.71 %
6	C	43.0 % / 19.15 %	22	A	53.61 % / 22.68 %	38	D	35.49 % / 20.47 %	54	A	27.98 % / 19.88 %	70	B	23.71 % / 24.01 %
7	C	24.89 % / 22.97 %	23	D	46.39 % / 7.51 %	39	C	61.86 % / 24.0 %	55	C	28.28 % / 17.08 %	71	C	46.69 % / 8.1 %
8	D	18.56 % / 22.38 %	24	C	39.18 % / 23.56 %	40	A	46.54 % / 23.12 %	56	A	20.03 % / 24.3 %	72	C	27.69 % / 13.99 %
9	C	42.27 % / 22.83 %	25	B	33.14 % / 23.12 %	41	B	24.89 % / 11.93 %	57	B	31.37 % / 24.01 %	73	D	36.97 % / 24.89 %
10	D	12.81 % / 20.18 %	26	B	61.12 % / 22.68 %	42	D	44.77 % / 23.12 %	58	A	54.79 % / 19.29 %	74	C	33.73 % / 21.35 %
11	C	63.48 % / 16.64 %	27	A	63.18 % / 10.6 %	43	A	36.23 % / 15.02 %	59	C	47.42 % / 17.53 %	75	C	11.34 % / 23.12 %
12	B	69.37 % / 22.09 %	28	D	50.66 % / 24.75 %	44	A	54.34 % / 23.57 %	60	A	68.63 % / 14.29 %	76	A	26.22 % / 18.11 %
13	C	18.7 % / 13.11 %	29	A	41.38 % / 13.26 %	45	D	19.0 % / 12.81 %	61	C	11.34 % / 24.3 %	77	B	29.16 % / 24.74 %
14	C	42.56 % / 22.83 %	30	A	54.93 % / 19.15 %	46	B	15.02 % / 23.27 %	62	A	20.77 % / 21.06 %	78	C	51.99 % / 21.94 %
15	D	37.7 % / 17.09 %	31	D	56.26 % / 16.94 %	47	A	36.82 % / 17.08 %	63	B	67.16 % / 17.67 %	79	A	46.54 % / 10.16 %
16	A	47.13 % / 16.2 %	32	C	33.14 % / 16.2 %	48	C	20.77 % / 23.56 %	64	B	29.46 % / 23.56 %	80	B	37.85 % / 15.61 %

Q.	Ans.	Correct		Q.	Ans.	Correct		Q.	Ans.	Correct		Q.	Ans.	Correct		Q.	Ans.	Correct
		Skipped				Skipped				Skipped				Skipped				Skipped
81	C	43.89 %		85	B	35.05 %		89	C	15.46 %		93	A	65.54 %		97	D	38.59 %
		12.52 %				24.89 %				23.72 %				12.96 %				24.74 %
82	C	25.48 %		86	C	30.19 %		90	A	33.28 %		94	B	20.77 %		98	D	14.14 %
		19.44 %				22.39 %				23.72 %				24.44 %				22.97 %
83	D	25.18 %		87	D	30.93 %		91	B	17.97 %		95	A	18.56 %		99	A	62.44 %
		23.57 %				23.56 %				23.71 %				18.11 %				17.38 %
84	A	55.26 %		88	B	35.05 %		92	A	17.97 %		96	D	48.9 %		100	C	45.66 %
		19.29 %				23.57 %				23.27 %				18.55 %				16.64 %

//Hints and Solutions//

1. The term plate was first used by the Canadian geophysicist J. Tuzo Wilson in 1965. Plates are broad rigid segments of lithosphere including the rigid upper part of upper mantle plus oceanic and continental crust that floats on the underlying asthenosphere.

Arthur Holmes suggested that the subcrustal convection currents involved the mechanism of thermal convection currents that acts as a driving force for movement of plates. Hot currents rise and then cool as they reach the surface. This convectional movement moves the crustal plates.

The process of breaking and bending of rocks of the entire lithosphere including the crust is known as tectonic activity. Plate tectonics refers to the whole mechanism of evolution, nature and motion of plates and the resultant processes and reactions.

There are 6 major plates which are 1.African Plate 2.American plate 3.Antarctica plate 4. Australian plate 5. Eurasian plate 6. Pacific plate.

2. The Convergence of plates or convergent boundaries refer to the situation where two plates moving from opposite directions come closer to each other. The Peru-Chile trench has been formed due to the convergence of the Nazca Oceanic plate and the South American continental plate. Here subduction of plates is a common thing and is a supporting reason for the formation of trenches.

3. Diastrophism refers to the endogenous forces which have deformed the earth's crust due to forces deep within the earth's crust. These forces work very slowly. So, Diastrophism is of two types which are Epeirogenetic and Orogenetic forces. Denudational forces are exogenous forces. Folding and faulting which occur due to compression and tension respectively are orogenetic forces or horizontal forces.

4. Gradation is nothing but the erosion of a rugged landscape into a level land. The gradation is achieved because of Degradation and Aggradation. Weathering and erosion have the capability to convert hard massive rocks into finer material. Hence for this, Weathering is often known as the first essential phase in the denudation or gradation of landscapes as it prepares the rock materials for transportation, depositional processes as well as provides for the degradation of landscapes.

5. All of the above sentences are correct. Talus and scree are like the by-products of granular disintegration which occur because of the insolation process and these are created because of insolation as well as the different mineral composition of rocks. Erosion, as the term indicates is the removal or transportation of weathered rock material from one place to another. Hence it is a dynamic process unlike weathering. However, Mechanical weathering involves the disintegration and breaking of rocks by frost action, freeze and thaw and pressure release.

6. L.C. King never gave any explanation regarding the presence of Yardangs or Zuegen. King said that the African Landscape consists of three basic elements, such as Rock pediments with a concave slope, scarps with a steep slope and inselbergs which are steep residual hills that vary in size and shape.

7. * Ash or Cinder cones are formed when the volcanic material thrown out of the volcano cools and form small solid pieces known as cinders. The solid particles that are rained down create a circular cone around the crater and a cinder cone is formed. These are also termed as central type of volcanoes. The cones of Krakatoa, Mt. Pele, Mt. Fuji are certain examples.

* The Acid Lava cone is formed by viscous lava and which has a presence of silica. This lava deposits itself near the neck of the crater just after an explosion and later forms a dome by solidification. Lessen Peak of California and Pary-de-dome of France are perfect examples.

* Basic lava cone or shield volcanoes are different from the acid lava cones in terms of material compositions and shape formation. The basaltic lava having low silica content flows out quietly and gives rise to the formation of a shield. A shield shaped volcano forms with a wide base and low slope in course of time. Best example is the Mauna Loa od Hawaiian Island.

* The composite are probably the largest and highest volcanic cones. They are formed by the deposition of lava and ash, layer after layer in a parallel format. Fujiyama, Mayen are the best examples of such cones.

8. Penck's geomorphic model divides the geomorphic process into three stage- Aufsteigende Entwickelung(waxing or accelerated development), Gleichformige Entwickelung(uniform development) and Absteigende Entwickelung(waning or decreasing rate development). The waning rate of development shows lateral erosion, absence of upliftment and decline in landforms. Vertical erosion is observed in the Aufsteigende Entwickelun or waxing rate of development.

Thus, the Correct answer is D.

9. The yardangs is an Aeolian landform. It is formed when rock is eroded forming ridges and furrows alternately in the direction of the wind. Turkistan and Mojave deserts have quite a number of yardangs.

Thus, the Correct answer is C.

10. The closed folds are formed due to intense compressive actions. Joints are fractures where no rock displacement takes place. The limbs of an asymmetrical fold are inclined at different angles and are irregular. The isoclinal folds have limbs parallel to each other, and they are formed when a compressive force is equally strong on both sides.

Thus, the Correct answer is D.

11. Kashmir saffron is a high value, low volume crop and the quality of saffron is among the best in the world particularly because of its rich color and flavour. A small area in the valley, Pampore has the virtual monopoly of saffron cultivation in the country.

Thus, the correct answer is A.

12. For cotton cultivation Black Soil is considered most suitable.

Thus, the correct answer is B.

13. Gujarat is the sole producer of agate, chalk, and perlite and is leading producer of fluorite (concentrate), fireclay, silica sand,

lignite, laterite, petroleum and natural gas and bauxite in the country. State is the sole holder of country's resources of perlite, 66% of fluorite, 28% of diatomite, 18% of bentonite and 12% of wollastonite. [Ministry of Mines]

So, the correct option is C.

14. Andhra Pradesh of Godavari Waters to Krishna Basin. The Project is located in Andhra Pradesh near Polavaram village about 34 KMs.

Thus, the correct answer is C.

15. Karnataka accounted for as much as 60% of the country's raw silk output.

Thus, the correct answer is D.

16.

- 21st March is the day of equinox. The sun is directly above the equator. The equinox also occurs on 23rd September. The day and night last 12 hours each on these days.

- 1st June is the day that is expected arrival of monsoon in India. Though this just expected date, usually monsoon arrives later.

- 22nd Dec is winter solstice. This is supposed to be the longest night. On this day, the sun is overhead at the tropic of Capricorn.

- 21st June the day of longest summer solstice. The sun is overhead the tropic of cancer on the day of summer solstice.

Thus, the correct answer is A.

17. Anti-cyclones are circular patterns of air movement. It has a high-pressure cell at its centre. Anti-cyclones are generally associated with calm weather. They show persistent and yield dry air. Cyclones are generally accompanied with violent thunderstorms. Thus, (A) is false and (R) is true.

Thus, the correct answer is D.

18. El Nino means Little Boy. It refers to warm ocean current which originates in the central and east-central Pacific, including area of pacific coast of South America. The phenomenon has effects on global climate.

Thus, the correct answer is B.

19. Global warming refers to increase in average temperature of the earth. Melting of glaciers and lack of snowfall are effects of global warming. Deforestation on the other hand leads to increase in carbon dioxide and ultimately to global warming.

Thus, the correct answer is D.

20. Sunspots are the most conspicuous feature on the solar surface which appears as dark spots. The sunspots are simply the huge magnetic storms that occur on the sun's surface. The number of sunspots increases and decreases in a cyclic manner.

Thus, the Correct answer is C.

21. The convergence of air towards the centre accompanied by lift of air and adiabatic cooling which produces cloudiness and precipitation in cyclone and on the other hand much fair and sunny weather is associated with travelling anticyclones in which the air tends to subside and spread outward, causing adiabatic warning, a progress that is unfavourable to the development of clouds and precipitation.

Thus, the Correct answer is A .

22. The quaternary or Pleistocene ice age witness the advance of huge glaciers or ice sheets from different centers. In north America, great glaciers spread out from the centers near the Hudson Bay which buried all set of eastern Canada, New England and much of middle west.

Thus, the Correct answer is A.

23. Thornthwaite's classification is based on precipitation effectiveness and thermal efficiency. Under this classification climatic types were subdivided using a term to denote the seasonal distribution of precipitation, the climatic types and characteristics of natural vegetation, soil and drainage pattern. Here,

A(wet) humidity province has rainforest.

B(humid) humidity province has Forest

C(sub humid) humidity province has grassland

D(semiarid) humidity province has steppe,

Thus, the Correct answer is D .

24. The carbon dioxide theory was advanced by T.C Chamberlin in the last decade of 19th century. According to this theory variations in the carbon dioxide content of the atmosphere play dominant role in causing worldwide climate change. Carbon dioxide and water vapour content of the atmosphere being the most important heat absorbers produce what is called greenhouse effect.

Thus, the Correct answer is C.

25. Radiosondes are balloons which fly at different levels to sense different weather phenomena, like stability and unstability of weather. Thus, radiosondes with help of radio waves measure the various weather formations.

Thus, the Correct answer is B.

26. As given in the passage above, temperature, density, salinity of water at the ocean's surface and wind are the reason for generation of ocean currents. An ocean current is a large body of water, primarily moving in horizontal direction. Due to the Coriolis Effect, the ocean currents in the Northern Hemisphere turn to right and the ones in the Southern Hemisphere turn to the left. Rock structure does not affect salinity.

Thus, the correct answer is B.

27. The North Equatorial current flows between 10^0 North and 20^0 North. It flows from west coast of Africa to east of South America. Although the current's name is North Equatorial current, it's not connected to the equator. It's a warm current. It is influenced by trade winds.

Thus, the correct answer A.

28. The North equatorial current gets deflected towards north in the higher latitudes and is called Gulf Stream in the area. It increases rainfall along the east coast of North America. As it nears the 40^0 N latitude, it drifts east and is called as North Atlantic Drift.

Thus, the correct answer is D.

29. The North Equatorial current is a warm current. Gulf Stream and North Atlantic Drift are the names for the North Equatorial current in Western North Atlantic and 40^0 North latitude respectively.

Hence, the correct option is (A).

30. The zonal westerly winds are also called prevailing winds or anti-trade winds. They flow from west to east direction in 30-60 degrees latitude. The zonal westerly winds in the northern hemisphere cause the warm Gulf Stream to drift westwards, where it is called as North Atlantic Drift.

Thus, the correct answer is A.

31. The sustainable development goals are set of 17 goals designed to achieve the measure and problems of society and the way to sustainable deal with the same. This was set in 2015 by the United Nation general assembly and intended to be achieved by the year 2030.

Thus, the Correct answer is D .

32. iii. Decomposition releases CH_4 or methane.
iv. Transpiration releases Water vapour.
i. Respiration releases CO_2 or carbon dioxide
ii. Photosynthesis releases O_2 or oxygen.

Thus, the Correct answer is C.

33. In February 1972, National environment planning and coordination (NEPC) was established. This was the body that looked after all the environmental issues, plans, and polities. It was established in the Department of Science and technology.

Hence, the correct option is (A).

34. Ocean acidification is the decrease in the level of pH of the ocean water, caused by the mixing of carbon dioxide. Ocean water absorbs a good amount of carbon dioxide making it acidic in nature and changing the chemical composition of the ocean water. This change in composition is called ocean acidification.

Thus, the Correct answer is D.

35. Deep ecology is an environmental philosophy promoting the worth of human beings. It states that the environment is a balance of complex interrelationship where the existence of organism is dependent on the existence of others within ecosystem. Thus, overuse and over utilization and destruction of environment not only disturbs the environment but also the other organisms in the ecosystem.

Thus, the Correct answer is A.

36. Walter Christaller, in his Central Place Theory gave three principles for proper arrangement and hierarchy. The Transport Principle is the scenario that denotes efficient transport network. It involves the connection of all central places in hierarchical order. The transport principle is given by k=4.

Thus, the correct answer is B.

37. The Satellite towns have a working administrative body of their own, generally municipalities. These towns have at least partial social and economic independence, but commute to city for is common. These areas develop beyond city's green belt and have a geographical barrier like river which separated the satellite town as a separate, but somewhat dependent entity from the main city.

Thus, the correct answer is C.

38. The rural urban fringe area that lies on the boundary, just outside the city area. It is where the urban and rural environments mix. The rural urban fringe has characteristics like cheap availability of land, lesser traffic with respect to city and space for development. The area develops due to suburbanization, but the rate of urbanization is clearly higher in the city.

Thus, the correct answer is D.

39. * The star-like pattern is where house are constructed in a pattern resembling a star.

* The house arranged in a circular shape is circular pattern.

* The houses are built along a line such as river, road, etc. in a linear pattern.

* In T-shaped pattern, the houses are built at a tri-junction.

Thus, the correct answer is C.

40. The sex ratio of India, as per the census of India of 2011 is 940 females per thousand males.

* Haryana is the state with lowest sex ratio of 879.

* Maharashtra ranks 22nd in the whole country with sex ratio of 929

* Bihar ranks 25th and has sex ratio of 918

* Uttar Pradesh has sex ratio of 912 and ranks 26th in India.

Thus, the correct answer is A.

41. The underdeveloped and developing countries lack resources and technology for sustainable development. Thus, they prove to be a major block in fighting climate change. The World Trade Organization has taken steps like formulation of Sustainable Development Goals under United Nations Development Program in collaboration with United Nations. Thus, both (A) and (R) are true, but (R) is not the correct explanation of (A).

Thus, the correct answer is B.

42. The gravity model has been named after Newton's Law of gravity. The principle of gravity has been applied to concepts such as migration, traffic flows, boundaries between areas, etc. The gravity model states that the attraction between two objects is proportional directly to their mass and inversely to their respective distance. Indices like alpha, beta and lamda are indices included in formulation of gravity model.

Thus, the correct answer is D.

43. The beta index is the level of connectivity in a given network. The beta index is calculated with the formula,

$\beta = e/v$

where 'e' is no. of edges or links and 'v' is the no of nodes. In the given figure, edges are 4 and nodes are 5. Thus, the beta index is

$4/5 = 0.8$

Thus, the correct answer is A.

44. * The Primary activities are dependent totally on the nature and natural resources. This includes agriculture, mining, quarrying, fishing, etc.

* The secondary economic activities process and produce finished output from the natural resources or raw materials from primary activities. These include factories of different kinds like metal and food processing.

* The tertiary activities are activities that contribute to transport of the goods and services produced by secondary sector. This is service sector which includes activities like transport, tourism, etc.

* Quaternary activities are based on skills of people. It includes knowledge-oriented activities like business consultancy, information technology, media, etc.

Thus, the correct answer is A.

45. M.E. Hurst was an American geographer who focused on transport geography and gave emphasis on behavioral geography. In his paper of the same name, he published the structure of movement and household travel behavior where he took into consideration the factors motivating household travels.

Thus, the correct answer is D.

46. The IDI ranking is published by United Nations International Telecommunications Union. It is an index which is a composite of ICT indicators. It is recognized all over the world. The leading country in this ranking is Iceland with the index value of 8.98 as of 2017. Switzerland, UK and USA hold third, fifth and sixteenth positions.

Thus, the correct answer is B.

47. The model is representation of Profit Maximization Theory given by August Losch. The primary objective of this theory was to decide the best possible location for industries. Losch rejected Weber's mode completely. He was of the opinion that industries would be located at a place where they would get maximum profit rather than the place with least cost.

Thus, the correct answer is A.

48. Alfred Weber's Industrial location theory is also called as least-cost theory. In this theory Weber explains how the industrial location will be based on the transport cost, labour cost and agglomeration cost. The assumptions made by him include things such as 'Raw materials will be taken from a fixed source location' and 'perfect competitive pricing'. But they also include stipulations like the demand and the market will be constant and transport rates will remain same everywhere, but transport cost will vary according to weight and distance.

Thus, the correct answer is C.

49. The behavioral matrix was developed by Allen Pred. He applied this matrix in a lot of different situations including industrial location. It takes into consideration decision-making process while deciding location for industry as would a common man do. It is based on ability to use the information and availability of information.

Thus, the correct answer is B.

50. Johann Heinrich von Thunen gave the agricultural land use model in early 1800s. The model contained four zones of concentric circles depicting land use around the marketplace. The assumptions of the theory are:- (i)There is only one common central market where all the produce is sold. (ii)The land is isolated, flat with uniform fertility and climate. (iii) Everyone has access to transport and farmers behave with economic rationality. The first zone, nearest to marketplace was of dairy farming, followed by forest, grains and field crops and livestock farming and ranching. As we go away from the central market, the cost of land decreases.

Thus, the correct answer is C.

51. The concept of agricultural productivity is not synonymous to fertility. Agricultural productivity can be measured by calculating the ratio of agricultural inputs such as land, labour, capital, etc. to the agricultural output such as produce yielded, measured in calories or monetary value. As per the 23rd Annual Conference of the Indian Society of Agricultural Economics, yield per hectare in a region is considers as a representation of agricultural productivity.

Thus, the correct answer is B.

52. Rafiullah is devised a crop combination method in 1965 in order to improve the crop combination method by Weaver. He D is represents D deviation, D_p is positive difference and D_n is negative difference and N is number of crops.

Thus, the correct answer is A.

53. John Friedmann presented his theory in 1966 about the difference central town and periphery. The theory makes two parts of developing town, as given by Francis Perroux. The theory divides a developing towns/poles into f types: Central cities, growth poles, development poles and integration poles. The development poles are urban districts which have diversified economic activities. The central town or pole is centre of development. The finished product is available here for input into tertiary activities and for consumption. It takes the required raw materials from towns in periphery.

Thus, the correct answer is A.

54. In his Theory of Unbalanced Growth Albert O. Hirschmann explains that profits and losses are symptoms of disequilibrium or imbalances in economy. He suggests that investment should be made in Social Overhead Capital (SOC) to create these imbalances. It has activities that support primary, secondary activities like education, transport and communication, drainage, etc. Investment in these leads to encouragement for investment in Direct Productive Activities (DPA). This provides cheap facilities for industries and agriculture like electricity and power supply.

Thus, the correct answer is A.

55. The Preferential Trade Area is the first step in economic integration. It gives preferred access regarding certain commodities to the participating countries. Free Trade Area is the second step gives reduced tariffs and lessened trade barriers which increases trade of goods and services. Customs Union is the next step after Free Trade area. It has common external tariff. It is designed to end re-exportation. A common market with a customs union forms an economic union. It is 6th stage in economic integration.

Thus, the correct answer is C.

56. George Wilson Hoke was the first person to use the term social geography. He published his paper titled " the study of social geography". It was published in the year 1907

Thus, the Correct answer is A.

57. According to the Global Climate Risk Index of 2020, published by German Watch, a think tank on North-South equity and preservation of livelihoods, India is the 5th most vulnerable country to climate change impacts. India's increasing vulnerability is due to severe rainfall, heavy flooding and landslide.

Thus, the Correct answer is B.

58. Zimmerman called his real-life theory, the functional theory of mineral resources. His followers coined the term resource ship. His methods taken account of the human, cultural and natural factors which helped in the production of resources.

Thus, the Correct answer is A.

59. Nearest neighbor analysis is the method used to study the distance between the nearest two points. It helps in studying the pattern of distribution of a settlement that is clustered, random or regular. Nearest neighbor analysis will produce a result between 0 and 2.5.

Thus, the Correct answer is C.

60. Cultural geography deals with study of cultural aspects of different ways and doings of the different countries and regions all around the world. Carl. O Sauer is known as the father of cultural geography. One of his best work is 'Agricultural origin and dispersal'.

Thus, the Correct answer is A.

61. Albert Damengean was a pupil of Vidal de la Blache. He produced a monograph "La Picardie et les regions veisines". He concentrated mainly on human geography. He wrote on transport geography, population and international economics. He prepared land use maps.

Thus, the Correct answer is C.

62. Richard Hartshorne was two persistent in noting a distinction within the fields between what he termed "systematic geography" and "regional geography". Regional geography of Hartshorne is the study of all the feature of a given region, any two-dimensional area of interest.

Thus, the Correct answer is A.

63. In the ancient period geography grew out of exploration, mapping of areas and materials collected. Some of the most prominent geographers of the ancient times were Arabs, Greeks, Chinese, Indians and Romans.

Odyssey is the work of Homer who is a Roman geographer.

Syntaxis is the work of Ptolemy who is a Greek geographer.

Kitab-Muraj-al-Dhahab is the work of Al Masudi who is an Arab Geographer

Qi Sheng is the work of Yu Qin who is a Chinese geographer

Thus, the Correct answer is B.

64. Aerial differentiation is the study of distribution of phenomena both human and physical and how they are casually related to other phenomena in proximity in a geographical region or area expressed in the space.

Thus, the Correct answer is B.

65. Leonardo da Vinci believed the rivers formed their vallies themselves through vertical erosion. Buffon opined that the rivers were the most powerful agent of erosion.

Targioni Tozetti stated that the rivers depend on the nature of the rocks through which they flow.

Guttenberg opined that not all the sediments eroded are deposited by the river in the sea rather some parts are also deposited in the course of river as the flood plain.

Thus, the Correct answer is B.

66. Schaefer questions the philosophy of exceptionalism which was advocated by Hettener and later argued by Hartshorne in his aerial differentiation. He argues for geography which is more scientific and analytical.

Thus, the Correct answer is A.

67. Positivism is a philosophical viewpoint that limits knowledge to the facts that can be observed to the relationships between these facts. Positivism is also called empiricism. This philosophy proclaims the unity of science, which is value free ideally, neutral, impartial and objective. Positivism is called hypothetic-deductive explanation because it's a kind of controlled speculation.

Thus, the Correct answer is B.

68. Structuration theory was majorly propounded by Giddens and Bourdieu. According to Giddens human agency and social structure are not two separate concepts or constructs, but these are together produced by social action and interaction. He states it as an outcome of a continuous process or flow of process.

Thus, the Correct answer is A.

69. Humanism in geography deals with creating human awareness and human agency. It developed as a criticism against positivism and quantitative revolution in geography. Its basic objection against quantitative revolution is that its tools and assumption do not adequately explain human world and human issues.

Thus, the Correct answer is B.

70. There has been good progress in the field of cartography in India with Years. Biggest contributors for the same were Survey of India and NATMO.

Planning Atlas of Andhra Pradesh was the work of SM Alam.

Resource atlas of Tamil Nadu is the work of A Ramesh

Planning atlas of Uttar Pradesh is the work of LR Singh

Census atlas of India is the work of BK Roy.

Thus, the Correct answer is B.

71. • Cartograms are representations of statistical data on a map in a diagrammatic way by purposefully distorting the original shape and appearance of the area concerned. World Distribution map is an example of a cartogram.

• In choropleth maps, the density of population, location factor for industries or the spatial distribution of the intensity or the density of an element is shown with the help of a system of graded shading or color, drawn following the boundaries of administrative units.

• In Quantitative dot maps, quantities or values are represented by dots of uniform sizes, each dot having a specific value. These are useful when the values are unevenly and sporadically distributed. Settlement maps show these characteristics.

• The spatial distribution of data is shown by a uniform scheme such as using letters, symbols, numbers, shapes, roman numerical in Choroschematic maps. e.g. the political maps are an example of choroschematic maps since various symbols are used for describing the political boundaries, districts, etc.

Thus, the Correct answer is C.

72. These are the most important forms of dynamic maps in which the movement of goods, information and people between and among places are shown. The flow maps are used to show the movement of almost anything such as people, products and natural resources. The actual route of movement on a map is considered and the quantitative impression is conveyed by the width of the line.

Speed at which the flow is occurring can also be shown with the help of flow maps, but they are a totally different thing. These are known as speed flow maps or isochronic cartograms. General flow maps do not show the speed.

Thus, the Correct answer is C.

73. Atlas and wall maps are intended for portraying the geography of large areas. These maps are described as small scale, which usually refer to scales smaller than 1:100,000. Small-scale maps show a large area on a single map sheet, but their contents are less detailed and include only major features like highways, railways, lakes, rivers, etc.

Thus, the Correct answer is D

74. The photograph that is taken with the optical axis deliberately tilted to show the earth's horizon is known as high oblique aerial photograph. These aerial photographs cover a large part of the earth's surface and are used for pictorial and illustrative purposes and are used in several reconnaissance surveys.

Thus, the Correct answer is C.

75. Unsupervised classification is a process whereby numerical operations are performed by the computer system itself that search for the natural groupings of the spectral properties of pixels in the multi spectral feature space. This method doesn't require much initial output and a priori knowledge of the scene as clustering does not involve training data.

Thus, the Correct answer is C.

76. For the NavIC system to provide real-time position and timing, three IRNSS satellites are in the geostationary orbits and the other four satellites are in geosynchronous orbits with required inclination.

Thus, the Correct answer is A.

77. Stratified Sampling is the only technique where all the sections of the population or sub-population are homogenously and adequately represented. Stratified sampling is generally used when the population is heterogenous but can be subdivided into strata within each of which the heterogeneity is not so prominent. If a proper stratification can be made such that the strata differ from one another as much as possible, but there is much homogeneity within each of them , then stratified sample will yield better results. Here the sub-sample sizes are made proportional to the sub population sizes.

Thus, the Correct answer is B.

78. Brahmaputra River when it flows out of India into Bangladesh is called as Jamuna River.

79. The stream order method by Strahler is the most common technique used in various applications. Here, the small permanent streams are called 1st order streams. Two 1st order streams join to form a larger order, second order stream; two 2nd order streams join to form a 3rd order and so on.

80. Rectangular streams are channel systems marked by right-angle bends and generally results from the presence of joints and fractures in massive rocks or foliation in metamorphic rocks. Such structures with their cross-cutting patterns have guided the directions of valleys.

The other two options depict a trellis pattern.

81. The state of Madhya Pradesh has tribal population of 1,53,16,784. This number is nearly 21.1% of the total population of the state. The tribes here include Gond, Mina, Oraon, Munda, Kol, Kawar, Korku, Habla, Saharia tribes among others. The states of Mahrashtra, Meghalaya and Mizoram have tribal population of 10510213, 2555861 and 1036115 respectively.

Thus, the correct answer is C.

82. The River Ganga originates at Gangotri glacier in the Himalayas. It is in its youthful stage in the mountains of Himalayas. A river does downward cutting in its youthful stage while it does lateral cutting in later stages. At Rishikesh, the channel of Ganga is narrow and deep due to downward cutting done by river Ganga.

Thus, the correct answer is C.

83. The Integrated Rural Development Program (IRDP) was launched by the Government of India during the financial year of 1978 and implemented during 1980. The main motto of the program was to provide employment opportunities to the poor community as well as opportunities to develop their skill sets so as to improve their living conditions.

84. The industrial region in Mumbai-Pune developed in the time of American Civil War due to high growth in cotton textile industry. The Chotanagpur industrial region has coal and iron ore deposits. Thus, it is called as Ruhr of India. The Kollam-Thiruvanathapuram industrial region is far away from the mineral deposits. Thus, industries here are agro-based and market oriented light industries. Same applies for the Gurgaon-Delhi-Meerut industrial regions. Thus, (d) is false and all others are true.

Thus, the correct answer is A.

85. Although there are mentions of Indian Monsoon in the *Rig Veda* and Al Masudi's works, the concept of Indian Monsoon was explained in 1686 by Sir Edmund Halley. Halley said that monsoon resulted due to thermal contrast between continents and oceans because of differential heating.

Thus, the correct answer is B.

86. The meteorological changes in Pacific Ocean and Indian Ocean are linked. When the surface level pressure over the Indian Ocean is high, the surface level pressure over the Pacific Ocean is low and vice versa. This phenomenon of intersection of high and low pressure is called as Southern Oscillation or S.O. The South-West Monsoon in Indian Ocean is stronger when the pressure over the Pacific Ocean in the winters is low.

Thus, the correct answer is C.

87. The groundwater level in the country is falling at an alarming rate in country due to over exploitation of the same. In some districts of Haryana and Punjab, the level is decreasing at over 1 meter per year. The Hilly terrains of Jammu and Kashmir make it very hard to develop the groundwater resources in the area. Thus, (R) is true and (A) is false.

Thus, the correct answer is D.

88. The union territory of Puducherry, also called as Pondicherry is has the highest sex ratio among the union territories of India. It has sex ratio of 1084 as per the census of 2011. The other Union Territories of Lakshadweep, Daman & Diu and Andaman & Nicobar have sex ratio of 946, 618 and 878 respectively.

Thus, the correct answer is B.

89. India ranks second in production of rice and wheat in world, after China. India holds third rank in world production of cotton. India has the largest area under Sesamum cultivation in world and is also the largest producer of the same, making for nearly one-third of the total produce of the oilseed in world.

Thus, the correct answer is C.

90. The Himalayas are a young mountain of soft rocks and there are still marks that imply that the process of uplift has not yet completed. To confirm this statement, there are certain evidences- 1. The Himalayan rivers are still in their youthful stage and have been rejuvenated in recent times. 2. The frequent occurrence of earthquakes in the Himalayan region shows that the Himalayas have not reached isostatic equilibrium and are still rising. 3. The Shivalik have been developed in the recent times during the post-Pliocene period.

91. The Lateritic soils are widely spread over an area of 2.48 lakh sq. km. and is found mainly on the summits of Western Ghats , eastern Ghats, the Rajmahal Hills, Vindhyas, Satpura and Malwa plateau. These soils are of little use in agriculture because of low fertility caused by intensive leaching and lack of lime, silica, potash. But these soils provide materials for building purposes as they are considered as the end product of weathering and are durable.

92. Plains are the most preferred agricultural sites due to their low altitude and because of this, certain practices such as ploughing, sowing, harvesting can be carried out with ease. They provide greater scope and environment for agricultural growth. Hence, Relief is sought as the major factor.

93. Among these factors, Humid climate is a major reason since this type of climate prevails in Mumbai and is essential as thread does not break frequently in such conditions. Other reasons include cheap hydroelectricity from the nearby areas and presence of black-cotton soil from the hinterland of Mumbai.

94. Pradhan Mantri Awas Yojana (Urban) Mission launched on 25th June 2015 which intends to provide housing for all in urban areas by year 2022. The Mission provides Central Assistance to the implementing agencies through States/Union Territories (UTs) and Central Nodal Agencies (CNAs) for providing houses to all eligible families/ beneficiaries. PMAY (U) has made a mandatory provision for the female head of the family to be the owner or co-owner of the house under this Mission.

95. The earthquakes that strike this zone are of moderate intensity of 6-6.5 . The extent of this zone runs to the south of the Himalayan zone and runs parallel to it. The earthquakes are quite devastating due to high density of population.

96. All three options are the primary objectives of the Agro-climatic regions. However, according to the Planning Commission of India, the primary objective of the Agro-climatic regions is:- 1. maximise the net income of the producers, 2. attempt a broad demand-supply balance of major commodities at the national level, 3. provide a framework for scientific and sustainable use of natural resources, particularly land, water and forests in the long run.

97. Wheat is a rabi crop and requires a temperature of 21-26 degree Celsius during the summer season. Annual rainfall of about 75 cm. is perfect for the cultivation of wheat. However, it can be grown in a variety of soils, well drained fertile and clay loams.

98. The period of stagnant population or the year of 1921 is referred to as the demographic divide. During most of the 19th century India witnessed a slow growth of population which continued till the year 1921. The population was more or less stagnant, and the high birth rate was counterbalanced by high death rate. Large scale abnormal deaths were present in this period. The census year of 1921 witnessed only a negative growth rate of -0.31% which was observed only once in India.

99. Infant mortality rate refers to the death rate among infants and is calculated for connoting mortality among the children of less than one year of age. IMR is the ratio of the number of deaths among children under one year of age to the number of live births.

Life expectancy at birth is a health indicator which indicates the number of years a person, whether a male or female would live after birth. Due to improvement in the medical field, the life expectancy has increased.

Crude death rate is the simplest measure of mortality indicating the number of deaths in a particular year per 1000 of population.

Total Fertility rate is known as the number of children born to a woman during her entire reproductive age and the TFR has decreased in India from 6 to 3 in 2003.

100. The high Yielding Variety(HYV) of seeds and agricultural universities are ways of optimizing agricultural output through advanced technology. It is a very important component of Green Revolution. Land Reforms such as abolishment of Raitwari and Zamindari system led to improvement in agricultural sector and was important for Green Revolution. The rural electrification guaranteed irrigation for agriculture and thus a part of Green Revolution. No Poverty as well as Employment guarantee, on the other hand , were not the components of Green Revolution.

Thus, the correct answer is C.

Q.1 Given below are two statements - one is labelled as Assertion (A) and the other is labelled as Reason (R):

Assertion(A)- Wegener was of the view that western and eastern coastlines of the Atlantic Ocean are in Jig-saw fit.

Reason(R)- The Continental drift theory was based primarily on two premises, which were polar wandering and matching of geological formations.

Choose the correct option:

A. Both A and R are true and R is the correct explanation of A

B. Both A and R are true but R is not the correct explanation of A

C. A is true but R is false

D. A is false but R is true.

Q.2 In which of the following states are the Aravalli mountains located

A. Jammu and Kashmir

B. Rajasthan

C. Himachal Pradesh

D. Madhya Pradesh

Q.3 The process in which the outer layers of rocks are peeled off from the main mass of the rock in the form of concentric shells is known as:

A. Granular Disintegration

B. Exfoliation

C. Block Disintegration

D. Pressure Release

Q.4 Which of the following option is correct regarding Penck's Theory?

A. The landforms of a region are related with the tectonic activity of that region.

B. Upliftment and degradation go on simultaneously.

C. Primarumpf refers to the landscape before the stage of upliftment.

D. All of the above

Q.5 Match List I with List II

List I (Mountain types)	List II(Examples)
a. Monoclinal folds	1. one side of the fold is gradual in slope but the other side is steep
b. Isoclinal folds	2. axis of the fold becomes tilted and the angle lies between axis and horizontal plane
c. Asymmetrical Folds	3. Both the limbs of the fold become parallel but not horizontal
d. Plunge folds	4. one limb of the fold is vertical

A. a-4 b-3 c-1 d-2

B. a-4 b-3 c-2 d-1

C. a-1 b-3 c-2 d-4

D. a-3 b-4 c-1 d-2

Q.6 Which of the following arrangement is in correct sequence in the case of elements of slope profile?

A. Summital convexity, Free face, Rectilinear, Basal concavity

B. Free face, Rectilinear, Summital convexity, Basal concavity

C. Summital convexity, Rectilinear, Free face, Basal concavity

D. Summital convexity, Basal concavity, Rectilinear, Free face

Q.7 The Glacial feature which is mostly found in groups and collectively known as 'basket of eggs topography' is known as-

A. Eskers

B. Moraines

C. Kettle

D. Drumlins

Q.8 Who postulated the paving stone hypothesis?

A. W. G. Wine and Mattheus

B. McKenzie and Parker

C. W. J. Moran and Le Pichon

D. Isacks and Sykes

Q.9 Which of the following is a divergent or constructive plate boundary?

A. The boundary between the Eurasian plate and Indian plate in North India

B. The boundary between the Pacific Plate and Mariana plate in the Western Pacific Ocean.

C. The boundary between the North American plate and Eurasian plate in the Atlantic Ocean

D. The boundary between the Australian Plate and the Pacific plate in New Zealand.

Q.10 Select the correct order of the following forms of mass movement as per the increasing amount of water in them.

A. Earth flow-Debris flow- Mud flow

B. Mud flow-Earth Flow-Debris Flow

C. Debris flow-Earth flow- Mud flow

D. Earth flow-Mud flow-Debris flow

Q.11 Consider the following statements-

a) Troposphere is also known as the convective region.

b) The Stratosphere is referred to as the point from where the decrease of temperature stops.

c) The most destructive gases that lower the effectiveness of the ozone are known as CFCs.

d) The three layers that fall under the Heterosphere are mesosphere, ionosphere, and exosphere.

Which of the following statements are correct?

A. a and c

B. a and b

C. b and d

D. a, b and c

Q.12 Which layer of the Ionosphere is also known as the Kennelly-Heaviside layer and is present between 99-130 km.?

A. E2 layer

B. F layer

C. Sporadic E layer

D. E layer

Q.13 Given below are two statements- one is labelled as Assertion (A) and the other is labelled as Reason (R):

Assertion(A)- Fogs, urban smog's, frost generally affect the economy.

Reason(R)- Inversion of temperature is known as the negative lapse rate.

Choose the correct options.

A. Both A and R are true and R is the correct explanation of A

B. Both A and R are true but R is not the correct explanation of A

C. A is true but R is false.

D. A is false but R is true.

Q.14 Match List-I with List-II:

List I	List II
a. Absorption	i. Diffusion of a portion of incoming solar radiation in different directions.
b. Diffusion	ii. Portion of the incident radiation reflected from the surface.
c. Reflection	iii. Scattering of incident radiation waves by dust and molecules of water vapour
d. Scattering	iv. Retaining of a portion of the incident energy by a substance.

Codes

A. a-iv b-iii c-i d-ii
B. a-iv b-iii c-ii d-i
C. a-i b-iii c-iv d-ii
D. a-ii b-iii c-i d-iv

Q.15 Which of the following option is correct in the case of fronts and frontogenesis?

A. The term frontogenesis used by Tor Bergeron means creation of altogether new fronts.

B. Fronts mostly lie on low pressure troughs and are associated with cloudiness and precipitation.

C. During the approach of a warm front, the clouds show a sequence of cirrus, cirrostratus, altostratus, stratus clouds.

D. All of the above

Q.16 In a tropical cyclone the pattern of isobars is

A. elliptical
B. semi-circular
C. circular
D. rectangular

Q.17 The systematic description of climatic conditions and climatic changes in the geological history of earth is known as -

A. Palynology
B. Climochronology
C. Glaciology
D. Dendrochronology

Q.18 Arrange the following belts from the centre of the cyclone towards the outer margin-

A. Eye, Eye wall, Spiral bands, Annular belt, outer convective belt, peripheral belt.

B. Eye, Eye wall, peripheral belt, annular belt, spiral bands, outer convective belt.

C. outer convective belt, eye, eye wall, annular belt, spiral bands, peripheral belt.

D. Eye wall, eye, spiral bands, outer convective belt, peripheral belt, annular belt.

Q.19 What does ENSO stand for?

A. El Nino Southern Oscillation
B. El Nino Surface Oscillation
C. El Nino Southern Ocean
D. El Nino Surfing organisation

Q.20 Given below are two statements. One is labelled as Assertion (A) and the other is labelled as Reason (R).

Assertion (A): The temperature increases in the stratosphere.

Reason (R) : The boundary between stratosphere and mesosphere is called as stratopause.

Select the correct answer from options given below:

A. Both (A) and (R) are true and (R) is the correct explanation of (A)

B. Both (A) and (R) are true, but (R) is not the correct explanation of (A)

C. (A) is true, but (R) is false

D. (A) is false, but (R) is true

Q.21 Match List-I with List-II

List-I (Type of climate)	List-II (Abbreviation)
(a) Humid warm summer	(i) Aw
(b) Dry Subtropical	(ii) BWh
(c) Tropical Desert	(iii) Cs
(d) Tropical Savannah	(iv) Da

Code:

A. (a)-(i), (b)-(ii), (c)-(iv), (d)-(iii)
B. (a)-(iv), (b)-(ii), (c)-(iii), (d)-(i)
C. (a)-(iv), (b)-(iii), (c)-(ii), (d)-(i)
D. (a)-(i), (b)-(ii), (c)-(iii), (d)-(iv)

Q.22 Read the following statements and choose correct answer from the code given below:

(a) El Nino current contributes to the global warming.

(b) El Nino is also associated with droughts in Australia.

(c) El Nino is a cold current.

(d) El Nino was discovered in the nineteenth century.

Code:

A. (a) and (b) are true
B. (a), (b) and (c) are true
C. (a), (b) and (d) are true
D. Only (a) is true

Q.23 Read the following statements and choose the correct answer from the code given below:

(a) Record of climatic data is available for the last three centuries.

(b) Trend of global warming set again in second decade of 20th century.

(c) Record breaking high temperatures have been observed since 1990.

(d) Harsh winters were observed in the first decade of 20th century in Western Europe.

Code:

A. Only (a) is true
B. (b), (c) and (d) are true
C. (a), (b) and (d) are true
D. (b) and (d) are true

Q.24 Rate at which solar radiation is received outside the earth's atmosphere on a surface perpendicular to sun's rays, when the earth is an average distance is called?

A. Albedo
B. Solar constant
C. Insolation
D. Angle of incidence

Q.25 Consider the following statement:

i. Air mass thunderstorm occur as a result of vertical displacement of air mass within an air mass.

ii. Local heat thunderstorm is a type of air mass thunderstorm

Choose the correct answer:

A. Only (i) is true

B. Only (ii) is true

C. Both (i) and (ii) are true

D. Neither (i) nor (ii) is true

Q.26 Given below are two statements. One is labelled as Assertion (A) and the other is labelled as Reason (R).The Egyptians used to call

Assertion (A): The density of oceanic water depends upon temperature and salinity.

Reason (R) : The density of water increases as the temperature increases.

Select the correct answer from options given below:

A. Both (A) and (R) are true and (R) is the correct explanation of (A)

B. Both (A) and (R) are true, but (R) is not the correct explanation of (A)

C. (A) is true, but (R) is false

D. (A) is false, but (R) is true

Q.27 Most tsunamis occur in

A. Indian Ocean

B. Arctic Ocean

C. Pacific Ocean

D. Atlantic Ocean

Q.28 In the northwestern Pacific Ocean, a tropical cyclone is called as

A. Hurricane

B. Sandstorm

C. Avalanche

D. Typhoon

Q.29 The major factors that decrease the ocean salinity are

a) Formation of Ice

b) Precipitation

c) River Runoff

d) Movement of Seawater

Choose the correct option:

A. a and c

B. b and c

C. a, b and c

D. a and d

Q.30 Given below are two statements- one is labelled as Assertion (A) and the other is labelled as Reason (R):

Assertion (A)- Ocean currents highly affect fishing, marine organisms.

Reason(R)- Mixing of the ocean currents leads to a phenomenon that suitable for the fishes.

Choose the correct option:

A. Both A and R are true, and R is the correct explanation of A

B. Both A and R are true, but R is not the correct explanation of A

C. A is true, but R is false

D. A is false, but R is true

Q.31 Given below are the two statements, one labelled as Assertion (A) and the other labelled as Reason (R). Select your answer from the code given below:

Assertion (A)- Habitat shifts provide important evidence of population changes.

Reason (R) - Habitats are ecological space that are composed of multiple dimensions, each representing a biotic or abiotic ecological variable.

A. Both A and R are true, and R correctly explains A

B. Both A and R are true but R does not explains A

C. A is true and R is false.

D. Both A and R are false

Q.32 Consider the following statements about ecological factors:-

i. Light and temperature are direct ecological factors.

ii. Indirect factors include soil structure, altitude, wind and slope.

iii. Edaphic factors and biotic factors can be included in physical factors.

Choose the correct option from below:

A. Only i

B. ii and iii

C. Only iii

D. i, ii and iii

Q.33 Who coined the term ecosystem?

A. Ritter

B. Tansley

C. Hettener

D. Ellenberg

Q.34 Match List-I with List-II and select the correct answer from the codes given below :

List-I(Author)	List-II(works on carbon cycle)
a)Riebeek	i) The age of wonder
b)Holmes	ii) The carbon cycle
c)Archer	iii) The carbon cycle and atmospheric carbon dioxide
d)Prentice	iv) The global carbon cycle

A. (a)-(iii), (b)-(ii), (c)-(i), (d)-(iv)

B. (a)-(ii), (b)-(i), (c)-(iv), (d)-(iii)

C. (a)-(i), (b)-(ii), (c)-(iii), (d)-(iv)

D. (a)-(iii), (b)-(i), (c)-(iv), (d)-(ii)

Q.35 Consider the following statements about human environment interaction and state which amongst the following is true:

i. The type of society has strong influence over the environment.

ii. Human characteristics have impact on the environment.

iii. Education is a key factor on people's view of life.

iv. Ecosystem services are important for human well-being.

Choose the correct option from below:

A. Only (i)

B. Only (ii)

C. (i) , (ii) and (iii)

D. (i), (ii), (iii) and (iv)

Q.36 Match the List-I with List-II

List-I (Primate city)	List-II (Secondary city)
a) Paris	(i) Nathaburi
b) London	(ii) Guadalajara
c) Mexico City	(iii) Birmingham
d) Bangkok	(iv) Marsallies

Code:

A. (a)-(iii), (b)-(i), c-(ii), d-(iv)

B. (a)-(iii), (b)-(iv), c-(i), d-(ii)

C. (a)-(iv), (b)-(iii), c-(ii), d-(i)

D. (a)-(iv), (b)-(ii), c-(i), d-(iii)

Q.37 Rank-size rule was given by

A. Christaller **B.** Zipf
C. Burgess **D.** Hoyt

Q.38 Which of the following is NOT a characteristic of slum?
A. High rates of criminal activities
B. High poverty
C. Low population
D. Lack of infrastructural facilities

Q.39 Given below are the two statements, one labelled as Assertion (A) and the other labelled as Reason (R). Select your answer from the code given below :

Assertion (A) : In the concentric zone model the rich high-class citizens live in the fourth zone.

Reason (R) : Detached homes are found in the fourth zone which is at quite a bit of distance from the Central Business District.

Code :

A. Both (A) and (R) are true and (R) is the correct explanation of (A).

B. Both (A) and (R) are true but (R) is not the correct explanation of (A).

C. (A) is true but (R) is false.

D. (A) is false but (R) is true.

Q.40 Which one of the following is the correct sequence of cultural change as given by Lewis Mumford?
A. Eopolis- Polis-Metropolis-Megalopolis
B. Polis-Eopolis- Metropolis-Megalopolis
C. Polis-Megalopolis-Metropolis-Eopolis
D. Polis-Metropolis-Megalopolis-Eopolis

Q.41 Direction: Read the passage carefully and answer the following questions:-

No country can be completely self-sufficient, and the trade between countries is however essential to ensure a supply of the country's needs. Many countries may produce a surplus of certain goods and if these are not required, they must be sold to the outside countries. The increasing condition of industrialization has increased the international trade. Industrial nations require raw materials for their labourers as well as for their factories. To meet their requirements the agricultural nations, need to import their surplus products. Similarly, the agricultural nations also need specialized machinery to run their farms and to meet their demands, industrial nations need to send their machinery. Countries which have a large international trade, can import large amount of various commodities which means that a much higher range of products such as raw materials, food stuffs are available than a single country could produce. Thus, the volume of international trade is taken as the economic barometer of a country. The world's greatest trading nations are U.S.A., Japan, West Germany, U.K., France which are also economically prosperous. India, Pakistan, Laos and Indonesia have a small volume of foreign trade per capita and are thus less economically developed nations. The volume of trade, the direction of trade and the types of goods traded differ greatly among the various continents and the countries of the world. Foodstuffs, Raw materials, Fuels, manufactured goods are some of the main commodities that enter the world trade. The world trade pattern of the major trading zones varies greatly from country to country.

Western Europe has a large world trade pattern because large imports of foodstuffs are required for the densely populated region. Inter-European trade also takes place. This continent is also highly industrialized and the most important mineral imported is oil. Also, a large volume of exports of manufactured and semi-finished goods takes place here. Next comes North America in foreign trade. In terms of the volume of trade, the U.S.A is the greatest country. The chief exports are machinery, iron and steel, etc. The major imports are iron ore, timber , newsprint, coal, etc. Canada was a major exporter of primary products during the 19th century. After these continents and countries, Latin America, Africa, Australia, U.S.S.R., And Asia comes accordingly. But this pattern changes according to the availability of the products and the volume of trade.

Which factor has increased the international or world trade patterns?
A. Transportation
B. Irrigation practices
C. Agricultural Practices
D. Industrialization

Q.42 Direction: Read the passage carefully and answer the following questions:-

No country can be completely self-sufficient, and the trade between countries is however essential to ensure a supply of the country's needs. Many countries may produce a surplus of certain goods and if these are not required, they must be sold to the outside countries. The increasing condition of industrialization has increased the international trade. Industrial nations require raw materials for their labourers as well as for their factories. To meet their requirements the agricultural nations, need to import their surplus products. Similarly, the agricultural nations also need specialized machinery to run their farms and to meet their demands, industrial nations need to send their machinery. Countries which have a large international trade, can import large amount of various commodities which means that a much higher range of products such as raw materials, food stuffs are available than a single country could produce. Thus, the volume of international trade is taken as the economic barometer of a country. The world's greatest trading nations are U.S.A., Japan, West Germany, U.K., France which are also economically prosperous. India, Pakistan, Laos and Indonesia have a small volume of foreign trade per capita and are thus less economically developed nations. The volume of trade, the direction of trade and the types of goods traded differ greatly among the various continents and the countries of the world. Foodstuffs, Raw materials, Fuels, manufactured goods are some of the main commodities that enter the world trade. The world trade pattern of the major trading zones varies greatly from country to country.

Western Europe has a large world trade pattern because large imports of foodstuffs are required for the densely populated region. Inter-European trade also takes place. This continent is also highly industrialized and the most important mineral imported is oil. Also, a large volume of exports of manufactured and semi-finished goods takes place here. Next comes North America in foreign trade. In terms of the volume of trade, the U.S.A is the greatest country. The chief exports are machinery, iron and steel, etc. The major imports are iron ore, timber , newsprint, coal, etc. Canada was a major exporter of primary products during the 19th century. After these continents and countries, Latin America, Africa, Australia, U.S.S.R., And Asia comes accordingly. But this pattern changes according to the availability of the products and the volume of trade.

What does the volume of international trade of a country imply?

A. Social Well-being

B. Economic Well-being

C. Material Well-being

D. Spiritual Well-being

Q.43 Direction: Read the passage carefully and answer the following questions:-

No country can be completely self-sufficient, and the trade between countries is however essential to ensure a supply of the country's needs. Many countries may produce a surplus of certain goods and if these are not required, they must be sold to the outside countries. The increasing condition of industrialization has increased the international trade. Industrial nations require raw materials for their labourers as well as for their factories. To meet their requirements the agricultural nations, need to import their surplus products. Similarly, the agricultural nations also need specialized machinery to run their farms and to meet their demands, industrial nations need to send their machinery. Countries which have a large international trade, can import large amount of various commodities which means that a much higher range of products such as raw materials, food stuffs are available than a single country could produce. Thus, the volume of international trade is taken as the economic barometer of a country. The world's greatest trading nations are U.S.A., Japan, West Germany, U.K., France which are also economically prosperous. India, Pakistan, Laos and Indonesia have a small volume of foreign trade per capita and are thus less economically developed nations. The volume of trade, the direction of trade and the types of goods traded differ greatly among the various continents and the countries of the world. Foodstuffs, Raw materials, Fuels, manufactured goods are some of the main commodities that enter the world trade. The world trade pattern of the major trading zones varies greatly from country to country.

Western Europe has a large world trade pattern because large imports of foodstuffs are required for the densely populated region. Inter-European trade also takes place. This continent is also highly industrialized and the most important mineral imported is oil. Also, a large volume of exports of manufactured and semi-finished goods takes place here. Next comes North America in foreign trade. In terms of the volume of trade, the U.S.A is the greatest country. The chief exports are machinery, iron and steel, etc. The major imports are iron ore, timber , newsprint, coal, etc. Canada was a major exporter of primary products during the 19th century. After these continents and countries, Latin America, Africa, Australia, U.S.S.R., And Asia

comes accordingly. But this pattern changes according to the availability of the products and the volume of trade.

Why is Western Europe considered to have a large world trade pattern?

A. Dense population

B. High Industrialization

C. Large volume of entrepot trade

D. All of the above

Q.44 Direction: Read the passage carefully and answer the following questions:-

No country can be completely self-sufficient, and the trade between countries is however essential to ensure a supply of the country's needs. Many countries may produce a surplus of certain goods and if these are not required, they must be sold to the outside countries. The increasing condition of industrialization has increased the international trade. Industrial nations require raw materials for their labourers as well as for their factories. To meet their requirements the agricultural nations, need to import their surplus products. Similarly, the agricultural nations also need specialized machinery to run their farms and to meet their demands, industrial nations need to send their machinery. Countries which have a large international trade, can import large amount of various commodities which means that a much higher range of products such as raw materials, food stuffs are available than a single country could produce. Thus, the volume of international trade is taken as the economic barometer of a country. The world's greatest trading nations are U.S.A., Japan, West Germany, U.K., France which are also economically prosperous. India, Pakistan, Laos and Indonesia have a small volume of foreign trade per capita and are thus less economically developed nations. The volume of trade, the direction of trade and the types of goods traded differ greatly among the various continents and the countries of the world. Foodstuffs, Raw materials, Fuels, manufactured goods are some of the main commodities that enter the world trade. The world trade pattern of the major trading zones varies greatly from country to country.

Western Europe has a large world trade pattern because large imports of foodstuffs are required for the densely populated region. Inter-European trade also takes place. This continent is also highly industrialized and the most important mineral imported is oil. Also, a large volume of exports of manufactured and semi-finished goods takes place here. Next comes North America in foreign trade. In terms of the volume of trade, the U.S.A is the greatest country. The chief exports are machinery, iron and steel, etc. The major imports are iron ore, timber , newsprint, coal, etc. Canada was a major exporter of primary products during the 19th century. After these continents and countries, Latin America, Africa, Australia, U.S.S.R., And Asia comes accordingly. But this pattern changes according to the availability of the products and the volume of trade.

Given below are two statements- one is labelled as Assertion (A) and the other is labelled as Reason (R):

Assertion (A)- The volume of International Trade is termed as the economic barometer of a country.

Reason (R)- The Latin America comes just after U.S.A in terms of the volume of world trade patterns.

Choose the correct option:

A. Both A and R are true and R is the correct explanation of A

B. Both A and R are true but R is not the correct explanation of A

C. A is true but R is false

D. A is false but R is true

Q.45 Direction: Read the passage carefully and answer the following questions:-

No country can be completely self-sufficient, and the trade between countries is however essential to ensure a supply of the country's needs. Many countries may produce a surplus of certain goods and if these are not required, they must be sold to the outside countries. The increasing condition of industrialization has increased the international trade. Industrial nations require raw materials for their labourers as well as for their factories. To meet their requirements the agricultural nations, need to import their surplus products. Similarly, the agricultural nations also need specialized machinery to run their farms and to meet their demands, industrial nations need to send their machinery. Countries which have a large international trade, can import large amount of various commodities which means that a much higher range of products such as raw materials, food stuffs are available than a single country could produce. Thus, the volume of international trade is taken as the economic barometer of a country. The world's greatest trading nations are U.S.A., Japan, West Germany, U.K., France which are also economically prosperous. India, Pakistan, Laos and Indonesia have a small volume of foreign trade per capita and are thus less economically developed nations. The volume of trade, the direction of trade and the types of goods traded differ greatly among the various continents and the countries of the world. Foodstuffs, Raw materials, Fuels, manufactured goods are some of the main commodities that enter the world trade. The world trade pattern of the major trading zones varies greatly from country to country.

Western Europe has a large world trade pattern because large imports of foodstuffs are required for the densely populated region. Inter-European trade also takes place. This continent is also highly industrialized and the most important mineral imported is oil. Also, a large volume of exports of manufactured and semi-finished goods takes place here. Next comes North America in foreign trade. In terms of the volume of trade, the U.S.A is the greatest country. The chief exports are machinery, iron and steel, etc. The major imports are iron ore, timber, newsprint, coal, etc. Canada was a major exporter of primary products during the 19th century. After these continents and countries, Latin America, Africa, Australia, U.S.S.R., And Asia comes accordingly. But this pattern changes according to the availability of the products and the volume of trade.

What kind of products were exported by Canada during the 19th century?

A. Forestry products

B. Manufactured products

C. Dairy Products

D. None of the above

Q.46 Deltas are formed where the shores are free of

A. Low tide

B. Hard rocks

C. High tide

D. Trees

Q.47 Consider the following statements:-

a) Weber's assumptions of a perfect competition with the spatial framework of a society has been criticized by many.

b) According to Losch, firms tend to locate at the most profitable of the production points.

c) E M Hoover used Isotims for joining places of equal transport costs.

d) D M Smith utilized the least cost approach of Weber with some of monopolistic -market area approach of Losch.

Which of the following options are correct?

A. a, b and d

B. b and c

C. c and d

D. a and c

Q.48 Which of the following are correctly matched?

a) **Gravity Model:** Measures interactions between all the possible locations pairs.

b) **Retail Model:** Measures the boundary of the market areas.

c) **Potential Model:** Measures interactions between central location and peripheral locations.

Choose the correct option:

A. only a

B. a and b

C. b and c

D. a, b and c

Q.49 Consider the following statements about Losch's theory of industrial location and choose which amongst them is true:

i. Goods have high demand with low prices.

ii. The demand curve rotated round the production point to give shape.

iii. As the competition increases, the market areas becomes hexagonal.

A. Only (i)

B. Only (ii)

C. (i) and (iii)

D. (i) , (ii) and (iii)

Q.50 Which country ranks first in ICT Development Index in 2017?

A. South Korea

B. Denmark

C. Iceland

D. United Kingdom

Q.51 The earliest arrivals in India are believed to be Negritos. At which one of the following places are they mainly found now?

A. Punjab

B. Rajasthan

C. Uttar Pradesh

D. Andaman Islands

Q.52 Given below are two statements- one is labelled as Assertion (A) and the other is labelled as Reason (R):

Assertion (A)- Over-dependence on one crop can lead to disastrous results to the Indian economy.

Reason (R)- Crop Diversification is a sound economic practice.

Choose the correct option:

A. Both A and R are true and R is the correct explanation of A

B. Both A and R are true but R is not the correct explanation of A

C. A is true but R is false

D. A is false but R is true

Q.53 Consider the following statements:-

a) Von Thunen put forward his theory of agricultural location because he thought that besides physical factors, economic forces of production and transport costs are factors in the land use.

b) According to Von Thunen, perishable items in strong demand get located close to the city.

c) The assumptions such as relative transport costs are still the same and are universally true.

d) In Von Thunen's original model, the 2nd land use ring was of livestock ranching.

Which of the following statements are correct?

A. a and b   **B.** c and d

C. a, b and c   **D.** c and d

Q.54 Shifting cultivation is known as _____ in Vietnam.

A. Chinook   **B.** Ray   **C.** Kumari   **D.** Masole

Q.55 Which of the following theories mention that the political and economic relationships between countries and regions of the world control and limit the economic development possibilities of the poor areas?

A. Rostow's Development Model

B. Theory of Balanced Development by Nurkse and Roden-Rodenstein.

C. Dependency Theory

D. Core periphery model

Q.56 Consider the following statements:-

a) Culture has no precise standard of measurement.

b) Brock and Webb has divided the world into 5 major and 3 minor cultural realms.

c) According to H. Robinson, the European cultural region is the most favourable continent.

d) Cultural regions and areas both are the same.

Which of the following options are correct?

A. a and c   **B.** a and b

C. b and d   **D.** b, c and d

Q.57 Consider the following statements:-

a) Society is a mosaic of various modes of social processes and interactions.

b) Industrialization has always been a positive force in modernizing the society.

c) Competition as a social process has always been an universal action.

d) Accommodation goes hand in hand with cooperation and conflict.

Which of the following options are correct?

A. a and c   **B.** b and d

C. a, c and d   **D.** c and d

Q.58 The first nuclear reactor of India is named

A. Urvashi   **B.** Apsara   **C.** Kamini   **D.** Rohini

Q.59 Direction: Read the following passage carefully and answer the following questions:-

Political geography's validity was recognized in the early 1920s. During that period, it was termed as the 'study of areal differentiation in political phenomena'. Political geography in the mid-1930s moved into the realm of the contemporary regional paradigm. In the post-second world war period, political geography retreated into the safer place of study at the scale of the individual state. By the early 1950s, there began a fast movement of the trend towards utilizing some of the environmental baggage of political geography and making it much more narrowly systematic. Hartshorne, Guttmann, Jones are some of the geographers who provided a new framework for analyzing the geography of political areas and modern state. It continued to be taught in various universities but there a lack of research to back up the teaching. Meanwhile, human geography started going through an expansion phase which was referred to as the quantitative revolution. The political geography sub discipline, during that period , consisted of boundaries, capital cities, territories, administrative areas, etc., but there was no specific coordination in these fields. The traditional political geography seemed to have lost its importance. The only solution was to follow the footsteps of the other sub disciplines of human geography.

Later the political incidents of the cold war period, particularly of the late 1960s, had a profound effect on all social sciences including the political geography. This sub discipline came into light due to the following reasons: economic and social geography included political variables in their analysis; the introduction of radical geography led to the creation of Marxist Geography. Initially, two main research areas came to dominate the growing political geography of the 1970s. Firstly, urban conflicts became a very common topic in human geography and in political geography, location of 'goods' and 'bads' with their respective externalities became an important part of a new urban political geography. Secondly, electoral geography started growing and were applied in the concepts of political geography. This growth led to the enhancement of its importance. Slowly, during the 1980s, political geography continued to prosper in various scales.

After which period the political geography came into limelight?

A. 1920   **B.** 1970   **C.** 2000   **D.** 1980

Q.60 Direction: Read the following passage carefully and answer the following questions:-

Political geography's validity was recognized in the early 1920s. During that period, it was termed as the 'study of areal differentiation in political phenomena'. Political geography in the mid-1930s moved into the realm of the contemporary regional paradigm. In the post-second world war period, political geography retreated into the safer place of study at the scale of the individual state. By the early 1950s, there began a fast movement of the trend towards utilizing some of the environmental baggage of political geography and making it much more narrowly systematic. Hartshorne, Guttmann, Jones are some of the geographers who provided a new framework for analyzing the geography of political areas and modern state. It continued to be taught in various universities but there a lack of research to back up the teaching. Meanwhile, human geography started going through an expansion phase which was referred to as the quantitative revolution. The political geography sub discipline, during that period , consisted of boundaries, capital cities, territories, administrative areas, etc., but there was no specific coordination in these fields. The traditional political geography seemed to have lost its importance. The only solution was to follow the footsteps of the other sub disciplines of human geography.

Later the political incidents of the cold war period, particularly of the late 1960s, had a profound effect on all social sciences including the political geography. This sub discipline came into light due to the following reasons: economic and social geography included political variables in their analysis; the introduction of radical geography led to the creation of Marxist Geography. Initially, two main research areas came to dominate the growing political geography of the 1970s. Firstly, urban conflicts became a very common topic in human geography and in political geography, location of 'goods' and 'bads' with their respective externalities became an important part of a new urban political geography. Secondly, electoral geography started growing and were applied in the concepts of political geography. This growth led to the enhancement of its importance. Slowly, during the 1980s, political geography continued to prosper in various scales.

Who provided a framework for analyzing the geography of political concepts?

A. Hartshorne

B. Col Friedman

C. D. Whittlesey

D. None of the above

Q.61 Direction: Read the following passage carefully and answer the following questions:-

Political geography's validity was recognized in the early 1920s. During that period, it was termed as the 'study of areal differentiation in political phenomena'. Political geography in the mid-1930s moved into the realm of the contemporary regional paradigm. In the post-second world war period, political geography retreated into the safer place of study at the scale of the individual state. By the early 1950s, there began a fast movement of the trend towards utilizing some of the environmental baggage of political geography and making it much more narrowly systematic. Hartshorne, Guttmann, Jones are some of the geographers who provided a new framework for analyzing the geography of political areas and modern state. It continued to be taught in various universities but there a lack of research to back up the teaching. Meanwhile, human geography started going through an expansion phase which was referred to as the quantitative revolution. The political geography sub discipline, during that period , consisted of boundaries, capital cities, territories, administrative areas, etc., but there was no specific coordination in these fields. The traditional political geography seemed to have lost its importance. The only solution was to follow the footsteps of the other sub disciplines of human geography.

Later the political incidents of the cold war period, particularly of the late 1960s, had a profound effect on all social sciences including the political geography. This sub discipline came into light due to the following reasons: economic and social geography included political variables in their analysis; the introduction of radical geography led to the creation of Marxist Geography. Initially, two main research areas came to dominate the growing political geography of the 1970s. Firstly, urban conflicts became a very common topic in human geography and in political geography, location of 'goods' and 'bads' with

their respective externalities became an important part of a new urban political geography. Secondly, electoral geography started growing and were applied in the concepts of political geography. This growth led to the enhancement of its importance. Slowly, during the 1980s, political geography continued to prosper in various scales.

Political Geography started to grow on different scales. Which were they?

A. Teaching and research

B. International and global perspectives

C. National and urban

D. All of the above

Q.62 Direction: Read the following passage carefully and answer the following questions:-

Political geography's validity was recognized in the early 1920s. During that period, it was termed as the 'study of areal differentiation in political phenomena'. Political geography in the mid-1930s moved into the realm of the contemporary regional paradigm. In the post-second world war period, political geography retreated into the safer place of study at the scale of the individual state. By the early 1950s, there began a fast movement of the trend towards utilizing some of the environmental baggage of political geography and making it much more narrowly systematic. Hartshorne, Guttmann, Jones are some of the geographers who provided a new framework for analyzing the geography of political areas and modern state. It continued to be taught in various universities but there a lack of research to back up the teaching. Meanwhile, human geography started going through an expansion phase which was referred to as the quantitative revolution. The political geography sub discipline, during that period , consisted of boundaries, capital cities, territories, administrative areas, etc., but there was no specific coordination in these fields. The traditional political geography seemed to have lost its importance. The only solution was to follow the footsteps of the other sub disciplines of human geography.

Later the political incidents of the cold war period, particularly of the late 1960s, had a profound effect on all social sciences including the political geography. This sub discipline came into light due to the following reasons: economic and social geography included political variables in their analysis; the introduction of radical geography led to the creation of Marxist Geography. Initially, two main research areas came to dominate the growing political geography of the 1970s. Firstly, urban conflicts became a very common topic in human geography and in political geography, location of 'goods' and 'bads' with their respective externalities became an important part of a new urban political geography. Secondly, electoral geography started growing and were applied in the concepts of political geography. This growth led to the enhancement of its importance. Slowly, during the 1980s, political geography continued to prosper in various scales.

Why was Political Geography termed as the 'wayward child of geographical sciences'?

A. lack of research analysis

B. elimination of environmental concepts

C. limiting its realm at the scale of the state

D. All of the above

Q.63 Direction: Read the following passage carefully and answer the following questions:-

Political geography's validity was recognized in the early 1920s. During that period, it was termed as the 'study of areal differentiation in political phenomena'. Political geography in the mid-1930s moved into the realm of the contemporary regional paradigm. In the post-second world war period, political geography retreated into the safer place of study at the scale of the individual state. By the early 1950s, there began a fast movement of the trend towards utilizing some of the environmental baggage of political geography and making it much more narrowly systematic. Hartshorne, Guttmann, Jones are some of the geographers who provided a new framework for analyzing the geography of political areas and modern state. It continued to be taught in various universities but there a lack of research to back up the teaching. Meanwhile, human geography started going through an expansion phase which was referred to as the quantitative revolution. The political geography sub discipline, during that period , consisted of boundaries, capital cities, territories, administrative areas, etc., but there was no specific coordination in these fields. The traditional political geography seemed to have lost its importance. The only solution was to follow the footsteps of the other sub disciplines of human geography.

Later the political incidents of the cold war period, particularly of the late 1960s, had a profound effect on all social sciences including the political geography. This sub discipline came into light due to the following reasons: economic and social geography included political variables in their analysis; the introduction of radical geography led to the creation of Marxist Geography. Initially, two main research areas came to dominate the growing political geography of the 1970s. Firstly, urban conflicts became a very common topic in human geography and in political geography, location of 'goods' and 'bads' with their respective externalities became an important part of a new urban political geography. Secondly, electoral geography started growing and were applied in the concepts of political geography. This growth led to the enhancement of its importance. Slowly, during the 1980s, political geography continued to prosper in various scales.

Which of the research areas led to the growth of urban political geography?

A. Urban social conflicts
B. Elections and voting patterns
C. Both A and B
D. Radical geography

Q.64 A tourist in Mumbai observes high tide near Gateway of India at 7.00 AM. At what time, he should expect another high tide on the same day?

A. 7.00 PM   **B.** 7.25 PM   **C.** 7.40 PM   **D.** 8.50 PM

Q.65 Read the following statements and select the correct answer from the code given below.

(a) Alexander Von Humboldt was the first geographer to describe the cause of human-induced climatic change.

(b) Humboldt discovered that the temperature fell as per increase in altitude.

(c) Humboldt supported the idea of behaviouralism.

(d) The Humboldt Current in South America was named after him.

Code:
A. (a) and (c) are true
B. (a), (b) and (d) are true
C. (c) and (d) are true
D. Only (a) is true

Q.66 Given below are two statements. One is labelled as Assertion (A) and the other is labelled as Reason (R).

Assertion (A): The double-humped camel found in cold desert of Ladakh is called as Bactrian camel.

Reason (R) : Greeks called the area of central Asia as Bactria.

Select the correct answer from options given below:
A. Both (A) and (R) are true and (R) is the correct explanation of (A)
B. Both (A) and (R) are true, but (R) is not the correct explanation of (A)
C. (A) is true, but (R) is false
D. (A) is false, but (R) is true

Q.67 Die Erdkunde was written by
A. Alexander Von Humboldt
B. Friedrich Ratzel
C. Carl Ritter
D. Carl Troll

Q.68 Read the following statements and select the correct answer from the code given below.

(a) Ratzel applied organic theory to biogeography.

(b) Humboldt was of the opinion that life of people living in islands, plains and mountains was similar.

(c) Kant described the impact of environment in late 18th century.

(d) Darwin's theory of origin of species is dependent on the idea that the nature changes with time.

Code:
A. (a) and (b) are true
B. (a), (b) and (c) are true
C. (a) and (d) are true
D. (c) and (d) are true

Q.69 Given below are two statements. One is labelled as Assertion (A) and the other is labelled as Reason (R).

Assertion (A): The Puranas name the region of Madagascar and Eastern Africa as Shalmali.

Reason (R) : The region of East-Africa is rich in silk-cotton trees.

Select the correct answer from options given below:
A. Both (A) and (R) are true and (R) is the correct explanation of (A)
B. Both (A) and (R) are true, but (R) is not the correct explanation of (A)
C. (A) is true, but (R) is false
D. (A) is false, but (R) is true

Q.70 Which of the following geographers has contributed to development of political geography in India?
A. Rias Akhtar   **B.** H. Ramachandran

C. Kashi Nath Singh   **D.** R.D.Dikshit

Q.71 The book 'Progress in Geography' is written by

A. Dr. B. Mukherji   **B.** S. P. Chatterjee
C. R. L. Singh   **D.** H. Ramachandran

Q.72 Match L st-I with List-II

List-I(Geographers)	List-II (Fields of study)
(a) Vidal de La Blache	(i) Geomorphology
(b) Albert Penck	(ii) la Terre
(c) Alexander Von Humboldt	(iii) Human geography
(d) Reclus	(iv) Physical geography

Code:

A. (a)-(ii),(b)-(iii),(c)-(iv),(d)-(i)
B. (a)-(iii),(b)-(iv),(c)-(i),(d)-(ii)
C. (a)-(iii),(b)-(i),(c)-(iv),(d)-(ii)
D. (a)-(iv),(b)-(iii),(c)-(ii),(d)-(i)

Q.73 Which one of the following is NOT an approach in physical geography?

A. Areal differentiation
B. Behavioralism
C. Spatial organization
D. Exploration and description

Q.74 Consider the following statements and state which of them is true about the types of maps-

(i). Political maps show the geographical boundaries between countries, states, districts etc.

(ii). Physical maps have green to brown and grey colour scheme for showing elevation.

(iii). Shallow water body is shown with light blue colour

(iv). Cities anc roads are not shown in physical map

A. Only (i) is correct
B. (i), (ii) and (iii) are correct.
C. Both (i) and (ii) are correct
D. (i), (ii), (iii) and (iv) is correct

Q.75 Match the List-I with List-II two.

List-I(Spectral Regions)	List-II(Wavelength)
a) Gamma-Ray region	i) 0.4-0.7µm
b) X- Ray region	ii) 0.3-0.4µm
c) Ultraviolet region	iii) 0.03-3.0nm
d) Visible region	iv) less than 0.03nm

Choose the correct answer form the code given below:

A. a-iv b-iii c-ii d-i   **B.** a-ii b-i c-iv d-iii
C. a-i b-ii c-iii d-iv   **D.** a-iii b-i c-iv d-ii

Q.76 Consider the following statements on digital image processing and choose which amongst them is true:

i. The process of digital image process is also called satellite image processing.

ii. Image pre-processing, Image enhancement and image classification are classification of digital image processing.

iii. The process is widely preferred.

iv. satellite images contain no errors. .

A. Only (i)   **B.** Only (ii)
C. (i) and(ii)   **D.** (i), (ii), (iii) and (iv)

Q.77 Consider the following statements on application areas of remote sensing and choose which amongst them is true:

i. Remote sensing is used in crop acreages estimation

ii. Different methods of remote sensing are used in soil categorization.

iii. Remote sensing is used in lithological discrimination

iv. Various methods of remote sensing are also used in major river valley projects. .

A. Only (i)   **B.** Only (ii)
C. (i) and(iii)   **D.** (i), (ii), (iii) and (iv)

Q.78 Which of the tests are used for comparison of differences of actual and expected frequencies-

A. Chi square test   **B.** Z test
C. T test   **D.** ANOVA

Q.79 Given below are two statements, one labelled as assertion(A) and other labelled as reason(R).

Assertion(A)- Principal component analysis identifies duplicate data over several datasets.

Reasoning(R)-It aggregates only essential information .

A. Both A and R are true and R correctly explains A
B. Both A and R are true but R does not explains A
C. A is true and R is false.
D. Both A and R are false

Q.80 Which curve is used to show the land elevations?

A. Clinograph   **B.** Hypsometric curve
C. Climograph   **D.** Hygrograph

Q.81 Consider the following statements about thematic map:

a. A special purpose map

b. Communicates geographical relationships

c. Shows single or multiple themes of a study

d. Depicts surface features of an area.

Which of the statements above are correct?

A. a,c,d   **B.** a,b,c   **C.** b,c,d   **D.** a,b,d

Q.82 Consider the following statements:-

a. GIS is an institutional entity, reflecting an organisational structure that integrates technology with a database, expertise and continuing financial support over time.

b. GIS is an internally referenced, automated, spatial information system.

c. GIS is any manual or computer-based set of procedures used to store and manipulate geographically referenced data.

d. GIS can present the results of information analyses using multimedia technologies

Which of the following statements above is /are correct?

A. a, b and d   **B.** a, b and c

C. a and c   **D.** All of the above

Q.83 Match List I with List II:-

List I (Drainage/watershed parameters)	List II (Explanation)
a. Stream Length Ratio(RL)	i. Total number of stream segments of all order in a basin per perimeter of the basin.
b. Bifurcation Ratio(Rb)	ii. The ratio of mean or average length of segment of order 'u' to the mean or average length of order 'u+1'.
c. Elongation Ratio(Re)	iii. The ratio of diameter of a circle of the same area as the basin to the maximum basin length.
d. Drainage Texture(T)	iv. The ratio of the number of streams of order(u) to the number of streams of higher order(u+1).

A. a-i b-iii c-iv d-ii   **B.** a-ii b-iv c-i d-iii
C. a-iv b-iii c-i d-ii   **D.** a-ii b-iv c-iii d-i

Q.84 Which fault line is the most active fault line in Himalaya system?
A. Main Central Thrust (MCT)
B. Indus Tsangpo Suture Zone (ITSZ)
C. Main Boundary Fault (MBF)
D. Himalayan Frontal Fold (HFF)

Q.85 Which of the following statements are true?
(a) The western coast of Mahrashtra is the region most prone to cyclonic storms.
(b) The river Chambal in the North Indian plain is susceptible to frequent flooding.
(c) The north-eastern states lie in the earthquake prone region.
(d) The eastern coast of India has most vulnerability to cyclones.
A. Only (a) true
B. (b) and (c) are true
C. (b), (c) and (d) are true
D. (c) and (d) are true

Q.86 Which union territory has the lowest population in India as per the census of 2011
A. Daman & Diu
B. Lakshadweep
C. Pondicherry
D. Andaman and Nicobar

Q.87 Match List-I with List-II :

List-I(Passes)	List II(States)
(a) Mana pass	(i) Sikkim
(b) Khardung la	(ii) Himachal Pradesh
(c) Rohtang	(iii) Jammu & Kashmir
(d) Nathu-la	(iv) Uttarakhand

Select the correct answer from the options given below:
A. (a)-(ii); (b)-(i); (c)-(iv); (d)-(iii)
B. (a)-(iv); (b)-(iii); (c)-(ii); (d)-(i)
C. (a)-(i); (b)-(ii); (c)-(iii); (d)-(iv)
D. (a)-(iv); (b)-(i); (c)-(ii); (d)-(iii)

Q.88 The East-West Corridor connects which of the following cities?
A. Mumbai-Kolkata
B. Surat-Tezpur
C. Srinagar-Kanyakumari
D. Silchar-Porbandar

Q.89 Read the following statements. Which of them are true? Select your answer from the code given below:
(a) The khaddar soils are found in the low areas of valley bottom of the North Indian plains.
(b) The black regur soils are found in the Deccan plateau.
(c) The tarai region is area in the Deccan plateau.
(d) The foothills of Sahyadris have bhabar soils.
A. Only (a) is true   **B.** (c) and (d) are true
C. (a) and (b) is true   **D.** (a) and (c) are true

Q.90 The high occurrence of floods in the Brahmaputra river region is due to which of the following reasons:-
A. High quantity of water
B. Less accommodating capacity of the river
C. Very high population pressure
D. All of the above

Q.91 Choose the correct option:-
A. The International trade of a country is 'Economic Barometer' of that country.
B. India is the 19th largest exporter in the world according to the WTO.
C. The value of exports has increased considerably.
D. All of the above

Q.92 Match List I with List II

List I (Indian railway types)	List II (Distance between two rails)
a. Broad gauge	1. 0.762m
b. Narrow gauge	2. 1.676m
c. Metre gauge	3. 1m

Choose the correct option:
A. a-2 b-1 c-3   **B.** a-1 b-2 c-3
C. a-3 b-1 c-2   **D.** a-3 b-2 c-1

Q.93 Which industry is known as the 'sunrise industry'?

A. Cement Industry	**B.** Petrochemicals
C. Plastic Incustry	**D.** Bicycle Industry

Q.94 Given below are two statements- one is labelled as Assertion (A) and the other is labelled as Reason (R):

Assertion(A)- The Sugar industry in southern regions of India is more productive.

Reason(R)- Sugar industry is gradual shifting from North India to the peninsular India.

Choose the correct option:

A. Both A and R are true, and R is the correct explanation of A
B. Both A and R are true, but R is not the correct explanation of A
C. A is true, but R is false
D. A is false, but R is true

Q.95 Arrange the following states according to the production of rice in descending order

a) Chhattisgarh

b) Odisha

c) Punjab

d) Uttar Pradesh

Choose the correct option:

A. d, c, b, a   **B.** a, b, d, c   **C.** d, b, c, a   **D.** a, b, c, d

Q.96 Given below are two statements- one is labelled as Assertion (A) and the other is labelled as Reason (R):

Assertion(A)- Green Revolution has a lot of drawbacks and several imbalances.

Reason(R)- Green revolution in India only brought about a Grain Revolution.

Choose the correct option:

A. Both A and R are true, and R is the correct explanation of A
B. Both A and R are true, but R is not the correct explanation of A
C. A is true, but R is false
D. A is false, but R is true

Q.97 Rainwater Harvesting is an effective technique to-

A. overcome the inadequacy of surface water
B. improve groundwater quality by dilution
C. increase the productivity of aquifer
D. All of the above

Q.98 Given below are two statements- one is labelled as Assertion (A) and the other is labelled as Reason (R):

Assertion (A)- The forest resources are unevenly distributed in India.

Reason(R)- Forest cover must be kept in check regularly.

Choose the correct option:

A. Both A and R are true, and R is the correct explanation of A
B. Both A and R are true, but R is not the correct explanation of A
C. A is true, but R is false
D. A is false, but R is true

Q.99 Which of the following statements represent the Peninsular River system?

a) This is a consequent drainage river system

b) The rivers receive water only from rainfall.

c) They follow more or less straight courses.

d) These rivers form big deltas at their mouths.

Select the correct option-

A. a and b   **B.** b and c
C. a, b and c   **D.** All of the above

Q.100 Which among the following is the largest Bay of the world?

A. Bay of Bengal
B. Hudson Bay
C. Blacksod Bay
D. Sandy Bay, Gibraltar

// Smart Answer Sheet //

Correct — Percentage of students who answered correctly. **Skipped** — Percentage of students who skipped.

Q.	Ans.	Correct / Skipped	Q.	Ans.	Correct / Skipped	Q.	Ans.	Correct / Skipped	Q.	Ans.	Correct / Skipped	Q.	Ans.	Correct / Skipped
1	C	18.97 % / 10.34 %	17	B	51.72 % / 25.87 %	33	B	68.97 % / 22.41 %	49	D	44.83 % / 27.58 %	65	B	55.17 % / 25.86 %
2	B	63.79 % / 24.14 %	18	A	51.72 % / 25.87 %	34	B	18.97 % / 25.86 %	50	C	44.83 % / 27.58 %	66	A	31.03 % / 25.87 %
3	B	58.62 % / 24.14 %	19	A	70.69 % / 17.24 %	35	D	62.07 % / 20.69 %	51	D	58.62 % / 25.86 %	67	C	51.72 % / 25.87 %
4	D	58.62 % / 25.86 %	20	B	43.1 % / 25.87 %	36	C	55.17 % / 25.86 %	52	A	34.48 % / 25.86 %	68	D	32.76 % / 27.58 %
5	A	27.59 % / 25.86 %	21	C	56.9 % / 20.69 %	37	B	63.79 % / 27.59 %	53	A	24.14 % / 27.58 %	69	A	29.31 % / 25.86 %
6	A	43.1 % / 24.14 %	22	A	12.07 % / 25.86 %	38	C	67.24 % / 27.59 %	54	B	43.1 % / 25.87 %	70	D	41.38 % / 27.59 %
7	D	53.45 % / 24.14 %	23	B	39.66 % / 20.68 %	39	D	20.69 % / 25.86 %	55	C	18.97 % / 27.58 %	71	B	32.76 % / 22.41 %
8	B	34.48 % / 25.86 %	24	B	37.93 % / 24.14 %	40	A	41.38 % / 29.31 %	56	A	17.24 % / 25.86 %	72	C	60.34 % / 25.87 %
9	C	56.9 % / 24.13 %	25	C	44.83 % / 25.86 %	41	D	63.79 % / 22.42 %	57	C	44.83 % / 25.86 %	73	B	51.72 % / 27.59 %
10	C	31.03 % / 24.14 %	26	C	36.21 % / 25.86 %	42	B	56.9 % / 27.58 %	58	B	31.03 % / 25.87 %	74	D	46.55 % / 25.86 %
11	A	31.03 % / 24.14 %	27	C	65.52 % / 20.69 %	43	D	50.0 % / 25.86 %	59	D	18.97 % / 27.58 %	75	A	58.62 % / 25.86 %
12	D	34.48 % / 25.86 %	28	D	44.83 % / 24.14 %	44	C	24.14 % / 25.86 %	60	A	63.79 % / 25.87 %	76	C	44.83 % / 27.58 %
13	B	46.55 % / 24.14 %	29	B	39.66 % / 20.68 %	45	A	39.66 % / 27.58 %	61	D	37.93 % / 27.59 %	77	D	60.34 % / 25.87 %
14	B	56.9 % / 25.86 %	30	A	67.24 % / 24.14 %	46	B	25.86 % / 27.59 %	62	D	37.93 % / 27.59 %	78	A	34.48 % / 27.59 %
15	D	55.17 % / 24.14 %	31	A	44.83 % / 24.14 %	47	A	51.72 % / 24.14 %	63	C	53.45 % / 27.58 %	79	A	39.66 % / 22.41 %
16	C	48.28 % / 24.13 %	32	D	53.45 % / 24.14 %	48	D	43.1 % / 27.59 %	64	B	43.1 % / 25.87 %	80	B	51.72 % / 25.87 %

Q.	Ans.	Correct		Q.	Ans.	Correct		Q.	Ans.	Correct		Q.	Ans.	Correct		Q.	Ans.	Correct
		Skipped				Skipped				Skipped				Skipped				Skipped
81	B	27.59 %		85	D	32.76 %		89	C	51.72 %		93	C	15.52 %		97	D	62.07 %
		24.13 %				25.86 %				25.87 %				25.86 %				27.59 %
82	D	51.72 %		86	B	34.48 %		90	D	48.28 %		94	A	46.55 %		98	B	39.66 %
		25.87 %				27.59 %				27.58 %				27.59 %				27.58 %
83	D	29.31 %		87	B	56.9 %		91	D	58.62 %		95	A	46.55 %		99	C	25.86 %
		25.86 %				25.86 %				25.86 %				27.59 %				29.31 %
84	A	29.31 %		88	D	39.66 %		92	A	48.28 %		96	A	37.93 %		100	A	34.48 %
		27.59 %				27.58 %				25.86 %				27.59 %				25.86 %

//Hints and Solutions//

1. Alfred Wegener based his theory of the basis of the following premises. Firstly, the geological formations and fossil remains of the present far away continents showed similarities. Secondly, some of the continents showed complementary coastlines, such as the East coast of South America matches the West coast of Africa. Polar Wandering or Paleomagnetism and geological matching are some of the evidences which were cited by Wegener to show that the continents were close once.

2. The Aravalli Hills are located in the Indian state of Rajasthan. The Aravalli hills are the range of mountains that stretch diagonally from Kotra in the northeast to Khetri in the southwest direction.

3. Exfoliation is one of the processes of Mechanical weathering where the expansion and contraction phases occur more on the outer rock layers than in the inner layers due to which the layers of concentric shells get peeled off from the main rock mass.

4. The German Geomorphologist, Walther Penck proposed that the geomorphic forms are an expression of the phase and rate of uplift and in relation to the rate of degradation or erosion. This explains that the interaction between upliftment and degradation are always coexistent. These are the basic premises of the Penckian model. Accordingly, Primarumpf is referred to as the formation which can be seen before the stage of upliftment. Similarly, just like the other theories, after continued upliftment and erosional factors, the landscape gets reduced to the low plain known as endrumpf. This theory contrasts with the Davisian cycle of erosion.

5. * Monoclinal Folds are referred to those where the compressional forces act in such a way that one limb of the fold is totally vertical.

* Isoclinal folds, also known as Overfolds are formed when the compressional forces are so strong that both the sides of the fold are inclined in the same direction. The short and steep side also dips in the same direction as the flat or gradual sloping side but the sides of the fold are not horizontal

* Asymmetrical folds are formed when one limb of the fold is pushed too far so that one side of the fold is long and gradual in slope while the other is short and steep. This shows a unilateral element.

* Plunge folds are found when the axis of the fold, instead of being parallel to the horizontal plane becomes tilted and forms plunge angle, which is the angle between the axis and the horizontal plane.

6. Most of the landforms have this type of arrangement. The Summital convexity is the topmost convex slope which supports waxing and the Basal concavity is the waning slope where the pediments or the weathered materials get deposited.

7. Drumlins are depositional features of glaciers and are peculiar type of low round hillocks which resemble the shape of an inverted boat or half egg split lengthwise. This is the reason they are collectively known as basket of eggs topography. Drumlins are basically smooth, oval-shaped ridge like features composed of mainly glacial till with some masses of gravel and sand. The long axes of drumlins are parallel to the direction of ice movement.

8. The term plate was first used by J.T. Wilson in 1965. McKenzie and Parker elaborated the mechanism behind the movement of plates in 1967. It was based on Euler's geometrical theorem. Based on this, they gave the paving stone hypothesis. It says that oceanic crust is formed at the ridges and destroyed at the trenches. Isacks and Sykes confirmed this hypothesis in 1967.

Thus, the Correct answer is B.

9. The Eurasian plate and North American plate are diverging or moving away from each other, forming the Mid-Atlantic range, the longest mountain range in the world. The Amid-Atlantic range is visible above sea level in Iceland and between North America and Africa.

Thus, the Correct answer is C.

10. The difference between the earth flow, mud flow and debris flow are the amount of water and the size of the particles. Debris flow has a minimum amount of water and particles coarse than sand. It is followed by earth flow and mud flow with more than 80 percent mud or sand. Mud flow has the maximum amount of water.

Thus, the Correct answer is C.

11. Troposphere is marked by turbulence and eddies. It is called as the convective region as all the convective activities cease at the upper limit of the troposphere. Various forms of clouds, thunderstorms, cyclones and anticyclones occur in this sphere because of the concentration of almost all the water vapour and aerosols in it.

CFCs or Chlorofluorocarbons are synthetic chemicals which, used as propellants, are released in the air and transported in the stratosphere by vertical atmospheric circulation. Chlorine when separated from CFCs reacts with water and thus depletes ozone rather breaks ozone into O_2 and O.

12. The E layer reflects the medium and high frequency radio waves and is much better defined than the D layer. It is produced by the ultraviolet photons from the sun interacting with nitrogen and nitrogen molecules. This layer does not exist during the nighttime.

13. We all know, temperature decreases with increasing altitudes in the troposphere at an altitude of 6.5 degree Celsius per 1000 meters but this trend sometimes gets reversed under special circumstances and hence is known as negative lapse rate. Thus, warm air layer lies over cold air layer. However, because of this inversion of temperature, several significant changes can be observed. The significance of this reversal is that there are al lot of climatic effects that affect the surrounding environment as well as the economy.

14. Absorption is defined as the process in which the incident energy is retained by a substance and is irreversibly converted into some other form of energy. Gases are selective absorbers. There is a certain amount of energy loss by the process of absorption in the atmosphere. Nitrogen is a poor absorber of incoming while oxygen and ozone are considered as good absorbers of solar radiation.

When the diameter of the particles is larger than the wavelength of the incident beam of light, true scattering does not occur and the effect of the particles is the nature of diffuse reflection or diffusion. As the process of diffusion s non-selective, component colours of the incident light do not get separated. This is the reason why the sun behind the observer is pure white. Also, the diffused light during twilight is due to this phenomenon.

Reflection refers to the part of the incident light which, falling on any surface is reflected. Thus, a certain amount of energy is lost and does not play a role in the heating of the atmosphere. The reflectivity of a substance is known as the albedo.

The atmosphere is composed of molecules of air, water molecules, and dust particles. These molecules scatter the shorter ultraviolet waves in different directions. This process, in meteorological terms, is known as scattering.

15. The term Frontogenesis was first used by Tor Bergeron for the creation of new fronts. Later, it was extended to include the process of regeneration of old and decaying fronts. The term is a Latin derived term. Frontogenesis occurs when the wind blows in such a way that the isotherms become packed along the leading edge of the intruding air mass.

Generally, the isobars in an air mass are smooth curves and there are no sharp bends in them. And frontal activity is always associated with cloudiness and precipitation. Since warm air moves up along the frontal surface, it cools adiabatically and thus results in cloudy condensation and precipitation.

The appearance of warm front is mostly observed by the presence of cirrus clouds.

16. The centre of the tropical cyclone is characterized by extremely low pressure. Isobars are more or less circular but are less in number. This is the reason why winds quickly rush up towards the centre and attain gale velocity. The air pressure at the centre sometimes becomes as low as 650 mm.

17. Climochronology is the description of the past climates of each period of the earth's history. The reconstruction of palaeoclimates, i.e., climochronology means rearranging of the climatic history of the globe or part, on the basis of indicators of palaeoclimates.

18. The eye of the cyclone refers to the central and core of the tropical cyclone which is characterized by minimum wind speeds, highest temperature and lowest pressure, etc. Eye wall is a narrow band of high wind speed and surrounds the eye of the cyclone. The characteristic features of this belt include high wind speed, intense thunderstorms, vertical motions, huge amount of rainfall. The spiral bands surround the eye and the eye wall of the cyclone and are called as rain bands because of dense cumulonimbus clouds and thunderstorms. Annular belt surrounds the spiral bands and are identified by low relative humidity, weak cloudiness, and little rainfall. Outer convective belt is characterized by intense convective activity and increased cloudiness and rainfall. And the last part, peripheral belt represents the outermost limit of the cyclone and is identified by scanty rainfall and less convectional activity.

19. ENSO refers to a condition where the rising air in the east Pacific cools above and turns west wards in the troposphere and ultimately descends in the tropical western Pacific giving birth to high pressure which drives war air towards the coasts of South America, Thus, in this manner a complete convective cell is formed and is known as ENSO.

20. The stratosphere has the additional ozone layer. This layer absorbs the harmful ultraviolet rays of the sun. That leads to increase in the temperature of the stratosphere. The boundary between mesosphere and stratosphere is called stratopause, which is located at about 50 km from the earth's crust. Thus, both (A) and (R) are true, but (R) is not the correct explanation of (A).

Thus, the correct answer is B.

21. · Humid Warm Summer climate is denoted by Da. It has hot summers. Summers are ideal for rapid growth of crops. Winters have very less vegetation.

· Dry subtropical climate is also called Mediterranean climate. It is shown by abbreviation Cs and covers 1.7% of world's total area. Winters here are mild and rainy while summers are hot and dry.

· Tropical desert is shown with abbreviation BWh. The average rainfall here is less than 35 cm. There is little vegetation and most of it is drought resistant. Thar Desert in Rajasthan is an example of BWh climate.

· The Aw is the Tropical Savannah Climate. It has alternate wet and dry seasons. The length of the day and night is nearly equal. Total annual rainfall is between 100 and 150 cm.

Thus, the correct answer is C.

22. The El Nino is warm water current that flows from Papua New Guinea towards Peru. It occurs every 3 to 8 years. It is considered to be one of the causes of global warming and also leads to droughts in Australia. It was discovered in the seventeenth century.

Thus, the correct answer is A.

23. The recorded climatic data has been available for the last 150 years. This data shows that the first decade of 20th century has seen harsh winters in Western Europe. In the winter of 1917-18, the Thames froze. In the second decade, began the trend of increase in global temperatures. Record breaking high temperatures have been observed since 1990.

Thus, the correct answer is B.

24. The amount of radiant energy has been found to be constant. There is little variation is the quantum of solar energy received at the outer margin of the atmosphere. It is a fact verified by observations made at various places on different occasions.

Thus, the Correct answer is B.

25. Air mass thunderstorm occur as a result of vertical displacement of air within an air mass and are not connected with frontal effects. Included in this type are the local heat thunderstorm, Orographic thunderstorm and advective or upper thunderstorm.

Thus, the Correct answer is C .

26. The density of ocean water is dependent on the temperature of water and amount of salts present in the water, i.e. salinity of water. Average density of ocean water is 1027 gm/ cc. As the salinity increases, the density of water also increases. As temperature of water increases, molecules of water move further apart, hence the density of water decreases. So, (A) is true and (R) is false.

Thus, the correct answer is C.

27. The Pacific Ocean is a geologically active area. There are many active fault lines in the area of ring of fire and several active volcanoes. Thus, the Pacific Ocean has the most number of tsunamis, nearly 80 %.

Thus, the correct answer is C.

28. A tropical cyclone has a low pressure centre, strong winds along with thunder and rains. It has different names in different places. In the Northwestern Pacific Ocean is called as typhoon. In Indian Ocean they are simply called severe cyclonic storms or tropical cyclones. In northeastern Pacific Ocean and Atlantic Ocean, they are called as hurricanes.

Thus, the correct answer is D.

29. Precipitation and river runoff are the major factors that decrease the ocean salinity to a large extent. Precipitation is inversely related to salinity. Due to heavy rainfall the ratio of salt to the total volume of water is reduced. This explains why the regions of equatorial zone record low salinity than the regions of sub-tropical zones. Similarly, the salinity decreases as the river bring down a large volume of water to the oceans. Due to this the mouths of the oceans have low salinity. This situation is more common in the enclosed seas. For instance, In the Baltic sea, many rivers from the land pour down fresh water in the Gulf of Bothnia and reduce the salinity. But if the evaporation is greater than the runoff, the salinity will be greater.

30. Ocean currents are of vital importance to the marine organisms, phytoplankton's and fishing grounds. The down welling and upwelling of water masses due to the ocean currents support the distribution of oxygen and nutrients on the ocean, hence leading to a situation suitable for the fishes. The down welling of cold-water mass take oxygen downwards and provide the growth for marine organisms and planktons. The upwelling and the convergence of warm and cold currents also promote the presence of rich nutrients. The places where cold and warm currents meet are rich in nutrients and various organisms. Hence, fishes thrive in these environments and thus form major fishing grounds. For instance, The Grand Banks off the Newfoundland is a major fishing ground due to the meeting of warm Gulf Stream and cold Labrador currents.

31. The habitat of specie describes the environment over which a species is known to occur and type of community that is formed as a result. Habitats can be defined as regions on ecological space that are composed of multiple dimensions, each representing a biotic or abiotic ecological variable. Habitat shifts gives the information about various population changes relative to habitats that most other individuals of species occupy.

Thus, the Correct answer is A.

32. The environment is an amalgamation of various features called factors. These are the product of forces and process of nature and are universal and inherent all over the earth. These factors are classified into two groups direct factors and indirect factors. The direct factors are light, temperature, soil air, water etc. and indirect factors include soil structure, soil organisms, altitude, wind, slope, etc.

Thus, the correct answer is D.

33. The term ecosystem was coined by Tansley in 1935. "eco" part means environment and the "system" part implies a complex of coordinate units. Ecosystem also called biocoenosis, geobiocoenosis, phytocoenosis, biosystem, etc.

Thus, the Correct answer is B.

34. Carbon cycle is a biogeochemical cycle where carbon is exchanged among the biosphere, geosphere, hydrosphere and atmosphere of the earth.

• Riebeek published their work in 2011 titled "The carbon cycle".

• Holmes published his work in 2008 entitled "the age of wonder"

• Archer published his work in 2010 named "the global carbon cycle'

• Prentice in 2001 published his work called "the carbon cycle and atmospheric carbon dioxide"

Thus, the Correct answer is B.

35. Human environment interaction involves understanding of human characteristics. The type of society strongly influences people's attitude towards nature, their behavior, and therefore their impact on ecosystem. Important characteristics of human social systems are population size, social organization, values, technologies etc.

Thus, the Correct answer is D.

36. The law of primate city was given by Mark Jefferson. The primate city is at least two times the size of the second city in terms of population. Examples of primate city include:-

* Paris is the primate city of France. The population here is 9.6 million (201C. and the city of Marseilles has the population of 1.3 million.

* In United Kingdom, London has population of 7 million and the second city, Birmingham has just the population of 1 million.

* Bangkok, in Thailand has the population of 7.5 million and the second city, Nathaburi has population of mere 4,18,000.

* Mexico City in Mexico has population of 8.6 million and the city if Guadalajara has population of 1.6 million.

Thus, the correct answer is C.

37. George Zipf gave the rank-size rule in 1949. The rank-size rule describes the relation between the size of the city and the rank of the city. This relation is shown by the formula, $P_r = P_1/r$. Here P_r is the population of the 'r' ranked city, P_1 is the population of the largest city and r is the rank of the city. For example, if the city X is ranked 4th, the population of X $P_1/4$.

Thus, the correct answer is B.

38. The slum is defined as a run-down area of the city characterized by substandard housing and squalor and lacking in

tenure security by the UN-Habitat. Slums have high rates of criminal activities, high poverty, lack of infrastructure, lack of basic health care facilities, etc. Population though is generally high in slums; one billion people worldwide live in slums.

Thus, the correct answer is C.

39. The Concentric zone model was given by Ernest Burgess. In this model he divided the structure of the city into 5 zones. These include the Central Business District, Transition zone, working class zone, residential zone and commuter's zone. The fourth or the residential zone is home to the middle-class people, who have amenities like parks, shops, gardens, lawns, etc. The houses here are detached. The rich, affluent people live in the commuter's zone, away from the city. These people can afford large houses and cost of the commute.

Thus, the correct answer is D.

40. Lewis Mumford gave 6 stage of cultural change of town in his theory of origin of towns. These were Eoplis is a rising village. Polis is a small market town. Metropolis has specialized activities and a sphere of influence. Megalopolis is wealth-dominant city. Tyrannopolis has wealth but also abundance of crimes. Necropolis is the city of dead, with environmental problems.

Thus, the correct answer is A.

41. The increasing tempo of Industrialization has made world trade or international trade much more important. Industries provide manufactured goods and machinery to the farms and houses. Moreover, it supports a lot of employment opportunities. And the most important point is that the industrialization increases the output or production capacity of several agricultural farms. Along with this, Industrialization increases self-sufficiency, diversification of economy, and raising of living standards.

42. Some countries only support self-sufficiency on food supplies, which means that there is little surplus for exports and hence can afford only a few imports. Whereas, on the other hand, countries which have a large international trade, can import a large amount of goods. This means that a wide range of products and manufactured goods are available as surplus. Thus, the volume of international trade is taken as a country's guide to economic well-being. As the economic well-being of a country increases, the number of employments, living standards, and others increase.

43. West Europe leads all other regions in the annual volume of world trade. Because the continent is small but very densely populated, there is a large import of foodstuffs such as tea, coffee, cocoa, sugar and fruits. Most of these come from the European countries themselves. As the continent is highly industrialized, many minerals and raw materials are imported such as cotton, wool, furs, jute, rubber and so on. There is also a large volume of entrepot trade by which goods are imported by one country for re-export to another either within Europe or further afield.

44. The volume of international trade is termed as the economic barometer or a guide to a country's economic well-being because of the imports and the exports. If a country has a large international trade, it is because it can import a large quantity of foodstuffs and manufactured goods.

In terms of the volume of trade, the U.S.A is the greatest country in the world because of its varied economy, rich mineral resources, rapid rate of industrial expansion, heavy overseas investments and liberal foreign aid to the underdeveloped countries.

45. During the 19th century, Canada was a major exporter of primary products, mainly to the United Kingdom. The greatest single export item is forest products which accounts for a third of the annual total. After that comes wheat and flour and many important minerals.

46. Deltas are formed where the shores are free of hard rocks. When a river reaches a lake or the sea the water slows down and loses the power to carry sediment . The sediment is dropped at the mouth of the river. Some rivers drop so much sediment that waves and tides can't carry it all away. It builds up in layers forming a delta.

47. Hoover proposed his theory of industrial location whose determinants of location of industries were transportation costs and extraction costs. The delivered price for the buyers will be the cost of extraction plus the transport costs. This was represented by isotims, which start from the point of production or extraction and joins the places containing the same delivered prices. Buyers will obtain the product from the source that offers the lowest delivered price.

48. Gravity model is defined as the level of interaction between two locations which is a function of their attributes based on their level of separation. The calculation of the Gravity model is given by $T_{ij} = V_i \ast W_j / S^2_{ij}$, where T_{ij} is the spatial interaction and this formulae explains the main notion of the Gravity model which basically says the gravitational attraction between 2 regions is directly proportional to the product of the masses of the two regions and inversely proportional to the square of the distance between the 2 regions.

The potential spatial model basically is the level of interaction between one location and all the others which is measured by the summation of the attributes of each other pondered by their level of separation, that is squared to reflect the friction of distance.

The retail model is a bit different than the others. Instead of interactions, it deals with the boundaries. It assumes that the market boundary between two locations is a function of their separation pondered by the ratio of their respective weights. Hence, the calculation is represented by $B_{ij} = S_{ij} / 1 + W_j / V_i$.

49. Losch's theory attempts to explain the size and shape of market area within which a location would command the largest revenue. It is assumed that the demand varies inversely with price. This gives us a demand pattern. The demand curve can be rotated round the production point to give the size and shape of the market space. With increasing competition, the size of the market area becomes hexagonal. They also become smaller as the markets are competed away.

Thus, the Correct answer is D.

50. The ICT Development Index (IDI) is an index published by the United Nations International Telecommunication Union based on

internationally agreed information and communication technologies (ICT) indicators. Iceland ranks first in 2017 ICT Development Index.

Thus, the Correct answer is C.

51. The earliest arrivals in India are believed to be Negritos. At Andaman Islands they are mainly found now. The Andaman Islands are home to four 'Negrito' tribes – the Great Andamanese, Onge, Jarawa and Sentinelese. The Nicobar Islands are home to two 'Mongoloid' tribes – the Shompen and Nicobarese. The 'Negrito' tribes are believed to have arrived in the islands from Africa up to 60,000 years ago.

52. Crop diversification is like crop rotation in which it helps to maintain soil fertility. depending on just one crop is disastrous to the national economy of a country as well as for an individual farm, such as the Brazil's coffee, or Ghana's cocoa, etc. Crop diversification reduces this problem as when one crop is only fetching low prices, another tends to be in good demand. A great advantage of this is that all types of land can be used. This overall leads to the most economic use of land.

53. Crops which are expensive to produce because they need skilled cultivation, much costly equipment or labour intensive picking, packing or processing for market are only profitable if transport costs can be kept low. Therefore, they must be located near city markets. Crops which require less intensive farming can stand higher costs in marketing, while crops or livestock produced on an extensive basis at low cost can stand higher transport costs and be grown at greater distance from the markets. This is the main notion of Von Thunen 's theory of Industrial location. Thus, perishable items in strong demand and those products with high transportation costs get located close to the city. Less perishable products with lower transport costs and lower market prices predominate with increasing distance from the markets.

54. Shifting cultivation is a primitive type of agriculture, still practiced around the world. In this system, the patch of forest or vegetation is burnt to make room for agricultural land. The land is abandoned after a few years and new land is selected. The abandoned patch of land is used again after its fertility is restored naturally. This type of cultivation is mostly done by nomadic people. It has different names in different parts of the world. It is called as Jhum in North-East India, Kumari in Western Ghats of Kerala, Podu in Andhra Pradesh and Dhavi, Kaman and Vinga in Odisha. Around the world, it has names like Masole in Congo, Ladang in Java & Indonesia, Roka in Brazil, Ray in Vietnam, etc.

Thus, the correct answer is B.

55. Dependency theory, another major body of the development theory, which holds that the political and economic relationships between countries and regions of the world control and limit the economic development possibilities of the poorer areas. Some theorists have stated, the colonialism created political and economic structures that caused the colonies to become dependent on the colonial powers. Many poorer countries tie their currency to a wealthy country's currency or by adopting the wealthy country's currency as their own, creating a important link between the poor and the wealthy country's economy.

56. Culture cannot be measured. The work standard of a person cannot be measured with another person's work. Culture is a social concept and is constantly changing and adapting.

Brock and Webb has divided the world into 4 major and 2 minor cultural realms. Occidental realm, Islamic, Indian and east Indian cultural realm are the major ones while south east Asian, Meso African are the minor cultural realms.

Europe has a large acre of agricultural land than any other continent and there are no deserts. Its mineral wealth is considerable and varied as well as the trade conditions exceed that of Europe. The mixing of European races results in a variety of energetic and inventive people.

Cultural area is a concept of cultural geography, in which a geographic region and time sequence is characterised by substantially uniform environment and culture. The present boundaries of states in India, which have been drawn on the basis of languages, generally represent cultural areas while cultural region is a portion of the Earth's surface that has common cultural elements.

57. Society is an expression of different social processes. Social processes, however, means those various modes of interactions between individuals or a number of groups which consist of cooperation, conflict, competition and assimilation. Competition is found in each society and in every class of society such as students, laborer's, artists, etc. It enables the development of both the individuals and the nation.

Accommodation is what leads to social harmony. It is close to cooperation and conflict and thus must take trends in both the areas into consideration. It checks conflicts and enables all to work in close cooperation with each other.

58. Apsara is the oldest of India's research reactors. The reactor was designed by the Bhabha Atomic Research Center (BARC) and built with assistance from the United Kingdom (which also provided the initial fuel supply consisting of 80 percent enriched uranium). Apsara first went critical on 4 August 1956.

59. Political Geography started to prosper during the 1980s. Two research areas dominated this field. Firstly, the urban conflicts and the location of 'goods' and 'bads'; secondly, the application of the concepts of electoral geography. These were identified during the 1970s and slowly this sub discipline grew because of its remarkable resurgence.

60. Richard Hartshorne, an American Geographer who specialized in economic and political geography, attempted to provide a new framework for analyzing the geography of political areas and the modern state in the 1950s as the sub discipline was becoming narrowly systematic. Hartshorne had a lot of contributions to this field such as "Political Geography in the Modern World", "The Politico-Geographic Pattern of the World".

61. Though political Geography was slowly gaining it's prominence, it could not overcome its uncoordinated nature and hence the lack of coherence increased. To correct this situation, the general reaction was to order political geography information in three separate scales: for teaching and research, international or global, national and urban.

62. Political Geography was termed as the wayward child of geographical sciences during the 1920s. The State-scale analysis had always been a major component of the Political Geography. It was being taught in the universities, but there was a lack of research to back up the teaching.

63. The two main research areas, urban conflicts and the development of the concepts of electoral geography such as the geography of voting, geographical influences in voting, the geography of representation led to the development of urban political geography. Radical geography was created as after the political events of the Cold war, the geography became more politicized and this also led to Marxist geography.

64. Most coastal areas experience two high and two low tides per day. One of these high tides is at the point on the earth which is closest to the moon (sub lunar) and other high tide is at the opposite point on the earth (antipodal). One tidal cycle comprises two high tides and two low tides. One tidal cycle completes in 24 hours and 50.4 minutes. This is because of the revolution of Moon around the earth and both earth's rotation and moon revolution are in same direction. (Moon is not stationary, so there is a difference, if moon were stationary the high tides would have occurred exactly in 12 hours). The high tides occur at an interval of 12 hours and 25.2 minutes. This means that if there is a high tide is at 7.00 am, next high tide would be at 7.25 pm and next would be at 7.50 am, and so on. The time difference between two high tides is called "Tidal Interval". The tidal cycle in this pattern is called semidiurnal. However, most of the enclosed water bodies or away from the open ocean such as Caribbean Sea or Caspian Sea, there are only one high tide and one low tide. This pattern is called Diurnal tides. At the coast of the oceans, there may be two high tides, of unequal length. This is called Mixed Tides.

65. Alexander von Humboldt was a German geographer who had travelled extensively. He was born in Berlin in 1769. He is famous for introducing the concept of human-induced climate change. His travels in South America, particularly Mt. Chimborazo led to discovery that the temperature falls with increasing altitude and air becomes rarified in higher altitudes. The current on west coast of South America, a cold-water current was named Humboldt current in his honor. It is nowadays called as Peru Current. Humboldt was a physical geographer and did not give his views on the idea of behaviouralism, which emerged in the 1900, years after his demise.

Thus, the correct answer is B.

66. The ancient Greeks believed that all area above the Caspian Sea is a cold desert. The ancient region of the parts of Central Asia was called as Bactria. The area extends from north of Hindu Kush mountains near Tibet to south of river Amo. The double-humped camel found in the Nubra valley is found in this region. Therefore, the camel is also called as Bactrian camel.

Thus, the correct answer is A.

67. 'Die Erdkunde' means Earth sciences. It is often used as translation of geography in German language. It is a collection of 19 volumes of books with over 20000 pages. It was written by Carl Ritter. It was intended to be complete geography of the world, but Ritter could complete only Asia and Africa in his lifetime.

Thus, the correct answer is C.

68. Ratzel developed the concept of Lebensraum (living space). In that he applied the concepts of organic theory to Political Geography. Humboldt travelled extensively through the world and noted that the mode of life was different in different places, such as coastal plains differed from islands, river basins or mountainous regions. Immanuel Kant, in 18th century concluded from his research that environment had a huge impact on human lifestyle. Charles Darwin, in his book Origin of species claimed that things in nature change with time.

Thus, the correct answer is D.

69. As per the Puranas, the East African and Madagascar region was called as Shalmali. The silk-cotton was called salmala and it was found in the said region. The area had moderate rainfall and was located on margin of equatorial region, which led to blossom of silk-cotton trees. Thus, both (A) and (R) are true and (R) is the correct explanation of (A).

Thus, the correct answer is A.

70. The field of political geography was explored in Indian context by R.D. Dikshit. He blended political theory with spatial analysis in case of Indian nation-state. R.N.P Sinha and Govind Saran Singh also made contributions to the political geography in India.

Thus, the correct answer is D.

71. 'Progress in Geography' was written by S.P. Chatterjee, in this book number studies related to economic geography were discussed. We can see in this book that although the industrial location, land-use variation, etc are still prevalent, there has been a definite increase in research upon quantitative techniques of regional economic analysis.

Thus, the correct answer is B.

72. * Vidal de La Blache was a famous French geographer who founded the school of human geography. He was also of the opinion that it was unreasonable to draw boundaries between physical and human phenomenon.

* Albert Penck was the first geographer to coin the term 'Geomorphology'.

He was also one of the two scientists to discover and name four ice ages of European Pleistocene period.

* Alexander von Humboldt travelled extensively throughout the world and focused on physical geography. He also emphasized the difference between lifestyle of people as per their different environments.

* Elisee Reclus was a disciple of Carl Ritter. He was interested in systematic physical geography which he called la Terre.

Thus, the correct answer is C.

73. While learning about physical geography, the most widely used way of obtaining data and information is by visiting, observation, exploration and description of the physical phenomenon. Further studies depend upon this approach rather than behaviouralism. Behaviouralism plays some part in human geography and in determining human behavior of humans.

Thus, the correct answer is B.

74. Physical maps are used to show the natural landscape feature of the earth. They use either colours or shades to show relief. They use green, brown and grey colours to show land elevation, dark green for near sea elevation. Shades of grey is used for highest elevation. Water bodies are often shades of blue. Glaciers and ice caps shown with white.

Political maps are used to show geographical boundaries of government units like countries, states, districts, cities etc. They show roads, cities and major water features such as oceans, rivers and lakes. Political maps are also called reference maps.

Thus, the correct answer is D.

75. In remote sensing technique, the electromagnetic radiation emitted or reflected from the objects must pass through atmosphere before it is detected by the remote sensor. Remote sensing by satellite involve atmospheric degradation. Hence the atmospheric conditions determine the effective use of electromagnetic spectrum for remote sensing.

* Wavelength of visible region is 0.4-0.7μm.

* Wavelength of ultraviolet region is 0.3 to 4μm.

* Wavelength of X ray region is 0.03to 3.0 nm.

* Wavelength of gamma ray region is less than 0.03nm.

Thus, the Correct answer is A.

76. Digital image processing is a technique which involves manipulation of digital image to extract information. When satellite images are being manipulated in such manner, this technique is also referred to as satellite image processing. It involves combination of software based image processing tools. There are three classification of digital image processing.

Thus, the correct answer is C.

77. Remote sensing is used to acquire the data of remotely sensed areas. It is used in the fields like crop acreages estimation, lithological discrimination, coral reef mapping, forest cover mapping, loss of biological diversity, wealth of oceans, oil fields detection, major river valley projects, management of wild rivers, environment impact analysis amongst many others.

Thus, the Correct answer is D.

78. The most popular test of statistical significance is chi square test. It is based on based on the comparison of the differences of observed and expected frequencies of a particular cell in the universe. In case both are same , it means that the attributes are completely independent of each other. If the observer and expected values are not equal in all the cells, the differences between the observed and expected frequencies of different cells are calculated.

Thus, the Correct answer is A .

79. Sometimes, variables are highly correlated in such a way that it would be duplicate information found in another variable. Principal component analysis identifies duplicate data over several datasets. It creates a new dataset with only the essential information.

Thus, the correct answer is A.

80. A hypsometric curve is a histogram or a cumulative distribution function of elevations in a geographic area. Differences in hypsometric curves between landscapes arise because the geomorphic process that shape the landscape may be different. Thus the differences in the shape show the differences in the elevation of the landscapes on the surface of the earth.

Thus, the correct answer is B.

81. The Thematic Maps are special category maps designed to show a particular theme with a specific geographic area and portray spatial variations of a single phenomenon or the relationship between phenomena prevalent at particular locations. The main purposes of thematic maps are to provide specific information about locations, provide general information about spatial patterns and can be used for comparing patterns on two or more maps. The General maps portray the surface features or data such as landforms, lines of transportation, settlements but the thematic maps show the most required thing i.e., spatial variation. Maps showing population density, climate natural vegetation are some examples of thematic maps.

Thus, the Correct answer is B.

82. All the above statements are correct, since GIS can be defined as a toolbox, as a database and as an organization. The first three statements explain GIS in terms of Database and Organization while the last statement is a characteristic feature of GIS. So, simply stated, GIS is a set of computer-based systems for managing geographical data and using these data to solve spatial problems.

Thus, the Correct answer is D.

83. Stream length ratio= Rl= Lu/Lu+i, where, Lu is the mean length of the streams or basins of order u; the suffix u+1 denotes the same for the next higher order.

Bifurcation Ratio, Rb= Nu/Nu+i, where Nu is the number of the streams or basin of order u; the suffix u+1 denotes the same for the next higher order.

Elongation ratio(Re)= P/π L

Where, P= basin perimeter, L is maximum basin length.

Drainage Texture may be defined as the total number of streams segments of all order in a basin per perimeter of the basin.

Thus, the Correct answer is d.

84. The Main Central Thrust (MCT) lies between Greater Himalayas and Lesser Himalayas. Many earthquakes have occurred along this fault line. Some of these include earthquakes at Srinagar in 2005, Kandla in 1905, Uttarkashi in 1993 and Kathmandu in 2015. It is the most active fault line in Himalayan mountain system.

Thus, the correct answer is A.

85. The eastern coast of India has always been prone to cyclonic storms. The major ones include like Fani and Gaja most recently. Western coast of Mahrashtra on the other hand does not have much vulnerability to cyclones. The coastline of Gujarat is more

vulnerable to cyclones. The north-eastern states lie in the Arkan Yoma mountain range and has had earthquakes like Tura(8.7-1897) and Cachar(7.5-1869) and more recently, on India-Nepal Border near Sikkim(7.1-2011). The river Chambal in North-Indian plains is not susceptible to floods on a frequent basis.

Thus, the correct answer is D.

86. The Union territory of Lakshadweep has total population of 64,473, which accounts for 0.01% of the total population of India according to census of 2011. The population density here is 382 persons per square km.

Thus, the correct answer is B.

87. • The Mana pass derives from a name of a village with the same name in Uttarakhand. It's last village on the border of Uttarakhand. Trade here is carried out with the help of mules.

• Khardung la is a pass in Jammu & Kashmir. At 18000 ft above the sea level, it's the highest motor able road in the world.

• The famous Rohtang pass in Himachal Pradesh connects the Kullu Valley with Spiti and Lahual Valley.

• Nathu la is a pass in Sikkim that lies in East Sikkim district and serves as one of the open trading posts on the border with China.

Thus, the correct answer is B.

88. The East-West corridor has been built to connect the cities of Silcher in Assam and Porbandar in Gujrat. The length of roads in the corridor is 3300 km. The corridor is a part of North-South-East-West Corridor, the largest ongoing highway project in the country.

Thus, the correct answer is D.

89. The khaddar soils are pale brown, sandy clays and loams. They are found in the lower areas of valley bottoms of North Indian plains. Black regur soils made of the basaltic rock are found in the Deccan plateau. The tarai region is the area swampy lowland of the north Indian plain, just below the Himalayas is called tarai tract. The foothills of Shiwaliks have the bhabar soils.

90. The floods are an annual feature in the Brahmaputra river region as rainfall amounting to over 250cm is observed here. Large amount of silt brought down by the rivers and its tributaries make the river channel shallow and hence the accommodating capacity is reduced. Thus, this results in heavy floods. Earthquakes are also a feature that lead to the river shape change.

91. The international trade is termed as the Economic barometer of a country because when one country exchanges goods with another country, it is known as foreign trade. This trade leads to economic prosperity and is important both as a source of imports and exports. The international trade is termed as an economic barometer as it shows the trend of the exports and imports and general economy.

From 2000-01, India's foreign trade grew up to a great extent, improved global growth and various policy initiatives were responsible for the improved exports. Another reason that led to this performance was that the value of exports had increased.

92. The Broad gauge has 1.676 m distance between the two rail tracks. About 82.49% length of the Indian Railways falls under the broad-gauge category.

The Metre gauge is indicated by the 1m distance between the two rails. About 13.24% of railways is under this category.

The narrow gauge has a distance of 0.762m and is only confined in the hilly regions as there is no flat terrain and sharp turns.

93. The plastic industry is considered as the sunrise industry because of its versatility, durability and increasing worldwide demand, easy processability, economic viability , non-corrosive and moisture resistant properties. There are a number of uses of plastics such as in packing industry, electrical accessories, etc.

94. There are a certain number of reasons behind this shifting which are:- Peninsular Indian comprises of a tropical climate which provides higher yield per unit area. Secondly, the sucrose content is high; Thirdly, large sugar lobby and better managed cooperative sugar mills in the south are also a reason.

95. Uttar Pradesh ranks 2nd in terms of rice production and has shown unprecedented progress in the recent years. About 13.82% of country's rice is produced here and availability of HYV seeds, irrigation facilities are the major factors for its development. After that, Punjab records an annual growth of over 12%. The major production comes Patiala, Ludhiana, Amritsar. Odisha produces about 7 % rice of India and Chhattisgarh comes right after that.

96. The effect of Green Revolution was primarily felt on the food grains, but the wheat benefitted the most. As a result, certain Inter crop imbalances, regional disparities, inter-personal inequalities took place. The major commercial crops such as cotton, jute, tea remained almost behind due to the green revolution. The most affected areas were Punjab, Haryana, Western Uttar Pradesh. For eliminating these problems caused by the green revolution, wider area and more crops and high yields must be considered for the green revolution. However, the Second Green Revolution was brought into life that covered all the demerits of the previous one.

97. The Rainwater Harvesting involves the collection and storage of rainwater at surface or sub-surface aquifers and is a very useful method, particularly for developing countries like India. The above sentences are some of the needs and advantages of rainwater Harvesting and is necessary in areas where ground water levels are declining on regular basis and inadequate.

98. The forests comprise only 23.28% of our geographical area and has a much less forest cover in comparison to the other countries. This is much below the average of 30.4% for the world. Uneven distribution of forests is also quite common in the Indian states. Madhya Pradesh has the largest area of about 76 thousand sq. km. under forests. The other states have a considerable area such as Arunachal Pradesh, Chhattisgarh, Odisha, Maharashtra and Andhra Pradesh. Each of these states vary considerably in terms of forest cover.

The thoughtless and rapid exploitation of the forest resources due to increasing demand of forest products and overgrazing practices has led to a lot of damage to the ecosystem. Thus,

forest conservation practices and social forestry practices must be considered.

99. Statements a, b and c are correct in the case of Peninsular Rivers as they have those characteristics. Firstly, these rivers flow in comparatively shallow and graded valleys. The rivers have little erosional activity to perform and hence these suggest a consequent drainage. Secondly, the rivers are seasonal and non-perennial. Water flows through these rivers only during the rainy season. Thirdly, the hard rock surface and non-alluvial character of the plateau does not allow for the formation of meanders and hence they follow a more or less straight course.

100. Bay of Bengal is the largest bay in the world. It is located to southeast of India. The Hudson bay comes second.

Q.1 According to Wegener, which of the following arrangements fall under the southern part of Pangaea?

A. South America, Africa, Europe, Asia

B. South America, Peninsular India, North America

C. Africa, Australia, Antarctica, South America

D. North America, Europe, Asia

Q.2 Consider the following statements:-

a) Davis along with erosional processes also stressed on biological processes as a contributing factor.

b) Davis' cycle of erosion is the most widely accepted theory and is also applicable in numerous approaches of landform development.

c) According to Penck, development of landscape is not time dependent.

d) The Youthful stage of Davisian cycle of erosion is characterized by vertical erosion and valley deepening.

Which of the following statement is correct?

A. a and b

B. b and c

C. a, b and c

D. c and d

Q.3 According to W.M. Davis, the landform that gets reduced to a low featureless plain due to vertical and horizontal erosion is known as

A. Peneplain

B. Pediplain

C. Pediment

D. Primarumph

Q.4 Among these, which one of the following variables will the slope character and formation depend on?

A. Lithology

B. Climate

C. Aspect and Base level changes

D. All of the above.

Q.5 Consider the following statements:-

a) Potholes and Plunge pools are found in the upper course of the river.

b) During the formation of meanders, the river does the erosional work on the convex bank and the depositional work on the concave bank.

c) A large number of tributaries joining the main river also lead to the formation of Deltas.

d) Braided stream is that which gets divided into several networks due to excess deposits on the river plain.

Which of the following statements are correct?

A. a and d

B. b and c

C. a, c and c

D. a and b

Q.6 Given below are the two statements, one labelled as Assertion (A) and the other labelled as Reason (R). Select your answer from the code given below:

Assertion (A): The gradual increase in depth of river valleys has occurred in the youthful stage of rivers.

Reason (R): The channel gradient is steep in the youthful stage of the river.

A. Both (A) and (R) are true and (R) is the correct explanation of (A).

B. Both (A) and (R) are true but (R) is not the correct explanation of (A).

C. (A) is true but (R) is false.

D. (A) is false but (R) is true.

Q.7 The part along with the line (a) in the following figure is

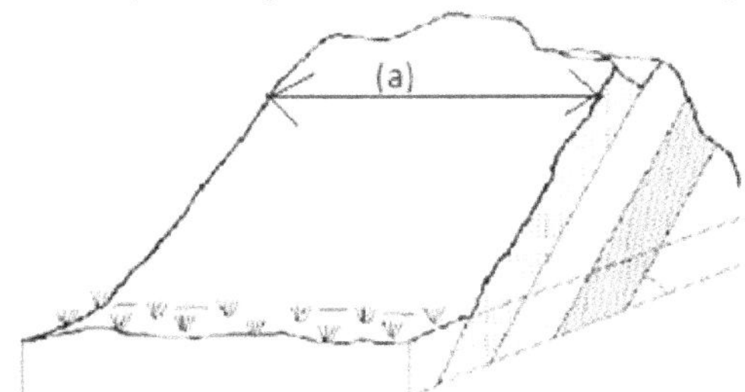

A. Dip

B. Strike

C. Anticline

D. Limb

Q.8 Which of the following is NOT an agent of weathering?

A. Frost

B. Soil

C. Oxygen

D. Carbon Dioxide

Q.9 Consider the following departments/ministries:

1. Ministry of Personnel, Public Grievances and Pensions

2. Department of Atomic Energy

3. Department of Space

Which of the above is/are under the direct charge of the Prime Minister of India?

A. 1 Only

B. 1 and 3 Only

C. 2 and 3 Only

D. 1, 2 and 3

Q.10 The model of cliff recession was developed by

A. A Strahler

B. A Young

C. O. Fisher and O. Lehman

D. L C King

Q.11 Which of the following statement is correct?

A. The three major gases in terms of volume in the atmosphere are nitrogen, carbon dioxide and argon.

B. The water vapour content in the atmosphere varies from 0.02%- 5%.

C. The greatest concentration of ozone is present between 50-80 km. in the atmosphere.

D. None of the above.

Q.12 Consider the following statements:-

a) Conduction is a slow process of heat transfer in terms of warming of the atmosphere.

b) The latent heat of evaporation and condensation are not quite responsible for the heating and cooling of the atmosphere.

c) Temperature over snow covered regions or grounds remain low even during daylight hours.

d) Loo is a typical example of the advection process.

Which of the following statements are correct?

A. a and c
B. a and b
C. b and d
D. a, c and d

Q.13 Given below are two statements- one is labelled as Assertion (A) and the other is labelled as Reason (R):

Assertion(A)- The other name for doldrums is subtropical high-pressure belt.

Reason(R)- Frequent calm conditions exist in the equatorial low-pressure belt.

Choose the correct option:

A. Both A and R are true and R is the correct explanation of A
B. Both A and R are true but R is not the correct explanation of A
C. A is true but R is false.
D. A is false but R is true.

Q.14 Consider the following statements:-

a) Close to the equator, tropical cyclones do not occur because of excessive humidity.

b) The largest number of temperate cyclones originate mostly over the North Atlantic Ocean.

c) The central low-pressure core of a tropical cyclone is called depression.

d) The Polar frontal theory or the wave theory provides an adequate explanation of the origin of extra tropical cyclones.

Which of the following statements are correct?

A. a and c
B. b and d
C. a, b and d
D. c and d

Q.15 Which among the following is / are correct statements with respect to Shifting Cultivation as practiced in India?

1. India's largest area under shifting cultivation is in the state of Arunachal Pradesh

2. In recent years, the cycle of shifting cultivation on a particular land has reduced drastically

Select the correct option from the codes given below:

A. Only 1
B. Only 2
C. Both 1 & 2
D. Neither 1 nor 2

Q.16 Match List-I with List-II:

List I (Drought definition)	List II (Precipitation parameters)
a. C.G. Bates	i. Rainfall for a week is half normal or less
b. J.C. Hoyt	ii. 0.25 inch precipitation in 24 hours
c. V.A. Conard	iii. Overall rainfall less than 85% of normal rainfall
d. D.A. Ramdas	iv. Annual precipitation 75% or less of normal rainfall

Choose the correct option from the code given below:

A. a-iv b-iii c-i d-ii
B. a-ii b-iii c-i d-iv
C. a-i b-iii c-iv d-ii
D. a-iv b-iii c-ii d-i

Q.17 Which of the following is NOT a reason for a glacial lake outburst flood?

A. Heavy rainfall
B. An avalanche
C. An earthquake under the ice
D. A volcanic eruption under the ice

Q.18 Over the last 100 years, the amount of CO_2 in the atmosphere has increased by

A. 10% **B.** 25% **C.** 30% **D.** 20%

Q.19 Which layer is called the Kennelly-Heaviside layer

A. D-layer **B.** E-layer **C.** F1-layer **D.** G-layer

Q.20 Two statements are given below. One is Assertion (A) and other is Reason (R):

Assertion(A)-El-Nino causes change in atmospheric circulation and water temperature.

Reasoning(R)-There is an increased Rainfall in eastern pacific.

Choose the correct answer:

A. Both A and R are true and R correctly explains A.
B. Both A and R are true but R does not explain A.
C. A is true and R is false.
D. Both A and R are false

Q.21 What is the average temperature of the oceanic water at the surface?

A. 10^0 C **B.** 15^0 C **C.** 17^0 C **D.** 25^0 C

Q.22 Match the following:-

List I (Major Oceans and Seas)	List II (Ocean bottom reliefs)
a. Atlantic Ocean	1. Algiers-Provencal Basin
b. Pacific Ocean	2. Fosse de Cape Breton Canyon
c. Mediterranean Sea	3. Cocos Keeling Basin
d. Indian Ocean	4. Tonga-Kermadec trench

Choose the correct option:

A. a-2 b-4 c-1 d-3
B. a-1 b-3 c-4 d-2
C. a-2 b-4 c-3 d-1
D. a-4 b-3 c-1 d-2

Q.23 Which of the following features provide major fishing grounds?

A. Continental Slope
B. Continental Rise
C. Continental Shelf
D. Deep Sea Plain

Q.24 Given below are two statements- one is labelled as Assertion (A) and the other is labelled as Reason (R):

Assertion (A)- Red Sea has a salinity of 40 ppt.

Reason (R)- The salinity is greatly influenced by the difference between evaporation and precipitation as well as sea water movement.

Choose the correct option:

A. Both A and R are true, and R is the correct explanation of A
B. Both A and R are true, but R is not the correct explanation of A
C. A is true, but R is false
D. A is false, but R is true

Q.25 Consider the following statements:-

a) Sea level Changes are only affected by Eustatic changes.

b) Marine sediments depict about global sea level change.

c) Evidences of sedimentary deposits of various sorts depict sea level changes during the pre-quaternary stages.

d) Sea level has risen by about 10 to 16 cm in the past 100 years.

Which of the following statements is correct?

A. a and b

B. b and c

C. a and c

D. b, c and d

Q.26 Given below are the two statements, one labelled as Assertion (A) and the other labelled as Reason (R). Select your answer from the code given below:

Assertion(A)- Nitrogen is used to stop things from reacting with oxygen

Reason (R)- Nitrogen compound is used in anesthetics.

A. Both A and R are true, and R correctly explains A

B. Both A and R are true but R does not explains A

C. A is true and R is false.

D. Both A and R are false

Q.27 Whose essay is "Exploring new ethics for survival"

A. Garett Hardin

B. Aldo Leopold

C. Rachel Carson

D. Murray Bookchin

Q.28 National Clean Air Programme (NCAP) was launched in

A. 2016 **B.** 2017 **C.** 2018 **D.** 2019

Q.29 Which article of the Indian constitution has the provision for the protection of environment, forest and wildlife in India by the state?

A. Article 46

B. Article 47

C. Article 48

D. Article 50

Q.30 Consider the following statement about Paris agreement:

i. Paris Agreement is known to combat climate change.

ii. Agreement aimed at global green house gas emission reduction.

iii. The conference held in 2015

Choose the correct option from below:

A. Only i

B. ii and iii

C. Only iii

D. All of the above

Q.31 Match the List-I with the List-II

List-I	List-II
(Model)	(Creator)
(a) Concentric Zone Model	(i) C.D. Harris and Edward Ullman
(b) Multiple Nuclei Model	(ii) Chauncy Harris
(c) Sector Model	(iii) Ernest Burgess
(d) Galactic City Model	(iv) Homer Hoyt

Code:

A. (a)-(iii), (b)-(i), c-(iv), d-(ii)

B. (a)-(iii), (b)-(iv), c-(i), d-(ii)

C. (a)-(iv), (b)-(iii), c-(ii), d-(i)

D. (a)-(iv), (b)-(ii), c-(i), d-(iii)

Q.32 A city which has direct effect on global affairs in social, economic, political and cultural terms is

A. Mega city

B. Global city

C. Central city

D. Edge city

Q.33 The idea of urban revolution due to growth of technology and presence of food surplus was stated by

A. Lewis Mumford

B. Karl Marx

C. V. Gordon Childe

D. Henri Pirenne

Q.34 Given below are the two statements, one labelled as Assertion (A) and the other labelled as Reason (R). Select your answer from the code given below :

Assertion (A) : According, to Lee's migration model, metropolitan areas are centers for immigration.

Reason (R) : The metropolitan areas have pull factors.

Code :

A. Both (A) and (R) are true and (R) is the correct explanation of (A).

B. Both (A) and (R) are true but (R) is not the correct explanation of (A).

C. (A) is true but (R) is false.

D. (A) is false but (R) is true.

Q.35 Which of the following is NOT a type of internal migration?

A. International migration

B. Intrastate migration

C. Interstate migration

D. Inter district migration

Q.36 Match the scholars (List-I) with the book/theory/concept/model (List-II) they propounded.

List – I (Scholar)	List – II (Theories/Model of development)
(a) A.G. Frank	(i) World System Theory
(b) Wallerstein	(ii) Dependency Theory
(c) John Friedman	(iii) Core Periphery Model
(d) Rostow	(iv) Historical Stage of Growth

A. (a)-(ii), (b)-(i), (c)-(iii), (d)-(iv)

B. (a)-(iii), (b)-(i), (c)-(ii), (d)-(iv)

C. (a)-(iv), (b)-(ii), (c)-(i), (d)-(iii)

D. (a)-(iv), (b)-(iii), (c)-(ii), (d)-(i)

Q.37 Given below are two statements. One is labelled as Assertion (A) and the other is labelled as Reason (R).

Assertion (A): Growth Centers may have a population ranging from 50000 to 500000.

Reason (R): Growth Poles would generally be the capital cities of the states.

Select the correct answer from options given below:

A. Both (A) and (R) are true and (R) is the correct explanation of (A)

B. Both (A) and (R) are true, but (R) is not the correct explanation of (A)

C. (A) is true, but (R) is false.

D. (A) is false, but (R) is true.

Q.38 "When a particular area starts developing, it attracts human as well as physical capital" these phenomena is called?

A. Spread effect   **B.** Backwash effect

C. Traditional effect   **D.** Drive to maturity

Q.39 Who among the following developed the formula

$$\sqrt{\frac{\Sigma d^2}{n}}$$ for delineating crop combination regions?

A. Doi   **B.** Rafiullah

C. Weaver   **D.** Thomas

Q.40 Which of the following agricultural system regions for the world are given by Whittlesey?

(a) Viticulture

(b) Rudimentary sedentary Tillage

(c) Specialized horticulture

(d) Commercial dairy farming

Choose the correct option from below:

A. Only (a)   **B.** (a), (b) and (c)

C. (b), (c) and (d)   **D.** (a), (b), (c), and (d)

Q.41 Which one of the following assumptions in Von Thunen's model of agriculture land use is not true?

A. An isolated estate

B. Isotropic surface

C. Uniform price for a particular crop in the market.

D. There are multiple markets for the surplus production from a single agricultural area

Q.42 People who work in the primary sector are called as

A. Blue-collar workers

B. Pink Collar workers

C. Red collar workers

D. White collar workers

Q.43 Which of the following is a potential natural resource for India?

A. Gold   **B.** Thorium

C. Diamond   **D.** Coal

Q.44 Area-Cost Curve Theory for industrial location was given by

A. Alfred Weber   **B.** Walter Christaller

C. August Losch   **D.** D . M. Smith

Q.45 Match the List - I with List - II and select the correct answer from the code given below :

List - I	List – II
(Industrial Centre)	(Industrial region)
(a) Cleveland	(i) Central eastern region
(b) Kazan	(ii) Central Europe and Russian region
(c) Busan	(iii) Western Europe
(d) Frankfurt	(iv) North American

A. (a)- (iv) ,(b)- (i) ,(c)- (iv) ,(d)- (iii)

B. (a)- (iv) ,(b)- (iii) ,(c)- (i) ,(d)- (ii)

C. (a)- (i) ,(b)- (ii) ,(c)- (iv) ,(d)- (iii)

D. (a)- (iv) ,(b)- (i) ,(c)- (ii) ,(d)- (i)

Q.46 Given below are two statements. One is labelled as Assertion (A) and the other is labelled as Reason (R).

Assertion (A): Development in ICT has led to increase in technical field of education in India.

Reason (R) : There has been increase in investment in ICT sector in India.

Select the correct answer from options given below:

A. Both (A) and (R) are true and (R) is the correct explanation of (A)

B. Both (A) and (R) are true, but (R) is not the correct explanation of (A)

C. (A) is true, but (R) is false

D. (A) is false, but (R) is true

Q.47 Given below are two statements. One is labelled as Assertion (A) and the other is labelled as Reason (R).

Assertion (A): Foreign Direct Investment is not beneficial for economic growth.

Reason (R) : Foreign Direct Investment increases trade in the economy.

Select the correct answer from options given below:

A. Both (A) and (R) are true and (R) is the correct explanation of (A)

B. Both (A) and (R) are true, but (R) is not the correct explanation of (A)

C. (A) is true, but (R) is false

D. (A) is false, but (R) is true

Q.48 Which of the following is NOT a function of the World Trade Organization?

A. To administer WTO trade agreements

B. To provide a forum for trade negotiations

C. To settle political disputes

D. To monitor national trade policies

Q.49 Consider the following statement about trade and growth and state which of them is true?

i. In the last century, the world economy has experienced positive economic growth.

ii. There is a visible direct relationship between the GDP and the trade growth.

A. Only (i) is true

B. Only (ii) is true

C. Both (i) and (ii) are true

D. Neither (i) nor (ii) are true

Q.50 Consider the following statement about gravity model and state which of them is true?

i. In gravity model of migration, as importance of location increases, there will also be a movement between them.

ii. There will be inverse relation between location and movement.

iii. The gravity model is used to estimate traffic flow.

A. Only (i) is true

B. Only (i) and (ii)

C. (ii) and (iii) are true

D. (i), (ii) and (iii) are true

Q.51 Read the passage and answer the following questions that follow.

Traditional Large-Scale Industrial Regions are based on heavy industry, often located near coal-fields and engaged in metal smelting, heavy engineering, chemical manufacture or textile production. These industries are now known as smokestack industries. Traditional industrial regions can be recognized by high proportion of employment in manufacturing industry, high-density housing, often of inferior type, and poor services, unattractive environment, for example, pollution, waste heaps, and so on... With the scientific advancement and technological improvements, the structure of industries changes. High technology, or simply high-tech, is the latest generation of manufacturing activities. It is best understood as the application of intensive research and development (R and D) efforts leading to the manufacture of products of an advanced scientific and engineering character. Professional (white collar) workers make up a large share of the total workforce. These highly skilled specialists greatly outnumber the actual production (blue collar) workers. High-tech industries which are regionally concentrated, self-sustained and highly specialized are called technopolies. The Silicon Valley near San Francisco and Silicon Forest near Seattle are examples of technopolies. ....Globalization has also caused the new international division of labour within the industry.

Which one of the following industries would be found in the traditional industrial region?

A. IT industry.

B. Knowledge based industries.

C. Cotton and Textile Industry

D. Entertainment Industry.

Q.52 Read the passage and answer the following questions that follow.

Traditional Large-Scale Industrial Regions are based on heavy industry, often located near coal-fields and engaged in metal smelting, heavy engineering, chemical manufacture or textile production. These industries are now known as smokestack industries. Traditional industrial regions can be recognized by high proportion of employment in manufacturing industry, high-density housing, often of inferior type, and poor services, unattractive environment, for example, pollution, waste heaps, and so on... With the scientific advancement and technological improvements, the structure of industries changes. High technology, or simply high-tech, is the latest generation of manufacturing activities. It is best understood as the application of intensive research and development (R and D) efforts leading to the manufacture of products of an advanced scientific and engineering character. Professional (white collar) workers make up a large share of the total workforce. These highly skilled specialists greatly outnumber the actual production (blue collar) workers. High-tech industries which are regionally concentrated, self-sustained and highly specialized are called technopolies. The Silicon Valley near San Francisco and Silicon Forest near Seattle are examples of technopolies. ....Globalization has also caused the new international division of labour within the industry.

Given below are two statements. One is labelled as Assertion (A) and the other is labelled as Reason (R).

Assertion (A): Traditional Industrial regions are also called regions of smokestack industries.

Reason (R): These industries rely upon obsolete technologies causing huge pollution to air and water.

Select the correct answer from options given below:

A. Both (A) and (R) are true and (R) is the correct explanation of (A)

B. Both (A) and (R) are true, but (R) is not the correct explanation of (A)

C. (A) is true, but (R) is false.

D. (A) is false, but (R) is true.

Q.53 Read the passage and answer the following questions that follow.

Traditional Large-Scale Industrial Regions are based on heavy industry, often located near coal-fields and engaged in metal smelting, heavy engineering, chemical manufacture or textile production. These industries are now known as smokestack industries. Traditional industrial regions can be recognized by high proportion of employment in manufacturing industry, high-density housing, often of inferior type, and poor services, unattractive environment, for example, pollution, waste heaps, and so on... With the scientific advancement and technological improvements, the structure of industries changes. High technology, or simply high-tech, is the latest generation of manufacturing activities. It is best understood as the application of intensive research and development (R and D) efforts leading to the manufacture of products of an advanced scientific and engineering character. Professional (white collar) workers make up a large share of the total workforce. These highly skilled specialists greatly outnumber the actual production (blue collar) workers. High-tech industries which are regionally concentrated, self-sustained and highly specialized are called technopolies. The Silicon Valley near San Francisco and Silicon Forest near Seattle are examples of technopolies. ....Globalization has also caused the new international division of labour within the industry.

Which of the following statements relating to industrial regions are correct?

(a) With shift in technology, there has been a shift in the structure of industries.

(b) The globalization has caused a new international division of labour.

(c) The high tech industrial regions have very little to no place for blue collar jobs.

(d) R&D is the most important feature of traditional large scale industrial regions.

Choose the correct option from below:

A. Only (a)   **B.** (a), (b) and (c)

C. (a) and (b)   **D.** (a), (b), (c), and (d)

Q.54 Read the passage and answer the following questions that follow.

Traditional Large-Scale Industrial Regions are based on heavy industry, often located near coal-fields and engaged in metal smelting, heavy engineering, chemical manufacture or textile production. These industries are now known as smokestack industries. Traditional industrial regions can be recognized by high proportion of employment in manufacturing industry, high-density housing, often of inferior type, and poor services, unattractive environment, for example, pollution, waste heaps,

and so on... With the scientific advancement and technological improvements, the structure of industries changes. High technology, or simply high-tech, is the latest generation of manufacturing activities. It is best understood as the application of intensive research and development (R and D) efforts leading to the manufacture of products of an advanced scientific and engineering character. Professional (white collar) workers make up a large share of the total workforce. These highly skilled specialists greatly outnumber the actual production (blue collar) workers. High-tech industries which are regionally concentrated, self-sustained and highly specialized are called technopolies. The Silicon Valley near San Francisco and Silicon Forest near Seattle are examples of technopolies. ....Globalization has also caused the new international division of labour within the industry.

Which of the following is not a feature of a technopolis?

A. Regional concentration

B. Self sustaining in nature

C. Highly polluted

D. Highly specialized

Q.55 Read the passage and answer the following questions that follow.

Traditional Large-Scale Industrial Regions are based on heavy industry, often located near coal-fields and engaged in metal smelting, heavy engineering, chemical manufacture or textile production. These industries are now known as smokestack industries. Traditional industrial regions can be recognized by high proportion of employment in manufacturing industry, high-density housing, often of inferior type, and poor services, unattractive environment, for example, pollution, waste heaps, and so on... With the scientific advancement and technological improvements, the structure of industries changes. High technology, or simply high-tech, is the latest generation of manufacturing activities. It is best understood as the application of intensive research and development (R and D) efforts leading to the manufacture of products of an advanced scientific and engineering character. Professional (white collar) workers make up a large share of the total workforce. These highly skilled specialists greatly outnumber the actual production (blue collar) workers. High-tech industries which are regionally concentrated, self-sustained and highly specialized are called technopolies. The Silicon Valley near San Francisco and Silicon Forest near Seattle are examples of technopolies. ....Globalization has also caused the new international division of labour within the industry.

Which of the following statement best characterizes New International Division of Labour?

A. A division of labour having complete mobility.

B. A system where the most specialized jobs are given to the industries in the third world countries.

C. A system of division of labour where the advanced economies export specialized services and the developing and under-developed countries taking up manufacturing and lower order services.

D. All of the above.

Q.56 Given below are two statements- one is labelled as Assertion (A) and the other is labelled as Reason (R):

Assertion (A)- Man is a captive in his culture.

Reason (R)- Culture is the product of human experience.

Choose the correct option:

A. Both A and R are true and R is the correct explanation of A

B. Both A and R are true but R is not the correct explanation of A

C. A is true but R is false

D. A is false but R is true

Q.57 Given below are two statements- one is labelled as Assertion (A) and the other is labelled as Reason (R):

Assertion (A)- Spykman argued that the Heartland theory appeared less important than the Rimland.

Reason (R)- Mackinder presented his model at the end of the railway age and did not mention about the superiority of air navigation as well as the railways.

Choose the correct option:

A. Both A and R are true and R is the correct explanation of A

B. Both A and R are true but R is not the correct explanation of A

C. A is true but R is false

D. A is false but R is true

Q.58 Consider the following statements:-

a) The Geographical Pivot of History was written by Sir Halford Mackinder in the year 1904

b) According to Spykman, aerial mobility is the new type of geopolitical structure.

Which of the following options are correct?

A. Only a   **B.** Only b

C. Both a and b   **D.** Neither a nor b

Q.59 Match List-I with List-II and select the correct answer from the codes given below :

List-I(Books)	List-II(Year)
a) Universal Geography	i) 1864
b) La reform sociale	ii) 1894
c) Du serment decisoir	iii) 1879
d) Histoire de France	iv) 1878

Choose the correct options from the following:

A. (a)-(i), (b)-(ii), (c)-(iii), (d)-(iv)

B. (a)-(iii), (b)-(iv), (c)-(i), (d)-(ii)

C. (a)-(iv), (b)-(iii), (c)-(ii), (d)-(i)

D. (a)-(ii), (b)-(i), (c)-(iv), (d)-(iii)

Q.60 According to census 2011, What is the sex ratio of Haryana? per thousand of males

A. 859   **B.** 860   **C.** 861   **D.** 879

Q.61 Which of the following statements about Indian Geography is not correct?

A. D N. Wadia has contributed in the field of geology of India.

B. R.P. Mishra has contributed in the field of regional planning and development in India.

C. S.P. Chatterjee has contributed in the field of regional geography of India

D. OHK Spate has contributed in the field of population geography in India.

Q.62 Sir Isaac Newton has improvised on the work of

A. Carl Ritter

B. Immanuel Kant

C. Alexander von Humboldt

D. Bernhardus Varenius

Q.63 Which of the following model is an example of spatial interaction?

A. Gravity Model

B. Demographic Transition Model

C. Industrial Location Model

D. Von Thunen's Land-use model

Q.64 Mentions of the earth-science tradition are found in works of

A. Aristotle

B. Strabo

C. Ptolemy

D. Posidonius

Q.65 The last decade of 19th century and early 20th century were focused on

A. Environmentalism

B. Environmental Determinism

C. Behaviouralism

D. Quantitative Revolution

Q.66 Consider the following statements:

i. With the technological advancement, the environment has affected beyond recognition.

ii. Mega cities and conurbation have not much affected the environmental conditions as they are developed in an environment friendly way.

iii. Global warming is an impact of technological advancement.

iv. Acid rain is due to the frontal formations.

Choose the correct option from below:

A. Only (i)

B. Only (ii) and (iii)

C. (i), (ii) and (iv)

D. None of them

Q.67 Consider the following statements about Dualism:

i. Dualism means difference in views.

ii. Dualism lies in methodology.

iii. It includes content of study, approach of study and method of study.

Choose the correct option from below:

A. Only (i)

B. Only (ii)

C. (i), (ii) and (iii)

D. (ii) and (iii)

Q.68 Who propounded the concept of paradigm?

A. Hagget   **B.** Kuhn   **C.** Darwin   **D.** Ritter

Q.69 In which decade feminist geography emerge in human geography?

A. 1960's   **B.** 1970's   **C.** 1980's   **D.** 1990's

Q.70 Match List-I with List-II and select the correct answer from the codes given below :

List-I(Geographers)	List-II(works)
a) Jean-Francois Lyotard	i) Approaches to human geography
b) Michel Foucault	ii) La Condition postmoderne
c) Zygmunt Bauman	iii) Madness and civilisation
d) Aitken S	iv) Postmodern Ethics

Choose the correct option from below:

A. a-iii b-ii c-i d-iv

B. a-i b-iv c-ii d-iii

C. a-iii b-ii c-iv d-i

D. a-ii b-iii c-iv d-i

Q.71 Mode > Median > Mean implies what kind of distribution?

A. Positively skewed distribution

B. Negatively skewed distribution

C. Unimodal distribution of moderate skewness

D. Normal distribution

Q.72 Given below are two statements. One is labelled as Assertion (A) and the other is labelled as Reason (R).

Assertion(A)- Standard Deviation is superior than the other measures of dispersion.

Reason(R)- It possesses almost all the requisites of a good measure of dispersion.

Select the correct answer from options given below:

A. Both A and R are true and R is the correct explanation of A

B. Both A and R are true but R is not the correct explanation of A

C. A is true but R is false

D. A is false but R is true.

Q.73 Consider the following statements:-

a. Geostationary satellites, at altitudes of approximately 29,000 km, revolve at speeds which match the rotation of the earth, so they seem stationary.

b. Weather and Communication satellites are commonly found in geosynchronous orbits.

c. Sun-synchronous satellites cover each area of the world at a constant local time of the day with almost no change in azimuth.

d. Geostationary satellites provide conditions for acquiring images in a specific season over successive years.

Which of the above statements are correct?

A. a and b

B. b, c and d

C. b and c are

D. All of the above

Q.74 Who conceptualized electromagnetic radiation as an electromagnetic wave that travels through space at the speed of light?

A. Leon Foucault

B. Albert A. Michelson

C. Max Planck

D. James Clerk Maxwell

Q.75 Which geographer used the altimetric analysis to study the nature of region effected by a single cycle of erosion?

A. Bauling

B. Darwin

C. Penk

D. Crickmay

Q.76 Consider the following statement of computation of composite index and state which of these are true-

i. The index has indicators like development vulnerabilities, exclusions etc.

ii. They compare country performances.

iii. They are not easy to interpret.

iv. It summarizes multi-dimensional realities.

A. Only (i) is true

B. Only (ii) and (iii) are true

C. (i), (ii) and (iv) are true

D. (iii) and (iv) are true

Q.77 Given below are two statements, one labelled as assertion(A) and other labelled as reason(R).

Assertion(A)- Aerial photographs are more useful when spatial detail is more critical than spectral information.

Reason(R)- Aerial photograph's spectral resolution is generally coarse.

A. Both A and R are true and R correctly explains A

B. Both A and R are true but R does not explain A

C. A is true and R is false.

D. Both A and R are false

Q.78 Read the following statements and choose the correct answer from the code given below:

(a) High drainage density means that the flood risk is minimal.

(b) If the drainage density is high, the bifurcation ratio too is high.

(c) Drainage density is dependent upon climate and physical characteristics of drainage basin.

(d) Drainage density is total length of river multiplied by the total area of the drainage basin.

Code:

A. (a) and (b) are true

B. (a), (b) and (c) are true

C. (a), (b) and (d) are true

D. (b) and (c) are true

Q.79 Read the following statements and choose the correct answer from the code given below:

(a) Altimetric frequency histograms and curves are two basic techniques to study high lands of geomorphological significance.

(b) Baulig suggested use of grid method to remove deficiencies in altimetric analysis.

(c) The accuracy of altimetric analysis depends upon the benchmarks.

(d) The grid method is used in altimetric analysis when there is deficiency in density of spot heights.

Code:

A. (a) and (b) are true

B. (a), (b) and (d) are true

C. (b) and (d) are true

D. (c) and (d) are true

Q.80 Which among the following is / are common features of the drainage pattern of Ganges river system?

1. Parallel Courses of rivers

2. Tributaries meeting their master streams at acute angles

3. Most rivers are of perennial nature

4. Lower reaches of rivers with steep gradient suitable for hydropower generation

Choose the correct option from the codes given below:

A. Only 1 & 2

B. Only 2 & 3

C. Only 1, 2 & 3

D. 1, 2, 3 & 4

Q.81 Palk Strait separates India from

A. Pakistan

B. China

C. Andaman Island

D. Sri Lanka

Q.82 Given below are two statements. One is labelled as Assertion (A) and the other is labelled as Reason (R).

Assertion (A): Peninsular Rivers have broad and shallow valleys.

Reason (R): Peninsular Rivers have a low capacity to carry load.

Select the correct answer from options given below:

A. Both (A) and (R) are true and (R) is the correct explanation of (A)

B. Both (A) and (R) are true, but (R) is not the correct explanation of (A)

C. (A) is true, but (R) is false

D. (A) is false, but (R) is true

Q.83 Read the following statements given below:

(a) Monsoon break is the phenomenon which means monsoon rainfall stops for a couple of days.

(b) Western Ghats receive orographic rain during the monsoon.

(c) First rain in a place is called as monsoon burst.

(d) The El Nino current decreases the temperature of water.

Select the correct option:

A. (a) and (b) are true

B. (a) and (d) are true

C. (a), (c) and (d) are true

D. (a), (b) and (c) are true

Q.84 Given below are two statements. One is labelled as Assertion (A) and the other is labelled as Reason (R).

Assertion (A): La Nina is the phenomenon that leads to droughts in India.

Reason (R): The Humboldt Current decreases temperature of water by 5-6^0 C

Select the correct answer from options given below:

A. Both (A) and (R) are true and (R) is the correct explanation of (A)

B. Both (A) and (R) are true, but (R) is not the correct explanation of (A)

C. (A) is true, but (R) is false

D. (A) is false, but (R) is true

Q.85 Match List-I with List-II

List-I(Crop)	List-II(State)
(a) Barley	(i) Uttar Pradesh
(b) Jute	(ii) Andhra Pradesh
(c) Sugarcane	(iii) Rajasthan
(d) Groundnut	(iv) West Bengal

Select the correct answer from the options given below:

A. (a)-(iii),(b)-(iv),(c)-(i),(d)-(ii)
B. (a)-(iv),(b)-(iv),(c)-(i),(d)-(iii)
C. (a)-(ii),(b)-(iii),(c)-(i),(d)-(iv)
D. (a)-(ii),(b)-(iii),(c)-(iv),(d)-(i)

Q.86 Given below are two statements. One is labelled as Assertion (A) and the other is labelled as Reason (R).

Assertion (A): India is the second largest irrigated country in the world.

Reason (R): The whole country of India is fully irrigated.

Select the correct answer from options given below:

A. Both (A) and (R) are true and (R) is the correct explanation of (A)
B. Both (A) and (R) are true, but (R) is not the correct explanation of (A)
C. (A) is true, but (R) is false
D. (A) is false, but (R) is true

Q.87 Given below are two statements. One is labelled as Assertion (A) and the other is labelled as Reason (R).

Assertion (A): Software industry has developed rapidly in India since 1990s.

Reason (R): India has a lot of technically skilled manpower.

Select the correct answer from options given below:

A. Both (A) and (R) are true and (R) is the correct explanation of (A)
B. Both (A) and (R) are true, but (R) is not the correct explanation of (A)
C. (A) is true, but (R) is false
D. (A) is false, but (R) is true

Q.88 Read the following statements and choose correct answer from the code given below:

(a) The laterite soils are used as building material.

(b) The forest soils are rich in humus.

(c) The forest soils are deficient in potash, phosphorus, and lime.

(d) Kari is a type of soil found in Kerala.

A. (a) and (c) are true
B. (b) and (c) are true
C. (a), (c) and (d) are true
D. All are true

Q.89 Which state in India has the least percentage of Scheduled Castes population?

A. Goa
B. Bihar
C. Himachal Pradesh
D. Kerala

Q.90 The swamp forests of India are found in delta of

A. Satluj
B. Tapi
C. Cauvery
D. Narmada

Q.91 Given below are two statements. One is labelled as Assertion (A) and the other is labelled as Reason (R).

Assertion (A): There is high density of population in Chotanagpur plateau.

Reason (R) : Various minerals are found in the Chotanagpur plateau.

Select the correct answer from options given below:

A. Both (A) and (R) are true and (R) is the correct explanation of (A)
B. Both (A) and (R) are true, but (R) is not the correct explanation of (A)
C. (A) is true, but (R) is false
D. (A) is false, but (R) is true

Q.92 Which of the following agro-climatic regions practices shifting agriculture?

A. Trans-Ganga plain
B. Eastern Himalaya
C. Lower Gangetic plain
D. Middle Gangetic Plain

Q.93 Match the following:-

List I (Geomorphological feature)	List II (Characteristics)
a. Bhabar	1. Characterised by clay soil
b. Bhangar	2. Composed of finer alluvium
c. Tarai	3. Found along the foot of the Shivalik
d. Khadar	4. Not much suited for cultivation

A. a-1 b-3 c-4 d-2
B. a-3 b-4 c-2 d-1
C. a-3 b-4 c-1 d-2
D. a-4 b-2 c-3 d-1

Q.94 Consider the following statements about the westerly jet stream:

a) Blows over the subtropical zone

b) has a significant influence over the Himalayan ranges

c) helps in the onset of the south-west monsoons

d) leads to the heating of the Tibetan Plateau

Choose the correct option:

A. a and b
B. c and d
C. b and c
D. a, b and c

Q.95 Consider the following statements about the achievements of the Five-Year Plans-

a) balanced regional development

b) Eradication of poverty

c) Increasing trend in life expectancy

d) Technological development

Choose the correct option:-

A. a and b
B. b and d
C. c and d
D. a, b and d

Q.96 Match the following:-

List I	List II
a. Meteorological Drought	1. Evaporation occurs more than usual
b. Hydrological Drought	2. Extreme moisture stress
c. Agricultural Drought	3. Deforestation
d. Soil Moisture Drought	4. prolonged monsoon breaks

Choose the correct option:

A. a-4 b-3 c-2 d-1
B. a-1 b-4 c-2 d-3
C. a-3 b-4 c-1 d-2
D. a-4 b-2 c-3 d-1

Q.97 The Chaudhary Charan Singh Airport is located in

A. Tamil Nadu
B. Uttar Pradesh
C. Madhya Pradesh
D. Rajasthan

Q.98 The class of population distribution which consist of areas having 251-500 persons/sq. km. is known as

A. Areas of high density
B. Areas of extremely low density
C. Areas of moderate density
D. Areas of extremely high density

Q.99 Which state has the highest share in leather production in India?

A. Uttar Pradesh
B. Maharashtra
C. West Bengal
D. Tamil Nadu

Q.100 First railway line in India was opened for public on

A. 1 May 1854
B. 16 April 1853
C. 12 May 1856
D. 1 May 1853

// Smart Answer Sheet //

Correct — Percentage of students who answered correctly.   **Skipped** — Percentage of students who skipped.

Q.	Ans.	Correct / Skipped
1	C	53.85 % / 15.38 %
2	D	36.54 % / 30.77 %
3	A	57.69 % / 28.85 %
4	D	59.62 % / 32.69 %
5	C	28.85 % / 34.61 %
6	A	59.62 % / 30.76 %
7	B	42.31 % / 32.69 %
8	B	44.23 % / 32.69 %
9	D	28.85 % / 34.61 %
10	C	21.15 % / 30.77 %
11	B	44.23 % / 28.85 %
12	D	38.46 % / 32.69 %
13	D	34.62 % / 28.84 %
14	B	13.46 % / 32.69 %
15	B	9.62 % / 28.84 %
16	D	15.38 % / 28.85 %
17	A	28.85 % / 34.61 %
18	C	38.46 % / 32.69 %
19	B	50.0 % / 17.31 %
20	A	46.15 % / 28.85 %
21	C	32.69 % / 28.85 %
22	A	38.46 % / 32.69 %
23	C	57.69 % / 25.0 %
24	A	44.23 % / 32.69 %
25	D	34.62 % / 34.61 %
26	A	34.62 % / 32.69 %
27	A	15.38 % / 26.93 %
28	D	21.15 % / 32.7 %
29	C	40.38 % / 28.85 %
30	D	61.54 % / 30.77 %
31	A	55.77 % / 28.85 %
32	B	48.08 % / 28.84 %
33	C	32.69 % / 26.93 %
34	A	57.69 % / 32.69 %
35	A	61.54 % / 25.0 %
36	A	46.15 % / 28.85 %
37	B	28.85 % / 34.61 %
38	B	25.0 % / 30.77 %
39	C	36.54 % / 34.61 %
40	C	26.92 % / 34.62 %
41	D	44.23 % / 28.85 %
42	C	53.85 % / 32.69 %
43	B	38.46 % / 30.77 %
44	D	34.62 % / 32.69 %
45	B	17.31 % / 30.77 %
46	A	36.54 % / 32.69 %
47	D	48.08 % / 28.84 %
48	C	50.0 % / 34.62 %
49	C	51.92 % / 34.62 %
50	D	36.54 % / 32.69 %
51	C	53.85 % / 28.84 %
52	A	51.92 % / 28.85 %
53	B	19.23 % / 34.62 %
54	C	42.31 % / 30.77 %
55	C	13.46 % / 28.85 %
56	A	59.62 % / 32.69 %
57	B	13.46 % / 36.54 %
58	A	23.08 % / 30.77 %
59	D	7.69 % / 28.85 %
60	D	42.31 % / 28.84 %
61	D	38.46 % / 32.69 %
62	D	19.23 % / 30.77 %
63	A	46.15 % / 30.77 %
64	A	23.08 % / 32.69 %
65	B	15.38 % / 30.77 %
66	A	23.08 % / 30.77 %
67	C	53.85 % / 34.61 %
68	B	53.85 % / 34.61 %
69	C	21.15 % / 32.7 %
70	D	9.62 % / 32.69 %
71	B	30.77 % / 26.92 %
72	A	65.38 % / 28.85 %
73	C	1.92 % / 34.62 %
74	D	28.85 % / 30.77 %
75	A	26.92 % / 32.7 %
76	C	46.15 % / 30.77 %
77	A	44.23 % / 32.69 %
78	D	17.31 % / 30.77 %
79	B	48.08 % / 26.92 %
80	C	28.85 % / 28.84 %

Q.	Ans.	Correct		Q.	Ans.	Correct		Q.	Ans.	Correct		Q.	Ans.	Correct		Q.	Ans.	Correct
		Skipped				Skipped				Skipped				Skipped				Skipped
81	D	65.38 %		85	A	42.31 %		89	A	32.69 %		93	B	15.38 %		97	B	40.38 %
		28.85 %				32.69 %				32.69 %				28.85 %				34.62 %
82	B	7.69 %		86	C	50.0 %		90	C	51.92 %		94	A	13.46 %		98	C	32.69 %
		30.77 %				32.69 %				32.7 %				32.69 %				32.69 %
83	D	38.46 %		87	B	15.38 %		91	A	36.54 %		95	C	13.46 %		99	D	19.23 %
		32.69 %				32.7 %				34.61 %				32.69 %				30.77 %
84	D	44.23 %		88	D	46.15 %		92	B	53.85 %		96	A	23.08 %		100	B	28.85 %
		30.77 %				32.7 %				32.69 %				32.69 %				30.77 %

//Hints and Solutions//

1. Alfred Wegener revealed that several continental landmasses together formed one Supercontinent during the Upper Carboniferous period and was hence termed as Pangaea by Wegener. However, continents such as South America, Africa, Peninsular India, Australia and Antarctica together formed the southern part of Pangaea while the northern part of Pangaea comprised of North America, Europe, and Asia. The northern part was known as Laurasia and the southern part was known as Gondwanaland.

2. The last two sentences do suggest correct explanation of the theory of geomorphic cycle. Davis neglected the biological processes completely. The cycle of erosion by Davis is not a widely accepted theory as the theory has a descriptive simplicity and is just a generalization useful only at the base level. Moreover, it is a deductive approach.

3. Peneplains, also known as Monadnocks, are a result of the continuous valley deepening and horizontal erosion processes. The Davisian erosional cycle goes through three stages. During the Youthful stage, as soon as the upliftment of landmass stops, vertical erosion as well as valley deepening kicks in. When the next Mature stage starts, horizontal erosion starts to take place. During this stage, mountain tops are well reduced and their heights lowered. And at the Old stage, the valley slopes, sides, divide crests are graded and waste materials formed by erosion are observed. Slowly, the whole surface comes closer and closer to the base level and the low featureless plains of soil creep or landmass forms known as Peneplain.

4. The slope characteristics will depend on these three factors along with Base-level changes, geomorphological changes, vegetation cover, tectonic movement. Rock types influence the slope angle directly and through its control on the nature of superficial deposits. Resistant rocks normally produce slopes that are steeper than these on weak rock types. Climate has been known to influence weathering and runoff processes, hence it can be said that it also influences slope form. But there is not much evidence regarding this factor.

5. A river follows a curved path. As a result, the speed of the river water slows down and the river does both the works of erosion and deposition. However, when the river starts to bend and swing in large curves, it does the erosional work on the concave bank of the river while deposition is done on the convex bank. This happens because the speed of the river water is more on the concave bank and less on the convex bank. This thing gradually increases and forms an S shape.

A large number of tributaries joining the main river are required for the formation of deltas as large amount of additional sediments are necessary. The more the number of steams, the more will the deposition of sediments which will consequently lead to delta formation.

6. As per W. M. Davis, the cycle of erosion is divided into three stages, namely, youthful stage, mature stage and old stage. In the youthful stage. the channel gradient and slope are very steep in the youthful stage. This leads to an increase in kinetic energy and velocity of the river. This causes the transportation capacity of the river to increase. The river can carry the big boulders due to their

high speed. These big boulders cause the vertical erosion of valleys. Thus, a gradual increase in depth of valleys is caused in the youthful stage of the river.

7. The direction of a horizontal line along the bedding plane is called a strike. The line (a) is a strike. The dip is the inclination of rock bed with respect to the horizontal plane. An anticline is an upfolded rock belt. The limb of the fold is the side of the fold.

8. When minerals in the rocks mix with the oxygen present in the water, oxides like iron oxide are formed, which weaken the rocks, causing weathering. Minerals in rock react to the presence of carbonate or bicarbonate, producing carbonic acid. This also leads to weathering. Frost cation weaken the rocks leading to block disintegration. Soil is formed due to weathering of rocks, but it is not an agent of weathering.

9. All the above mentioned departments/ministries are under the direct charge of the Prime Minister.

10. The cliff recession model, also known as Fisher- Lehman model, explains the process of cliff recession. Fisher in 1866 examined and interpreted the chalk cliffs in coastal areas and collection of basal debris apron. Lehmann in 1933 added the various stages of weathering to this Fisher's model.

11. Water vapour is one of the most variable gases in the atmosphere, which is found in small amounts, but however very important. Water vapour is always present in some proportion in the lower atmosphere. The water vapour content of air varies from 0.02% in a cold dry climate to nearly 4% in the humid tropics. Water vapour plays a significant role in the insulating action of the atmosphere as well as absorbs not only the long wave terrestrial radiation but also a part of the incoming solar radiation. It is an important control in regulating the energy transfer through the atmosphere.

12. Conduction is a slow process and hence is least important. As air is a very poor conductor of heat, the conduction affects only the uppermost layers of the lowermost layers of air closest to the earth's surface.

Temperature over snow covered grounds remain low during daylight as snow reflects a larger part of the incident solar radiation which is not available for heating the layers of the air lying adjacent to the surface.

Advection as a process of heat transfer is very important. Advection refers to the horizontal convection transport of heat. In the middle latitude regions, most of the diurnal variations in the daily weather are caused by advection itself. Hence, the scorching winds blowing during the summer in the northern plains of India are known as loo, a typical example of advection.

13. The other name for doldrums is Equatorial low-pressure belt. It is the zone of convergence of trade winds blowing equator ward from the sub-tropical belts of high-pressure belts of high pressure in the northern and southern hemispheres. Within this belt the winds are light, variable and feeble with frequent calm conditions. That is why this belt is known as the belt of calms or doldrums. This belt is in the vicinity of the equator between latitudes 5-degree S and 5 degree north.

14. In the North Atlantic region high frequencies of tropical cyclones are found in the months of August, September and

October. The period from December to May is free from cyclones. In the south western North Pacific greatest frequency is seen from July to October. There are no cyclones in the South Atlantic and the reason behind the absence of the tropical cyclones is that the intertropical convergence zone remains to the north of the equator so that no weak tropical disturbance develops over this ocean. Moreover, the sea surface temperature is comparatively low in the low latitudes.

15. The current practice of shifting cultivation in the eastern and north-eastern regions of India is an extravagant and unscientific form of land use. According to a recent estimate, India's 0.59 percent of the total geographical area is under shifting cultivation. The effects of shifting cultivation are devastating and far-reaching in degrading the environment and ecology of these regions. The earlier 15–20 years cycle of shifting cultivation on a particular land has reduced to two or three years now. This has resulted in large-scale deforestation, soil and nutrient loss, and invasion by weeds and other species. The indigenous biodiversity has been affected to a large extent. The current statistics say that India's largest area under shifting cultivation is in the state of Odisha.

16. C.G. Bates in 1935 proposed that drought happens when the annual precipitation is 75% or less than normal precipitation and monthly precipitation is 60% or less than of normal monthly precipitation.

J.C. Hoyt in 1936 explained that drought occurs when annual and monthly rainfall is less than 85% of normal rainfall.

According to V.A. Conard in 1944, period of 20 or more consecutive days without 0.25 inch precipitation in 24 hours during the months of march -September.

D.A. Ramdas in 1950 claimed that drought occurs when the rainfall for a week is half normal or less.

17. The Glacial Lake outburst flow (GLOF) occurs when the dam that contains the glacial lake falls. It can occur due to an avalanche of heavy snow and rock, an earthquake or volcanic eruption under the ice, erosion, pressure due to buildup of water, etc.

18. The amount of CO_2 has been increasing rapidly since the 1970s. In the last 100 years, the amount of carbon-dioxide has increased by 30% from 270 ppm to 350 ppm. The increase of carbon dioxide leads to increase in surface temperature.

19. E-layer is also called the Kennelly-Heaviside layer. It reflects the medium and high frequency radio waves. It is much better defined than the D-layer. It is produced by ultraviolet photons from the sun interacting with nitrogen and nitrogen molecules. This layer also does not exist at night.

20. The change in the atmospheric circulation and water temperature results in increased rainfall in the eastern pacific and decreased rainfall in the western pacific. This effects the monsoon current over the Indian sub-continent resulting in low rainfall during the monsoon season.

21. The top layer of the ocean is called as surface layer. The sun heats the water in the surface layer and thus the temperature of the surface layer is higher than the lower layers. The average temperature at the surface is 17^0 C. This temperature also varies in polar and equatorial areas.

22. • The Atlantic Ocean has several great canyons. Among them, the Fosse de Cape Breton canyon is one that is found along the western continental shelves of the European continent. It lies on the floor of the Bay of Biscay, near the coast of south-western France. The canyon is in front of an old river, Adour.

• The Pacific Ocean has about 32 deeps, among which most of them are trenches. The Tonga Kermadec trench is a trough like depression extending from north east to south west along the Tonga and Kermadec islands. They are measured to be 8000m deep.

• The Mediterranean Sea has deep elongated basins which extend from east to west. Because of a ridge the sea is divided into western and eastern parts. The Algiers-Provencal basin lies in the western part of the western Mediterranean. This basin is bound by 2700m contour showing deepest areas not crossing 2900m.

• The Indian Ocean is also divided by the central ridge into several basins. Among them the Cocos-Keeling basin is the most extensive basin found on the eastern side of the central ridge, extending from 10-degree N to 50-degree S. The average depth ranges from 2000-4000m. This basin is also known as the Indo-Australian Basin.

23. The Continental Shelves are very significant ecologically as these provide ideal habitats for marine life including both plants and animals as well as micro-organisms. These in turn lead to ideal fishing grounds as they support the presence of the planktons and fishes. The coral reefs in the continental shelves promote all these factors. The shallow continental shelves also support the growth of rich mangroves.

24. As we all know, the Evaporation, precipitation and some other are prime driving factors that are responsible for the spatial and regional distribution of sea and ocean water. In the partially enclosed seas of the Indian Ocean at the head of the Persian Gulf the salinity is 37ppt. whereas in the interior it amounts to 40.0ppt. The Red Sea, however, records the highest salinity among the enclosed seas because of high evaporation, less precipitation and mixture of the runoff water from the land.

25. The sea level changes are not only affected by eustatic changes such as the melting of ice and global warming but also by tectonic changes such as Isostatic changes, epeirogenetic and orogenetic changes. Various other evidences such as elevated shorelines, the deposition of organic and inorganic deposits in the continental shelves support the sea level changes. But recently, the change in the sea level has mostly been due to the factors such as global warming due to anthropogenic conditions and melting of glaciers and ice sheets.

26. Nitrogen is a nonmetal and chemical compound. Nitrogen has many uses like anesthetics, explosives, cleansers, meat and planes. It is also used to stop or prevent other compound's reaction with oxygen. Lithium is one of the few chemical elements that react with nitrogen without being heated. Magnesium can burn in nitrogen.

27. Environmental ethics got involved in academic field in response to the works of Rachel Carson and Murray Bookchin. First earth day was celebrated in 1970. Thereafter various writers, philosophers, environmentalists started contributing their works to the field. One of them was the essay written by Garrett Hardin titled "Exploring new ethics for survival"

28. National Clean Air Programme (NCAP) was launched on 10th January 2019 by the Ministry of Environment, Forest and Climate Change. The tentative national level target of 20%–30% reduction of PM2.5 and PM10 concentration by 2024 is proposed under the NCAP taking 2017 as the base year for the comparison of concentration.

29. In the directive principle of state policy, article 48 of the Indian constitution says, "the state shall endeavour to protect and improve the environment and safeguard the forests and wildlife of the country". India is one of the parties in convention of biological diversity treaty.

30. Paris agreement is an international agreement to control climate change. From 30 November to 11 November 2015, over 195 nation governments gathered in Paris, France and discussed a possible new global agreement on climate change aimed at reducing global green house gas emission. It is a 32 page agreement with 29 articles widely recognized as a historic deal to stop global warming.

31. * Concentric Zone Model was given by Ernest Burgess. The zones have been divided into CBD, transition zone, working class zone, residential zone and commuter zone.

* Multiple Nuclei Model was given by C. D. Harris and Edward L. Ullman. There are 9 zones in the model. The 9 zones are all nuclei for city's development.

* Sector Model was given by Homer Hoyt. Homer made five sectors namely CBD, Transport and industry, low0class residential, middle-class residential and high-class residential.

* The Galactic City model was given by Chauncy Harris. It was based on the spread of the galaxy. Urban sprawl plays a dominant role in the development of the city.

32. The word global city was first used by Saskia Sassen in the paper 'The Global City' for the cities of London, New York and Tokyo. The global cities have a tangible and direct impact on the cultural, socio-economic and political scenario of the world. Emerging cities like Sydney, Mexico City, Frankfurt are looking to emerge as global cities.

33. Gordon V. Childe was a famous archeologist. He gave theory about Urban Revolution. The origin and development of cities was part of this theory. This theory described the transition of pre-literate agricultural civilization into civilized societies. The causes for Urban Revolution were growth of revolution, food surplus and availability of capital.

34. The metropolitan areas have forces which attract people who want to migrate. These forces include better lifestyle, employment opportunities, educational facilities, etc. These forces were termed as pull factors by Lee. Thus, metropolitan areas have pull factors and have high rates of immigration. Thus, (A) and (R) are true and (R) is the correct explanation of (A).

35. Migration can be defined as the movement of people from one place to another. Migration, based on place of migration is divided into two types, internal migration and international migration. Internal migration is further divided into interstate, intrastate migration. Inter district migration is a type of intrastate migration.

36. Andre G. Frank is a German-American scholar who promoted the dependency theory by his famous work "the development of the underdevelopment". In 1974, in his book 'The Modern World System', Wallerstein gave the world system theory. In his paper 'The stages of Economic Growth' in 1959, W.W. Rostow gave the modernization theory based on the historical stages of economic growth. John Friedmann has given the concept of core-periphery in his book "Regional Development policy: A case study of Venezuela" in the year 1966.

37. RP Mishra conceived in his theory of growth foci that central villages, service centers, growth point, growth centers and growth poles, ascending order in terms of their size, are all parts of the system of growth foci. According to this theory, growth poles would be the capital cities and therefore cater to the services of large number of people in the state. And next in size would be growth centers, with a population size from 50000 to 500000, which would be district headquarters.

38. Swedish economist Gunnar Myrdals propagated an economic development effect model namely backwash effect. Backwash effect basically means that if one particular area in a country starts growing or developing, it causes human capital as well as physical capital from other parts of the country to gravitate to this part of the country.

39. JC Weaver gave this formula $\sqrt{\dfrac{\Sigma d^2}{n}}$ for delineating crop combination region, when studied crop combination for the Middle-East countries. Here, n means the number of crops and d refers to the difference or deviation between the actual and hypothetical area covered in the region by the specific number of crop. Σd^2 is the summation of square of the deviation, and the number of crops where this value is lowest, would be suitable for the region.

40. D Whittlesey in 1936 gave a 13 regions classification for the agricultural system regions of the world. Rudimentary sedentary Tillage constituted the few pockets in and around regions of shifting cultivation, which relatively more settled agriculturists lived than the former. E.g. S.E. Asia, Central and South America. Commercial dairy farming is practiced in the most developed parts of the world like Northern and western Europe, Australia. Specialized horticulture is practiced in the densely populated industrial districts of Denmark, Britain, France, Germany etc.

41. Johann Heinrich Von Thunen developed a crop theory in 1826 in which he took various assumptions like an isolated estate, isotropic surface, uniform price for a crop in the market and there would be only one market for one agricultural area where the surplus of the agricultural area will be sold.

42. People in primary sector do most of their jobs in the outdoors. This is the reason that they are called red collar workers. Secondary and tertiary sectors workers are called as blue collar and white-collar workers respectively.

43. India has the largest reserves of thorium, but it has not yet been utilized. It is said that it can replace Uranium in the nuclear power sector. Thus, it's a potential natural resource for India that has power to be utilized.

44. D. M. Smith gave theory of industrial location which was a combination of Weber's and Losch's Model. This theory is called as Area-Cost Curve theory. The theory has simplified world conditions. It states that the despite of lower revenue, entrepreneur is likely to choose a location which cost less.

45. * Cleveland lies in the North American Industrial region. It has many steel and manufacturing industries. The other centers in this region include Detroit, Boston, Baltimore, etc.

* Kazan has petrochemical, mechanical engineering, chemical, light and food industries. It belongs to Central European and Russian industrial region.

* Busan is a logistic hub and financial centre in South Korea. It belongs to Central Asian industrial region.

* Frankfurt is in Germany and belongs to western European industrial region. Essen, Dusseldorf, etc. are other centers in German province. A variety of financial industries are present in Frankfurt.

46. The Information and communication is a sector developing at a stupendous rate globally. The Foreign Direct Investment in India has been done most in the ICT sector. Thus, investment in the area has increased considerably. This has led to requirement of skilled workforce for ICT. So, there has been progress in technical education in India, specifically ICT sector due to enormous employment opportunities. Thus, (R) is the correct explanation of (A).

47. Foreign Direct Investment means that companies from other countries invest in the companies in the host country. This provides employment to workers and increases the foreign currency in the country. Utilization of available resources is also done. The FDI facilitates trade as the amount of finished product increase. Thus, it is helpful for economic growth. Thus, (R) is true and (A) is false.

48. The WTO comprises of 164 members. It represents nearly 98% of the world's trade. The WTO's functions include settling international trade disputes, providing a forum for trade negotiations, monitoring national trade policies and administration of trade agreements under WTO among others as listed on website of WTO. The settlement of political disputes is not as function of WTO.

49. Over the last couple of centuries, the world economy has experienced sustained positive economic growth, and over the same period , this process of economic growth has been accompanied by even faster growth in global trade. Also the country level data has a positive correlation between GDP and trade growth.

50. The gravity model of migration deals with degree of migration interaction between two places. The gravity model of migration is based on the idea that as the importance of one location increases, there will also be an increase between them. The farther the two locations are, the movement between them will be less.

51. Industries like Cotton Textile Industries, Iron and Steel industries, Sugar industries are characterized by higher proportion of workers in semi-skilled categories, using old obsolete technology, causing huge pollution unlike modern high tech industries. IT industries and the knowledge-based industries do not fall under traditional large-scale industries.

52. Traditional industrial regions has industries involving heavy manufacturing with stages like blast furnaces, smelting which causes a lot of smoke. The pollution is also, in part the result of obsolete unclean technologies. Hence, they are called regions of smokestack industries.

53. With the shift in technology, the structure of industries has changed considerably with the manufacturing low grade industries being shifted to the southern countries like Bangladesh, India. The advanced economies have kept the high-paying research intensive jobs within the same industries. The globalization and the unrestricted flow of capital has induced a new international division of labour where specialized goods and service is produced by workers of specific economies. Blue collar workers are characteristic of traditional heavy industries and the gold collar workers engaged R&D are characteristic of the hi-tech industries.

54. High-tech industries which are regionally concentrated, self-sustained and highly specialised are called technopolis. Silicon Valley is an example. They are clean, environment friendly with most of the jobs pertaining to Research and Development sector.

55. The New International Division of Labour (NIDL), is the consequence of globalization and is referred to as the characteristic feature of the Post-Fordist era. The high paying jobs are still concentrated in the core economies and the low-paying jobs within the same industry is concentrated in the third world countries. Example, the shoemaking will be done in cottage industries of Bangladesh for large MNCs whose headquarter and the R&D wing is situated in United States.

56. Culture is a sum of what a human being or a group has learnt about living together within certain circumstances since his birth. Culture is basically what creates a human. It teaches us various things such as communication and transmission of certain values and norms. Culture is what directs and confines the behaviour of an individual as well as providing him certain tasks and objectives. The main work of culture is that it not only controls but also liberates human energy. Hence, Culture exists because of the presence of human beings.

57. One of the serious faults of Mackinder's Heartland theory is that, though he had presented his model during the railway age, he never mentioned the presence of this huge transport facility. During that time railways had almost dominated quite several years. He also did not make any attempt to elaborate the impacts of air mobility on his newer versions of the model. However, during his model the role of technology had a major impact on the power potentials. Mackinder failed to recognize the effect of the role of changing technology. The Rimland theory by Spykman tends to cover up these weaknesses that were present in the Heartland theory.

58. Mackinder presented his model, ' The Geographical Pivot of History' in front of the Royal Geographical Society in London in

1904. This model was developed during a period when Britain was losing her political and economic significance to the world economy.

Maritime mobility, according to Spykman, was the fundamental fact that was responsible for the development of the world politics. The development of ocean navigation and sea routes to various parts of the world has led a new structure of great power and enormous extent.

59. Universal Geography is the work of Elisee Recule published in the year 1894

La reform Sociale is the work by Le play published in the year 1864

Du serment decisoir is the work by Paul de Rousiers published in the year 1878

Histoire de France is the work of Edmond demolins published in the year 1879

60. The structure of population in terms of density, age, sex, literacy and occupational structure is an important part of federalism. The sex ratio in different pats and different cultural groups varies from each other. According to census 2011, the sex ratio of Haryana is 879 females per 1000 males.

61. OHK Spate was a British Geographer who has contributed in the regional geography of India. He is best known for his book titled "India and Pakistan: A General and Regional Geography" published in 1954.

62. Varenius is famous for his book *Geographica Generalis*. It is divided into three sections of absolute geography, comparative geography and relative geography. It is head as an important addition to the knowledge about comparative and scientific geography. Sir Isaac Newton made a lot of improvisation on the 1672 Cambridge edition of this book.

63. Spatial interaction models aim to explain the flow of people, resources or ideas from one geographical space to another. The gravity model is a type of models based on Sir Isaac Newton's low of gravitation. It can show trade, migration, between two cities. The gravity model is thus an example of spatial interaction.

64. The earth science tradition emerged in ancient Greece. It is seen in the works of Aristotle. He outlined the study of geography as study of natural processes in and near surface of the earth.

65. In the last decade of 19th century and early years of 20th century, social Darwinist thought was prevalent. It was reflected in Ratzel ad his contemporaries' thought. Geography rejected physical geography and environmentalism and focused mostly on environmental determinism that was Darwin's thoughts.

66. Environment change is a continuous process that has been in operation from a very long time. Right from the primeval stage of human development man has been interacting with environment. With the advancement of technologies, the environment of earth has been transformed beyond recognition. Mega cities, Conurbation, modern towers are some of examples of these technological advancement.

67. Dualism means difference in views, in geography dualism lies in its methodology which includes content of study, approach of study and method of study. Content is the subject matter, approach is the point of view to look at a problem, method is the way to deal with the problem.

68. There have been various evolutionary phases in geography. It passed from descriptive and teleological phase to the quantitative radical and dialectical materialism stage. There was a shift of approaches that were conventionally used to a set of new ways of approaches. This was called paradigm which was for the first time propounded by Thomas Kuhn in 1962.

69. Feminist geography emerged to inculcate women geographers and scholars in the field of geography. It focused on bringing out equality in the domain and giving equal opportunities to everyone irrespective of gender, class, creed, sexuality etc. Feminist geography emerged in 1980s as a new move.

70. Post modernism is an approach in human geography. It is against the concept of modernism and rejects all the statements the theory gives.

La condition postmorderne was the work of Jean Francois Lyotard.

Madness and civilization is the work of Michel Foucalt.

Postmodern Ethics is the work of Zygmunt Bauman.

Approaches to human geography is the work of Aitken S.

71. The above condition implies negatively skewed distribution with its tail on the left side of the frequency curve. Skewness refers to the extent of asymmetry in the shape of the frequency distribution curve. Any asymmetry distribution is a skewed distribution. Basically, it measures the extent by which the bulk of the values in a distribution are concentrated on one or the other side of the mean.

72. Standard Deviation is truly superior than the other measures of dispersion as it contains all the properties of a good measure of dispersion. Some properties are:- 1. It is rigidly defined. 2. It is based on all the observations as even if one observation is changed, S.D. changes. Range and Quartile Deviation do not possess this property. 3. Although not so simple as range or Q.D., the calculation of S.D. is not so difficult and doesn't require any special technique. 4. It is amenable to algebraic treatment.

73. Geostationary satellites are placed at altitudes of about 36,000km, and revolve at speeds which match the rotation of the earth. Hence, always view the same portion of the earth's surface E.g., METEOSAT, GOES-e. etc.,

Due to the position of the sun-synchronous satellites and consistent illumination conditions as they cover each area of the world at a constant local time of the day, images can be acquired in a specific season over successive years. This is an important factor for monitoring the changes between images as they do not have to be corrected for different illumination conditions.

74. James Clerk Maxwell was the one who conceptualized the wave nature of the EMR and stated that Electromagnetic energy propagates in harmonic sinusoidal wave motion, consisting of inseparable revolving electric and magnetic fields that are always perpendicular to one another and to the direction of propagation. All EM radiation travel with the same speed in a particular medium and equal to the velocity of light in a vacuum. Hence it can be stated as c=f*(lambda). Where, c= speed of light, f =frequency, lambda= wavelength.

75. Bauling's device is used to pervade some deficiencies in the spot heights. In his device bauling has used a square grid in which frequency distribution of the highest and lowest point is counted and plotted on the graph. He drew he concave curve in an altimetric plot indicate the mature stage. The inflexions and curves produced in the curve show the different cycles or polycyclic nature of landform.

76. The computation of composite index is a composite phenomenon like development, vulnerabilities, exclusion etc. Composite indicators also compare country performances which are increasingly being recognized as useful in policy analysis and public communication. It is easy to interpret and can summarize multi-dimensional realities with a view to support decision making.

77. Aerial photographs are most useful when fine spatial detail s more critical than spectral information, as their spectral resolution is generally coarse when compared to data captured with electronic sensing devices. The geometry of vertical devices is well understood and it is possible to make very accurate measurements from them.

78. The drainage density is the total length of streams and rivers is divided by the total area. High drainage density means that the flood risk is high. If the drainage density is high, the bifurcation ratio, too is high. Drainage density is dependent upon the climate and physical characteristics of drainage basin.

79. Altimetric analysis is the use of altimetric frequency histograms and curves for study of geomorphological significance. The accuracy of altimetric analysis depends on the density of spot-heights in an area. The grid method was suggested by Baulig to remove the deficiencies in density of spot-height. It is common to use grid method when there is deficiency in density of spot-heights.

80. The drainage of the Gangetic region is dendritic with parallel courses and acute angle functions of tributaries with their master stream s. Most of the rivers are perennial streams with well-defined courses and gentle gradient. While the upper reaches of the rivers are suitable for generating hydel power. the mainstreams in the plains provide water for canal irrigation and are also used for navigation purposes.

81. Palk Strait separates India from Sri Lanka. Palk Strait, inlet of the Bay of Bengal between southeastern India and northern Sri Lanka. It is bounded on the south by Pamban Island (India), Adam's (Rama's) Bridge (a chain of shoals), the Gulf of Mannar, and Mannar Island (Sri Lanka).

82. Rivers in Indian peninsula have almost reached base level of their erosion. They are in the mature stage which is evident through their broad and shallow valleys and the deltas that they make. The velocity of water in their channel and their capacity to carry load is also less. The reason for this is that the peninsular rivers have existed for a much longer period of time as compared

to the Himalayan Rivers. Thus, both (A) and (R) are true but (R) is not the correct explanation of (A).

83. Western Ghats lie near the western coast of India. They occur as a hindrance for the winds of South-west monsoon winds and lead to orographic rain in the area. First occurrence of rain in an area is called as monsoon burst. During the Monsoon season, there are periods when there are sharp decrease in rainfall over most parts of the country, this is called monsoon break. The El Nino is a warm current and hence it leads to increase in temperatures by 3-4 degree Celsius.

84. La Nina means the little girl. The Humboldt Current in the South Pacific Ocean is a cold current that brings ice bergs from Antarctica and the temperature of the water decreases by $5\text{-}6^0$ C. This leads to the Indian monsoon being accelerated and causes floods and landslides in India. Thus, (A) is false and (R) is true.

85. • The largest producer of Barley in the country is Rajasthan. It produces nearly 40% of the total production. Tonk, Sawai Madhopur, Bharatpur are major Barley producing region of the Rajasthan.

• West Bengal is the largest producer of jute. It produces three-fourths of the total jute of the country and has two-third of the total area under jute production.

• Uttar Pradesh is the largest producer of sugar cane In India. It accounts for 36% of the total production and has nearly 43% of the total area in sugar cane production.

• Andhra Pradesh leads in the production of groundnut. It produces nearly 23%of the total production of India. Chitoor, Kunoor and Anantapur districts are the districts which have groundnut.

86. India is the second largest irrigated country in the world. But only one-third of the total area of the country is irrigated. Majority of the country is still dependent upon the rains for water for agriculture. The Indian monsoon is highly erratic and unpredictable. Therefore, it is necessary to develop irrigation in India. Thus, (A) is true and (R) is false.

87. The software industry is one of the leading industries in India. This industry had a breakthrough and has developed rapidly since 1990s. The reason for such unprecedented development is that there is abundance of skilled technicians in India who are very skilled at software development.

88. The forest soils are rich in humus and lack potash, phosphorus, and lime. Therefore, they require a good deal of fertilizers for high yields. The laterite soils are used as building material. Kari is a type of Peaty soil in the Kottayam and Alappuzha districts of Kerala.

89. The state of Goa has the least percentage of Scheduled Tribes population among the states of India. The total ST population in Goa is just 566 as per the census of 2011, which accounts for 0.0% of the total population of 1,347,668.

90. The swamp forests are found in and around deltas, estuaries and creeks. In India, they are confined to deltas of Ganga, Mahanadi, Godavari, Krishna and Cauvery. The can survive in fresh as well as brackish waters. The most prominent example is Sunderban forest in the delta of Ganga River.

91. The Chotanagpur plateau of Jharkhand has abundance of minerals such as iron, coal, copper, bauxite, etc. The area thus provides employment opportunities in mining and other heavy industries. This has led to high density of population in the Chotanagpur plateau. Thus, both (A) and (R) are true and (R) is the correct explanation of (A).

92. The Eastern Himalayan region has rugged topography, steep slopes, thick forests and swift flowing rivers. The area has red brown soil and has shifting cultivation. It is called jhumming locally. Rice, maize, potato and fruits are the main crops here.

93. The bhabar lies along the foothills of the Shivalik from the Indus river to the Tista. It consists of pebble-studded rocks in the shape of porous beds and due to the porosity of this zone all the stream disappears here.

The Bhangar is not much suitable for cultivation due to the presence of older alluvium and it forms the alluvial terrace above the level of flood plains. One major characteristic of bhangar is that it is impregnated with calcareous deposits, Kankar.

The Tarai is situated to the south of the Bhabar and has alluvium deposits that are much finer than that present in bhabar. It is an area of excessive dampness. Most of the Tarai land has been reclaimed for agriculture.

The khadar represents the flood plain with newer alluvium. The khadar is characterised by clay and fertile soil and as a result intensive agriculture is practiced here.

94. The westerly jet stream has a lot of significance. It blows during winter over the sub-tropical zone. This jet stream is the one that is responsible for influencing the winter weather conditions in India. It is bifurcated by the Himalayan ranges. Thus, this jet stream is responsible for bringing western disturbances from the Mediterranean region into India. For these disturbances, winter rain and heat storms in the north-western plains and occasional snowfall in the hilly regions are prevalent.

95. The five-year plans were not able to achieve numerous fixed targets, but there has been constructive and socio-economic development. The failures were that the plans did not achieve any kind of balanced regional development. The eradication of poverty was also not achieved. Even during the year 2011-12, 21.9% of population of India was below the poverty Line.

96. Meteorological drought is caused by lean monsoons and below average rainfall. It is also caused by late onset and early withdrawal of monsoons and prolonged breaks. However, it is described as a situation where there is a decrease in rainfall for a particular time period.

Hydrological droughts are observed after two meteorological droughts set in. large scale deforestation, unwanted human activities, quarrying or excessive pumping of the groundwater are the causes of such drought.

Agricultural drought takes place when soil moisture and rainfall conditions are not enough for backing up the crop requirements. This causes extreme moisture stress and wilting of major crop. This drought occurs even when there is no meteorological drought.

Soil moisture drought is particularly seen in the rainfed areas where the water supply is less and water loss by evaporation is more. It also occurs in the condition of meteorological drought.

97. Chaudhary Charan Singh International Airport is located in Uttar Pradesh and serves Lucknow. It was earlier known as Amausi airport.

98. The areas of moderate density include the class which have a spatial distribution of population of about 251-500 persons per sq. km. The average for whole of India falls in this class. Odisha, Gujarat, Andhra Pradesh, Tripura, Karnataka, Maharashtra fall in this category.

99. Nearly 40% of country's leather production is concentrated in the state of Tamil Nadu, making it the highest leather producing state in India. In state of Tamil Nadu the major leather production centers are Vellore, Chennai, Ambur, Trichy, Vaniyambadi and Erode.

100. The British Government constructed the first railway line from Mumbai to thane for a distance of about 34 km. It opened for public service on 16th April 1853. This line was further extended to Klayn on 1st May 1854 and to Khopoli on 12th May 1856. The Haora-Hugli line in Bengal was inaugurated on 15th August 1854.

Q.1 Which one of the following option is responsible for the formation of volcanic eruptions?

A. High Temperature in the Earth's Interior
B. Plate Tectonics
C. Presence and the formation of gases
D. All of the above

Q.2 Lines joining places which experience the earthquake at the same time are known as

A. Isoseismal lines
B. Homoseismal lines
C. Mercalli Scale
D. Isohyets

Q.3 Which of the following scientists tried to explain the drift of the continents before Wegner's Continental Drift Theory?

A. Harry Hess
B. Frank Taylor
C. J. Tuzo Wilson
D. S. W. Wooldridge

Q.4 According to Walther Penck, geomorphic forms are an expression of the phase and rate of uplift in relation to the rate of

A. Degradation
B. Transformation
C. Subduction
D. Transportation

Q.5 Read the following statements and select the correct answer using the code given below :

a) The diastrophic forces include both vertical as well as horizontal movements of the earth's crust.

b) The diastrophic forces occur suddenly, and their effects are immediately observed.

c) The orogenetic movements lead to mountain building.

d) The diastrophic forces lead to the formation of Meso-level landforms like mountains, plateaus, big faults, etc.

A. Only (a) is correct
B. (a) and (d) are correct
C. (a), (b) and (c) are correct
D. (a), (b) and (d) are correct

Q.6 The clouds that occur at the highest level are:

A. Cumulus   B. Stratus   C. Cirrus   D. Nimbus

Q.7 Volcanic activity is prominently found near the

A. Convergent plate boundaries
B. Divergent plate boundaries
C. Mid-oceanic ridges
D. All the above

Q.8 Match List-I with List-II :

List-I	List -II
(a) Earthquake	(i) Mumbai, 2000
(b) Landslide	(ii) Gujrat, 2004
(c) Avalanche	(iii) Barren Island, 2017
(d) Volcanic Eruption	(iv) Jammu and Kashmir, 2017

Select the correct answer from the options given below :

A. (a)-(ii); (b)-(i); (c)-(iv); (d)-(iii)
B. (a)-(iv); (b)-(iii); (c)-(ii); (d)-(i)
C. (a)-(i); (b)-(ii); (c)-(iii); (d)-(iv)
D. (a)-(iv); (b)-(i); (c)-(ii); (d)-(iii)

Q.9 Read the following statements and select the correct answer using the code given below :

a) L C King based his model of hillslope theory on field observations alone.

b) As per L C King, subtropical semi-humid regions are most normal for the evolution of the landscape.

c) He was in favour of the theory that forms of slope vary from one climate to another.

d) He said that the natural slope was the product of normal processes of mass movement and/or fluvial processes.

A. Only (a) is correct
B. (a) and (d) are correct
C. (a), (b) and (c) are correct
D. (a), (b) and (d) are correct

Q.10 Given below are the two statements, one labelled as Assertion (A) and the other labelled as Reason (R). Select your answer from the code given below:

Assertion (A): The place of occurrence of an earthquake is called as an epicenter.

Reason (R): The epicenter of an earthquake is perpendicular to the focus.

A. Both (A) and (R) are true and (R) is the correct explanation of (A).
B. Both (A) and (R) are true but (R) is not the correct explanation of (A).
C. (A) is true but (R) is false.
D. (A) is false but (R) is true.

Q.11 Given below are two statements. One is labelled as Assertion (A) and the other is labelled as Reason (R).

Assertion (A): Carbon dioxide is largely responsible for the greenhouse effect.

Reason (R): It absorbs a part of the outgoing terrestrial radiation and reflects back some part of it towards the earth's surface.

Select the correct answer from options given below:

A. Both (A) and (R) are true and (R) is the correct explanation of (A)
B. Both (A) and (R) are true, but (R) is not the correct explanation of (A)
C. (A) is true, but (R) is false
D. (A) is false, but (R) is true

Q.12 Read the following statements and choose your answer from the code given below:

(a) The coldest point in the atmosphere is the stratopause.

(b) The thickness of troposphere is greatest at the poles.

(c) The ozone layer is concentrated maximum in the stratosphere.

(d) Radio waves operation is a facilitated by the ionosphere.

A. Only (a) is true

B. (c) and (d) are true

C. (a), (b) and (d) are true

D. (a), (c) and (d) are true

Q.13 Given below are two statements. One is labelled as Assertion (A) and the other is labelled as Reason (R).

Assertion (A): Water vapour is a variable gas in the atmosphere.

Reason (R): It ranges from 4 per cent to less than 1 per cent by volume in different parts of the atmosphere.

Select the correct answer from options given below:

A. Both (A) and (R) are true and (R) is the correct explanation of (A)

B. Both (A) and (R) are true, but (R) is not the correct explanation of (A)

C. (A) is true, but (R) is false

D. (A) is false, but (R) is true

Q.14 Which term is used to describe the conversion of a gas directly to a solid, without passing through the liquid state ?

A. Evaporation

B. Deposition

C. Condensation

D. Sublimation

Q.15 Lower part of the atmosphere is mostly heated by

A. Direct solar radiation

B. Incoming shortwave radiation

C. Absorption of radiation by aerosols

D. Outgoing long-wave radiation

Q.16 Wind moves from tropical regions to equatorial regions in a curved path because of

A. The shape of the earth

B. The blow pressure at the equator

C. The earth's rotation from west to east

D. Coriolis force

Q.17 Which of the following statements regarding wind is/are not correct?

(a) The pressure gradient force and the Coriolis force affects the wind movement.

(b) Geostrophic wind is the wind which moves parallel to the pressure gradient force.

(c) The Coriolis force is maximum at the equator and keeps decreasing towards poles.

(d) The wind speed is measured through barometer.

A. Only (a)

B. (a), (b) and (c)

C. (b) and (c)

D. (b), (c) and (d)

Q.18 Match List-I with the List-II and select the correct answer from the code given below:

List - I (Fronts/Airmass)	List - II (Characteristics)
(a) Warm Front	(i) Warm air moving towards cold air
(b) Occluded Front	(II) warm oceans in the tropics
(c) Cold Front	(iii) cold air moving towards warm airmass
(d) Maritime Tropical Airmass	(iv) steep gradient in temperature & pressure

A. (a)-(i), (b)-(iii), (c)-(iv), (d)-(ii)

B. (a)-(ii), (b)-(iii), (c)-(iv), (d)-(i)

C. (a)-(i), (b)-(iv), (c)-(iii), (d)-(ii)

D. (a)-(iv), (b)-(iii), (c)-(ii), (d)-(i)

Q.19 According to Koppen's Scheme of climatic classification 'B' (Dry) type climatic is found in:

A. Rajasthan

B. Assam

C. West Bengal

D. Arunachal

Q.20 'Positive Southern Oscillation Index' refers to which of the following ?

A. Favourable condition for El Nino

B. Favourable condition for La Nina

C. Favourable conditions both for El Nino and La Nina

D. Unfavourable conditions both for El Nino and La Nina

Q.21 The centre of a mature tropical cyclone is called as

A. Eye

B. Dip

C. Epicenter

D. Mouth

Q.22 Read the following statements and select the correct answer from the code given below:

(a) The tsunami is caused by volcanic eruption or earthquake under the sea.

(b) The speed of the tsunami waves depends upon the distance of the source of the wave.

(c) A tsunami can be caused by a giant meteor impacting with the ocean.

(d) Tsunamis are tidal waves.

A. Only (a) is true

B. (a) and (b) are true

C. (a) and (c) are true

D. (a), (b) and (d) are true

Q.23 The semi-diurnal tidal cycle consists of

A. Two high and two low tides with different cycles every lunar day

B. Two nearly equal high and low tides every lunar day

C. Three high and three low tides with different cycles every lunar day

D. One high and one low tide every lunar day.

Q.24 Read the following statements and select the correct answer from the code given below:

(a) The North Equatorial current is flows from equator to the north.

(b) The Gulf Stream is a warm current flowing towards the North.

(c) The Peru Current is responsible for the scanty rainfall in western Peru.

(d) The West Wind Drift is a warm current in Southern Hemisphere.

A. (a) and (d) are true

B. (a) and (b) are true

C. (b) and (c) are true

D. (c) and (d) are true

Q.25 Match the List - I with List - II and select the correct answer from the code given below :

List - I (Relief features in ocean)	List-II(Depth)
(a) Continental Shelf	(i)2000 – 3000 m
(b) Abyssal plains	(ii)4000 – 10000 m
(c) Oceanic Trenches	(iii)4000 – 6000 m
(d) Continental Slope	(iv)0 – 200 m

A. (a)-(iii),(b)-(i),(c)-(ii),(d)-(iv)
B. (a)-(iv),(b)-(iii),(c)-(ii),(d)-(i)
C. (a)-(iv),(b)-(i),(c)-(ii),(d)-(iii)
D. (a)-(iii),(b)-(iv),(c)-(i),(d)-(ii)

Q.26 Diamond, graphite and fullerenes are three forms of ?

A. carbon
B. Silicon
C. Beryllium
D. Uranium

Q.27 Given below are the two statements, one labelled as Assertion (A) and the other labelled as Reason (R). Select your answer from the code given below:

Assertion(A)- The biomass of producers is at the maximum

Reason (R)- Biomass pyramids have large base of primary producers.

A. Both A and R are true, and R correctly explains A
B. Both A and R are true, but R does not explain A
C. A is true and R is false.
D. Both A and R are false

Q.28 Given below are the two statements, one labelled as Assertion (A) and the other labelled as Reason (R). Select your answer from the code given below:

Assertion(A)- 80% of world's water gets flowed back to the environment without reused or treated.

Reason(R)- There is production of 34% billion gallons of wastewater every day.

A. Both A and R are true and R correctly explains A
B. Both A and R are true but R does not explains A
C. A is true and R is false.
D. Both A and R are false

Q.29 Where was 18th conference of parties related to Kyoto protocol held?

A. Doha
B. Italy
C. Canada
D. India

Q.30 The development of city was due to commercial revival in 11th and 12th century was said by

A. Karl Marx
B. V. Gordon Childe
C. Henri Pirenne
D. Lewis Mumford

Q.31 If the number of villages is equal to half of hamlet number, it is a

A. Dispersed settlement
B. Hamleted Settlement
C. Isolated settlement
D. Compact settlement

Q.32 Which of the following countries has the highest rural population?

A. China
B. South Africa
C. India
D. Bangladesh

Q.33 The rate of rural to urban migration in India as per census of 2011 was

A. 6.2%
B. 14.6 %
C. 20.1%
D. 12.3%

Q.34 Given below are the two statements, one labelled as Assertion (A) and the other labelled as Reason (R). Select your answer from the code given below :

Assertion (A) : China changed its one-child policy to two-child policy in 2015.

Reason (R) : China has population shrinking and ageing in recent times.

Code :

A. Both (A) and (R) are true and (R) is the correct explanation of (A).
B. Both (A) and (R) are true but (R) is not the correct explanation of (A).
C. (A) is true but (R) is false.
D. (A) is false but (R) is true.

Q.35 In which year was the first census of Independent India conducted?

A. 1957
B. 1972
C. 1951
D. 1961

Q.36 Match List-I with List-II

list-I	List-II
(a) Infant Mortality rate	(i) Average no of children a woman will bear through her Child-bearing years
(b)Total fertility rate	(ii) Number of death of children under $0-1$ years per 1000 live births
(c) Crude birth rate	(iii) Number of deaths per 1000 people.
(d) Crude death rate	(iv) Number of live births per 1000 people

Code:

A. (a)-(i), (b)-(iii),(c)-(iv),d-(ii)
B. (a)-(ii),(b)-(i),(c)-(iv),d-(iii)
C. (a)-(iii),(b)-(iii),(c)-(i),(d)-(iv)
D. (a)-(ii),(b)-(iv), (c)-(ii), (d)-(i)

Q.37 Read the passage and answer the following questions that follow.

....On the one hand, it is clear that many resources currently being used are non-renewable, and that the use of some resources destroys others. On the other hand, many elements which are currently considered as resources might be appraised differently in the future as new resources are developed. As a result, there are many different ways of assessing resource prospects. One extreme is the Malthusian view which sees the stock of resources as a finite supply rapidly being depleted by large and increasing demands resulting from uncontrolled population growth and increasing aspirations. The consequence of this will be the exhaustion of resources and the impoverishment or even destruction of man. At the other extreme is the technological view which concedes that although the stock of resources is ultimately finite, the bounds of possibility within these limits are so extensive that the exhaustion of resources is not a practical problem. Technology

may deplete some resources, but it also has a capacity for creating others, and as a result all problems can be solved if technical progress is maintained and economic and social constraints can be overcome... "Resources are not, they become"...

"Resources are not, they become" is a famous quote given by

A. Erich Zimmerman

B. Carl Sauer

C. Richard Hartshorne

D. David Harvey

Q.38 Read the passage and answer the following questions that follow.

....On the one hand, it is clear that many resources currently being used are non-renewable, and that the use of some resources destroys others. On the other hand, many elements which are currently considered as resources might be appraised differently in the future as new resources are developed. As a result, there are many different ways of assessing resource prospects. One extreme is the Malthusian view which sees the stock of resources as a finite supply rapidly being depleted by large and increasing demands resulting from uncontrolled population growth and increasing aspirations. The consequence of this will be the exhaustion of resources and the impoverishment or even destruction of man. At the other extreme is the technological view which concedes that although the stock of resources is ultimately finite, the bounds of possibility within these limits are so extensive that the exhaustion of resources is not a practical problem. Technology may deplete some resources, but it also has a capacity for creating others, and as a result all problems can be solved if technical progress is maintained and economic and social constraints can be overcome... "Resources are not, they become"...

Which of the following features do not correspond to the Malthusian view?

A. Resources are scarce.

B. Resource must be used judiciously.

C. Technology can expand the scope of resources.

D. None of the above.

Q.39 Read the passage and answer the following questions that follow.

....On the one hand, it is clear that many resources currently being used are non-renewable, and that the use of some resources destroys others. On the other hand, many elements which are currently considered as resources might be appraised differently in the future as new resources are developed. As a result, there are many different ways of assessing resource prospects. One extreme is the Malthusian view which sees the stock of resources as a finite supply rapidly being depleted by large and increasing demands resulting from uncontrolled population growth and increasing aspirations. The consequence of this will be the exhaustion of resources and the impoverishment or even destruction of man. At the other extreme is the technological view which concedes that although the stock of resources is ultimately finite, the bounds of possibility within these limits are so extensive that the exhaustion of resources is not a practical problem. Technology may deplete some resources, but it also has a capacity for creating others, and as a result all problems can be solved if technical progress is maintained and economic and social

constraints can be overcome... "Resources are not, they become"...

Which of the following statements related to the technological view is not true?

(a) It talks about infinite stock of resources from which to choose.

(b) It claims technology has the capacity of creating resources.

(c) Progress in the society by eliminating socio-economic barriers is possible with the help of technology.

(d) The rate of demand will exceed the supply of resources and would lead to resource crisis.

A. Only (a)

B. (a), (b) and (d)

C. (a) and (d)

D. (a), (b), (c) and (d)

Q.40 Read the passage and answer the following questions that follow.

....On the one hand, it is clear that many resources currently being used are non-renewable, and that the use of some resources destroys others. On the other hand, many elements which are currently considered as resources might be appraised differently in the future as new resources are developed. As a result, there are many different ways of assessing resource prospects. One extreme is the Malthusian view which sees the stock of resources as a finite supply rapidly being depleted by large and increasing demands resulting from uncontrolled population growth and increasing aspirations. The consequence of this will be the exhaustion of resources and the impoverishment or even destruction of man. At the other extreme is the technological view which concedes that although the stock of resources is ultimately finite, the bounds of possibility within these limits are so extensive that the exhaustion of resources is not a practical problem. Technology may deplete some resources, but it also has a capacity for creating others, and as a result all problems can be solved if technical progress is maintained and economic and social constraints can be overcome... "Resources are not, they become"...

Read the following statements and choose your answer from the code given below:

(a) The advent of shale gas and biofuels can be attributed to the technological point of view of looking at resources.

(b) The population growing at an arithmetic growth rate and resources growing at geometric growth rate is a Malthusian view.

(c) 'Resources are not, they become' essentially indicates the level of technology and the socio-cultural processes for a material to become resource.

(d) Petroleum and solar energy are non-conventional resources.

A. Only (a) is true

B. (a) and (c) are true

C. (a), (b) and (c) are true

D. (a), (c) and (d) are true

Q.41 Read the passage and answer the following questions that follow.

....On the one hand, it is clear that many resources currently being used are non-renewable, and that the use of some resources destroys others. On the other hand, many elements

which are currently considered as resources might be appraised differently in the future as new resources are developed. As a result, there are many different ways of assessing resource prospects. One extreme is the Malthusian view which sees the stock of resources as a finite supply rapidly being depleted by large and increasing demands resulting from uncontrolled population growth and increasing aspirations. The consequence of this will be the exhaustion of resources and the impoverishment or even destruction of man. At the other extreme is the technological view which concedes that although the stock of resources is ultimately finite, the bounds of possibility within these limits are so extensive that the exhaustion of resources is not a practical problem. Technology may deplete some resources, but it also has a capacity for creating others, and as a result all problems can be solved if technical progress is maintained and economic and social constraints can be overcome… "Resources are not, they become"…

Match List-I with the List-II and select the correct answer from the code given below:

List - I (Energy Resources)	List - II (Areas of concentration)
(a) Petroleum	(i) Ruhr basin
(b) Uranium	(ii) Krishna-Godavari Basin
(c) Shale gas	(iii) Olympic Dam
(d) Coal	(iv) Safaniya

A. (a)-(ii), (b)-(i), (c)-(iii), (d)-(iv
B. (a)-(ii), (b)-(iii), (c)-(iv), (d)-(i)
C. (a)-(iv), (b)-(ii), (c)-(i), (d)-(iii)
D. (a)-(iv), (b)-(iii), (c)-(ii), (d)-(i)

Q.42 Match List-I with List-II

List - I(Economic Activity)	List - II (Sector of Economy)
(a) Quarrying	(i) Secondary
(b) Construction	(ii) Primary
(c) Researcher	(iii) Quaternary
(d)Policy Making	(iv) Quinary

A. (a)-(ii), (b)-(i), (c)-(iii), (d)-(iv)
B. (a)-(ii), (b)-(iii), (c)-(iv), (d)-(i)
C. (a)-(iv), (b)-(ii), (c)-(i), (d)-(iii)
D. (a)-(iv), (b)-(iii), (c)-(ii), (d)-(i)

Q.43 Which of the following statements relating to Weber's industrial location theory are correct?

(a) Linear location of industry occurs when the industry is located between the source of one raw material and the market.

(b) Non-linear location of industry occurs when the industry is located between market and the source more than one raw material.

(c) It is also called as area-market curve theory.

(d) The theory does not take into account the labour cost for an industry's optimal location.

Choose the correct option from below:

A. Only (a)
B. (a), (b) and (c)
C. (a) and (b)
D. (a), (b), (c) and (d)

Q.44 Match the List - I with List - II and select the correct answer from the code given below :

List -I
(a) Gold
(b) Coal
(c) Uranium
(d) Diamond

List -II
(i) United States of America
(ii) Russia
(iii) South Africa
(iv) Australia

A. (a)- (iv) ,(b)- (i) ,(c)- (iv) ,(d)- (iii)
B. (a)- (iv) ,(b)- (iii) ,(c)- (i) ,(d)- (ii)
C. (a)- (i) ,(b)- (ii) ,(c)- (iv) ,(d)- (iii)
D. (a)- (iii) ,(b)- (i) ,(c)- (iv) ,(d)- (ii)

Q.45 Given below are two statements. One is labelled as Assertion (A) and the other is labelled as Reason (R).

Assertion (A): Complementarity basis of spatial interaction refers to the idea that deficit or demand for an object/service at one location is fulfilled by supply or surplus in another location

Reason (R) : Complementarity relationship is same for every commodity.

Select the correct answer from options given below:

A. Both (A) and (R) are true and (R) is the correct explanation of (A)
B. Both (A) and (R) are true, but (R) is not the correct explanation of (A)
C. (A) is true, but (R) is false
D. (A) is false, but (R) is true

Q.46 Which of the following is NOT a member of the World Trade Organization?

A. China
B. South Korea
C. Kiribati
D. Afghanistan

Q.47 Match List-I with List-II of Transportation networks Indices with their formula's and select the correct answer from the codes given below :

List-I (Indices)	List-II (Formulas)
a. Beta	i) $\dfrac{u}{2v-5}$
b. Alpha	ii) $\dfrac{e}{v}$
c. Network Density	iii) $\dfrac{e}{3(v-2)}$
d. Gamma	iv) $\dfrac{L}{S}$

A. a-iii b-ii c-i d-iv
B. a-ii b-i c-iv d-iii
C. a-i b-ii c-iii d-iv
D. a-iii b-i c-iv d-ii

Q.48 Consider the following statements about spatial interaction and choose which amongst them is true:

i. There must be a supply and demand between interacting location.

ii. The residential zones are default to the industrial zones.

A. Only (i)
B. Only (ii)
C. both (i) and (ii)
D. Neither (i) nor (ii)

Q.49 Consider the following statements about world industrial regions and choose which amongst them is true:

i. The industrial region of New York and Mid Atlantic provides variety of manufacturing items.

ii. The region of New York has greatest concentration of ferrous industries.

iii. Detroit have motor vehicle industries.

A. Only (i)
B. Only (ii)
C. (ii) and (iii)
D. (i) , (ii) and (iii)

Q.50 Which of the following statement is correct?

A. Spatial interaction is a dynamic flow process which may refer to the daily commuters or the daily movement of human beings or the flow of tangible or intangible items such as information.

B. Edward Ullman shifted his focus on situation, instead of sites with his spatial interaction model.

C. Ullman used 3 parameters to explain the pattern of movement and interaction between 2 areas.

D. All of the above.

Q.51 Which of the following is not a factor affecting the interaction between regions as per the flow theory?

A. Complementarity
B. Government's fiscal policy
C. Intervening Opportunities
D. Transferability

Q.52 Given below are two statements. One is labelled as Assertion (A) and the other is labelled as Reason (R).

Assertion (A): Monocrop region delineated on the basis of Weaver's method means it is best suited to grow more than 1 crop.

Reason (R): For a monocrop region to be delineated, the square of the deviation is lowest for single crop vis-à-vis multiple crops.

Select the correct answer from options given below:

A. Both (A) and (R) are true and (R) is the correct explanation of (A)
B. Both (A) and (R) are true, but (R) is not the correct explanation of (A)
C. (A) is true, but (R) is false.
D. (A) is false, but (R) is true.

Q.53 According to Von Thunen, which zone had crop farming without fallow land?

A. Zone I **B.** Zone II **C.** Zone III **D.** Zone IV

Q.54 Which of the theories were taken as the basic assumptions in R.P. Mishra's theory of growth foci?

a) Central Place Theory
b) Growth Pole Theory
c) Spatial Diffusion Theory
d) Sector Theory

Choose the correct option from below:

A. Only (a)
B. (a), (b) and (c)
C. (b), (c) and (d)
D. (a), (b), (c), and (d)

Q.55 Which of the following is not one of the dimensions used to calculate Human Development index?

A. Life Expectancy at birth
B. Literacy ratio
C. Education Index
D. GNI per capita

Q.56 Match the List - I with List - II and select the correct answer from the code given below :

List - I (Social Group)	List - II(Example)
(a) Religion	(i) Marathi
(b)Language	(ii) Santhal
(c) Tribe	(iii) Muslim
(d) Caste	(iv) Brahmin

A. (a)-(iii),(b)-(i),(c)-(ii),(d)-(iv)
B. (a)-(iv),(b)-(iii),(c)-(ii),(d)-(i)
C. (a)-(iv),(b)-(i),(c)-(ii),(d)-(iii)
D. (a)-(iii),(b)-(iv),(c)-(i),(d)-(ii)

Q.57 Given below are two statements. One is labelled as Assertion (A) and the other is labelled as Reason (R).

Assertion (A): The city of Chennai is called as India's Health capital.

Reason (R) : There are several super-specialty hospitals in the city.

Select the correct answer from options given below:

A. Both (A) and (R) are true and (R) is the correct explanation of (A)
B. Both (A) and (R) are true, but (R) is not the correct explanation of (A)
C. (A) is true, but (R) is false
D. (A) is false, but (R) is true

Q.58 Read the following statements and choose the correct answer from the code given below:

(a) Rimland theory was given in the 1950s.

(b) Rimland theory was given by Nicholas Spykman.

(c) As per Rimland theory, the world is divided into 5 types.

(d) Spykman says that who controls Rimland, controls Eurasia.

A. (Only (a) is true
B. (a) and (b) are true
C. (b) and (c) are true
D. (b) and (d) are true

Q.59 For how much distance does the Exclusive economic zone extends in the ocean?

A. 12 nautical miles
B. 100 nautical miles
C. 200 nautical miles
D. 300 nautical miles

Q.60 Which of the following statement is correct?

A. Cultural region is divided into formal, functional and vernacular cultural regions.
B. The spread of culture can also be reciprocal.
C. Cultural ecology refers to the adaptive processes by which cultural societies adjust with the parameters of their habitat.
D. All of the above.

Q.61 Match the scholars (List-I) with the book/theory/concept/model (List-II) they are associated with.

List-I (Scholars)	List-II (Field of contribution)
(a) Aijazuddin Ahmad	(i) Gender geography
(b) Saraswati Raju	(ii) Regional Geography
(c) R.L. singh	(iii) Social Geography
(d)SM Rafiullah	(iv) Agricultural Geography

A. (a)-(i), (b)-(iii), (c)-(ii), (d)-(iv)
B. (a)-(iii), (b)-(i), (c)-(ii), (d)-(iv)
C. (a)-(iv), (b)-(ii), (c)-(i), (d)-(iii)
D. (a)-(iv), (b)-(iii), (c)-(ii), (d)-(i)

Q.62 Who among the following geographers is known for the distinction between general and special geography?

A. Varenius   **B.** Pattrick Geddes
C. Hartshorne   **D.** Schaefer

Q.63 Sense of Place is a concept propounded by which of the following Geographer?

A. Hartshorne   **B.** Derek Gregory
C. William Bunge   **D.** Yi-Fu Tuan

Q.64 Which of the following statements are correct regarding the literary works of the following geographers?

(a) Kosmos is written by Alexander von Humboldt to search for a universal science.

(b) Muqadimmah is written by Al Idrisi.

(c) Erdkunde is written by Carl Ritter where he has talked about the concept of unity in diversity.

(d) Freidrich Ratzel has written the book Anthropogeographie.

Choose the correct option from below:

A. Only (a)   **B.** (a) and (c)
C. (a), (b) and (c)   **D.** (a), (c) and (d)

Q.65 Man is a product of the earth's surface. This means not merely that he is a child of the earth, dust of her dust; but the earth has mothered him, fed him, set him tasks, directed his thoughts, confronted him with difficulties that have strengthened his body..........
Who among the following geographer has said this?

A. Ratzel
B. Issiah Bowman
C. Ellen Churchill Semple
D. Elsworth Huntington

Q.66 Which of the following statements are correct about the scholars regarding the dualism in physical versus human geography?

(a) Febvre was the one of earliest scholars's who talked about man's active role in shaping the physical earth.

(b) Vidal de la Blache is considered to be the founder of human geography.

(c) H.H Barrows was an adherent of physical geography.

(d) The philosophy of the followers of human geography was to establish a mutual man-nature relationship where the concept of dominance of nature was rejected.

Choose the correct option from below:

A. Only (b)   **B.** (a), (b) and (d)
C. (a), (c) and (d)   **D.** (b), (c) and (d)

Q.67 Match the scholars (List-I) with the book/theory/concept/model (List-II) they are associated with regards to the various dualisms in geography.

List-I (Scholars)	List-II (Works/Approaches)
(a) Hartshorne	(i) Exceptionalism in Geography
(b) Schaefer	(ii) Human Geography
(c) Vidal de la Blache	(iii) Quantitative Geography
(d) Peter Haggett	(iv) The Nature of Geography

A. (a)-(i), (b)-(iii), (c)-(ii), (d)-(iv)
B. (a)-(iii), (b)-(i), (c)-(ii), (d)-(iv)
C. (a)-(iv), (b)-(i), (c)-(ii), (d)-(iii)
D. (a)-(iv), (b)-(iii), (c)-(ii), (d)-(i)

Q.68 Read the following statements and select the correct answer from the code given below.

(a) As per Varenius, general geography deals with formulation theories, principles.

(b) Regional geography deals with one world as one unit.

(c) Regional geography describes various areas as spatial units.

(d) Humboldt was the first geographer to give the term uranography.

Code:

A. Only (a) is true
B. (a), (b) and (c) is true
C. (a) and (b) is true
D. (a), (b) and (d) is true

Q.69 Given below are two statements. One is labelled as Assertion (A) and the other is labelled as Reason (R).

Assertion (A): Humanism grew as a criticism against historical approach.

Reason (R) : Humanism studies human awareness.

Select the correct answer from options given below:

A. Both (A) and (R) are true and (R) is the correct explanation of (A)
B. Both (A) and (R) are true, but (R) is not the correct explanation of (A)
C. (A) is true, but (R) is false
D. (A) is false, but (R) is true

Q.70 Read the following statements. Which of the following statements are objectives of behavioral approach? Select the correct answer from the code given below.

(a) To elaborate the spatial dimension of human decision-making and behavior

(b) To bring about quantitative revolution

(c) To unfold spatial dimensions of social and psychological theories

(d) To develop models for humanity

(e) To emphasize structural explanation of human activity and physical environment.

(f) To generate primary data for human behavior

Code:

A. (a) and (b) are true
B. (a), (b), (c) and (d) are true
C. (b),(d), (e) and (f) are true
D. (a), (c), (d) and (f) true

Q.71 Match List-I with List-II

List-I(Name of test)	List-II(Critical Value)
(a)Chi-square test	(i) Value of D

(b)z-test	(ii) Value of z
(c) KS Test	(iii) Value of F
(d) ANOVA	(iv) Value of X2 2 ^(2)

Code:

A. (a)-(ii),(b)-(iii),(c)-(iv),(d)-(i)
B. (a)-(iv),(b)-(ii),(c)-(i),(d)-(iii)
C. (a)-(iii),(b)-(ii),(c)-(i),(d)-(iv)
D. (a)-(iii),(b)-(i),(c)-(ii),(d)-(iv)

Q.72 Number of Principal Components can be _______ the number of original attributes.

A. More than
B. Less than
C. Equal to
D. Less than or equal to

Q.73 Which of the following is NOT a part of a regression equation?

A. Principal Component
B. Dependent variable
C. Covariates
D. Error terms

Q.74 In GIS, non-spatial data is also called as

A. Quantitative Data
B. Attribute data
C. Raster data
D. Vector data

Q.75 In a pie diagram, the total of all the angles is

A. 180^0
B. 90^0
C. 360^0
D. 100^0

Q.76 Read the following statements and choose the correct answer from the code given below:

(a) An advantage about the remote sensing data is that the data is consistent.

(b) Maps, aerial photographs, and images are scanned to use as raster data.

(c) Remote sensing is used to capture vector data.

(d) Ground surveying is a source of vector data.

Code:

A. (a) and (b) are true
B. (a), (b) and (d) are true
C. (b) and (d) are true
D. (c) and (d) are true

Q.77 Which of the following is NOT a form of interaction when the radiation of the sun interacts with earth's surface?

A. Scattering
B. Absorption
C. Reflection
D. Transmission

Q.78 Read the following statements and choose the correct answer from the code given below:

(a) The area-height curve gives a more realistic picture of area-height relationship than the hypsometric curve.

(b) A hypsometric curve only represents the vertical distribution of land.

(c) An area height curve gives the relationship between the area and elevation.

(d) A hypsometric curve records average slope between contours.

Code:

A. (a), (b) and (c) are true
B. (a), (b) and (d) are true
C. (b) and (d) are true
D. (c) and (d) are true

Q.79 Which map shows the movement of objects from one location to another?

A. Flow maps
B. Chorchromatic
C. Isorhythmic
D. Dasymetric

Q.80 Match the List-I with List-II two.

List-I(Author)	List-II(books)
a) Rhind	i) Computer aided cartography
b) Dale	ii) The Unique dualities of geographic information system
c) Parker	iii) Land information management
d) Reddy	iv) remote sensing and geographical information system

Choose the correct option from the code given below:

A. a-iii b-ii c-i d-iv
B. a-ii b-i c-iv d-iii
C. a-i b-iii c-ii d-iv
D. a-iii b-i c-iv d-ii

Q.81 Match List-I with List-II

List-I (Rivers)	List-II (Origin)
(a) Sutlej	(i) Multai
(b) Narmada	(ii) Mansarovar
(c) Tapi	(iii) Amarkantak
(d) Ravi	(iv) Rohtang

Select the correct answer from the options given below:

A. (a)-(iii),(b)-(iv),(c)-(i),(d)-(ii)
B. (a)-(iv),(b)-(ii),(c)-(i),(d)-(iii)
C. (a)-(ii),(b)-(iii),(c)-(i),(d)-(iv)
D. (a)-(ii),(b)-(iii),(c)-(iv),(d)-(i)

Q.82 Read the following statements and choose your answer from the code given below:

(a) Gujarat is the leading producer of cotton in India.

(b) India ranks second in wheat production in the world.

(c) Punjab ranks first among the wheat producing states in India.

(d) India is the leading producer of rice in the world.

A. (a) and (d) are true
B. (a) and (b) are true
C. (a), (c) and (d) are true
D. (a), (b) and (d) are true

Q.83 During which five-year plan period Indian economy entered the 'take-off stage'?

A. Third Five Year Plan
B. Ninth Five Year Plan
C. Fourth Five Year Plan
D. Sixth Five Year Plan

Q.84 Given below are two statements- one is labelled as Assertion (A) and the other is labelled as Reason (R):

Assertion(A)- Sex ratio in India is low in comparison to developed countries.

Reason(R)- Literacy and living standards are poor in the rural and in some urban areas.

Choose the correct option:

A. Both A and R are true, and R is the correct explanation of A

B. Both A and R are true, but R is not the correct explanation of A

C. A is true, but R is false

D. A is false, but R is true

Q.85 Arrange the districts on the basis of lowest decadal growth rate in 2001-2011:-

a) Ratnagiri

b) Lahul and Spiti

c) Mumbai

d) Mokokchung

A. d, c, b, a   **B.** a, b, d, c   **C.** a, b, c, d   **D.** b, c, d, a

Q.86 Which state has the highest cropping intensity in India?

A. Punjab   **B.** Assam

C. Haryana   **D.** West Bengal

Q.87 Match List-I with List-II :

List-I (Crops)	List II (States with highest production)
(a) Rice	(i) Assam
(b) Cotton	(ii) West Bengal
(c) Wheat	(iii) Gujarat
(d) Tea	(iv) Uttar Pradesh

Select the correct answer from the options given below:

A. (a)-(ii); (b)-(i); (c)-(iv); (d)-(iii)

B. (a)-(iv); (b)-(iii); (c)-(ii); (d)-(i)

C. (a)-(i); (b)-(ii); (c)-(iii); (d)-(iv)

D. (a)-(ii); (b)-(iii); (c)-(iv); (d)-(i)

Q.88 Which of the following is NOT a reason for growth of population?

A. Immigration

B. Outmigration

C. Increase in birth rate

D. Decrease in death rate

Q.89 Given below are two statements. One is labelled as Assertion (A) and the other is labelled as Reason (R).

Assertion (A): The period of World War I proved to be beneficial for Indian industries.

Reason (R) : The cotton textile industry developed in Mumbai in the period of World War I.

Select the correct answer from options given below:

A. Both (A) and (R) are true and (R) is the correct explanation of (A)

B. Both (A) and (R) are true, but (R) is not the correct explanation of (A)

C. (A) is true, but (R) is false

D. (A) is false, but (R) is true

Q.90 Given below are two statements. One is labelled as Assertion (A) and the other is labelled as Reason (R).

Assertion (A): Floods occur almost annually in Brahmaputra valley.

Reason (R): The river channel of Brahmaputra is very narrow.

Select the correct answer from options given below:

A. Both (A) and (R) are true and (R) is the correct explanation of (A)

B. Both (A) and (R) are true, but (R) is not the correct explanation of (A)

C. (A) is true, but (R) is false

D. (A) is false, but (R) is true

Q.91 Match List-I with List-II

List-I(Characteristics)	List-II(State)
(a) State with highest sex ratio	(i) Bihar
(b) State with highest tribal population	(ii) Arunachal Pradesh
(c) State with lowest literacy rate	(iii) Madhya Pradesh
(d) State with lowest density	(iv) Kerala

Select the correct answer from the options given below:

A. (a)-(iv),(b)-(ii),(c)-(iii),(d)-(i)

B. (a)-(iv),(b)-(iii),(c)-(i),(d)-(ii)

C. (a)-(ii),(b)-(iii),(c)-(i),(d)-(iv)

D. (a)-(ii),(b)-(iii),(c)-(iv),(d)-(i)

Q.92 Match List-I with List-II

List-I(National Park)	List-II(State)
(a) The Silent Valley	(i) Uttarakhand
(b) Panna	(ii) Himachal Pradesh
(c) Rajaji	(iii) Kerala
(d) Simbalbara	(iv) Madhya Pradesh

Select the correct answer from the options given below:

A. (a)-(iii),(b)-(iv),(c)-(ii),(d)-(i)

B. (a)-(iii),(b)-(iv),(c)-(i),(d)-(ii)

C. (a)-(ii),(b)-(iii),(c)-(i),(d)-(iv)

D. (a)-(ii),(b)-(iii),(c)-(iv),(d)-(i)

Q.93 The first aircraft industry in India was set up in

A. Chennai   **B.** Jamshedpur

C. Bangalore   **D.** Delhi

Q.94 Arrange the flowing ports of India in the order that of their location from North to South

A. Kolkata-Mumbai-Kandla-Marmugao

B. Kandla-Kolkata-Mumbai-Marmugao

C. Kandla-Kolkata- Marmugao-Mumbai-

D. Kolkata-Kandla-Marmugao-Mumbai

Q.95 Read the following statements and choose your answer from the code given below:

(a) Karnataka is the leading producer of coffee.

(b) Western India has most tea plantations in the country.

(c) India produces 9 % of the total rubber in world.

(d) India is the largest producer of Ginger in the world.

A. (a) and (d) are true

B. (a) and (b) are true

C. (a), (c) and (d) are true

D. (a), (b) and (d) are true

Q.96 Read the passage below and answer questions that follow:

The 73rd and 74th constitutional amendments have provided for fund collection by the Panchayat at the local level for local development for which state governments are supposed to provide matching giant. Till now, not even a single state government has taken initiative to generate resources at the Panchayat level. At the maximum, the Panchayat can identify the problems at the local level which can provide guidelines to our planning process. Unfortunately, no one at the administrative level is willing to share any power which creates great practical hindrances in decentralization of the planning process and give much needed thrust to regional planning. The success of regional planning primarily depends upon:

• Quality of planning education

• Degree of public awareness about the rationale for a planned effort

• Efficiency of planning institutions

• Proper comprehension and appreciation of the basic issues in regional planning by society itself.

In India, regional planning is still at its nascent stage and is not very popular with our planners. It has a long way to go in terms of its content and implementations before it is able to show its utility and be some use to people at the regional level.

Which amendments provided fund to local Panchayat for local development?

A. 72nd

B. 73rd and 74th

C. 75th

D. 74th and 75th

Q.97

Read the passage below and answer questions that follow:

The 73rd and 74th constitutional amendments have provided for fund collection by the Panchayat at the local level for local development for which state governments are supposed to provide matching giant. Till now, not even a single state government has taken initiative to generate resources at the Panchayat level. At the maximum, the Panchayat can identify the problems at the local level which can provide guidelines to our planning process. Unfortunately, no one at the administrative level is willing to share any power which creates great practical hindrances in decentralization of the planning process and give much needed thrust to regional planning. The success of regional planning primarily depends upon:

• Quality of planning education

• Degree of public awareness about the rationale for a planned effort

• Efficiency of planning institutions

• Proper comprehension and appreciation of the basic issues in regional planning by society itself.

In India, regional planning is still at its nascent stage and is not very popular with our planners. It has a long way to go in terms of its content and implementations before it is able to show its utility and be some use to people at the regional level.

Success of regional planning is NOT dependent upon

A. Quality of education planning

B. Efficiency of planning institutions

C. Degree of public awareness about the rationale for planned effort.

D. Proper paperwork for planning

Q.98

Read the passage below and answer questions that follow:

The 73rd and 74th constitutional amendments have provided for fund collection by the Panchayat at the local level for local development for which state governments are supposed to provide matching giant. Till now, not even a single state government has taken initiative to generate resources at the Panchayat level. At the maximum, the Panchayat can identify the problems at the local level which can provide guidelines to our planning process. Unfortunately, no one at the administrative level is willing to share any power which creates great practical hindrances in decentralization of the planning process and give much needed thrust to regional planning. The success of regional planning primarily depends upon:

• Quality of planning education

• Degree of public awareness about the rationale for a planned effort

• Efficiency of planning institutions

• Proper comprehension and appreciation of the basic issues in regional planning by society itself.

In India, regional planning is still at its nascent stage and is not very popular with our planners. It has a long way to go in terms of its content and implementations before it is able to show its utility and be some use to people at the regional level.

Which of the following is the reason for lack of local development?

A. Lack of funds

B. Lack of industrialization

C. Lack of initiative by state government

D. Illiteracy

Q.99

Read the passage below and answer questions that follow:

The 73rd and 74th constitutional amendments have provided for fund collection by the Panchayat at the local level for local development for which state governments are supposed to provide matching giant. Till now, not even a single state government has taken initiative to generate resources at the Panchayat level. At the maximum, the Panchayat can identify the problems at the local level which can provide guidelines to our planning process. Unfortunately, no one at the administrative level is willing to share any power which creates great practical hindrances in decentralization of the planning process and give much needed thrust to regional planning. The success of regional planning primarily depends upon:

• Quality of planning education

• Degree of public awareness about the rationale for a planned effort

• Efficiency of planning institutions

• Proper comprehension and appreciation of the basic issues in regional planning by society itself.

In India, regional planning is still at its nascent stage and is not very popular with our planners. It has a long way to go in terms of its content and implementations before it is able to show its utility and be some use to people at the regional level.

What is the hindrance in the decentralization of planning process?

A. Lack of funds

B. Unwillingness to give up power at administrative level

C. Poverty

D. Unemployment

Q.100

Read the passage below and answer questions that follow:

The 73rd and 74th constitutional amendments have provided for fund collection by the Panchayat at the local level for local development for which state governments are supposed to provide matching giant. Till now, not even a single state government has taken initiative to generate resources at the Panchayat level. At the maximum, the Panchayat can identify the problems at the local level which can provide guidelines to our planning process. Unfortunately, no one at the administrative level is willing to share any power which creates great practical hindrances in decentralization of the planning process and give much needed thrust to regional planning. The success of regional planning primarily depends upon:

• Quality of planning education

• Degree of public awareness about the rationale for a planned effort

• Efficiency of planning institutions

• Proper comprehension and appreciation of the basic issues in regional planning by society itself.

In India, regional planning is still at its nascent stage and is not very popular with our planners. It has a long way to go in terms of its content and implementations before it is able to show its utility and be some use to people at the regional level.

India is placed at which stage of Regional planning?

A. Beginning

B. Middle

C. Last

D. Second

// Smart Answer Sheet //

Correct — Percentage of students who answered correctly. **Skipped** — Percentage of students who skipped.

Q.	Ans.	Correct / Skipped
1	D	59.26 % / 12.96 %
2	B	18.52 % / 33.33 %
3	B	38.89 % / 31.48 %
4	A	42.59 % / 37.04 %
5	B	35.19 % / 35.18 %
6	C	27.78 % / 35.18 %
7	D	50.0 % / 33.33 %
8	A	55.56 % / 37.03 %
9	D	24.07 % / 37.04 %
10	D	24.07 % / 33.34 %
11	A	62.96 % / 33.34 %
12	B	40.74 % / 37.04 %
13	A	61.11 % / 31.48 %
14	B	12.96 % / 35.19 %
15	D	38.89 % / 33.33 %
16	D	42.59 % / 33.34 %
17	D	16.67 % / 37.03 %
18	C	48.15 % / 37.04 %
19	A	66.67 % / 24.07 %
20	B	31.48 % / 31.48 %
21	A	64.81 % / 27.78 %
22	C	20.37 % / 37.04 %
23	B	27.78 % / 29.63 %
24	C	24.07 % / 37.04 %
25	B	40.74 % / 35.19 %
26	A	46.3 % / 37.03 %
27	A	64.81 % / 27.78 %
28	A	24.07 % / 35.19 %
29	A	57.41 % / 27.78 %
30	C	20.37 % / 35.19 %
31	B	25.93 % / 33.33 %
32	C	42.59 % / 33.34 %
33	A	11.11 % / 29.63 %
34	A	50.0 % / 35.19 %
35	C	46.3 % / 27.77 %
36	B	64.81 % / 35.19 %
37	A	44.44 % / 35.19 %
38	C	29.63 % / 33.33 %
39	C	12.96 % / 35.19 %
40	B	16.67 % / 35.18 %
41	D	24.07 % / 29.63 %
42	A	55.56 % / 35.18 %
43	C	22.22 % / 33.34 %
44	D	22.22 % / 35.19 %
45	C	20.37 % / 29.63 %
46	C	38.89 % / 35.18 %
47	B	48.15 % / 33.33 %
48	C	38.89 % / 37.04 %
49	D	40.74 % / 37.04 %
50	D	51.85 % / 33.34 %
51	B	38.89 % / 31.48 %
52	D	24.07 % / 31.49 %
53	C	44.44 % / 35.19 %
54	B	33.33 % / 35.19 %
55	B	16.67 % / 33.33 %
56	A	57.41 % / 35.18 %
57	A	53.7 % / 35.19 %
58	D	51.85 % / 35.19 %
59	C	51.85 % / 33.34 %
60	D	61.11 % / 31.48 %
61	B	40.74 % / 33.33 %
62	A	46.3 % / 37.03 %
63	D	16.67 % / 31.48 %
64	D	55.56 % / 35.18 %
65	C	40.74 % / 33.33 %
66	B	24.07 % / 33.34 %
67	C	33.33 % / 37.04 %
68	D	33.33 % / 35.19 %
69	D	27.78 % / 35.18 %
70	D	29.63 % / 37.04 %
71	B	29.63 % / 27.78 %
72	D	18.52 % / 33.33 %
73	A	16.67 % / 37.03 %
74	B	38.89 % / 35.18 %
75	C	64.81 % / 33.34 %
76	A	9.26 % / 35.18 %
77	A	12.96 % / 33.34 %
78	A	22.22 % / 35.19 %
79	A	61.11 % / 29.63 %
80	C	16.67 % / 31.48 %

Q.	Ans.	Correct / Skipped		Q.	Ans.	Correct / Skipped		Q.	Ans.	Correct / Skipped		Q.	Ans.	Correct / Skipped		Q.	Ans.	Correct / Skipped
81	C	57.41 % 29.63 %		85	C	14.81 % 35.19 %		89	C	14.81 % 33.34 %		93	C	42.59 % 27.78 %		97	D	50.0 % 35.19 %
82	B	35.19 % 35.18 %		86	A	44.44 % 37.04 %		90	A	48.15 % 37.04 %		94	B	31.48 % 37.04 %		98	C	40.74 % 37.04 %
83	A	25.93 % 35.18 %		87	D	57.41 % 35.18 %		91	B	59.26 % 35.18 %		95	C	46.3 % 35.18 %		99	B	51.85 % 33.34 %
84	A	24.07 % 35.19 %		88	B	44.44 % 37.04 %		92	B	44.44 % 35.19 %		96	B	55.56 % 35.18 %		100	A	46.3 % 35.18 %

//Hints and Solutions//

1. All the three factors are responsible for the creation of volcanic eruptions. The temperature increases with the increase in depth below the surface of the Earth. This results in the melting of rock and other materials at a high pressure in the interior of the Earth. Later this ejects at the surface of the Earth.

The presence of gases and especially water vapour is a prime factor that cause the volcanic eruptions as heat and pressure increases highly when water get converted into water vapour and this comes out from a weak joint.

Similarly, plate tectonics is a major reason behind this kind of process. Collision of plates and subduction of the continental plate and melting of the plate due to heat are primary factors responsible for the volcanic eruptions.

2. Lines joining places which experience earthquakes at the same time are known as Homoseismal Lines. These are oval and elliptical in shape and run around the epicenter.

3. Frank. B. Taylor, in the year 1910, postulated his theory about the horizontal displacement of the continents. According to Taylor, the primary reason for the movement of the continents was the tidal force of the moon. That led to the movement of continents towards the equator beginning in the Cretaceous period.

4. Walther Penck was a German scientist who rejected the Davision model of erosion. He stated that the landform development can be explained by taking into consideration the ratio between the endogenetic (uplifting) processes and exogenetic (degradation) processes. The tectonic activity plays an essential role in the characteristics of landforms.

5. The forces affecting the earth's crust are divided into two types, endogenetic forces and exogenetic forces. The endogenetic forces are further divided into two types based on their intensity, diastrophic movements and sudden movements. The diastrophic movements occur on a global level, leading to the creation of mountains, plains, plateaus, etc. Sudden movements cause rapid events and the destruction of the earth's crust. The vertical movement of diastrophic forces is called epirogenetic movement, which causes upliftment or subsidence of the crust. The horizontal movement is called orogenetic movement, which leads to warping of the crust and formation of folds, faults, fractures, cracks, etc.

6. At the highest level, there are cirrus clouds. The pectorals are thin and distinct clouds with a slender appearance. They are always white in colour. These clouds form at high altitudes (8,000 - 12,000 m).

A cloud is a mass of small water droplets or ice formed by the condensation of water vapor in abundant free air. As clouds form at certain altitudes on Earth's surface, they take on different shapes.

Hence, the correct option is (C).

7. Volcanic activity occurs in active plate boundaries. These can be both converging and diverging plate boundaries. The mid-oceanic ridges are generally a part of the divergent plate boundaries. Examples of volcanoes in converging and diverging plate boundaries include Mt. Kilimanjaro in Kenya and Nevados Ojos del Salado on Chile-Argentina Border respectively.

8. • The earthquake in Gujrat in 2004 was of magnitude 7.7 on the Richter scale. It occurred at 8:56 am on 26th January, the Republic Day of India.

• The landslide occurred on 12th July 2000 at Ghatkopar in Mumbai. Seventy-eight people were killed, and seven were injured in this landslide.

• A series of four avalanches occurred in Gurez sector of Jammu and Kashmir on 25th January 2017. It killed 24 people, 20 of whom were soldiers.

• The Barren Island, the only active volcano of India spewed ash and lava on 23rd January 2017. The volcanic activity was continuation of eruptions of 2005.

9. L.C. King did field observations as the basis for his hillslope model. He did not take into consideration any measurements. He was against the theory that climatic variation caused variation in the form of the slope. He maintained a belief that basic physical processes in landform formation remain same in all types of climate. His concept of normal/ideal slope consisted of summital, rectilinearity, free face and basal concavity. Such normal slope was formed due to fluvial processes and mass movement in normal conditions. His observations in the South African landscape led him to believe that sub-tropical, semi-humid regions have most normal slopes, while humid regions do not.

10. The place of occurrence of an earthquake, usually in the earth's interior is called a focus. The epicenter is the place where the seismic event begins. The epicenter is always perpendicular to the focus. So. (R) is true, and (A) is false.

11. Carbon dioxide is transparent to the incoming solar radiation but is opaque to the outgoing terrestrial radiation. Its opaqueness can be seen in two ways as it absorbs part of the outgoing terrestrial radiation and reflects back to earth some part of it. This effect is called greenhouse effect. Carbon dioxide (CO_2) is a greenhouse gas.

12. The layering of the atmosphere is done on the basis if temperature. The troposphere is the lowest layer of the atmosphere. Its average height is greater at equator than poles because of the higher transport of heat at equator due to strong convective currents. Above troposphere is stratosphere which is also the layer of maximum ozone concentration because of which it is also called ozonosphere. The coldest point in the atmosphere is mesopause above which temperature continues to increase. Due to the electrical properties of the ionosphere, radio communications are made possible through sending radio waves.

13. Water vapour is the most variable gas in the atmosphere and also the most important greenhouse gas. It can be found in different amount by volume in different parts of the atmosphere. It is almost negligible in deserts while it is maximum above warm and wet tropics. Also, it decreases with altitude.

14. Deposition refers to the conversion of gas to solid in extreme cold conditions, without passing through the liquid state. It is just the opposite phenomena of sublimation. This process along with freezing and condensation is known to warm their surrounding due to release of latent heat during change in state.

15. The atmosphere is largely transparent to incoming solar radiation. The insolation after passing through the atmosphere heats the earth surface, after which the earth itself becomes a radiating body. It transmits the heat to the atmospheric layers near the surface in long-wave radiation form.

16. Coriolis force is a fictitious force which originates as a result of the rotation of the earth and causes any moving object to deflect to its right in the northern hemisphere and to its left in the southern hemisphere. It is primarily this reason why the trade winds that moves from the tropical region to equatorial regions are called North East Trade Winds and South East Trade Winds in the northern hemisphere and the southern hemisphere, respectively.

17. Pressure Gradient Force is the force produced by the difference in atmospheric pressure. Wind moves from high pressure to low pressure area. Coriolis force is produced by the rotation of the earth and thus wind deflects to its right and left in the direction of its movement in the northern hemisphere and southern hemisphere respectively. It is maximum at poles and zero at equator. The wind speed is measured by anemometer.

18. Warm front is the contact zone when a warm air mass moves towards cold air mass. Similarly, cold front develops in the contact zone where cold air moves towards warm air mass. Occluded front develops when an air mass is fully lifted above the land surface by other air mass and it is marked by steep pressure and temperature changes. Maritime Tropical (mT) air mass is named after the source region of warm tropical and sub tropical oceans.

19. The letter code B in Koppen's climatic classification represents *dry climates* group where the potential evaporation is higher than the precipitation. It is further divided into semi arid (BS) and desert (BW) climates and further can be divided into subtropical steppe (BSh) and sub-tropical desert (BWh) climates where *h* is for sub-tropical region (15°-30° latitudes) and mid-latitude steppe (BSk) and mid-latitude desert (BWk) climates where *k* is for mid-latitude region (35°-60° latitudes). Rajasthan falls in the sub-tropical desert climate (BWh).

20. Southern Oscillation Index (SOI) is an index which gives an indication of the development and the intensity of El Nino or La Nina events. The SOI is calculated based on the pressure differences between Tahiti in French Polynesia in central Pacific and Darwin, Australia. A positive SOI refers La Nina conditions and in the same manner a negative SOI indicates El Nino condition.

21. Cyclones have inward motion of the winds towards centre of low pressure. It is a very large-scale air mass. The winds in a cyclone are spiraling around the centre, which is also called as eye of the cyclone. They are called as typhoon in northwestern Pacific Ocean.

22. The tsunami is a series of huge waves caused by volcanic eruption or earthquake under the sea. Tsunami can also be caused by a meteor falling from the sky and entering the ocean. The tsunami is NOT a tidal wave. The speed of the waves of tsunami waves depends upon the depth of the ocean rather than the distance of the source of the wave.

23. In the Semi-diurnal tidal cycle, there are two nearly equal high tides and low tides every lunar day. The east coast of India has semi-diurnal tides. They have a period of 12 hours 25 min. They have wavelength of more than half the circumference of the earth.

24. The North Equatorial Current is a warm current flowing between 10^0 and 20^0 N. It is not connected to Equator despite its name. The West Wind Drift is a cold current that flows in the Southern Hemisphere. The Peru Current is a cold current. It causes fog and scanty rainfall in the western Peru. The Gulf Stream is a warm current in the Northern Hemisphere.

25. • Continental Shelf is the first of the oceanic relief features. It extends at depth of 0-200 m. It has width of 70-80 km average.

• Abyssal Plains are plains of the ocean. They are found in deep seas. They have depth of 4000-6000 m. They have very gentle relief.

• Oceanic trenches are deep U-shaped valleys in the ocean. Trenches are the deepest points in the ocean. They can have depth from 4000-10000 m.

• The continental slope lies after the continental shelf. It can have depth from 2000-3000m.

26. Carbon is a nonmetallic chemical element found in group 14 of periodic table. Carbons form diamond and graphite are crystalline in structure but differ in physical properties. Fullerenes contains many molecules formed entirely of carbons.

27. Pyramid of biomass is representation of biomass present in a unit area of various tropic levels. It shows the relationship between biomass and its levels showing the amount in each level at a time. Ecosystems of biomass have mostly pyramids of bio mass with large base containing primary producers and small tropic level perched on the top. Hence the pyramid looks upright.

28. Wastewater in the environmental terms is defined as any water that has come into the usage of human beings. wastewater comes from sinks, toilets, showers and toilets. More than 80% of world's waste water flows back into the environment and in some of the least developed countries, the figure reaches 95%.

29. Kyoto protocol is an international treaty which focuses on the reduced green house gas emission by the countries. It is an initiation by United Nation. This protocol was adopted in 1997 and entered into force in 2005. The first commitment treaty was from 2005-2012. The 18th conference of parties was held in Doha.

30. Henri Pirenne has studied the history and development of cities for his whole life. The main reason that is given for development of towns by Pirenne is the revival of commerce in the eleventh and twelfth century. The original nuclei of the towns were settlement of merchants. In his second attempt, Pirenne explained his theories in his book 'Les villes du moyen age' in 1927.

31. If number of villages is equal to half of hamlet numbers, the settlement is a hamleted settlement. The hamleted settlement has a large area and intervening fields. Mostly, central or main settlement is absent or has very low influence on the area.

Settlements of this type are found in Madhya Pradesh, West Bengal, Uttar Pradesh and coastal plains.

32. According to United Nations, the total rural population of the world is nearly 3.4 billion. It is expected to decline to 3.1 billion by 2050. The country with highest rural population in the world is India with 893 million. It is followed by China with rural population of 578 million.

33. The total number of migrants' intra-state and inter-state in 2011 was around 97.5 million. Approximately, the number of rural to rural migrants was 53 million, urban to rural was 20 million, urban to urban was 14 million and rural to urban was 6 million. Thus, the rate of rural to urban migration was 6.2%

34. The population policies of China have been strict since 1970s. There was one-child policy in China. But the population in China has seen to be decreasing. In number of people in the non-working age of 60 years and plus has also increased. Thus, population policy was changed in 2015 to two-child policy to overcome these setbacks. Both (A) and (R) are true and (R) is the correct explanation of (A).

35. The first census conducted in India was in 1871, the first complete census in 1881. After independence and partition, Census was conducted for the first time in 1951. It was conducted under 1948 census act of India and was the 9th census of India.

36. * Infant mortality rate is the number of death of children under 0-1 years per 1000 live births. India's Infant mortality rate was 43 as per census of 2011.

* Average no of children a woman will bear through her childbearing years is the total fertility rate. India's TFR is 2.4 as of 2011.

* Crude birth rate is the number of live births per 1000 population in the year. It was 21.8 in 2011.

* Crude death rate is the number of deaths per 1000 of population.

37. Erich Zimmerman was an economist who gave the functional theory of mineral resources. It is his quote "Resources are not, they become" which implies that it is the society and the level of technology the society possesses, would determine what will be called resources.

38. Malthusian view of assessing resource prospects is based on the assumption that the stock of resources are finite and the rate at which population is growing is greater than the rate at which the resources are produced. Hence, resources must be used judiciously, else there would be instances of famines, catastrophes etc.

39. Technological view of assessing resource prospects considers although the stock of resources to choose from is finite, but there is no limit to the possibilities of creating new resources with the help of technology. It questions the basic assumptions of any future projections by current level of technology. It argues that any projections to the future must also consider that the level of technology would never be the same, rather improve.

40. The technological view of looking at resources claimed that new resources would be created from the very finite stock with the improvement of technology. The improvement of technology led to the discovery of shale gas and biofuels too are recent improvements in the field of energy. Malthusian view suggests that population grows at geometric rate while food production (resources) grow at arithmetic rate. Petroleum is a conventional source of energy and the reserves would exhaust in the future if the rate of consumption remains unchanged, while solar energy is a non-conventional and renewable source of energy.

41. Safaniya is the largest off-shore oil field in the world operated by Saudi Arabia. Olympic Dam in Australia has one of the largest extractable uranium deposits. In India, Krishna-Godavari basin has deposits of shale gas along with Gulf of Cambay, Assam-Arakan Basin etc. Ruhr Basin is in Germany and is famous for its coal reserves.

42. Primary activities are directly associated with the utilization of earth's resources while secondary activities involves processing of the materials into a finished product. Hence quarrying refers to extraction of useful minerals from earth's surface and construction involves the use of building materials like bricks, cement, stones, rods as raw materials to build houses, apartments etc as finished product. Researcher is involved in the creation of knowledge, hence quaternary activities. Policy making requires decision making and has an impact upon the lives of others directly and are therefore quinary activities.

43. Weber's theory of industrial location takes into account transportation cost, labour cost and the cost of agglomeration. As far as the transportation cost is concerned, for industries using one raw material, the industry would be located in any of the three locations: at the source of raw material, at or near market and any point between the first two. Hence, a linear location. For two raw materials, there would be a non-linear location.

44. * South Africa has the most gold deposits in the world. The Witwatersrand basin here has the largest deposit currently. It is said that40% of the basin is still yet to be mined.

* The leading country in coal deposits is United States of America. It has nearly 24% of the total coal deposits of the world.

* Uranium is found most in Australia. It has almost 30% of the total deposits of uranium in the world which can be recovered.

* Russia has richest and largest diamond deposits of the world.

45. Edward Ullman, a French geographer gave the three bases for spatial interaction two locations. They were complementarity, transferability and intervening opportunity. Based on complementarity, the two location interact when one location has need or deficit for a commodity while the other location has surplus or supply of the same. But this relation is commodity specific. So, (A) is true and (R) is false.

46. Afghanistan became the 164th member nation of WTO on 29th July 2016. South Korea has had the membership of WTO since 1995. China became a member nation of World Trade Organization on 11 December 2001. Kiribati is one of the sixteen nations which do not have membership in the World Trade Organization.

47. Transportation networks are composed of many nodes and links, and as they rise in complexity their comparison becomes challenging. Indices are more complex methods to represent the

structural properties of graph since they involve the comparison of a measure over another.

Formula of beta index is $\dfrac{e}{v}$

Formula of Alpha index is $\dfrac{u}{2v-5}$

Formula of Network Density is $\dfrac{L}{S}$

Formula of Gamma is $\dfrac{e}{3(v-2)}$

48. Edward Ullman was the leading transportation geographer of twentieth century for formally addressed interaction as complementarity. There must be a supply and demand between interacting locations. A residential zone is complementary to the industrial zone because the first is supplying workers while the second is supplying workers.

49. The New York and Mid Atlantic region extends from York to Baltimore. In Middle Atlantic States, industrial centers are scattered over New Jersey, Pennsylvania, Maryland, Delaware, Philadelphia and Baltimore. It contributes many manufacturing items. The region has greatest concentration of ferrous industries. In cities like Detroit, several industries have developed including motor vehicles, machinery, fabricated metals, machine tools and electronics.

50. Spatial interaction is a dynamic flow process from one location to another. It is a realized movement of people, freight or information and traffic between an origin and destination. The concept of spatial interaction was mostly developed as a fundamental concept with the contribution of Edward Ullman. With the spatial interaction model, Ullman shifted his focus on situation as an important locational attribute. So, there are 3 parameters or bases for spatial interaction on the basis of which things move: complementarity, transferability, intervening opportunity.

51. In Ulman's flow theory the interaction between regions is determined by three factors: complementarity, both regions must be complimentary in nature to each other; intervening opportunities, which means the availability or non-availability of any other source which influences the complementarity of two regions; and transferability, the viability of the movement, and is mainly determined by the costs of the movement.

52. Only those regions according to Weaver's minimum deviation method of crop combination are considered Monocrop region, whose square of the deviation is the lowest for the first crop compared to the sum of the square of deviation of two, or three or more crops. In other words, as we try to delineate for more than one crop, the value of $\dfrac{\sum d2}{n}$ keeps increasing. Hence mono crop region is best suited for the cultivation of a single crop only.

53. The earliest attempts to explain agricultural land use pattern in economic terms is contained in a model of agricultural location proposed by J.H Von Thunen. The model was designed to explain the factors governing the prices of farm products and the principles by which sure price variations are translated into patterns of land use. Zone I deals with the production of fresh milk and vegetables, Zone II was used for the production of

wood, Zone III used for cropping without fallow land and in zone IV the farmers used a seven years crop rotation in which rye occupied only one-seventh of the fallow land.

54. R.P. Mishra's Growth Foci theory was based on the assumptions of Christaller's Central Place theory, Perroux's Growth pole Theory and Hager strand's theory of cultural diffusion. The key concepts of these theories were taken as major assumptions in Mishra's theory.

55. While calculating the Human Development Index, three dimensions are used. They include the Life expectancy at birth, education index consisting of mean years of schooling and expected years of schooling, GNI per capita or PPP. Literacy ratio is NOT used while calculating the HDI.

56. • Religion is a basis for social classification in India. A large number of people in India belong to Hinduism. Other religions include Muslim, Jainism, Christianity, etc.

• Language is used for the dividing the country into states. Officially 23 languages in the country. Marathi, Hindi, Assamese, Gujrati, etc. are some of the languages in the country.

• Tribes are social divisions of society as per economic. Cultural, religious traditions. Tribes in India include Gond, Bhil, Santhal, etc.,

• Caste is a subset of a religion. There are numerous castes in Indian religions. These include Brahmin, Maratha, etc.

57. The city of Chennai is the India's Health capital. It is a large number of super-specialty hospitals. It brings about 150 international patients daily. 30-40% of domestic and 45% of international health tourists are treated the city of Chennai. Thus, (A) and(R) are true and (R) is the correct explanation f (A).

58. The Rimland theory was given by Dutch American political geographer Nicholas Spykman in the year 1942. Rimland is the coastal strip of land that encircles Eurasia. As per this Theory, Spykman says that who controls Rimland, controls the Eurasia and who controls Eurasia controls destiny of the world. Spykman divided world into three categories.

59. The area from coast up to 12 nautical miles is the territorial water belonging to the coastal country. The area up to 200 nautical miles is part of the exclusive economic zone. The coastal country has exclusive rights for fishing, drilling and other economic activities in this region.

60. Formal cultural region refers to an area inhabited by people who have one or more cultural traits in common. An Eskimo cultural region may consist of multiple traits such as language, religion, type of economy , typical form of dwelling. A functional cultural region denotes an area that has been organized to function politically, socially or economically. For instance, a city, a church, a trade area. Vernacular cultural region often lacks the organisation necessary for functional regions. Vernacular region, like other cultural regions, generally lack sharp borders and the inhabitants of any given area may claim residence in more than one such region.

Culture may always not spread from more advanced to less advanced regions. Rather, it is sometimes reciprocal. The Americans have in most cases carried a number of cultural items from Indians like maize, potato, beans. Cultural ecology includes the adaptive processes that can be explored through a cultural core of human activities such as typical folk culture, etc.

61. Aijazuddin Ahmed is best known for his work on Social geography of India. He has also published a book with the same name. Saraswati Raju is one of the pioneers in Gender geography in India. R.L. Singh has given the physiographic regionalization of India. SM Rafiullah is known for his contribution in the field of agricultural geography. He has also modified J.C. Weaver's method of delineating crop combination regions.

62. Bernhard Varenius (1622-1650), a young and futurist geographer is credited with distinguishing between general and special geography; and the mutual dependence of these approaches. This distinction later manifested in the form of systematic and regional geography by the German scholars.

63. Yi-Fu Tuan is a Chinese Geographer who is known for humanistic perspectives in Geography. His famous paper, "Space and Place" in 1974 presented the concept of Sense of Place.

64. Muqaddimah is a monumental work from Arab geographers. It is written by Ibn Khaldun. Kosmos was written by Humboldt. Erdkunde which meant science of Earth, was written by Carl Ritter and Friedrich Ratzel wrote his book Anthropogeogrraphie which essential means Human Geography.

65. It was Ellen Churchill Semple, a determinist American geographer who said that so. She was influenced by Ratzel's first volume of *Anthropogeographie*. She wrote her famous book "Influences of Geographic Environment in 1911.

66. H.H. Barrows was an American human geographer. In his address to the Association of American Geographers, he said that geographers should work at a unifying theme, which is human ecology. Human ecology, according to him, should be used for the study of man and environment, not in a deterministic sense, but for man's place in the web of life.

67. Richard Hartshorne is known for his famous work "The Nature of Geography" (1939) where he has talked about the importance of unique place-based idiographic concept of areal differentiation. In response to it, F. Schaefer published his famous paper "Exceptionalism in Geography: A Methodological Explanation" (1953) where he criticized Hartshorne and presented a case for law making approach in geography. Vidal de la Blache's monumental book "Human Geography" was published posthumously. Peter Haggett is associated with quantitative geography.

68. Varenius was the first geographer to give distinction between systematic or general geography and regional or particular geography. General geography treats the whole world as one single unit. It formulates theories, principles, laws applicable everywhere in the world. Regional geography has description of small areas as spatial units. Humboldt distinguished geography and uranography. Uranography is descriptive astronomy.

69. Among other things, human awareness, human consciousness, human agency and human creativity are major areas of study in humanism. It takes historical approach while studying understanding of man in his environment. It also deals with art history, literary criticism and aesthetics. Thus, (A) is false, (R) is true.

70. The behavioral approach was a psychological turn in human geography, emphasizing cognition in humans as a factor in joining environment and spatial behavior. The objectives of this approach include explanation of spatial dimension in human decision-making and behavior, unfolding of spatial dimension in social and psychological theories, developing models for humanity as an alternative to quantitative revolution, generating primary data for human behavior. They also include emphasis on processing rather than structural explanation of human activity and physical environment.

71. • The chi-square is a non-parametric test the observed results to the expected results. The critical value for chi-square test is of X^2.

• The z-test is used when the sample size is large and variance is known. It is primarily used to test if the means of the two populations are different but it can also be used for hypothesis testing. The critical value is shown using z.

• The KS-test is also a non-parametric test used to test nature of distribution in single sample and the difference in the distribution of independent variables. The critical value is measured as value for no of the samples are less than 30 and X^2 for those who have more than 30.

• ANOVA is the test for analysis of variance. It is a parametric test used for simultaneously the difference between several samples. The critical value used here if that of t.

72. Principal Component Analysis was invented by Karl Pearson. It is a method to select the most important of the given attributes and is used to reduce the dataset. The maximum number of Principal Components can be either less than or equal to the original number of attributes.

73. Regression analysis is done to estimate the relationship between the two variables. These two variables are dependent variable and the independent variables or the covariates. They are one the main components of regression analysis. The error terms are used to cover the errors in the equation.

74. Data about the location is called as spatial data. Non-spatial data is also called as attribute data. It is a type of qualitative data as it gives more information about any point, line, or polygon on the map other than the Locational data. It can be numeric, character, time /date or in BLOB form.

75. The pie diagram is a circular diagram which is divided into slices to illustrate proportion. The central angle is proportional to the quantity it represents. The total of all the central angles is 360^0. The pie diagrams are used in business and mass media.

76. The geographical data for GIS comes through aerial photographs, remote sensing, surveying, LiDAR, etc. Raster data is obtained through remote sensing. An advantage of remote sensing is that data is consistent. Maps, remote sensing, and aerial photographs are scanned and used as raster data. Ground surveying measures angles and distances between points. It is used as a source of vector data.

77. When the Incident rays of the sun, hit their target, the earth's surface, three kinds of interactions take place. These three are reflection, transmission, and absorption. Scattering occurs when the rays of sun interact with the atmosphere.

78. The area-height curve and hypsometric curve are graphs used in hypsometric analysis. A hypsometric curve represents vertical distribution of land but it does not record average slope between contours. The area-height curve gives the relationship between the area and elevation. It is similar to a hypsometric curve but they both differ in aspect that the area-height curve gives a more realistic picture of the area than the hypsometric curve.

79. Flow maps are the maps hat show movement of objects from place to another. It shows entities like number of people immigrated and migrated, the amount of resources being transferred from one state to another, number of goods carried in trains from one location to another etc. There are various types of flow maps like baker flow maps, blood flow maps and traffic flow maps.

80.

- Author of computer aided cartography is David Rhind.
- Author of unique dualities of geographic information system is Parker.
- The author of land information management is Dale.
- The author of remote sensing and geographical information system is Reddy.

81. • The Sutlej River is a west flowing river, a tributary of the Indus river. It originates at Mansarovar Lake near Darma Pass in western Tibet nearly 80 km from the origin of the Indus river itself.

• The Narmada rises near western side of Amarkantak plateau at elevation of 1057 m. It is one of the largest rivers of the Indian Peninsula.

• Tapi River (Tapti) is also called as the twin of Narmada river. It originates from Multai on Satpura Plateau. Total length of the river is 730 km.

• The Ravi rivers rises near Rohtang pass in Himachal Pradesh. It enters Punjab near Madhopur and enters Pakistan 26 km below Amritsar.

82. Gujarat is the leading producer of cotton in India. It also has many cotton industries. India ranks second in world in production of wheat. China ranks first. Uttar Pradesh is the leading producer of wheat in India. Punjab ranks second. India also ranks second in rice production as well as consumption in world after China.

83. After the first two five-year plans helped in generating infrastructural facilities, India entered this stage. Later this plan aimed at securing self-relaince, self-generating economy and self-sustainable growth.

84. The sex ratio of India is low due to several sociological factors and regional disparities. Some factors that lead to this trend are negligence of the female child in terms of treatment, education, status, health, many women die while giving birth to child. A few states like Kerala , Pondicherry have a sex ratio favourable to females, but the other states comprise of low sex ratio.

85. Ratnagiri of Maharashtra with a decadal growth rate of -4.96, Lahul and Spiti of Himachal Pradesh with -5.10, Mumbai of Maharashtra with a rate of -5.75 and Mokukchung of Nagaland with a rate of -16.77. This negative growth rate is mostly due to the decline in natural growth rate and outmigration.

86. Cropping Intensity is calculated as **Total Cropped Area/Net Sown Area * 100.** It is given in percentage. Punjab has the highest cropping intensity in India with 189.4%. Assam, Haryana and West Bengal have cropping intensity of 145.9, 178.9 and 181.3 % respectively.

87. • The largest producer of rice in the country is West Bengal. It produces almost 14% of the country's total rice. The average yield per hectare is 2755 kg.

• The largest producer of cotton in the country is Gujarat. It produces almost 26% of the total cotton of the country. The average yield is 549 kg/ hectare.

• The largest producer of wheat in the country is Uttar Pradesh. It produces almost 33% of country's total wheat. The average yield per hectare is 3114 kg.

• The largest producer of tea in the country is Assam. It produces almost 51% of the country's total tea. The average yield per hectare is 17.4 quintals.

88. Immigration is inflow of population in a place. Thus, it is one of the reasons for growth of population. Increase in birth rate and decrease in death rate also lead to growth of population. Outmigration, on the other hand, means outflow of population from a place, which leads to decline in population, not growth.

89. The Indian industries developed tremendously in the period of World War I. The industries of paper, iron and steel, sugar, cement and textile grew rapidly. The cotton industry developed so well that India stood fourth after USA, UK and Japan in cotton manufacturing during the World War I. The decentralization of the textile mills in Mumbai happened during World War I and the industries shifted from Mumbai. There were 61.7% of cotton mills in Mumbai in 1938-39 and only 17.5 % remained there after the War. Thus, (A) is true and (R) is false.

90. The Brahmaputra River flows through Assam and the other North Eastern states of India. The floods occur almost every year in the river valley due to many reasons. There are heavy rains in the hills and Brahmaputra has 34 tributaries. The channel of the river is also very narrow. The maximum width of the channel is 81 km. The silt brought by the river due to erosion has made the channel very shallow, too. Thus, the capacity of the river to accommodate water is very less which leads to annual floods. Hence, both (A) and (R) are true and (R) is the correct explanation of (A).

91. • Kerala is the state with highest sex ratio in India as per census of 2011. The sex ratio of Kerala in 2011 was 1084 and 1058 in 2001.

• State with highest tribal population as of 2011 is Madhya Pradesh. The tribal population of Madhya Pradesh is 3122528.

• Bihar is the state with the lowest literacy rate in India as per 2011. The literacy rate of Bihar is 61.80. Male literacy is 71.20 and female literacy was 51.50.

• The state with lowest population density is Arunachal Pradesh. It has population of 1383727. It has the population density of 17 persons per square km.

92. • The Silent Valley National Park is located at foothills of Nilgiri Mountains in the state of Kerala. It is home to birds like black-and-orange-flycatcher and black bulbul. Animals here include Nilgiri Langur, Malabar Giant Squirrel, etc

• Panna National park is in the state of Madhya Pradesh in the districts of Panna and Chhatarpur. It is primarily a tiger reserve.

• Rajaji National Park too is a tiger reserve and national park. It is at the foothills of Himalayas, encompassing a large area of Shivalik's. It lies in the state of Uttarakhand.

• Simbalbara National Park was established in the year 1958. Its located in the state of Himachal Pradesh. It is a wildlife sanctuary too. It is filled with thick Sal forests.

93. The first aircraft industry of the country was set up under the name of Hindustan Aircrafts Ltd in Bangalore. It was set up in 1940. In the beginning, it was a private company but was soon taken over by the government in the year 1942. This factory later merged into Aeronautics India Ltd.

94. The port of Kandla is located at 23.0081° N (approximately). The port of Kolkata lies a little further south.The city of Mumbai has two ports-Mumbai Port Trust and Jawaharlal Nehru Port Trust. These are further south in Mahrashtra. The port of Marmugao lies in Goa state below Mahrashtra.

95. Tea production in India is concentrated in North-eastern, north-western, and southern parts of India. North-eastern region has the majority of tea plantations. Karnataka ranks first in the country among coffee producing states and produces 71% of the country's total production. India ranks third in rubber production and produces 9% of the world's total produces. India is the leading producer of Ginger and produces 80% of the total ginger in the world.

96. India's planning began with Five Year Plans. It was formulated in 1951, after four years of independence. As per the 73rd and 74th constitutional amendment funds have been provided for local development.

97. Regional planning is can be achieved only when the public is aware of planning institutions rationale about planning, good quality of education about planning, efficient planning institutions and proper comprehension and appreciation of basic issues by society. It is not dependent on paperwork for planning.

98. Most of the regional plans are formulated according to state boundaries. But the state governments lack initiative for the local development. The state government has to provide funds for the local development to the Panchayat. But most of the state governments have not taken the step.

99. The decentralization of planning process is necessary for proper implementation of the plans But the administrative authorities are often unwilling to share power which makes decentralization of the process extremely difficult.

100. The regional planning in India started with the first Five Year Plan (FYP). This process began in the year 1951. But still planning is a relatively new activity in India. Thus, India is still in the beginning stage of planning.

Q.1 Which of the following is not a minor plate?

A. Cocos Plate

B. Nazca Plate

C. Indo Australian Plate

D. Arabian Plate

Q.2 Given below are two statements. One is labelled as Assertion (A) and the other is labelled as Reason (R).

Assertion (A): There is the formation of a constructive plate margins between Indian plate and the Eurasian plate.

Reason (R): Convergent boundaries form when two plates come towards each other.

Select the correct answer from options given below:

A. Both (A) and (R) are true and (R) is the correct explanation of (A)

B. Both (A) and (R) are true, but (R) is not the correct explanation of (A)

C. (A) is true, but (R) is false.

D. (A) is false, but (R) is true.

Q.3 Match the concepts (List-I) relating to volcanism with features (List-II) which best characterizes them.

List -I (Vulcanism)	List - II (Features)
(a) Mafic magma	(i) Highly viscous
(b) Felsic magma	(ii) less viscous
(c) Plutonic rocks	(iii) cooling at the surface
(d) Volcanic rocks	(iv) cooling within the crust

Code:

A. (a)-(ii), (b)-(i), (c)-(iv), (d)-(iii)

B. (a)-(i), (b)-(ii), (c)-(iv), (d)-(iii)

C. (a)-(iv), (b)-(ii), (c)-(i), (d)-(iii)

D. (a)-(iv), (b)-(iii), (c)-(ii), (d)-(i)

Q.4 The concept of cycle of erosion was first given by:

A. Penck

B. Crickmay

C. Hutton

D. None of the above.

Q.5 Who characterized valleys as insequent, obsequent and resequent?

A. Davis **B.** Johnson **C.** Penk **D.** Powell

Q.6 Obstruction on the peneplane are called?

A. Inselberg **B.** Valley

C. Fault **D.** Monadnocks

Q.7 Karst topography is mainly found in which region?

A. Equatorial region

B. Tropical Region.

C. Mediterranean Region

D. Polar region.

Q.8 Match List-I with List-II:

List-I	List - II (Work)

(Author)	
(a) Bagnold	i) Pedestal rocks formed by differential erosion
(b) Bryan	(ii) A further journey through the Libyan desert
(c) Gautier	(iii) Loess and Quaternary geology of lower Mississippi
(d) Fisk	(iv) The great desert

A. a- iii b-ii c-i d-iv

B. a-ii b-i c-iv d-iii

C. a-i b-ii c-iii d-iv

D. a-iii b-i c-iv d-ii

Q.9 Whose Classification of eruption of a volcano is most commonly used?

A. Lacroix **B.** Nichols **C.** Cotton. **D.** Williams

Q.10 Honeycombed rocks formed by?

A. Weathering **B.** erosion

C. Mass wasting **D.** Denudation

Q.11 Which of the following concepts was used by C.W. Thornthwaite in 1948 in his attempt to classify the climate of the world?

A. Evaporation

B. Transpiration

C. Evapotranspiration

D. Potential Evapotranspiration

Q.12 The phenomenon in which the warm waters of the Central Pacific shifts eastward to replace the cool Peruvian Current off the West Coast of Peru is called:

A. La Nina **B.** El Nino

C. Southern oscillation **D.** Northern oscillation

Q.13 Which of the following statements relating to cyclones are correct?

(a) Tropical Cyclone does not develop near to the equator

(b) A strong Coriolis effect retards development of tropical cyclones.

(c) Large sea surface with temperature higher than 27°C is required for the tropical cyclone to form.

(d) Extra tropical cyclones can originate over both sea and land.

Choose the correct option from below:

A. (a) and (c) **B.** (a) and (b)

C. (a), (b) and (d) **D.** (a), (c) and (d)

Q.14 Match List-I with the List-II and select the correct answer from the code given below:

List - I (Tropical Cyclone Names)	List - II (Places associated)
(a) Cyclone	i) Atlantic and eastern North Pacific
(b) Hurricane	(ii) Indian Ocean
(c) Typhoons	(iii) Australia
(d) Willy-Willies	(iv) Western North-Pacific

A. (a)-(ii), (b)-(i), (c)-(iv), (d)-(iii)

B. (a)-(ii), (b)-(iii), (c)-(iv), (d)-(i)

C. (a)-(iii), (b)-(iv), (c)-(i), (d)-(ii)

D. (a)-(iv), (b)-(iii), (c)-(ii), (d)-(i)

Q.15 On the basis of various thermodynamic and mechanical modifications, air masses were further divided into how many numbers of classes-

A. 14   **B.** 13   **C.** 16   **D.** 15

Q.16 Which of the following statement is correct?

A. El Nino is also known as Christ Child in Spanish.

B. The El Nino events of 1982-83 and 1997-98 are the most disastrous weather phenomena.

C. La Nina is a condition where the water temperature in the Eastern Pacific gets colder than normal.

D. All of the above.

Q.17 Select the correct arrangement of atmospheric layers from the options given below:

A. Troposphere-Stratosphere-Mesosphere-Thermosphere

B. Stratosphere-Troposphere-Thermosphere-Mesosphere

C. Troposphere-Stratosphere-Mesosphere-Thermosphere

D. Stratosphere-Troposphere-Mesosphere-Thermosphere

Q.18 Match List-I with List-II

List - I (Local Wind)	List-II(Country)
(a) Loo	i) Australia
(b) Brick fielder	(ii) Libya & Algeria
(c) Norte	(iii) Canada
(d) Sirocco	(iv) India

Code:

A. (a)-(iv),(b)-(i),(c)-(iii),(d)-(ii)

B. (a)-(iv),(b)-(ii),(c)-(i),(d)-(iii)

C. (a)-(iv),(b)-(iii),(c)-(ii),(d)-(i)

D. (a)-(i),(b)-(iii),(c)-(ii),(d)-(iv)

Q.19 Which are the most variable gases in atmosphere

A. Nitrogen   **B.** Oxygen

C. Water Vapour   **D.** Argon

Q.20 What is the density of ocean water at sea surface?

A. 1025 gm/m³   **B.** 1055 gm/m³

C. 1035 gm/m³   **D.** 1027 gm/ m³

Q.21 Consider the following statements and select the correct answer from the code given below:

(a) The temperature of the sea water does not affect density of sea water.

(b) The density of water decreases as the temperature of water increases.

A. Only (a)   **B.** Only (b)

C. Both (a) and (b)   **D.** Neither (a) nor (b)

Q.22 Which of the following statements is not correct?

A. The Temperature of the land becomes more than the sea.

B. The temperature of the open seas in low latitudes becomes higher.

C. Surface Water temperature of seas decreases from the equator towards the poles.

D. Trade winds cause low temperature along the eastern margins of the oceans.

Q.23 Consider the following statements:-

a) The Oyashio Current is a warm current of the Pacific Ocean.

b) The Californian Current is almost similar to the Canary current.

c) The Sargasso Sea has the highest salinity of the Atlantic Ocean

d) The Brazil current is a North-Atlantic Current.

Choose the correct option:

A. a and b   **B.** a, b and c

C. b and c   **D.** c and d

Q.24 Which scale is used for measuring the wind speeds of tropical cyclones or hurricanes and their impacts and intensity?

A. Beaufort Scale

B. Anemometer

C. Fujita Scale

D. Saffir-Simpson Scale

Q.25 Which of the following sentences explains the term Ecosystem?

A. Energy moves in a multidirectional manner through the ecosystems and is ultimately lost irretrievably.

B. Ecosystems exist independently of specific components and also exist in space and time.

C. A natural ecosystem never attains a stable equilibrium state as it is dynamic.

D. The hierarchy and aggradation of world's ecosystem is collectively termed as Ecology.

Q.26 What does BOD stand for?

A. Biochemical Oxygen Demand

B. Bill on Demand

C. Biodegradable Oxygen Demand

D. Biomagnified Oxygen Demand

Q.27 Match the following:-

List I	List II
a. Vienna Convention	1. making 5.2% cut in carbon emissions
b. Toronto Summit	2. checking the emission of greenhouse gases
c. Second World Climate Summit	3. reduction in CO2 emissions by 20%
d. Kyoto Agreement	4 , conservation of ozone layer

A. a-4 b-2 c-3 d-1   **B.** a-4 b-3 c-2 d-1

C. a-2 b-3 c-1 d-4   **D.** a-1 b-2 c-3 d-4

Q.28 What is Agenda 21?

A. a global action plan for sustainable development

B. a policy for migrant workers

C. a policy to increase women literacy

D. None of the above

Q.29 Read the text carefully and answer the questions given below: -

The communication of chemical elements involves biological organisms and their geological environment. This communication is collectively considered a biochemical cycle. In a group of these cycles, the atmosphere produces a large reservoir of elements present in the gaseous state, known as the gaseous nutrient cycle. Among the preliminaries, the major reservoir is the lithosphere, from which elements emerge by weathering. Carbon and androgens are the major gases of the biochemical cycle in the major gaseous state. Elements from atmospheric and vermilion reservoirs accumulate in the soil. The inorganic elements of the mean and gaseous states accumulate in the soil reservoir, which are ingested by root osmosis. These elements are then modified into forms that are used in the development of plant tissues by biochemical processes. Thus nutrients driven by energy flow pass through different components of biological groups through the process of biochemical cycles. These nutrients or organic matter from plants and animals are released in various ways. The carbon cycle involves the movement of carbon within the biosphere. Includes 2 routes or cycles such as gases and abiotic cycles. However, the level of carbon dioxide in the environment has increased by 20% since the beginning of the Industrial Revolution. In contrast to the simplicity of the carbon cycle, the nitrogen cycle consists of 4 major phases, such as nitrogen fixation, ammonization, nitrification, and denitrification: each containing some number of different organisms, some free living.

Which is the pathway through which the circulation pattern of the carbon cycle takes place?

A. Gaseous cycle

B. Non-gaseous cycle

C. Both A and B

D. None of the above

Q.30 Given below are two statements. One is labelled as Assertion (A) and the other is labelled as Reason (R).

Assertion (A)- There has been a rapid growth of population in many Asian and African nations in the 20th century.

Reason(R) - Death rates, birth rates and infant mortality rates have had a profound effect on the population growth.

Select the correct answer from options given below:

A. Both (A) and (R) are true and (R) is the correct explanation of (A)

B. Both (A) and (R) are true but R is not the correct explanation of (A)

C. (A) is true but (R) is false

D. (A) is false but (R) is true

Q.31 Which of the following reasons do support that the views of Malthus are pessimistic?

A. Rapid and efficient means of transportation

B. Advancement in agriculture in underdeveloped countries

C. Elimination of economic inequality

D. All of the above

Q.32 Match List-I with List-II:-

List-I (Terms related to population structure)	List-II (Definitions)
(a) Natural Increase	(i) Number of deaths below 1year of age per 1000
(b) Net reproduction ratio	(ii) The average age at which people die
(c) Life expectancy	(iii)Rate at which women are
(d) Infant mortality rate	replaced by daughters
	(iv) Excess of births over deaths per 1000

A. a-i b-ii c-iv d-iii

B. a-ii b-iii c-iv d-i

C. a-iv b-ii c-i d-iii

D. a-iv b-iii c-ii d-i

Q.33 Consider the following statements:-

a) The most restrictive factors affecting rural settlement patterns are terrain and water source.

b) Villages of Gujarat and Uttarakhand are prime examples of agglomeration that are formed by the need for defense factor.

c) The commonest form of village form is the rectangular village which is found in the northern plains of India.

d) Nucleation can take place around more than one point.

Which of the following statements are correct?

A. a and b

B. b and c

C. a, b, and c

D. a, c, and d

Q.34 According to Burgess' Concentric zone model, which Zone is also known as the twilight zone or the urban blight?

A. Loop

B. Zone of transition

C. Zone of Workingmen's home

D. Zone of Residence

Q.35 Given below are the two statements, one labelled as Assertion (A) and the other labelled as Reason (R). Select your answer from the code given below:

Assertion (A) : Population density is high in North Indian plains.

Reason (R) : North Indian Plains have fertile land and availability of water.

Code :

A. Both (A) and (R) are true and (R) is the correct explanation of (A)

B. Both (A) and (R) are true but (R) is not the correct explanation of (A)

C. (A) is true but (R) is false.

D. (A) is false but (R) is true.

Q.36 The average Total Fertility rate of the world population is

A. 1.2 live births per woman

B. 1.5 live births per woman

C. 2.5 live births per woman

D. 2.0 live births per woman

Q.37 Choose the correct order of states in decreasing levels of literacy from the ones given below:

A. Mizoram- Maharashtra-Goa-Tripura

B. Mizoram-Goa-Tripura-Maharashtra

C. Tripura-Goa-Maharashtra-Mizoram

D. Goa-Tripura-Mizoram-Maharashtra

Q.38 Given below are the two statements, one labelled as Assertion (A) and the other labelled as Reason (R). Select your answer from the code given below:

Assertion (A) : Sadler rejected Malthus' increase of population in geometric progression.

Reason (R) : Adam Sadler states that population density increases with industrialization

Code :

A. Both (A) and (R) are true and (R) is the correct explanation of (A).

B. Both (A) and (R) are true but (R) is not the correct explanation of (A).

C. (A) is true but (R) is false.

D. (A) is false but (R) is true.

Q.39 Which are the major reasons for the development of social segregation in urban cities?

A. Rearrangement of residential pattern

B. Increased acceptance of market-based land and basic services

C. Spatial Isolation

D. All of the above

Q.40 Match List-I with List-II

List-I (Type of Industry)	List-II (Example)
(a)Agro-based industry	(i) Pump manufacturing industry
(b) Mineral based industry	(ii) Cotton textile
(c) Marine-based industry	(iii)Paper production
(d) Forest-based Industry	(iv) Oil plant

A. (a)-(ii),(b)-(iii),(c)-(iv),(d)-(i)

B. (a)-(iii),(b)-(iv),(c)-(i),(d)-(ii)

C. (a)-(ii),(b)-(i),(c)-(iv),(d)-(iii)

D. (a)-(iv),(b)-(iii),(c)-(ii),(d)-(i)

Q.41 Which of the following is NOT a geographical factor influencing location of industries?

A. Water   **B.** Labour

C. Raw materials   **D.** Capital

Q.42 Which of the following country has the highest share of Information and Communication Technology (ICT) sector in her economy?

A. France   **B.** South Korea

C. Germany   **D.** India

Q.43 The following formula was given by

$$I_{i,j} = \frac{p_i p_j}{d_{i,j}^{\beta}}$$

A. EM Hurst   **B.** Edward Ulman

C. Gunnar Myradal   **D.** Albert Hirschmann

Q.44 Given below are two statements. One is labelled as Assertion (A) and the other is labelled as Reason (R).

Assertion (A): If one raw material is localized and impure while the other is ubiquitous, the industry will be located near the raw material which is localized and impure.

Reason (R): The industry will locate near market if both raw materials are ubiquitous.

Select the correct answer from options given below:

A. Both (A) and (R) are true and (R) is the correct explanation of (A)

B. Both (A) and (R) are true, but (R) is not the correct explanation of (A)

C. (A) is true, but (R) is false.

D. (A) is false, but (R) is true.

Q.45 Which of the factors generally do not affect the transport costs?

A. Type of Commodity

B. Type of Carrier

C. Degree of competition from other carriers

D. Religion of the shipper

Q.46 Which among the following is India's biggest regional broadcaster?

A. Sun TV   **B.** Gemini TV

C. Manorama News   **D.** Asianet

Q.47 Given below are two statements, one labelled as assertion(A) and other labelled as reason(R).

Assertion- According to A. Weber's industrial location theory, when there is one market and one raw material, there are three possible situations.

Reason- When the raw material is available everywhere, the best location is market.

Select the correct answer from options given below :

A. Both A and R are true and R correctly explains A

B. Both A and R are true but R does not explain A

C. A is true and R is false.

D. Both A and R are false

Q.48 Given below are two statements, one labelled as assertion(A) and other labelled as reason(R).

Assertion(A)- Increase in world population increases demand for fuel.

Reason(R)-Trading of all products require energy resources.

Select the correct answer from options given below :

A. Both A and R are true and R correctly explains A

B. Both A and R are true but R does not explain A

C. A is true and R is false.

D. Both A and R are false

Q.49 Which region is called as Orchard Lands of the World?

A. African region

B. Mediterranean region

C. Polar Region

D. Tropical Region

Q.50 Which of the following is NOT an assumption to Von Thunen's Model of Agricultural land use?

A. The city is isolated state.

B. The city is self-sufficient.

C. The land of the city has mountains, plains, and plateaus.

D. Farmers in the city act to maximize profits.

Q.51 According to land capability classification, what does yellow colour class indicate on map?

A. Good cultivable land, deep slope

B. Good cultivable land, gentle slope

C. Good soil on steep slope

D. Rough eroded soil with shallow erosion

Q.52 Match the List - I with List - II and select the correct answer from the code given below :

List - I (Theory)	List-II Profounder
(a) Growth Pole Theory	(i) Albert O. Hirschmann
(b) Matter of Centre Vs. Periphery	(ii) Gunnar Myradal
(c) Theory of Unbalanced Growth	(iii)John. R. Friedmann
(d) Circular Cumulative Causation	(iv) Francois Perroux

A. (a)- (iii) ,(b)- (iv) ,(c)- (i) ,(d)- (ii)
B. (a)- (iv) ,(b)- (iii) ,(c)- (i) ,(d)- (ii)
C. (a)- (iii) ,(b)- (ii) ,(c)- (iv) ,(d)- (i)
D. (a)- (ii) ,(b)- (iii) ,(c)- (i) ,(d)- (iv)

Q.53 The strategy for Unbalanced Growth was given by
A. Francis Perroux **B.** Gunnar Myrdal
C. W.W. Rostow **D.** Albert Hirschmann

Q.54 Which of the following is NOT one of the four types of Growth poles?
A. Technical **B.** Statistical
C. Geographical **D.** Psychological

Q.55 The Somasila Dam is located in which state?
A. Madhya Pradesh **B.** Himachal Pradesh
C. Andhra Pradesh **D.** Uttar Pradesh

Q.56 Aranmula Kannadi is a GI protected tag of Kerala. It is a _______?
A. Sweet **B.** Handicraft
C. Plantation Product **D.** Soft Drink

Q.57 In India the states with more than 80 percent of the population are schedule tribe are
A. Mizoram, Nagaland, and Meghalaya
B. Arunachal Pradesh, Meghalaya, Mizoram
C. Mizoram, Nagaland, and Manipur
D. Mizoram and Meghalaya

Q.58 Which country has shown an increased presence in the Indian Ocean in the recent decades?
A. China **B.** U.S.A . **C.** Australia **D.** Japan

Q.59 In which year was the 1st National Health Policy initiated?
A. 2002 **B.** 1983 **C.** 1995 **D.** 2005

Q.60 The theory of uniformitarianism was given by which of the following scholar?
A. W.M. Davis **B.** James Hutton
C. Humboldt **D.** Strahler

Q.61 Bharachukki Falls are in which state of India?
A. Karnataka **B.** Andhra Pradesh
C. Telangana **D.** Tamil Nadu

Q.62 The Farakka Barrage issue is an issue between India and Bangladesh, related to distribution of water of which among the following rivers?
A. Ganga **B.** Brahmputra
C. Teesta **D.** Damodar

Q.63 At which among the following places, India's first rail coach factory was built with PPP:
A. Secundarabad **B.** Gwalior

C. Patiala **D.** Palakkad

Q.64 Approximately what fraction of world's tea output comes from Assam?
A. 10% **B.** 15% **C.** 20% **D.** 25%

Q.65 Blatter Herbarium in India is located in:
A. Mumbai **B.** Kolkata
C. Chennai **D.** Bangalore

Q.66 Time geography was developed by
A. Tosten Haggerstand
B. Albrecht Penck
C. Alexander von Humboldt
D. Vidal de la Blache

Q.67 Whose work is Erdkunde?
A. Ritter **B.** Humbolt **C.** Hettener **D.** Ratzel

Q.68 Given below are two statements. One is labelled as Assertion (A) and the other is labelled as Reason (R).
Assertion(A): Study of an element or element complex concentrates on one kind of phenomena or phenomenon-association.
Reasoning(R): Systematic approach is generally related to natural factors like the climatic factors, landforms, soils etc.
Select the correct answer from options given below:
A. Both A and R are true, and R correctly explains A
B. Both A and R are true, but R does not explain A
C. A is true, and R is false.
D. Both A and R are false

Q.69 Consider the following statements about Behavioral geography:
i) It is responsible for human spatial behaviour
ii) It was developed in the opposition of quantitative revolution.
iii) In behaviouralism a man is a responder to stimuli
iv) It has relationship with statistical approach of study.
Choose the correct option from below:
A. Only (i) **B.** (i), (ii) and (iii)
C. (ii) and (iii) **D.** (i), (ii), (iii) and (iv)

Q.70 The Gandhi Sagar Dam is built on which river in Madhya Pradesh?
A. Narmada **B.** Chambal **C.** Son **D.** Tapti

Q.71 Which of the following statements about the satellite Landsat-8 are correct?
(a) It has a sun-synchronous orbit.
(b) It has an altitude of 705 km.
(c) The revisit time of Landsat-8 is 16 days.
(d) It cannot see the poles well as its orbit is above the equator.
Code:
A. Only (a) is true
B. (a) and (c) are true
C. (a), (b) and (c) are true
D. (a), (c) and (d) are true

Q.72 In the visible spectrum, the longest wavelength is

A. Yellow   **B.** Violet   **C.** Red   **D.** Blue

Q.73 Will be incorrectly excluded from the wrong location:

A. Pasteur Institute of India: Coonoor

B. National TB Training Institute - Bangalore

C. Central Leprosy Training and Research Institute - Chengalpattu

D. Kasturba Health Society - Ahmedabad

Q.74 Watson's Hotel or Esplanade Mansion, India's oldest surviving cast iron building, is located in which of the following cities?

A. Mumbai   **B.** Kolkata   **C.** Surat   **D.** Chennai

Q.75 Which one of the following is a river (inland river) port?

A. Chennai   **B.** Kandla   **C.** Kolkata   **D.** Tuticorin

Q.76 How the intensive farming is different from extensive farming?

1. While intensive farming results in maximum output per unit of land, production per unit of land is low in extensive farming

2. While extensive farming is not found in India, Intensive farming is common in high grain producing states of India

Select the correct option from the codes given below:

A. Only 1   **B.** Only 2

C. Both 1 & 2   **D.** Neither 1 nor 2

Q.77 Match the List-I with List-II two.

List-I(Authors of work on morphometry)	List-II(Year)
(a) Bagyaraj M	(i) 2012
(b) Magesh N.S	(ii) 2011
(c) Nag S.K	(iii) 2005
(d) Sreedevi P.D	(iv) 2003

Choose the correct option from the code given below:

A. a- iii b-ii c-i d-iv   **B.** a-ii b-i c-iv d-iii

C. a-i b-iii c-ii d- iv   **D.** a-iii b-i c-iv d-ii

Q.78 Which diagrammatic method is useful for representing the distribution of a total among its components?

A. Horizontal Bar diagram

B. Pie diagram

C. Line Diagram

D. Vertical Bar Diagram

Q.79 Which of the following phenomenon is responsible for the bluish appearance of the sky during the day?

A. Mie Scattering

B. Non-selective scattering

C. Rayleigh scattering

D. None of the above

Q.80 Which of the following is not correctly matched ?

A. Roopkund — Uttarakhand

B. Chandra Taal — Himachal Pradesh

C. Tso Moriri — Ladakh

D. Gurudongmar — Assam

Q.81 The eastward extension of peninsular plateau is called?

A. Bhagelkhand   **B.** Malabar Plain

C. Northern Circar   **D.** Coromandel Coast

Q.82 By which date the southwest monsoon covers the whole India?

A. 1 June   **B.** 15 June   **C.** 15 July   **D.** 30 July

Q.83 Which of the following factors is not responsible for causing the monsoon type of climate in India?

A. Location

B. Thermal Contrast

C. Upper Air Circulation

D. El Nino

Q.84 Which of the following statements relating to Waterways in India is not correct?

A. National Waterway 1 has been divided into 3 parts.

B. National Waterway 2 is the longest waterway within a state.

C. The task of development and regulation of inland waterways has been entrusted to Inland Waterways Authority of India.

D. National Waterway 16 over Barak River is shortest operational waterway.

Q.85 Which of the following plan or scheme is not related to the construction of the roadways in India?

A. Bombay Plan

B. Twenty Year Plan

C. Build Operate Transfer

D. Nagpur Plan

Q.86 India is largest producer of which of the following crops?

A. Groundnut   **B.** Sesame

C. Sugarcane   **D.** Rice

Q.87 Which of the following states is the highest producer of iron ore?

A. Jharkhand   **B.** Orissa

C. Chhattisgarh   **D.** Goa

Q.88 How much percentage of the world's population resides in India?

A. 15.2%   **B.** 19.4%   **C.** 17.5%   **D.** 16.8%

Q.89 Match List-I and List-II

List-I(river)	List-II(Tributary)
(a) Ganga	(i) Chandra
(b) Yamuna	(ii) Sharada
(c) Chenab	(iii) Dras
(d) Indus	(iv) Ken

A. (a)-(iii), (b)-(iv), (c)-(ii),(d)-(i)

B. (a)-(iv), (b)-(ii), (c)-(iii),(d)-(i)

C. (a)-(ii), (b)-(iv), (c)-(i),(d)-(iii)

D. (a)-(iii), (b)-(i), (c)-(ii),(d)-(iv)

Q.90 Which among the following rivers is an example of superimposed drainage system?

A. Banas   **B.** Chambal

C. Saraswati   **D.** Gomti

Q.91 Match List-I with List-II

List-1 (Railway Zone)	List II (Headquarter)
(a) North Eastern Railway	(i) Mumbai CST
(b) Central Railway	(ii) Gorakhpur
(c) Metro Railway	(iii) New Delhi
(d) Northern Railway	(iv) Kolkata

A. (a)-(iii), (b)-(i), (c)-(iv),(d)-(ii)
B. (a)-(iv), (b)-(ii), (c)-(iii),(d)-(i)
C. (a)-(ii), (b)-(i), (c)-(iv),(d)-(iii)
D. (a)-(iii), (b)-(i), (c)-(ii),(d)-(iv)

Q.92 Jet streams Meandering through the upper stratosphere is called?
A. Tropical Easterly jet stream
B. Sub tropical jet streams
C. tropical westerly jet stream
D. Polar Night jet stream

Q.93 Given below are two statements, one labeled as assertion(A) and other labeled as reason(R).

Assertion(A)-Green revolution aimed towards excess mechanization of agriculture.

Reason(R)- Income oriented crops were yielded during Green revolution.

A. Both (A) and (R) are true and (R) is the correct explanation of (A)
B. Both (A) and (R) are true, but (R) is not the correct explanation of (A)
C. (A) is true, but (R) is false
D. (A) is false, but (R) is true

Q.94 About how much percent of world trade does India accounts currently?
A. 2.7%   **B.** 4.3%   **C.** 1.0%   **D.** 6.1%

Q.95 Direction: Earthquake is a violent tremor in the earth's crust, sending out a series of shock waves in all directions from its place of origin. Earthquakes constitute one of the worst natural hazards which often turn into disaster causing widespread destruction and loss of human lives. India has a very long history of earthquake occurrences. The most vulnerable areas according to the present seismic zone map of India are located in Himalayan and sub-Himalayan regions, Kachchh and the Andaman and Nicobar Islands. Depending on the varying degrees of seismicity, the entire country can be divided into following seismic regions:

• Kashmir and Western Himalayas: The region covers the state of Jammu & Kashmir, Himachal Pradesh, and sub-mountains areas of Punjab. This is the zone of maximum intensity.

• Central Himalayas: The region includes the mountainous and sub-mountainous region of Uttarakhand, Uttar Pradesh, and the sub-conscious parts of Punjab.

• Northeast India: This region comprises the whole of Indian Territory to the east of northern West Bengal.

• Indo-Gangetic Basin and Rajasthan: This region comprises of Rajasthan, plains of Punjab, Haryana, Uttar Pradesh, and West Bengal. This is called the zone of comparative intensity.

• Khambhat and Rann of Kachchh.

• Peninsular India including the islands of Lakshadweep: This zone is called zone of minimum intensity.

• The Andaman & Nicobar Islands

The state of Mahrashtra is included in which seismic region?
A. Central India
B. Indo-Gangetic Plains
C. Peninsular India
D. North-East India

Q.96 Direction: Earthquake is a violent tremor in the earth's crust, sending out a series of shock waves in all directions from its place of origin. Earthquakes constitute one of the worst natural hazards which often turn into disaster causing widespread destruction and loss of human lives. India has a very long history of earthquake occurrences. The most vulnerable areas according to the present seismic zone map of India are located in Himalayan and sub-Himalayan regions, Kachchh and the Andaman and Nicobar Islands. Depending on the varying degrees of seismicity, the entire country can be divided into following seismic regions:

• Kashmir and Western Himalayas: The region covers the state of Jammu & Kashmir, Himachal Pradesh, and sub-mountains areas of Punjab. This is the zone of maximum intensity.

• Central Himalayas: The region includes the mountainous and sub-mountainous region of Uttarakhand, Uttar Pradesh, and the sub-conscious parts of Punjab.

• Northeast India: This region comprises the whole of Indian Territory to the east of northern West Bengal.

• Indo-Gangetic Basin and Rajasthan: This region comprises of Rajasthan, plains of Punjab, Haryana, Uttar Pradesh, and West Bengal. This is called the zone of comparative intensity.

• Khambhat and Rann of Kachchh.

• Peninsular India including the islands of Lakshadweep: This zone is called zone of minimum intensity.

• The Andaman & Nicobar Islands

The zone of maximum intensity is
A. Peninsular India
B. Kashmir & Western Himalayas
C. Northeast India
D. Andaman & Nicobar Islands

Q.97 Direction: Earthquake is a violent tremor in the earth's crust, sending out a series of shock waves in all directions from its place of origin. Earthquakes constitute one of the worst natural hazards which often turn into disaster causing widespread destruction and loss of human lives. India has a very long history of earthquake occurrences. The most vulnerable areas according to the present seismic zone map of India are located in Himalayan and sub-Himalayan regions, Kachchh and the Andaman and Nicobar Islands. Depending on the varying degrees of seismicity, the entire country can be divided into following seismic regions:

• Kashmir and Western Himalayas: The region covers the state of Jammu & Kashmir, Himachal Pradesh, and sub-mountains areas of Punjab. This is the zone of maximum intensity.

• Central Himalayas: The region includes the mountainous and sub-mountainous region of Uttarakhand, Uttar Pradesh, and the sub-conscious parts of Punjab.

• Northeast India: This region comprises the whole of Indian Territory to the east of northern West Bengal.

• Indo-Gangetic Basin and Rajasthan: This region comprises of Rajasthan, plains of Punjab, Haryana, Uttar Pradesh, and West Bengal. This is called the zone of comparative intensity.

• Khambhat and Rann of Kachchh.

• Peninsular India including the islands of Lakshadweep: This zone is called zone of minimum intensity.

• The Andaman & Nicobar Islands

India is divided into seismic regions according to which criteria?

A. Mountain systems

B. River valleys

C. Seismic risk

D. Varying degrees of seismicity

Q.98 Direction: Earthquake is a violent tremor in the earth's crust, sending out a series of shock waves in all directions from its place of origin. Earthquakes constitute one of the worst natural hazards which often turn into disaster causing widespread destruction and loss of human lives. India has a very long history of earthquake occurrences. The most vulnerable areas according to the present seismic zone map of India are located in Himalayan and sub-Himalayan regions, Kachchh and the Andaman and Nicobar Islands. Depending on the varying degrees of seismicity, the entire country can be divided into following seismic regions:

• Kashmir and Western Himalayas: The region covers the state of Jammu & Kashmir, Himachal Pradesh, and sub-mountains areas of Punjab. This is the zone of maximum intensity.

• Central Himalayas: The region includes the mountainous and sub-mountainous region of Uttarakhand, Uttar Pradesh, and the sub-conscious parts of Punjab.

• Northeast India: This region comprises the whole of Indian Territory to the east of northern West Bengal.

• Indo-Gangetic Basin and Rajasthan: This region comprises of Rajasthan, plains of Punjab, Haryana, Uttar Pradesh, and West Bengal. This is called the zone of comparative intensity.

• Khambhat and Rann of Kachchh.

• Peninsular India including the islands of Lakshadweep: This zone is called zone of minimum intensity.

• The Andaman & Nicobar Islands

Which of the following is NOT an effect of earthquake?

A. Destruct on of buildings

B. Afforestation

C. Destruct on of roads

D. Loss of Human life

Q.99 Direction: Earthquake is a violent tremor in the earth's crust, sending out a series of shock waves in all directions from its place of origin. Earthquakes constitute one of the worst natural hazards which often turn into disaster causing widespread destruction and loss of human lives. India has a very long history of earthquake occurrences. The most vulnerable areas according to the present seismic zone map of India are located in Himalayan and sub-Himalayan regions,

Kachchh and the Andaman and Nicobar Islands. Depending on the varying degrees of seismicity, the entire country can be divided into following seismic regions:

• Kashmir and Western Himalayas: The region covers the state of Jammu & Kashmir, Himachal Pradesh, and sub-mountains areas of Punjab. This is the zone of maximum intensity.

• Central Himalayas: The region includes the mountainous and sub-mountainous region of Uttarakhand, Uttar Pradesh, and the sub-conscious parts of Punjab.

• Northeast India: This region comprises the whole of Indian Territory to the east of northern West Bengal.

• Indo-Gangetic Basin and Rajasthan: This region comprises of Rajasthan, plains of Punjab, Haryana, Uttar Pradesh, and West Bengal. This is called the zone of comparative intensity.

• Khambhat and Rann of Kachchh.

• Peninsular India including the islands of Lakshadweep: This zone is called zone of minimum intensity.

• The Andaman & Nicobar Islands

The Peninsular India is

A. Zone of minimum intensity

B. Zone of maximum intensity

C. Zone of comparative intensity

D. Zone of no intensity

Q.100 Which among the following activities are included in the group of tertiary economic activities?

1. Trade

2. Transport

3. Services

Select the correct code from the options given below:

A. Only 1

B. Only 2 & 3

C. Only 1 & 3

D. 1, 2 & 3

// Smart Answer Sheet //

Correct Percentage of students who answered correctly.   **Skipped** Percentage of students who skipped.

Q.	Ans.	Correct / Skipped	Q.	Ans.	Correct / Skipped	Q.	Ans.	Correct / Skipped	Q.	Ans.	Correct / Skipped	Q.	Ans.	Correct / Skipped
1	C	53.06 % / 6.12 %	17	A	51.02 % / 24.49 %	33	D	36.73 % / 24.49 %	49	B	53.06 % / 22.45 %	65	A	16.33 % / 24.49 %
2	D	34.69 % / 24.49 %	18	A	46.94 % / 24.49 %	34	B	36.73 % / 24.49 %	50	C	48.98 % / 24.49 %	66	A	46.94 % / 24.49 %
3	A	34.69 % / 24.49 %	19	C	55.1 % / 22.45 %	35	A	67.35 % / 18.36 %	51	B	44.9 % / 22.45 %	67	A	63.27 % / 22.44 %
4	D	34.69 % / 24.49 %	20	D	34.69 % / 22.45 %	36	C	22.45 % / 24.49 %	52	B	57.14 % / 22.45 %	68	B	20.41 % / 22.45 %
5	A	16.33 % / 22.45 %	21	B	48.98 % / 24.49 %	37	B	32.65 % / 22.45 %	53	D	48.98 % / 22.45 %	69	B	40.82 % / 24.49 %
6	D	57.14 % / 24.49 %	22	B	22.45 % / 24.49 %	38	B	22.45 % / 22.45 %	54	B	24.49 % / 24.49 %	70	B	36.73 % / 24.49 %
7	C	42.86 % / 22.45 %	23	C	32.65 % / 24.49 %	39	D	61.22 % / 24.49 %	55	C	24.49 % / 22.45 %	71	C	42.86 % / 22.45 %
8	B	16.33 % / 22.45 %	24	D	20.41 % / 22.45 %	40	C	57.14 % / 22.45 %	56	B	26.53 % / 24.49 %	72	C	53.06 % / 22.45 %
9	A	20.41 % / 22.45 %	25	B	26.53 % / 22.45 %	41	D	53.06 % / 22.45 %	57	A	26.53 % / 24.49 %	73	D	4.08 % / 24.49 %
10	A	36.73 % / 24.49 %	26	A	51.02 % / 24.49 %	42	B	30.61 % / 24.49 %	58	A	46.94 % / 24.49 %	74	A	24.49 % / 24.49 %
11	D	55.1 % / 22.45 %	27	B	30.61 % / 22.45 %	43	B	32.65 % / 22.45 %	59	B	26.53 % / 24.49 %	75	C	36.73 % / 22.45 %
12	B	48.98 % / 22.45 %	28	A	55.1 % / 24.49 %	44	B	34.69 % / 24.49 %	60	B	65.31 % / 24.49 %	76	A	8.16 % / 22.45 %
13	D	48.98 % / 22.45 %	29	C	26.53 % / 24.49 %	45	D	57.14 % / 24.49 %	61	A	34.69 % / 24.49 %	77	B	18.37 % / 24.49 %
14	A	61.22 % / 24.49 %	30	A	44.9 % / 24.49 %	46	A	22.45 % / 24.49 %	62	A	42.86 % / 24.49 %	78	B	59.18 % / 24.49 %
15	C	28.57 % / 22.45 %	31	D	53.06 % / 24.49 %	47	B	32.65 % / 24.49 %	63	D	14.29 % / 22.44 %	79	C	51.02 % / 24.49 %
16	D	67.35 % / 22.45 %	32	D	59.18 % / 22.45 %	48	B	16.33 % / 22.45 %	64	B	24.49 % / 22.45 %	80	D	28.57 % / 24.49 %

Q.	Ans.	Correct		Q.	Ans.	Correct		Q.	Ans.	Correct		Q.	Ans.	Correct		Q.	Ans.	Correct
		Skipped				Skipped				Skipped				Skipped				Skipped
81	A	30.61 %		85	A	18.37 %		89	C	42.86 %		93	A	32.65 %		97	D	46.94 %
		22.45 %				24.49 %				22.45 %				24.49 %				24.49 %
82	C	26.53 %		86	B	46.94 %		90	B	28.57 %		94	A	32.65 %		98	B	53.06 %
		24.49 %				24.49 %				24.49 %				24.49 %				24.49 %
83	D	38.78 %		87	B	28.57 %		91	C	46.94 %		95	C	51.02 %		99	A	51.02 %
		22.44 %				24.49 %				22.45 %				22.45 %				22.45 %
84	D	24.49 %		88	C	44.9 %		92	D	20.41 %		96	C	0 %		100	D	57.14 %
		22.45 %				22.45 %				22.45 %				100 %				22.45 %

//Hints and Solutions//

1. Indo Australian plate is a major plate which is located between the Eurasian plate and the Antarctic plate. Cocos plate is located between Central America and the Pacific plate while Nazca plate is located between South America and the Pacific Plate. Arabian Plate is mostly the Saudi Arabian landmass.

2. Where Indian plate and Eurasian plates meet, it forms a convergent boundary. It is also called as destructive plate margins. Contrary to this constructive plate margins is used for divergent boundaries when two plates move apart from each other. The best example of the constructive plate margins is the mid-Atlantic ridges.

3. There are three basic types of magma. Mafic magma is also known as basaltic magma and are less viscous while Felsic magma is the type of magma which is highly viscous. When magma starts moving towards crust or when it reaches the crust it is called lava. When the lava comes out on the surface and cools down, the rocks forming out of it is called volcanic rocks. On the other hand, if the lava cools down within the crustal portion, it is called plutonic rocks.

4. The concept of cycle of erosion was first given by an American geomorphologist William Morris Davis in 1899. He was influenced by the ideas of both Charles Darwin and James Hutton. He tried to present a genetic classification and systematic description of landforms through the concept of geographical cycle, also known as cycle of erosion. Walther Penck rejected Davisian model and tried to give his own theory of landform development. Crickmay much later in 1932 suggested modifications in Davisian model of geographical cycle.

5. Davis characterized valleys as being insequent, obsequent and resequent. Insequent valleys are those which shown no apparent adjustment to structural or lithological control. The valleys which presumably drain in a direction opposite to that of original consequent valley are defined as obsequent. The valleys with a lower topographic level were designated as resequent.

Thus, the Correct answer is A.

6. W.M Davis gave the theory of cycle of erosion in the year 1899. He explained the three stages of erosion these are youthful stage, mature stage and old stage. The hillocks present in the plains after the third stage or the mature stage of erosion is called the monadnocks. Monadnocks in India are found in coastal states like West Bengal, Orissa, Andhra Pradesh etc.

Thus, the Correct answer is D.

7. Most of the notable Karst areas are in the region where limestone underlie the surface., although in some localities the rocks are dolomites or dolomitic limestone. Solution features may develop upon other soluble rocks such as gypsum and rock salt. Karst topography is majorly found in Mediterranean regions.

Thus, the Correct answer is C .

8. Bagnold authored the work "A further journey through the Libyan desert" in 1933.

Bryan authored the work "Pedestal rocks formed by differential erosion "in 1926.

Gautier authored the work "The great desert" in 1935.

Fisk authored the work "Loess and Quaternary geology of lower Mississippi "in 1951.

Thus, the Correct answer is B.

9. Numerous classifications of volcanoes according to their mode of eruption have been proposed. The most commonly used classification is that originally proposed by Lacroix in 1908. According to it, there are four principal types of eruptions-the Hawaiian, Strombolian, Vulcanian and Pelean types.

Thus, the Correct answer is A.

10. Honeycombed rocks are the result of differential weathering which is of differential weathering. Some of the results of differential weathering are hardly to be classed as landforms but rather are geological features which add variety to topographic surfaces. Features like lattice and honeycombed rocks are formed by differential etching of thinly bedded rocks.

Thus, the Correct answer is A.

11. Charles Warren Thornthwaite was an American geographer who devised a climatic classification of the world based on precipitation effectiveness index in 1931. He revised it in 1948 when he used potential evapotranspiration for computing moisture index, a modification to his 1931 classification.

12. El Nino is the phenomena when the pressure system changes along the equator and low pressure develops in the eastern Pacific and high pressure develops in the western pacific. The equatorial counter current gets stronger which brings warm water from the west to the eastern pacific and replace the cool Peruvian current and also prevent upwelling. It is a deviation from the general Walker Circulation.

13. Tropical cyclone gets its name because it originates and intensifies over warm tropical oceans. It cannot originate near the equator because the Coriolis force is zero in the equator and it is with the help of Coriolis force that cyclone formation is possible. They require vast sea surface with high temperature for the moisture as the supply of energy in the cyclone development. On the other hand, mid-latitude cyclones can originate over both land and sea-surface and it forms along polar front.

14. Tropical cyclone is the general term which is used to refer to all hurricane like storm and/or cyclonic systems originating over tropical waters by international agreement. Cyclone is a common name for the tropical cyclone in India and the Indian Ocean region, whereas it is called Willy-willies in Australia. It is called hurricane in the Atlantic region and the eastern North-pacific region while Typhoons is used in the western North – Pacific region and the South China Sea.

15. There are four principal types of air mass on the basis of source regions and the nature of the surface which are 1. continental polar air masses 2. Maritime polar air masses 3. Continental tropical air masses 4. Maritime tropical air masses. Thermodynamic modifications include modifications like W and K which are warm and cold respectively while mechanical modifications include s and u air masses which are upper level instability and upper level stability respectively. Hence, on all

these modifications and the principal types, air masses can be divided further into 16 types.

16. El Nino is a well-known weather-related phenomenon which occurs off the west coast of South America, mainly outside the Peruvian Coast. El Nino is related to the increase of temperature of the East Pacific Ocean off Peruvian coast.

The 1982-83 El Niño events led to the rise of the normal temperature of the in the north western parts of Canada and Alaska, rise in the winter normal temperature in the eastern parts of U.S.A. and several other drastic environmental conditions like drought, less rainfall, coral bleaching, etc. The 1997-98 event caused a rise in the normal sea surface temperature by 5 degree C in the Pacific Ocean and Indian Ocean which led to coral bleaching and destruction.

The La Nina is the opposite of El Nino.

17. The Troposphere extends from the ground to the distance of about 18 km. It varies according to latitude. The boundary between the troposphere and stratosphere is called as tropopause. The Stratosphere extends from tropopause up to 50 km from the ground. Its height is about 32 km. The upper layer of stratosphere has ozone layer and boundary between stratosphere and mesosphere is called as stratosphere. The mesosphere extends from stratopause until height of 85 km from ground. Above the mesosphere lies the thermosphere between around 90 km to 500 km.

Thus, the correct answer is A.

18. The Loo winds are prevalent in central Thar and north Indian plain and Pakistan. The wind has drying effect on vegetation. Brick fielder is a wind that blows in Southeastern Australia in summer season. It destroys injurious gems from the interior of the desert.
Norte is a cool wind that blows from the polar area. It blows from central Canada to USA. It is laden with snow.
 Sirocco is a form of sandstorm in Libya and Algeria. It has iron oxides which lead to red colored rains in the southern slopes of Alps.

Thus, the correct answer is A.

19. Water vapour is the most variable gas in atmosphere. It is present in smal amounts but is very important. It is always present in some proportion in the lower atmosphere. The water vapour content varies from 0.2% in cold dry climate to 4% in humid tropics.

Thus, the Correct answer is C.

20. Density of pure water is 1000 gm/m^3. The density of water is affected by the temperature and salinity of water. The cold water is denser than the warmer water. It is so because as the temperature increases, molecules of water get farther apart from each other. Increase salinity also reads to increased density. The density of oceanic water is 1027 gm/ m^3.

Thus, the correct answer is D.

21. The density of water is affected by the salinity of water and temperature of water. Increased temperature means the molecules of water spread far away from each other. Hence, the density of water decreases. Hence, the temperature of water is inversely proportional to the density of water.

Thus, the correct answer is B.

22. The temperature of the enclosed seas in low latitudes is higher comparatively because of the influence of the surrounding lands areas and movement of sea water. For instance, the average annual temperature of the surface water of the equator is 26 degree C while it is 37.7 in the Red Sea.

The other statements imply that even though the insolation is equal, the land surface takes a longer time as the insolation falling on the water surface has to heat a large volume of water and to a greater depth. Similarly, due to the slanting of the sun's rays, the amount of insolation decreases towards the poles.

23. The Oyashio current is a cold current of the Pacific Ocean, also known as the Kurile Current. Bering Sea is the only communication of this current through which the Arctic water enters the Pacific along the eastern coasts of Kamchatka.

The Brazil current is a South Atlantic Current and is generated because of the bifurcation of the south equatorial current. It is a comparatively feeble current with an average velocity ranging between 20to 24 sea miles per day. It is a warm current.

24. The Saffir Simpson Hurricane Wind scale is a 1 to 5 categorization based on the hurricane's intensity at the indicated time. The scale, originally developed by wind engineer Herb Saffir and meteorologist Bob Simpson, has been a perfect tool for alerting the public about the possible impacts of various intensity hurricanes. Category Five hurricanes are the catastrophic ones. This scale however does not provide any knowledge regarding the potential of other hurricane-related events like storm surges, tornadoes, etc.

25. Ecosystems are organizations consisting of a unified group of components forming a systematized whole. Ecosystem is a functional unit composed of the biotic and the abiotic components which are intimately related to each other through a series of large scale of cyclic mechanisms. For instance, an individual tree may die, but the forest's organization remains intact. Similarly ecosystems occur in space as well as in time; they also have width, depth, height. A summer sample will be usually very different from a winter sample, generally in areas with freezing temperatures and samples taken many years ago could be totally different, mostly in young ecosystems. These dimensional properties pose problems in studying the ecosystems.

26. When domestic, industrial and agricultural wastes are mixed with fresh water, it creates a demand of extra oxygen for the decomposition of the present organic waste in water. This demand of oxygen for the decomposition of organic waste in per unit volume of water is known as BOD. It is generally expressed as milligram of oxygen consumed for the degradation of the organics present in one litre of water.

27. • The Vienna Convention was held in Austria in the year 1985 and its primary objective was the protection and maintenance of the ozone layer.

• The Toronto Summit that was held in the Toronto city of Canada was created for the reduction in the emission of CO_2. It aimed at 20% reduction by the year 2005 but the developed countries backed out from this summit because of the non-availability of data.

• The Second World Climate Summit which was organized in 1990 to search for effective measures in order to keep a check on the emission of greenhouse gases.

• The Kyoto Protocol, with a primary aim to reduce global warming, was signed during the period of December 1-10, 1997 in the Kyoto city of Japan. The main item of this treaty was that a 5.2% cut in the CO_2 emissions by the developed countries was signed.

28. It is a non-binding action plan on global environment and development and covers more than 100 programme plans intended to promote sustainable development.

29. Gaseous cycle includes the movement of carbon as CO2 as free gas in the atmosphere and as a dissolved gas in the water bodies while the non-gaseous or inorganic cycle involves the solid phase of carbon wherein it resides in carbohydrate molecules in organic matter and as hydrocarbon and mineral carbonate compounds.

30. More than half of the world's population live in Asia which accounts for only 1/5th of the world's land area while the African countries account for a quarter of the land surface which is over 1/10th of the world population. However, the population growth of these countries during the 20th century was still higher. Death rates had declined rapidly during the 20th century, though they were still higher than the European countries because of lower standards of hygiene, nutrition, and disease control. The proportions of old people in the population were very small. The moderate decline in the death rate however has not been matched by the change in the birth rate which still remains very high. Hence the population contained many young people. Therefore, in many of these countries it will take a long time to overcome the traditional attitudes and the lack of knowledge of family planning techniques, though some countries such as India give great publicity and prominence to family planning.

31. All the above reasons support that the theory of Malthus are from a pessimistic pint of view. Rapid and efficient means of transportation have benefitted not only Europe but the rest of the world. Thus, if there is famine in one area food supplies can usually be brought in from elsewhere. Tremendous advances have been made in agriculture in underdeveloped countries which, with foreign aid and technical advice, are growing more stable crops and are introducing more nutritious crops not grown previously. Research into plant varieties has produced improved hybrids which have a number of advantages over climatic situations. The biggest problem, economic inequality, has gradually been reduced by the development of natural resources, agriculture, and industries in underdeveloped countries, which in turn earns foreign exchange and provides them with financial resources for further development. Such improvements eventually lead to better incomes and standards of living and more and better foods.

32. Natural Increase refers to the excess of births over deaths per 1000 of population. This does not include increases in population due to immigration. However, the rate of natural increase or growth rate of population refers to the difference between the birth rate and the death rate. When the difference is 0 then the population has stabilized or has reached the replacement level.

Net reproduction ratio is the rate at which women are replaced by daughters who will have children. More boys are born than girls- this is a natural way of keeping population even, for mortality is higher among men. The ratio is 1050: 1000. Thus if 1000 girls are born per 1000 women in the present population the Gross Reproduction ratio is 1. But if we assume that only 800 of these girls will survive to bear the children the Net Reproduction Ratio is only 0.8 and this population would decline.

Life Expectancy is the average age at which people die. Moreover, it refers to the estimated number of years that an average person is expected to survive. It is calculated on the basis of data on age-specific death rates in a given area over a period of time.

The infant mortality rate is the number of deaths of babies before the age of 1 year per 1000 live births.

33. Since rural settlements are associated with low technology levels, it is difficult for them to overcome the restrictions imposed by the ruggedness of the terrain. Buildings are generally found on the gentler slopes and exist individually or in small groups. It is unusual for a village in a rugged terrain to be compact. In some places the houses are dispersed totally, that is, they occur individually or in very small groups.

The commonest form in India is the rectangular village of Lineated form. The houses are close-shaped and face more or less the same cardinal direction. Enayat Ahmed explains this form with reference to the rectangular field patterns common to most of the Northern plains of India.

Nucleation can take place around more than one point. Examples of double nucleation are found in several areas of India. A new railway station built a little away from the main village usually leads to secondary nucleation resulting in a double village. The Rampur settlement in Almora district is an example of double nucleation.

34. The concentric zone model suggests that as cities expand, the interaction of people and their economic social and political organizations create rings of urban growth. These expand outwards from the city centre which is the main area of commercial activity or the Central Business District (CBD). The zone of transition is also known as the twilight zone or the urban blight which lies around the CBD. This is the intermediate zone between the commercial and the residential areas, consisting of wholesaling or light manufacturing activity. This zone is called so due to its association with factories, slums, and poor ethnic enclaves. Sometimes this area gets occupied by the CBD by converting the older houses into commercial purposes.

35. North Indian Plains have gentle slope and fertile land due to alluvium brought by rivers from Himalayas. The water is also available due to presence of perennial rivers like Ganga and Yamuna. Due to these factors, the area becomes suitable for agriculture and settlement. Hence, population density is high in the area. So, both (A) and (R) are true and (R) is the correct explanation of (A).

Thus, the correct answer is A.

36. The Total Fertility Rate for world population on average is 2.5 live births per woman. It is expected to fall to 2.2 live births per woman in 2050. The sub-Saharan African regions have the fertility rate higher than average at 4.6 in 2019. It is expected that this will drop down to 3.1 in 2050 and 2.1 in 2100.

Thus, the correct answer is C.

37. The literacy rate of India as per the census of 2011 was 74. 04%. The state of Mizoram stood third among all the states and union territories with literacy rate of 91.8 %. Goa was 4th and Tripura was 5th with literacy rates of 88.7 % and 87.2 % respectively. Maharashtra was 12th with literacy rate of 82.3 %.

Thus, the correct answer is B.

38. Adam Sadler wrote his ideas about population in his book, Law of Population. He strongly opposed Malthus' views that population increased in geometric progression. He said that population cannot increase or decrease in mathematic terms. He believed as industrialization increases, society becomes literate and civilized and population density increases. Thus, both (a) and (R) are true, but (R) is not the correct explanation of (A).

Thus, the correct answer is B.

39. Social Segregation, as we all know, refers to the process in which the urban population becomes more and more divided into various social groups mostly in terms of income, social status, and other reasons. Social Segregation has been seen in large cities or towns. This division takes place due to rearrangement of residential pattern and also due to spatial isolation. Residential segregation is nowadays observed in many places which widens the social distance between various localities. Segregation also takes place due to the increasing acceptance of market-based land and basic services. This tends to draw a line between the poor, marginalized people, and the better off societies. Such differences might be due to the kind of accommodations occupied by the people. Influences on the behaviours with the people of different status have also some form of effect on the segregation part. This kind of segregation also occurs in the pre-industrial societies

40. • The Agro-based industry is dependent upon the raw material from agricultural sector. It also includes animal-based products. The examples of this include cotton textile, leather industry, and food processing and dairy products.

• Mineral based industry is dependent on minerals ore extracted from mining as its raw material. These industries provide tools for other industries. Examples of this type include the ore industry, pump manufacturing units, etc.

• Sea and ocean are primary sources of raw material in case of the marine based industry. Oil plants which extract oil from the below the ocean or fishing industry are examples of this type.

• The forest-based industries, as we can know from the name are dependent on forests. They use raw materials from forests. The examples of this type include lumber production and paper production.

Thus, the correct answer is C.

41. Industries in any area are dependent upon facilities there. The availability of raw material, water and labour are some of the geographical factors affecting the decision of location of industries. The capital availability is a non-geographical factor, although it does affect location of industries.

Thus, the correct answer is D.

42. South Korea or the republic of Korea has 10.7% as its share of Information and Communication Technology (ICT) in its economy, as per the report of OECD. Germany, India, and France have 4.84, 5.87 and 4.33% respectively.

Thus, the correct answer is B.

43. Edward Louis Ullman was an American geography, a student of University of Chicago. He gave spatial interaction models. As per the Ullman the above formula could be used to determine level of interaction. In this formula,

• I: Level of interaction between i,j. alternatively, quantity of trade between i,j.

• P_i = population of i

• $d_{i,j}$ = distance separating i,j

• β = impedance factor

Thus, the correct answer is B

44. In case of two raw materials which are pure and ubiquitous the location of industry would be at market. However, if one of the two is localized and impure, the material index of such raw material would be higher than the pure and ubiquitous raw material. The material index of any raw material is the ratio between quantity of raw material used and the quantity of finished product. Therefore, the industry would locate near the localized and impure raw material.

45. Transport costs will be affected by the type of commodity as perishable and fragile commodities require more overhead costs than raw and bulky items. In the same manner The type of carrier also determine the transport costs as trains and ships and trucks all have different terminal and line-haul costs. Also, the competition from other carriers for the same distance can also check the transport costs as the shipper would go to the carrier with low cost.

46. Sun TV is India's biggest regional broadcaster.

47. According to A. Weber, when there is one market and one raw material, there are three possible situations. If the raw material is available everywhere, the best location in this case is market, as that will eliminate the transportation cost for manufacturing unit.

If the raw material is fixed, and pure then the manufacturing unit should be located either at the market or at the source. If the raw material fixed and gross (Loses Weight On Processing) then the best location will be at source.

Thus, the correct answer is A.

48. There are many reasons for the reduction of energy resources from the environment. One such reason is over population and its demand for fuel and fuel products. Every product's transportation require fuel . All these products are transported with a significant drain on our energy products.

Thus, the correct answer is B.

49. The Mediterranean region is having wet winters and dry summers. It is suitable for farming of loves, grapes, and citrus fruits. The area is thus also dubbed as Orchard Lands of the World. The region is also heart of wine production.

Thus, the correct answer is B.

50. The Agricultural Land use model given by Von Thunen uses the central part of the city as market area. The theory goes by assuming that this central city is an isolated state and self-sufficient. The land here is plain, without mountains and obstructions. The farmers aim to make maximum profits of the available resources.

Thus, the correct answer is C.

51. According to the land capability classification, yellow colour represent good cultivable land on almost level plain or on gentle slope, moderate depths, subject to occasional overland flow, may require drainage, moderate risk of damage when cultivated, use crop rotation, water control system or special tillage practices to control erosion.

Thus, the Correct answer is B.

52. * Francois Perroux gave the Growth Pole Theory in 1955. The Growth Pole Theory tells that growth occurs in poles rather than happening everywhere at the same time. He tries to explain that modern development has deviated from stationary equilibrium of growth.

* Matter of Centre Versus Periphery was discussed by John. O. Friedmann in the year 1966. The theory explains how presence physical and human advantages lead to growth in some areas turning them into core and lack of them makes turns the area into periphery.

* The theory of unbalanced growth was given by Albert O. Hirschmann in 1950s. according to Hirschmann, 'Development is a chain of disequilibria that must be kept alive rather than eliminate the disequilibrium of which profits and loss are symptoms in a competitive economy.

* Circular Cumulative Causation was given by Gunar Myrdal in the year 1956. The model explains that wealth is further enhanced by wealth and poverty is promoted by poverty.

Thus, the correct answer is B.

53. Albert Hirschmann gave the strategy for unbalanced growth. It is suitable for shutting down the vicious circle of poverty in developing and underdeveloped countries. As per Hirschmann the disequilibria should be promoted rather than eliminated. The development policy should be to maintain tension, disproportion, and disequilibria.

Thus, the correct answer is D.

54. Francis Perroux gave the Growth Pole Theory. As per this theory, growth does not take place simultaneously everywhere. It occurs in poles. The four poles given by Perroux include geographical poles, psychological poles, technological or technical poles and income poles.

Thus, the correct answer is B.

55. The Somasila Dam is a dam constructed across the Penna River near Somasila in Nellore district of Andhra Pradesh. The reservoir impounded by the dam has a surface area of 212.28 km2 with live storage capacity of 1.994 km3. It is the biggest storage reservoir in Penna River basin and can store all the inflows from its catchment area in a normal year.

Thus, the correct answer is C.

56. Aranmula Kannadi is a GI protected tag of Kerala. It is a Handicraft.

Thus, the correct answer is B.

57. According to the 2011 Census reports Schedule Tribe population: Mizoram (94.4%), Nagaland (86.5%), and Meghalaya (86.1%). Tribes display a high amount of clustering in the hilly and the forested tracts of the country while unevenly distributed between the Indian states. Mizoram consists of about 94.4% of tribal proportion, but the numerical strength of the tribes in not very large. In terms of population Madhya Pradesh, ranks 1st, has about 14.70% of the state's population.

58. In the recent years, the Chinese presence has increased in the Indian Ocean region. Indian Ocean is considered as geopolitically significant as several unexplored lands still remain which have not been exploited, huge amount of oil trade occurs through this ocean and the sea route links various parts of the world. However, the increased presence of China can be identified by certain ways like- the development of maritime silk trade route and the development of various ports of Pakistan, Bangladesh and Myanmar so that oil transports go smoothly, engagement of African countries so as to get support. With various investment strategies, China is making a strong position in the Indian Ocean Region.

59. With the formulation of the National Health Policy in 1983, there was shift from committees to policy-based approaches. The major aim of this policy was to provide universal, comprehensive primary health services. Population stabilization, medical and health education are some of the elements of this policy.

60. James Hutton has given the theory of uniformitarianism where he has said that 'the present is the key to the past'. According to this idea, the same processes of earth which are operating today has been operating in the past. This theory came as a response and counter to the then prevailing theory of diastrophism.

61. The Bharachukki Falls is situated at a distance of about 130 km from Bangalore. This waterfall is actually a part of the Shivanasamudram Falls.

62. The Farakka Barrage issue is an issue between India and Bangladesh, related to distribution of water of Ganga river.

63. At Palakkad places, India's first rail coach factory was built with PPP.

64. Approximately 15% of world's tea output comes from Assam.

65. Blatter Herbarium in India is located in Mumbai.

66. Time geography was developed by Tosten Haggerstand, who was a Swedish geographer. As per Haggersand, "Every situation in inevitably rooted in past situation."Time geography

emphasizes on connectedness and continuity of sequences of events. Space and time are resources that contain activity.

Thus, the correct answer is A.

67. Carl Ritter is known as the founders of modern geography who believed in empirical research. He developed the concept of unity in diversity. He declared geography to be Erdkunde or an earth science which deals with local conditions and embraces the attributes of places with respect to tropical, formal and material characteristics.

Thus, the Correct answer is A.

68. Systematic approach is related to natural factors like climatic factors, landforms, soils etc. The study of an element or element-complex concentrates on one kind of phenomena or phenomenon association. As it leads naturally, therefore the establishment of generic concepts for each element: a logical system of types may be established.

Thus, the Correct answer is B.

69. Behavioral geography is an approach to human geography and in particular to the process responsible for human spatial behavior, which especially draws on behaviouralism or on cognition, as a key to understand human spatial behavior.

Thus, the Correct answer is B.

70. The Gandhi Sagar Dam is built on Chambal river and is located in the Mandsaur & Neemuch district of Madhya Pradesh. It is a masonry gravity dam, standing 62.17 metres (204.0 ft) high, with a gross storage capacity of 7.322 billion cubic metres from a catchment area of 22,584 km2. The dam sports a 115-MW hydroelectric power station at its toe, with five 23-MW generating units each providing a total energy generation of about 564 GWh. The dam's reservoir area is the second-largest in India (after the Hirakud Reservoir), and attracts a large number of migratory and non-migratory birds throughout the year.

71. Landsat-8 is a remote sensing satellite which has a sun-synchronous and near polar orbit. Hence, the orbital path of Landsat-8 is near polar and not above equator. But the geostationary satellites which are generally used for weather and meteorological information moves exactly with the speed of the earth and orbits over the equator.

72. The earth receives energy from the sun in the form of electromagnetic radiation. The part of the electromagnetic spectrum visible to our eyes is called as visible spectrum. This consists of colours red, indigo, blue, green, yellow, orange and red. The color red has the longest wavelength of 0.7 $\times 10^{-6}$.

Thus, the correct answer is C.

73. Kasturba Health Society - Ahmedabad

Kasturba Health Society is in Wardha This is the correct answer.

Thus, the correct answer is D.

74. Watson's Hotel or Esplanade Haveli, India's oldest surviving cast iron building, is located in Mumbai.

Thus, the correct answer is A.

75. A river (inland river) is Kolkata port.

Thus, the correct answer is C.

76. Extensive farming is done on large patches of land. The large swathes are able to output huge amount of produce but production per unit of land may be low. Such farming is done in those countries where large size of landholding is available e.g. United States, Canada etc. Extensive farming is almost absent in India except in some states such as Punjab, Haryana and Uttar Pradesh. The focus of intensive farming is to produce maximum output per unit of land. It is common in India as well as South East Asian countries such as Thailand, Vietnam, and Indonesia etc.

Thus, the Correct answer is A.

77. * M. Bhagyaraj and B Gurungnanam's book significance of morphometry studies were published in the year 2011.

* Magesh N.S work GIS based morphometric evolution of chimney and supply watershed was published in the year 2012.

* Nag S.K's work influence on rock type and structure in the development of drainage network in hard rock area was published in the year 2003.

* P.D Sreedevi's work the significance of morphometric analysis for obtaining ground water potential zones in a structurally controlled terrain was published in 2005.

Thus, the Correct answer is B.

78. Pie Diagram is best suited for showing the above condition. When statistical data are given for several categories and we are interested in the comparison of various categories or between a part and the whole, pie diagrams are very helpful for effectively displaying the data. The other methods are useful for showing the frequency of distribution of individual items or doing a time series graph.

Thus, the Correct answer is B.

79. Rayleigh scattering takes place when the atmospheric particles are very small as compared to the wavelength of the radiation. Rayleigh scattering causes shorter wavelengths of energy to be dispersed more than the longer wavelengths. It is a dominant scattering mechanism in the upper atmosphere. And as EMR or radiant energy passes through the atmosphere, the shorter wavelength of the visible spectrum i.e., blue portion, are scattered more than the other longer wavelengths. Therefore, the sky appears blue in colour.

Thus, the Correct answer is C

80. * Roopkund lake is located in the Uttarakhand state of India. It is a part of the Himalayas and is located at a height of 4800m.

* Chandrataal lake is located in the Himachal Pradesh state of India. It is present in the Lahaul and Spiti district at a height of 4250m.

* Tso Moriri lake is located in Ladakh. It is present at a height of 4522m.

* Lake Guudongmar is located in the Sikkim. It is one of the highest lakes in the world located at a height of 5425m.

Thus, the Correct answer is D .

81. The peninsular plateau is the table land composed of old crystalline, igneous, and metamorphic rocks. It was formed due to the breaking and drifting of Gondwana land and thus, making it a part f the oldest landmass. The plateau consists of two broad divisions namely the central highlands and the deccan plateau. The eastward extension of this plateau is locally known as the Bhagelkhand.

Thus, the Correct answer is A .

82. Wind from southwest carrying heavy moisture brings rainfall to southern Asia during the summer. the period of southwest monsoon is June to September. This is the monsoon season of India. Monsoon in Kerala commences by around 31st May. It takes time to cover the entire India. The normal date by which it covers the entire India is 15th July.

Thus, the Correct answer is C.

83. El Nino is only a modifier to the Monsoon climate of India and not a factor causing it, which is why monsoon occurs even when there is no el-nino as such. The unique location of the Indian subcontinent and the thermal contrast of the sea-land aided by the shifting ITCZ are decisive factor in causing monsoon type climate in India. Upper Air Circulation in terms of westerly jet streams causing western disturbances enhances the monsoonal character.

84. The Allahabad-Haldia Stretch Waterway or NW 1 is the longest waterway and is divided into 3 parts. They are a) Haldia-Farakka; b) Farakka-Patna; c) Patna-The IWAI (Inland Waterway Authority of India) was set up at Noida in 1987 and is responsible for the development and regulation of the National Waterways.

NW-2 or the Sadiya Dhubri stretch is on the Brahmaputra River entirely in Assam. The NW 16 has not been operational and has been taken up for construction by IWAI.

85. Nagpur Plan was the first serious attempt to develop roadways in 1943. Twenty Year (Road) Plan was drawn in 1961 after having met the objectives of the Nagpur plan. Build Operate Transfer (BOT) is a scheme in which private operators are invited to construct roads and bridges who are allowed to collect toll tax from the users. However, the Bombay Plan was to decide about the post-independence economic development of the country.

86. India ranks second in production of groundnut, sugarcane, and rice. China holds the first place for groundnut and rice while Brazil holds the same for sugarcane. India has the largest area under cultivation of sesame in the world as well as the leading producer of sesame. West Bengal is the leading producer of sesame in India.

Thus, the correct answer is B.

87. According to Indian Minerals Yearbook 2018 (released in 2019) state of Orissa produces nearly 40% of the total iron ore production in India. Sambalpur, Mayurbhanj, Koraput, Cuttack are some of the highest iron ore producing iron ore in India. Goa, Chhattisgarh, and Jharkhand are other major Iron ore producing state in India.

Thus, the correct answer is B.

88. The population of India as per the census of 2011 is 1210.2 million. India stands second in the ranking of total population in the world. This number is 17.5% of the world's population. China represents 19.4%. After India, USA has population of 308.7 million which represents 4.5% of the world's population.

Thus, the correct answer is C.

89. • The river Ganga originates at Gomukh glacier near Gangotri. The river has a number of tributaries like Kosi, Gandak, Mahanadi, etc. The river Sharada joins Ganga near Ayodhya.

• Yamuna is a tributary of river Ganga. It originates at Yamunotri near Bander punch. The river Ken is a right-bank tributary of the river Yamuna.

• The river Chenab originates near Barlacha la pass. The important tributaries of the river include Chandra and Bhaga that lie in Himachal Pradesh.

• The Indus River flows through Ladakh and Zaskar range. It originates near Siachen glacier. The tributaries of river include Jhelum, Chenab, Ravi, Suru, Dras among others.

Thus, the correct answer is C.

90. Chambal river is an example of superimposed drainage. A superimposed river does not adjust with the structure of its place of origin. First of all the river valley is built on upper part and then the river develops and expands such structure in the lower part.

Thus, the correct answer is B.

91. • The North Eastern Railway zone officially became a railway zone in 1952. It has three main divisions which include Izzatnagar Railway Station, Lucknow NER Railway Station and Varanasi City Railway Station. Its headquarters are located at Gorakhpur.

• The Central Railway zone has its headquarters at Mumbai CST. It was formed in 1951. It is the largest railway zone in India in terms of area, staff and track mileage.

• Metro railway was first started in Kolkata on 24 December 1984. The headquarters of Indian Metro railway zone is also at Kolkata.

• The Northern Railway zone is the northern-most railway zone in India. It officially became a railway zone in 1952. Its headquarters are located at Baroda House in New Delhi.

Thus, the correct answer is C.

92. Jet streams are the geostrophic winds. They are present at high altitudes as high as 20000-50000 feet. They blow horizontally in the upper stratosphere. There are majorly three types of jet stream. These are sub-tropical, polar night and polar easterly. Polar Nigh travels through the upper stratosphere. They are present above the sub polar low-pressure belt.

Thus, the Correct answer is D.

93. Green revolution which majorly aimed at profit maximization. The features of green revolution are led to excess mechanization of agriculture. More crops were grown for the market that is market-oriented crop were given major priority. Also, hybrid varieties of seeds were made available to the farmers which would help them yield the required product.

Thus, the correct answer is A.

94. Globalisation is the process where humans from all over the world or globally are integrated by various sharing of goods, services, and commodities. India felt globalization with increasing trade volumes, investment, and growth. Globalisation in India was first introduce in 1990s. India currently accounts 2,7% of world trade up from 1.2% in in 2006 according to WTO.

Thus, the Correct answer is A.

95. The state cf Mahrashtra lies in the peninsular part of India and is a part of the seismic zone. The most prominent earthquake in the state of Maharashtra occurred at C.56 am on 30 September 199C. The magnitude of the earthquake was 6.2 on the Richter scale. It affected Latur and Osmanabad districts.

Thus, the correct answer is C.

96. The zone cf Kashmir & Western Himalayas has a number of earthquakes w th high intensity, even with earthquakes of magnitude more than 8.0 on Richter scale. The fault line of Main Central Thrust passes through this area.

Thus, the correct answer is C.

97. India has 7 seismic regions, divided according to the varying intensity of seismicity. These zones include Kashmir and Western Himalayas, Central Himalayas, Northeast India, Indo-Gangetic Basin, Peninsular India, Khambhat and Kutch area and Andaman & Nicobar Islands.

Thus, the correct answer is D.

98. Earthquake is violent tremor of the earth's crust. Its effects include destruction of roads, buildings, loss of human and animal life. Earthquake triggers other natural disasters like volcanic eruption, tsunami, etc. Afforestation is increasing the number of trees in any area, which is not an effect of earthquake.

Thus, the correct answer is B.

99. The country of India has been divided into 7 seismic regions and 3 zones. These three zones are zone of maximum intensity, zone of comparative intensity and zone of minimum intensity. The peninsular India along the islands of Lakshadweep makes the zone of minimum intensity.

Thus, the correct answer is A.

100. Trade, transport and services are included in the group of tertiary economic activities. These activities are not concerned with production of tangible goods directly, however, they play an important role in the performance of the primary and secondary activities producing such goods.

Q.1 Which of the following movement refers most appropriately to continent building?

A. Diastrophic movement

B. Epeirogenic movement

C. Orogenic movement

D. Exogenetic movement

Q.2 Which one of the following is not true for a transcurrent fault?

A. Movement is horizontal

B. No scarp is formed.

C. Only a thin line or narrow trench may be formed

D. Landform graben is thus created.

Q.3 Which of the following statements regarding volcanism are correct?

(a) In case of mafic magma, the solidified plutonic rock is Gabbro.

(b) In case of felsic magma, the solidified plutonic rock is Granite.

(c) Depending on size, tephra can be classified into bombs, blocks, lapilli or ash.

(d) Higher gas content and higher temperature of the magma indicates higher viscosity.

Code:

A. Only (a)

B. (a), (b) and (c)

C. (b), (c) and (d)

D. (a), (b), (c) and (d)

Q.4 Given below are two statements. One is labelled as Assertion (A) and the other is labelled as Reason (R).

Assertion (A): Shield Volcanoes are formed of mafic or basalt lava and have gentle slopes.

Reason (R): Mafic lava is not viscous and can travel long distances to spread out in thin layers.

Select the correct answer from options given below:

A. Both (A) and (R) are true and (R) is the correct explanation of (A)

B. Both (A) and (R) are true, but (R) is not the correct explanation of (A)

C. (A) is true, but (R) is false.

D. (A) is false, but (R) is true.

Q.5 Which among the following is not included in mass movement processes?

A. Avalanches

B. Tsunami

C. Rockfall

D. Slump

Q.6 Which among the following statement about weathering and mass movement is not correct?

A. Weathering and mass wasting are both part of denudation process.

B. Frost action, thermal action, exfoliation are different types of physical or mechanical weathering.

C. Hydrolysis, Oxidation, Salt-crystal growth, acid action are types of chemical weathering.

D. Solifluction is a type of mass wasting that occurs when soil becomes thoroughly saturated with water.

Q.7 Flowstone is a typical feature in which of the following?

A. Fluvial landform

B. Volcanic landform

C. Aeolian landform

D. Karst landform

Q.8 Which of the following scholars is associated with the concept of primarumpf?

A. W.M. Davis

B. C.D. Crickmay

C. Walther Penck

D. Albrecht Penck

Q.9 Match the seismic waves (List-I) and the characteristics (List-II) they are associated with.

List-I (seismic waves)	List-II (characteristics)
(a) P-waves	(i) shadow zone beyond $105°$
(b) S-waves	(ii) fastest surface waves
(c) Love Waves	(iii) fastest seismic waves
(d) Rayleigh waves	(iv) most destructive waves

Code:

A. (a)-(i), (b)-(iii), (c)-(ii), (d)-(iv)

B. (a)-(iii), (b)-(i), (c)-(ii), (d)-(iv)

C. (a)-(iii), (b)-(i), (c)-(iv), (d)-(ii)

D. (a)-(iv), (b)-(iii), (c)-(ii), (d)-(i)

Q.10 Which among of the following geomorphologists gave the concept of slope replacement?

A. W.M. Davis

B. L. King

C. W. Penck

D. Playfair

Q.11 Which of the following statements are correct?

a) Plate tectonic theory explains the formation of volcanoes.

b) Tectonic plates are composed of continental and oceanic lithosphere.

A. only a

B. only b

C. Both a and b

D. Neither a nor b

Q.12 Who used the term "gradation" primarily ?

A. Penk

B. Sharpe

C. Reiche

D. Chamberlin

Q.13 Match List-I with List-II:

List-I (Author)	List-II (works)
(a) Blackwelder	(i) The reaction principle in petrogenesis
(b) Bowen	(ii) Exfoliation as a phase of rock weathering
(c) Chapman	(iii) Geological process and their results
(d) Chamberlin	(iv) Spheroidal weathering of igneous rocks

A. a- iii b-ii c-i d-iv

B. a-ii b-i c-iv d-iii

C. a-i b-ii c-iii d-iv

D. a-iii b-i c-iv d-ii

Q.14 Which river "does not" flow through a rift valley?

A. Tapti

B. Damodar

C. Mahi   **D.** Luni

Q.15 Match List-I with List-II:

List-I (Extinct Volcanoes)	List-II (Places)
(a) Huascaran	(i) Northwest Pacific Ocean
(b) Kyushu-Palau Ridge	(ii) Peru
(c) Mount Buninyong	(iii) Philippine Sea
(d) Tamu Massif	(iv) Australia

A. a- iii b-ii c-i d-iv   **B.** a-ii b-i c-iv d-iii
C. a-i b-ii c-iii d-iv   **D.** a-ii b-iii c-iv d-i

Q.16 A rapidly rotating column of air that blows around a small area of intense low pressure with a circulation that reaches the ground is called

A. convective storms   **B.** hurricane
C. eddies   **D.** tornado

Q.17 Which of the following option is correct?

A. On the basis of Precipitation Effectiveness Indices and boundary values, 6 humidity provinces have been identified by Thornthwaite.

B. Thermal Efficiency index is the sum of 12 monthly values of (T-32)/4, where T is the mean monthly temperature in degree F.

C. 30 climatic types have been shown on Thornthwaite's 1931 classification.

D. None of the above

Q.18 Read the following statements and choose your answer from the code given below:

(a) Precipitation efficiency and temperature effectiveness were two parameters for delineation of climatic classification by Thornthwaite

(b) On the basis of precipitation efficiency Index, Thornthwaite made 6 humidity zones.

(c) Precipitation efficiency ratio was calculated by dividing monthly evaporation by monthly precipitation.

(d) Precipitation efficiency index is the average of precipitation efficiency ratios for the year.

Code:

A. Only (a) is true
B. (a) and (d) are true
C. (a), (b) and (d) are true
D. (a), (c) and (d) are true

Q.19 Read the following statements. Choose the correct answer from the words given below:

(a) In India, a heat wave occurs when the temperature rises by 5-6⁰ C above the normal temperature.

(b) A heat wave in India in 2015 led to death of nearly 2500 people.

(c) World Meteorological Department defines heat wave as rise in temperature by 8-10⁰ C.

(d) Heat exhaustion, dehydration and heatstroke may be health-related effects of a heat wave.

Code:

A. (a) and (b) are true
B. (a), (b)and (c) are true
C. (a), (b) and (d) are true
D. (a) and (d) are true

Q.20 Match the List -I with List-II

List-I(Surface)	List-II(percent Albedo)
a) Fresh Snow	i) 50-60
b) Old Snow	ii) 20-30
c) Sand	iii) 20-25
d) Grass	iv) 80-85

A. a –iii b –ii c –i d –iv   **B.** a –iv b –i c –ii d –iii
C. a –i b –ii c –iii d –iv   **D.** a –iii b –i c –iv d –ii

Q.21 Match the following

List-I(Koppen classification system)	List -II(Climate type)
a. Aw	i) Tundra Climate
b. DF	ii) Desert Climate
c. Bw	iii) Tropical Savanna
d. ET	iv) Cold Snowy Forest

Choose the correct answer:

A. a –iii b –ii c –i d –iv   **B.** a –i b –iv c –ii d –iii
C. a –iii b –iv c –ii d –i   **D.** a –iii b –i c –iv d –ii

Q.22 Intertropical fronts are formed in the meeting ground of the:-

A. South west and North west trade winds
B. South east and North west trade winds
C. North east and south east trade winds
D. North and south trade winds.

Q.23 Two statements are given below. One is Assertion (A) and other is Reason (R):

Assertion(A)-High pressure cells develop over the places with oceans where temperature is relatively low in July over the tropic of cancer.

Reason(R)- The high-pressure cells which develop in north pacific is called the 'pacific high'.

Choose the correct answer:

A. Both A and R are true and R correctly explains A
B. Both A and R are true but R does not explain A
C. A is true and R is false.
D. Both A and R are false

Q.24 Match the following

List-I(Major affected Regions)	List-II(2019 Indian Ocean cyclone)
a. Bangladesh	i) Bulbul
b. Maldives	ii) Hikaa
c. India	iii) Fani
d. Pakistan	iv) Vayu

Choose the correct answer:

A. a – iii b – ii c – i d – iv
B. a – i b – iv c – ii d – iii
C. a – iii b – ii c – iv d – i
D. a – iii b – i c – iv d – ii

Q.25 Which of the following coastal zones of India suffered the maximum damage during the Sumatra Tsunami of 2004?

A. Andhra Pradesh   **B.** Kerala
C. Orissa   **D.** Tamil Nadu

Q.26 Read the following passage and answer the questions given below it.

Tsunamis are caused by sudden changes in the topography of the ocean floor, such as glide with an error in the depth of the water, rapid currents from landslides in the ocean floor, or large ocean volcanic eruptions and underwater volcanoes The destruction of, etc. These processes that cause tsunamis are usually seismic events, so tsunamis are accurately called seismic ocean waves. Once a tsunami is generated, its stability (ratio of wavelength to height) is extremely low. Due to this absence, they are interwoven with long-term waves, due to which they are not detected even when passing under the sea vessels. When the tsunami comes in shallow water, the energy from the entire oceanic water column is compressed into a shallow region, and the tsunami forms a series of rapid waves of incoming and withdrawing seawater on the coast. It exerts its energy which brings great destruction. Like shallow water waves, seismic ocean waves are affected by the contour of the floor and are usually refracted, sometimes in an unpredictable manner. A detailed analysis of the events of 2004 and 2011 showed that the central oceanic ridges act as topographic waves. A tsunami in Hawaii in 1946 caused a tsunami warning system to be installed throughout the Pacific Ocean.

Which among the following is not a cause of a tsunami?
A. sudden vertical movement along faults
B. Landslides
C. Icebergs falling from glaciers
D. None of the above.

Q.27 When the tide is channeled between islands or into bays and estuaries they are called:
A. Amphidromic tides   **B.** Surges
C. Tidal Currents   **D.** Flow Tides

Q.28 Consider the following statements regarding ocean circulation and ocean currents and answer the question below:
(a) Ocean currents help in temperature and salinity redistribution over the oceans.
(b) Shape of the continent has no impact on ocean circulation.
(c) Indian Ocean witness seasonal reversal of ocean currents.
Which of the above statements is/are correct?
A. (a) and (c) only   **B.** (b) and (c) only
C. (c) only   **D.** (a), (b) and (c)

Q.29 Which of the following statements is/are correct about the distribution of temperature over the oceans?
(a) Offshore winds drive warm surface water away from the coast resulting in upwelling of the cold water.
(b) Isotherms are more regular and follow latitudes in northern hemisphere as compared to the southern hemisphere
(c) The enclosed seas in lower latitudes have higher temperature as compared to the open seas because of landmass.
A. (b) only   **B.** (a) and (c) only
C. (b) and (c) only   **D.** (a), (b) and (c)

Q.30 Read the passage carefully and answer the following questions given below: -

The movement of chemical elements involves the biological organisms and their geological environment. These movements are collectively referred to as biogeochemical cycles. In one group of these cycles, the atmosphere constitutes a major reservoir of the element that exists in gaseous phase, which are known as gaseous nutrient cycles. In the sedimentary phase, the major reservoir is the lithosphere, from which the elements are released by weathering. Carbon and nitrogen are prime representatives of biogeochemical cycles with a prominent gaseous phase. The elements derived from the atmospheric and sedimentary reservoirs are pooled into soils. The inorganic elements of the sedimentary and gaseous phase that are pooled in the soil reservoir are taken up by the plants by root osmosis. These elements are then converted in such forms that they are used in the development of plant tissues by biochemical processes. Thus the nutrients driven by energy flow pass into various components of biotic communities through the process of biogeochemical cycles. These nutrients or organic matter of plants and animals are released in a variety of ways. The carbon cycle involving the circulation of carbon within the biosphere includes 2 pathways or cycles such as gaseous and the inorganic cycle. However, the level of CO_2 in the atmosphere has increased by 20% since the beginning of the industrial revolution. In contrast to the simplicity of carbon cycle, the nitrogen cycle involves 4 major steps, as for e.g. Nitrogen fixation, ammonification, nitrification, and denitrification: each involving a number of different organisms, some free-living.

Match the following:-
List
a) nitrogen fixation
b) ammonization
c) Nitrification
d) denitrification
List II
1) Nitrate deficiency in a gaseous nitrogen species such as N2
2) Conversion of ammonia to nitrite or nitrate
3) Conversion of organic nitrogen to ammonia
4) Conversion of nitrogen gas to any form of nitrogen compound
A. a-4 b-2 c-3 d-1   **B.** a-4 b-3 c-2 d-1
C. a-2 b-3 c-1 d-4   **D.** a-1 b-2 c-3 d-4

Q.31 Read the passage carefully and answer the following questions given below: -

The movement of chemical elements involves the biological organisms and their geological environment. These movements are collectively referred to as biogeochemical cycles. In one group of these cycles, the atmosphere constitutes a major reservoir of the element that exists in gaseous phase, which are known as gaseous nutrient cycles. In the sedimentary phase, the major reservoir is the lithosphere, from which the elements are released by weathering. Carbon and nitrogen are prime representatives of biogeochemical cycles with a prominent gaseous phase. The elements derived from the atmospheric and sedimentary reservoirs are pooled into soils. The inorganic elements of the sedimentary and gaseous phase that are pooled in the soil reservoir are taken up by the plants by root osmosis. These elements are then converted in such forms that they are used in the development of plant tissues by biochemical processes. Thus the nutrients driven by energy flow pass into various components of biotic communities through the process of biogeochemical cycles. These nutrients or organic matter of plants and animals are released in a variety of ways. The carbon cycle involving the circulation of carbon within the biosphere includes 2 pathways or cycles such as gaseous and the inorganic cycle. However, the level of CO_2 in the atmosphere has increased by 20% since the beginning of the industrial revolution. In contrast to the simplicity of carbon cycle, the nitrogen cycle involves 4 major steps, as for e.g. Nitrogen fixation, ammonification, nitrification, and denitrification: each involving a number of different organisms, some free-living.

How are organic elements of plants and animals released?

A. Decomposition of leaf falls

B. Forest fires

C. Excretion of waste materials

D. All of the above

Q.32 Read the passage carefully and answer the following questions given below: -

The movement of chemical elements involves the biological organisms and their geological environment. These movements are collectively referred to as biogeochemical cycles. In one group of these cycles, the atmosphere constitutes a major reservoir of the element that exists in gaseous phase, which are known as gaseous nutrient cycles. In the sedimentary phase, the major reservoir is the lithosphere, from which the elements are released by weathering. Carbon and nitrogen are prime representatives of biogeochemical cycles with a prominent gaseous phase. The elements derived from the atmospheric and sedimentary reservoirs are pooled into soils. The inorganic elements of the sedimentary and gaseous phase that are pooled in the soil reservoir are taken up by the plants by root osmosis. These elements are then converted in such forms that they are used in the development of plant tissues by biochemical processes. Thus the nutrients driven by energy flow pass into various components of biotic communities through the process of biogeochemical cycles. These nutrients or organic matter of plants and animals are released in a variety of ways. The carbon cycle involving the circulation of carbon within the biosphere includes 2 pathways or cycles such as gaseous and the inorganic cycle. However, the level of CO_2 in the atmosphere has increased by 20% since the beginning of the industrial revolution. In contrast to the simplicity of carbon cycle, the nitrogen cycle involves 4 major steps, as for e.g. Nitrogen fixation, ammonification, nitrification, and denitrification: each involving a number of different organisms, some free-living.

Which of the following are important carbon storage reservoirs of the biosphere?

A. Forests

B. Oceans

C. Icebergs

D. Lakes bottoms

Q.33 Read the passage carefully and answer the following questions given below: -

The movement of chemical elements involves the biological organisms and their geological environment. These movements are collectively referred to as biogeochemical cycles. In one group of these cycles, the atmosphere constitutes a major reservoir of the element that exists in gaseous phase, which are known as gaseous nutrient cycles. In the sedimentary phase, the major reservoir is the lithosphere, from which the elements are released by weathering. Carbon and nitrogen are prime representatives of biogeochemical cycles with a prominent gaseous phase. The elements derived from the atmospheric and sedimentary reservoirs are pooled into soils. The inorganic elements of the sedimentary and gaseous phase that are pooled in the soil reservoir are taken up by the plants by root osmosis. These elements are then converted in such forms that they are used in the development of plant tissues by biochemical processes. Thus the nutrients driven by energy flow pass into various components of biotic communities through the process of biogeochemical cycles. These nutrients or organic matter of plants and animals are released in a variety of ways. The carbon cycle involving the circulation of carbon within the biosphere includes 2 pathways or cycles such as gaseous and the inorganic cycle. However, the level of CO_2 in the atmosphere has increased by 20% since the beginning of the industrial revolution. In contrast to the simplicity of carbon cycle, the nitrogen cycle involves 4 major steps, as for e.g. Nitrogen fixation, ammonification, nitrification, and denitrification: each involving a number of different organisms, some free-living.

Which of the following element has a prominent sedimentary phase?

A. Carbon

B. Nitrogen

C. Water

D. Phosphorus

Q.34 This policy had adopted some fundamental principles such as prevention of pollution at source, promotion of the best available technology to reduce pollutants and decision making. Which of the following policies have these guidelines?

A. Indian Environmental Policy

B. Central Pollution Control Board

C. National Conservation Strategy

D. Forest Policy

Q.35 Given below are two statements. One is labelled as Assertion (A) and the other is labelled as Reason (R).

Assertion (A)- Migration only assumed international importance during the 19th and early 20th centuries.

Reason (R)- Most significant factor in European migration in 19th century was the development of transport.

Select the correct answer from options given below:

A. Both (A) and (R) are true and (R) is the correct explanation of (A)

B. Both (A) and (R) are true but (R) is not the correct explanation of (A)

C. (A) is true but (R) is false

D. (A) is false but (R) is true

Q.36 Which of the following statements are correct regarding the population composition and structure of various countries?

A. During the 20th century, the population pyramid of Britain had a narrow base and a broad bulge in the old-age groups.

B. According to recent trends, Japan holds the lowest death

and infant mortality rates.

C. Population structure of Latin America and African Countries are still different from the European countries.

D. All of the above

Q.37 The reason why there has been a wide gap between the developed and developing countries are-

A. prevalence of environmental hazards rather than infectious diseases in developing countries

B. Less prioritization in basic health services in developing countries

C. Minimum Infrastructural facilities in developing countries

D. All of the above

Q.38 Which of the following are correctly Matched?

Shape of rural houses	Distribution
1. Rectangular ground plan and horizontal roof	Uttar Pradesh and Rajasthan
2. Rectangular ground plan and inclined roof	Orissa, Tamil Nadu, Kerala
3. Circular ground plan and conical roof	Tribal belt of Andhra Pradesh and Nilgiris

Select the correct option from the code given below:

A. Only 1   **B.** 1 and 2

C. 2 and 3   **D.** 1, 2 and 3

Q.39 Based on which areas was the Hoyt's Sector theory presented?

A. France   **B.** Germany

C. U.K   **D.** U.S.A

Q.40 Which of the following are the major problems of rural-urban fringe areas?

A. Lack of ownership rights

B. Development of slum areas

C. Garbage and sewage dumping site

D. All of the above

Q.41 Which of the following is NOT a factor affecting location of industries?

A. Machines   **B.** Capital

C. Insurance   **D.** Climate

Q.42 Read the following statements and select the correct answer from the code given below:

(a) The communication industry is not considered as part of the knowledge industry.

(b) The emergence of knowledge industry has led to decline in capitalism.

(c) The pharmaceutical industry is a major knowledge industry.

(d) The pharmaceutical industry employs highly educated people.

A. Only (a) is true

B. (a) and (b) are true

C. (c) and (d) are true

D. (b), (c) and (d) are true

Q.43 Which of the following are the tasks of any product in the Information and Communication Technology (ICT) sector? Select your answer from the code given below:

(a) Storage of data

(b) Retrieval of data

(c) Planning for data

(d) Manipulation of data

(e) Creation of data

A. (a) and (b)   **B.** (a), (b) and (c)

C. (a), (b) and (d)   **D.** (a), (c) and (e)

Q.44 Which among the following is not associated with the Pacific Ocean?

A. Albatross Plateau   **B.** Challenger Deep

C. Challenger Rise   **D.** Fiji Basin

Q.45 Given below are two statements, one labelled as assertion(A) and other labelled as reason(R).

Assertion- Cultivation, agricultural labour, forestry represents primary activities.

Reason- This classification of workers closely corresponds to the standard industrial classification of workers at the first digit level.

Select the correct answer from options given below :

A. Both A and R are true and R correctly explains A

B. Both A and R are true but R does not explain A

C. A is true and R is false.

D. Both A and R are false

Q.46 Direction: Read the passage and answer the following questions that follow.

A **region** is an area on Earth's surface marked by a degree of formal, functional, or perceptual homogeneity of some phenomenon. The three main types of regions are formal, functional, and vernacular regions. A **formal region,** also known as a uniform or homogeneous region, is an area in which everyone shares in common one or more distinctive characteristics. This common characteristic could be a cultural value such as language, an economic activity such as production of a certain crop, or an environmental property such as climate and weather patterns. Whatever the common characteristic is, it is present throughout the selected region. A **functional region,** also known as a nodal region, is a region organized around a node or focal point. The characteristic chosen to define a functional region dominates at a central focus or node and diminishes in importance outward. The region is tied to the central point by transportation, communication systems or by economic or functional associations. An example of a functional region is the circulation area of a newspaper. That area is centered around the city in which the newspaper is published in. The farther away from the city of circulation, the less people that read the newspaper. A **vernacular region,** also known as perceptual region, is a place that people exists as part of their cultural identity. Perceptual regions vary from person to person. They emerge from a person's informal sense of place. An example of a vernacular region would be the South.

An area on the earth marked by homogeneity is called as

A. District   **B.** Town   **C.** Region   **D.** Village

Q.47 Direction: Read the passage and answer the following questions that follow.

A **region** is an area on Earth's surface marked by a degree of formal, functional, or perceptual homogeneity of some phenomenon. The three main types of regions are formal, functional, and vernacular regions. A **formal region,** also known as a uniform or homogeneous region, is an area in which everyone shares in common one or more distinctive characteristics. This common characteristic could be a cultural value such as language, an economic activity such as production of a certain crop, or an environmental property such as climate and weather patterns. Whatever the common characteristic is, it is present throughout the selected region. A **functional region,** also known as a nodal region, is a region organized around a node or focal point. The characteristic chosen to define a functional region dominates at a central focus or node and diminishes in importance outward. The region is tied to the central point by transportation, communication systems or by economic or functional associations. An example of a functional region is the circulation area of a newspaper. That area is centered around the city in which the newspaper is published in. The farther away from the city of circulation, the less people that read the newspaper. A **vernacular region,** also known as perceptual region, is a place that people exists as part of their cultural identity. Perceptual regions vary from person to person. They emerge from a person's informal sense of place. An example of a vernacular region would be the South.

Which of the following is NOT a main type of region?

A.   Formal region
B.   Functional Region
C.   Vernacular Region
D.   Administrative region

Q.48 Direction: Read the passage and answer the following questions that follow.

A **region** is an area on Earth's surface marked by a degree of formal, functional, or perceptual homogeneity of some phenomenon. The three main types of regions are formal, functional, and vernacular regions. A **formal region,** also known as a uniform or homogeneous region, is an area in which everyone shares in common one or more distinctive characteristics. This common characteristic could be a cultural value such as language, an economic activity such as production of a certain crop, or an environmental property such as climate and weather patterns. Whatever the common characteristic is, it is present throughout the selected region. A **functional region,** also known as a nodal region, is a region organized around a node or focal point. The characteristic chosen to define a functional region dominates at a central focus or node and diminishes in importance outward. The region is tied to the central point by transportation, communication systems or by economic or functional associations. An example of a functional region is the circulation area of a newspaper. That area is centered around the city in which the newspaper is published in. The farther away from the city of circulation, the less people that read the newspaper. A **vernacular region,** also known as perceptual

region, is a place that people exists as part of their cultural identity. Perceptual regions vary from person to person. They emerge from a person's informal sense of place. An example of a vernacular region would be the South.

In a functional region, the whole region is Not tied to a central point by

A.   Transportation
B.   Climate
C.   Communications systems
D.   Economic association

Q.49 Direction: Read the passage and answer the following questions that follow.

A **region** is an area on Earth's surface marked by a degree of formal, functional, or perceptual homogeneity of some phenomenon. The three main types of regions are formal, functional, and vernacular regions. A **formal region,** also known as a uniform or homogeneous region, is an area in which everyone shares in common one or more distinctive characteristics. This common characteristic could be a cultural value such as language, an economic activity such as production of a certain crop, or an environmental property such as climate and weather patterns. Whatever the common characteristic is, it is present throughout the selected region. A **functional region,** also known as a nodal region, is a region organized around a node or focal point. The characteristic chosen to define a functional region dominates at a central focus or node and diminishes in importance outward. The region is tied to the central point by transportation, communication systems or by economic or functional associations. An example of a functional region is the circulation area of a newspaper. That area is centered around the city in which the newspaper is published in. The farther away from the city of circulation, the less people that read the newspaper. A **vernacular region,** also known as perceptual region, is a place that people exists as part of their cultural identity. Perceptual regions vary from person to person. They emerge from a person's informal sense of place. An example of a vernacular region would be the South.

Which of the following regions **can not** be considered as a vernacular region?

A. North-Eastern India   **B.** South India
C. Deccan plateau   **D.** North India

Q.50 Direction: Read the passage and answer the following questions that follow.

A **region** is an area on Earth's surface marked by a degree of formal, functional, or perceptual homogeneity of some phenomenon. The three main types of regions are formal, functional, and vernacular regions. A **formal region,** also known as a uniform or homogeneous region, is an area in which everyone shares in common one or more distinctive characteristics. This common characteristic could be a cultural value such as language, an economic activity such as production of a certain crop, or an environmental property such as climate and weather patterns. Whatever the common characteristic is, it is present throughout the selected region. A **functional region,** also known as a nodal region, is a region organized around a node or focal point. The characteristic chosen to define a functional region dominates at a central

focus or node and diminishes in importance outward. The region is tied to the central point by transportation, communication systems or by economic or functional associations. An example of a functional region is the circulation area of a newspaper. That area is centered around the city in which the newspaper is published in. The farther away from the city of circulation, the less people that read the newspaper. A **vernacular region,** also known as perceptual region, is a place that people exists as part of their cultural identity. Perceptual regions vary from person to person. They emerge from a person's informal sense of place. An example of a vernacular region would be the South.

Climatic region is a type of

A. Formal region

B. Functional Region

C. Vernacular region

D. Linguistics region

Q.51 Tea is cultivated by

A. Mixed farming

B. Mediterranean agriculture

C. Shifting Cultivation

D. Commercial Plantation

Q.52 Match List-I with List-II

List-I (Method)	List-II(Formula)
(a) Weaver's crop combination	i. $D = \dfrac{\Sigma D^2 p - D^2 n}{N^2}$
(b) Doi's crop combination	ii. $\dfrac{r_1 + r_2 + r_3 + \cdots \ldots + \cdots + r_n}{n}$
(c) Rafiuulah's crop combination	iii. Σd^2
(d) Ranking Coefficient Index	iv. $d = \dfrac{\Sigma d^2}{n}$

A. (a)-(iv),(b)-(iii),(c)-(i),(d)-(ii)

B. (a)-(iii),(b)-(iv),(c)-(i),(d)-(ii)

C. (a)-(ii),(b)-(i),(c)-(iv),(d)-(iii)

D. (a)-(iv),(b)-(iii),(c)-(ii),(d)-(i)

Q.53 Select the correct arrangement of rings of various activities as per the updated model by Von Thunen.

A. Milk production-Firewood Production-Livestock Farming-Crop farming without fallow

B. Crop farming without fallow-Milk Production-Firewood Production-Livestock farming

C. Firewood production-Milk Production-Crop farming without fallow-Livestock farming

D. Milk production-Firewood Production-Crop farming without fallow-Livestock farming

Q.54 When was the first international organization of oceanography created as the International Council for the Exploration of the Sea?

A. 1902　　**B.** 1903　　**C.** 1904　　**D.** 1905

Q.55 Which of the following option is correct?

A. Mackinder presented his Heartland theory by using the Mercator projection system which also created a false picture of the world.

B. The outer or insular crescent consists largely of North and South America, Australia, British Isles, Japanese Islands, and Africa.

C. Events such as the rise of Germany as a major continental

power in Europe and the collapse of Russian state led to the development of the Heartland theory.

D. All of the above

Q.56 Given below are two statements. One is labelled as Assertion (A) and the other is labelled as Reason (R).

Assertion (A): The Environment and Human Health are interdependent

Reason (R): Environment and Human Health are determined by the interplay and integration of the internal environment and the external environment which surrounds humans.

Select the correct answer from options given below:

A. Both (A) and (R) are true and (R) is the correct explanation of (A)

B. Both (A) and (R) are true, but (R) is not the correct explanation of (A)

C. (A) is true, but (R) is false.

D. (A) is false, but (R) is true.

Q.57 Given below are two statements. One is labelled as Assertion (A) and the other is labelled as Reason (R).

Assertion (A): Cultural ecology tries to understand adaptation of humans to the environment

Reason (R) : It applies idea from systems theory and ecology.

Select the correct answer from options given below:

A. Both (A) and (R) are true and (R) is the correct explanation of (A)

B. Both (A) and (R) are true, but (R) is not the correct explanation of (A)

C. (A) is true, but (R) is false

D. (A) is false, but (R) is true

Q.58 Match List-I with List-II:

List I (Branch)	List II (Language)
a. Munda	1. sindhi/Kachchhi
b. Assam-Burmese	2. Gondi
c. Central Dravidian	3. Tripuri
d. Indo-Aryan	4. Korku

Choose the correct option:

A. a-4 b-3 c-2 d-1

B. a-3 b-4 c-1 d-2

C. a-1 b-2 c-3 d-4

D. a-2 b-3 c-4 d-1

Q.59 Match List-I with List-II and select the correct answer from the codes given below :

List-I (authors)	List-II (books)
a) Agnew	i) Social problems in India
b) Ahuja	ii) Place and politics
c) Maxwell	iii) Partition of Punjab
d) Satya	iv) India China War

Choose the correct options from the following:

A. a-iii b-ii c-i d-iv

B. a-i b-iv c-ii d-iii

C. a-ii b-i c-iv d-iii

D. a-iii b-i c-iv d-ii

Q.60 Which of the following geographers was NOT in support of human geography?

A. Carl Ritter

B. Strabo

C. Ptolemy

D. Fredrick Ratzel

Q.61 Match List-I with List-II

List-I (Geographers)	List-II(Field of study)
(a) Alexander Von Humboldt	(i) Regional Geography
(b) Hartshorne & Hettner	(ii) Deterministic Geography
(c) Ellen Semple	(iii) Possibilistic
(d) Vidal de la Blache	(iv) General Geography

Select the correct answer from the options given below:
A. (a)-(iv),(b)-(ii),(c)-(iii),(d)-(i)
B. (a)-(iv),(b)-(i),(c)-(ii),(d)-(iii)
C. (a)-(ii),(b)-(iii),(c)-(i),(d)-(iv)
D. (a)-(ii),(b)-(iii),(c)-(iv),(d)-(i)

Q.62 Read the following statements and select the correct answer from the code given below:
(a) The term 'Paradigm' was crafted by Richard Hartshorne.
(b) Kuhn was of the opinion that science undergoes periodic revolutions which are called as paradigm shifts.
(c) The paradigm is defined as universally recognized scientific achievements that for a time provide a model problems and solutions to a community of practitioners.
(d) According to Kuhn, the scientific knowledge progresses and develops like a mountain.
Code:
A. (b) and (d) are true
B. (a) and (d) are true
C. (a), (b) and (d) are true
D. (a) and (c) are true

Q.63 Given below are two statements. One is labelled as Assertion (A) and the other is labelled as Reason (R).
Assertion (A): Earth science as a tradition is regarded with respect in the scientific community.
Reason (R): The earth science tradition has concrete objects that can be studied.
Select the correct answer from options given below:
A. Both (A) and (R) are true and (R) is the correct explanation of (A)
B. Both (A) and (R) are true, but (R) is not the correct explanation of (A)
C. (A) is true, but (R) is false
D. (A) is false, but (R) is true

Q.64 The Nomothetic and Ideographic approaches to geography was given by
A. Anaximander
B. Homer
C. Thales
D. Hecataeus

Q.65 Given below are two statements. One is labelled as Assertion (A) and the other is labelled as Reason (R).
Assertion (A): The North-South Line was identified by the Egyptians.
Reason (R): Egyptians developed ways of measuring land.
Select the correct answer from options given below:
A. Both (A) and (R) are true and (R) is the correct explanation of (A)
B. Both (A) and (R) are true, but (R) is not the correct explanation of (A)

C. (A) is true, but (R) is false
D. (A) is false, but (R) is true

Q.66 Select the incorrect pair among the ones given below:
A. NATMO-Thematic mapping
B. Geological Survey of India-Gseological maps
C. Naval Hydrographic Office-Topographic maps
D. Indian Meteorological Department- Climatic maps

Q.67 Given below are two statements. One is labelled as Assertion (A) and the other is labelled as Reason (R).
Assertion (A): CARTOSAT-2 had a single high-resolution panchromatic camera.
Reason (R): It was developed for use in industrial purposes.
Select the correct answer from options given below:
A. Both (A) and (R) are true and (R) is the correct explanation of (A)
B. Both (A) and (R) are true, but (R) is not the correct explanation of (A)
C. (A) is true, but (R) is false
D. (A) is false, but (R) is true

Q.68 Which of the following is NOT a characteristic of post-modernism?
A. It stresses openness in social and geographical enquiry
B. It opposes the idea of structuralism
C. It focuses on generalization
D. It emphasizes heterogeneity

Q.69 Who made the first behavioral model?
A. Wolpert **B.** Kirk **C.** Reclus **D.** Wright

Q.70 Match List I with List II

List I (Measures of central Tendency)	List II (properties)
a. Arithmetic Mean	i. Particularly suitable for averaging ratios, rates and percentages
b. Mode	ii. Applicable to qualitative data.
c. Median	iii. Easy and does not involve any laborious numerical calculations.
d. Geometric mean	iv. Large number of observations are required to perform.

A. a –i b – iv c – iii d - ii
B. a –iv b – iii c – i d - ii
C. a –iii b – iv c – ii d - i
D. a –iii b – iv c – i d - ii

Q.71 A dimensionless number denoting the ratio of streams of two orders is called?
A. Bifurcation Ratio
B. Slope analysis
C. Drainage density
D. Drainage frequency

Q.72 What is the measure of relative size of streams called?
A. Stream Order
B. Bifurcation ratio
C. Hypsographic curve
D. slope analysis

Q.73 Which among the following concepts means drawing of contours on the basis of known heights of neighbouring points?
A. Contour interpolation

B. Contour interpretation

C. Contours extrapolation

D. Form lining

Q.74 Which among the following refers to the diagrammatic representation of statistical map, where purposeful distortion is sought, to put the distribution pattern of the particular element represented into bold relief?

A. Cartogram   **B.** Pyramidal Diagram

C. Pictogram   **D.** Riband

Q.75 There are four individuals whose average height is 170 cm. If the height of first three persons are 160 cm, 180 cm and185 cm respectively, what is the height of the fourth person?

A. 155 cm   **B.** 162.5 cm

C. 165 cm   **D.** 145 cm

Q.76 Which among the following means the same as the total length of the streams draining that area divided by the area?

A. Elongation Ratio

B. Stream Order

C. Stream Length Ratio

D. Drainage Density

Q.77 Which of the following concepts in morphometric analysis refers to the overall steepness of the drainage basin?

A. Relief Ratio   **B.** Stream Order

C. Drainage Density   **D.** Circulatory Ratio

Q.78 Which of the following projection was used by the Survey of India toposheets prior to the National Map Policy, 2005?

A. Polyconic Projection

B. Mercator

C. Azimuthal

D. Stereographic Projection

Q.79 Which of the following is an example of non-spatial data?

A. Point   **B.** Line

C. Polygon   **D.** Temperature

Q.80 Given below are two statements, one labeled as assertion(A) and other labeled as reason(R).

Assertion(A)- Convectional rainfall is more common in equatorial region.

Reason(R)- Rainfall in equator and nearby region occur in late afternoon.

A. Both (A) and (R) are true and (R) is the correct explanation of (A)

B. Both (A) and (R) are true, but (R) is not the correct explanation of (A)

C. (A) is true, but (R) is false

D. (A) is false, but (R) is true

Q.81 What is the amount of present fish production in India?

A. 5.6 mmt   **B.** 13.7 mmt

C. 9.5 mmt   **D.** 11.8 mmt

Q.82 The Sahyadris commence in ________.

A. Maharashtra   **B.** Kerala

C. Karnataka   **D.** Delhi

Q.83 Match the List-I with List-II.

List-I (State)	List-II (Infant Mortality rate)
a) a) Andhra Pradesh	(i) 36
b) Arunachal Pradesh	(ii) 34
c) Assam	(iii) 44
d) Bihar	(iv) 38

Code:

A. a-i b-iii c-ii d-iv   **B.** a-ii b-i c-iii d-iv

C. a-i b-ii c-iii d-iv   **D.** a-iii b-i c-iv d-ii

Q.84 What amount of rainfall is witnessed by eastern Himalayan region?

A. 200cm-400cm   **B.** 75cm-150cm

C. 100cm-200cm   **D.** >40cm

Q.85 What is the full form of DPIIT?

A. Department of promotion of industry and internal trade

B. Daily promotion of industrial and internal trade.

C. Demand product increasing initiative team

D. Demand promotion and index of investment team

Q.86 In July of 1991 the Indian government devalued the rupee by

A. 19%   **B.** 25%   **C.** 30%   **D.** 50%

Q.87 Kutch region of Gujarat comes under which earthquake zone?

A. Very high damage risk zone

B. High damage risk zone

C. Moderate damage risk zone

D. Low damage risk zone

Q.88 In Bay of Bengal, cyclones mostly develop during the months of

A. July and August

B. October and November

C. March and April

D. May and June

Q.89 Match List-I with the List-II and select the correct answer from the code given below:

List - I (Tribes)	List - II (States)
(a) Todas	(i) Arunachal Pradesh
(b) Adis	(ii) Rajasthan
(c) Garasia	(iii) Himachal Pradesh
(d) Gaddis	(iv) Tamil Nadu

Code:

A. (a)-(i), (b)-(iii), (c)-(iv), (d)-(ii)

B. (a)-(ii), (b)-(iii), (c)-(iv), (d)-(i)

C. (a)-(i), (b)-(iv), (c)-(iii), (d)-(ii)

D. (a)-(iv), (b)-(i), (c)-(ii), (d)-(iii)

Q.90 Given below are two statements on urbanization in India as per Census of India, 2011. One is labelled as Assertion (A) and the other is labelled as Reason (R).

Assertion (A): Goa has the highest percentage of urban population among the states in India.

Reason (R): Goa experienced the highest negative decadal growth in its rural population among all the states.

Select the correct answer from options given below:

A. Both (A) and (R) are true and (R) is the correct explanation of (A)

B. Both (A) and (R) are true, but (R) is not the correct explanation of (A)

C. (A) is true, but (R) is false

D. (A) is false, but (R) is true

Q.91 Which of the following statements are correct about the Himalayas?

(a) Himalayas play a significant role in the case of Indian monsoons.

(b) The doons are important features of the middle Himalayas.

(c) Siachen glacier is the largest glacier of the Greater Himalayan range.

(d) Bara Shigri is an important glacier in the Pir Panjal range.

Code:

A. (a) and (d)
B. (a) and (c)
C. (b) and (c)
D. (b), (c) and (d)

Q.92 Which of the following states has the highest proportion of their geographical area under forests?

A. Madhya Pradesh
B. Himachal Pradesh
C. Uttarakhand
D. Arunachal Pradesh

Q.93 Which of the following statements relating to the vegetation in India are correct?

(a) Kanchenjunga National Park is the first mixed heritage site of India declared by UNESCO.

(b) The Sunderbans is the largest biosphere reserve in India.

(c) Panna is the smallest biosphere reserve in India.

(d) The Forest policy of India aimed at bringing 25 per cent of area under forest cover.

Code:

A. (b) and (c)
B. (a) and (c)
C. (a), (c) and (d)
D. (b), (c) and (d)

Q.94 Which of the following statements about Indian agriculture is not correct?

A. The Soil and Land Use Survey of India conducts soil survey in the country for national land-based developmental programme.

B. India is experiencing a decline in the average size of operational land holdings in India.

C. However, in the case of land holdings in the Large category (with size of 10 hectares and above), it is experiencing an increase both in terms of area and average size of the land holdings.

D. Agricultural land is the most dominant land use in the country followed by the forest area.

Q.95 Given below are two statements. One is labelled as Assertion (A) and the other is labelled as Reason (R).

Assertion (A): *Zaid* is a short duration summer cropping season while Rabi and Kharif and Rabi are long cropping seasons.

Reason (R): Such distinction of cropping seasons is present in the southern part of India.

Select the correct answer from options given below:

A. Both (A) and (R) are true and (R) is the correct explanation of (A)

B. Both (A) and (R) are true, but (R) is not the correct explanation of (A)

C. (A) is true, but (R) is false

D. (A) is false, but (R) is true

Q.96 Which state is the largest producer of fertilizer in India?

A. Gujarat
B. Maharashtra
C. Uttar Pradesh
D. Madhya Pradesh

Q.97 Given below are two statements. One is labelled as Assertion (A) and the other is labelled as Reason (R).

Assertion (A): There are urgent need for development of road capacity in India.

Reason (R): The population of India is increasing at a high rate.

Select the correct answer from options given below:

A. Both (A) and (R) are true and (R) is the correct explanation of (A)

B. Both (A) and (R) are true, but (R) is not the correct explanation of (A)

C. (A) is true, but (R) is false

D. (A) is false, but (R) is true

Q.98 Match List-I with the List-II relating to regions and dominant industries and select the correct answer from the code given below:

List - I (Region)	List - II (Industries)
(a) Rourkela	(i) Petrochemical
(b) Ahmedabad	(ii) Software Tech Parks
(c) Noida	(iii) Iron and Steel
(d) Jamnagar	(iv) Cotton textile

Code:

A. (a)-(iii), (b)-(i), (c)-(ii), (d)-(iv)
B. (a)-(ii), (b)-(iii), (c)-(iv), (d)-(i)
C. (a)-(i), (b)-(iv), (c)-(iii), (d)-(ii)
D. (a)-(iii), (b)-(iv), (c)-(ii), (d)-(i)

Q.99 The Great Bath of Indus Valley civilisation is found at

A. Harappa
B. Mohenjo-Daro
C. Ropar
D. Kalibangan

Q.100 The Social System of the Harappans was

A. Fairly egalitarian
B. Slave Labour based
C. Colour Varna based
D. Caste based

// Smart Answer Sheet //

Correct — Percentage of students who answered correctly. **Skipped** — Percentage of students who skipped.

Q.	Ans.	Correct	Skipped	Q.	Ans.	Correct	Skipped	Q.	Ans.	Correct	Skipped	Q.	Ans.	Correct	Skipped	Q.	Ans.	Correct	Skipped
1	B	35.56 %	15.55 %	17	B	22.22 %	44.45 %	33	D	11.11 %	35.56 %	49	C	28.89 %	44.44 %	65	A	33.33 %	44.45 %
2	D	22.22 %	37.78 %	18	A	0 %	100 %	34	A	11.11 %	40.0 %	50	A	33.33 %	37.78 %	66	C	42.22 %	37.78 %
3	B	15.56 %	35.55 %	19	C	31.11 %	24.45 %	35	A	33.33 %	33.34 %	51	D	57.78 %	35.55 %	67	C	15.56 %	44.44 %
4	A	42.22 %	42.22 %	20	B	46.67 %	35.55 %	36	D	51.11 %	35.56 %	52	A	44.44 %	35.56 %	68	C	22.22 %	42.22 %
5	B	26.67 %	44.44 %	21	C	53.33 %	35.56 %	37	D	46.67 %	44.44 %	53	D	35.56 %	44.44 %	69	B	37.78 %	44.44 %
6	C	8.89 %	37.78 %	22	C	33.33 %	40.0 %	38	D	42.22 %	37.78 %	54	A	15.56 %	37.77 %	70	C	17.78 %	42.22 %
7	D	22.22 %	42.22 %	23	B	22.22 %	35.56 %	39	D	15.56 %	42.22 %	55	D	44.44 %	37.78 %	71	A	44.44 %	35.56 %
8	C	37.78 %	40.0 %	24	C	33.33 %	42.23 %	40	D	48.89 %	40.0 %	56	A	46.67 %	42.22 %	72	A	40.0 %	35.56 %
9	B	6.67 %	44.44 %	25	D	26.67 %	44.44 %	41	A	6.67 %	35.55 %	57	B	13.33 %	44.45 %	73	A	33.33 %	44.45 %
10	B	15.56 %	37.77 %	26	D	24.44 %	40.0 %	42	C	22.22 %	42.22 %	58	A	35.56 %	37.77 %	74	A	15.56 %	37.77 %
11	C	48.89 %	37.78 %	27	C	15.56 %	35.55 %	43	C	24.44 %	35.56 %	59	C	26.67 %	37.77 %	75	A	26.67 %	44.44 %
12	D	13.33 %	40.0 %	28	A	37.78 %	44.44 %	44	C	11.11 %	42.22 %	60	C	31.11 %	35.56 %	76	D	31.11 %	37.78 %
13	B	17.78 %	35.55 %	29	B	31.11 %	35.56 %	45	B	22.22 %	35.56 %	61	B	33.33 %	44.45 %	77	A	28.89 %	44.44 %
14	D	37.78 %	40.0 %	30	B	26.67 %	37.77 %	46	C	42.22 %	42.22 %	62	A	33.33 %	37.78 %	78	A	13.33 %	40.0 %
15	D	6.67 %	37.77 %	31	D	48.89 %	37.78 %	47	D	37.78 %	37.78 %	63	A	40.0 %	37.78 %	79	D	53.33 %	35.56 %
16	D	31.11 %	35.56 %	32	A	26.67 %	35.55 %	48	B	44.44 %	42.23 %	64	D	20.0 %	44.44 %	80	B	13.33 %	35.56 %

Q.	Ans.	Correct		Q.	Ans.	Correct		Q.	Ans.	Correct		Q.	Ans.	Correct		Q.	Ans.	Correct
		Skipped				Skipped				Skipped				Skipped				Skipped
81	B	24.44 %		85	A	42.22 %		89	D	37.78 %		93	B	24.44 %		97	A	24.44 %
		35.56 %				44.45 %				44.44 %				35.56 %				44.45 %
82	A	40.0 %		86	A	17.78 %		90	C	4.44 %		94	C	37.78 %		98	D	48.89 %
		37.78 %				40.0 %				42.23 %				42.22 %				40.0 %
83	B	13.33 %		87	A	24.44 %		91	A	13.33 %		95	B	13.33 %		99	B	42.22 %
		44.45 %				44.45 %				44.45 %				37.78 %				37.78 %
84	A	33.33 %		88	B	22.22 %		92	D	11.11 %		96	A	20.0 %		100	A	35.56 %
		37.78 %				42.22 %				42.22 %				37.78 %				37.77 %

//Hints and Solutions//

1. Epeirogenic movement or epeirogenetic movement are also called as continent building processes. Epeirogenetic movements cause upliftment and subsidence of continental masses through upward and downward movements, respectively. On the other hand orogenic or orogenetic movement refers to mountain building. It consists of forces movements like folding and faulting. Both orogenic and epeirogenic movements are part of diastrophic movements.

2. Transcurrent faults are the kind of faults where the movement is nearly horizontal and crustal blocks slide past each other and unlike other kind of faults does not cause conspicuous deformation like horst or graben. It is the parallel normal faults which can drop a block of crust down into a graben , or push a block up, into a horst.

3. Mafic magma is also called basaltic magma because the when the lava solidifies outside the crust, it becomes basalt. But, the mafic magma turns into gabbro if it solidifies inside the crust. Similarly the felsic or rhyolitic magma is named after rhyolite volcanic rocks. The solidified plutonic rock for felsic magma is granite. Tephra is nothing pyroclastic material of smaller sizes where bombs and blocks are the largest in size followed by lapilli and the smallest particles being ash. Higher gas content of the magma indicates higher viscosity but higher temperature indicates less viscosity.

4. Shield volcanoes are formed of mafic and basalt lava. They have gentle to less steep slopes because the basaltic lava is characterized with less silica content and thus less viscosity and travel long distances. Hawaiian volcanoes are a good example of shield volcanoes.

5. Tsunami is not included in mass movement process because it is the result of sudden endogenic force and not exogenetic force. Moreover, the tsunamis are not earthquake in itself, rather the waves generated by the tremors of an earthquake. Tsunamis would only occur if the epicenter of the earthquake is below oceanic waters and the magnitude of the earthquake is sufficiently high.

6. Salt-crystal growth is a physical weathering process. Except salt-crystal growth all other types of weathering mentioned are chemical weathering processes. However, salt-crystal growth is similar to frost cracking, but occurs in dry climates where salt crystal growth in crevices and pores builds up pressure and can disintegrate rock.

7. Flowstone is a typical feature of a karst landform. They are structures most commonly found in caverns where there is a flow of water along with calcite minerals down the walls or along the floor of the caves. When the flowing water carries dissolved minerals like calcium carbonate or gypsum, it might deposit the minerals on walls and floors and these deposits will soon develop in layers to form flowstones.

8. Walther Penck, a German geomorphologist is known to have criticized key elements of Davisian cycle of erosion and in the response to which he tried to present his "Morphological analysis of landforms". In his morphological analysis of landforms, primarumpf is used to denote the initial geomorphic unit (low height and relief) for beginning of the development of all sorts of landforms.

9. The earthquake waves are of two types: Body waves and Surface waves. Body waves are faster than surface waves. Primary waves (p-waves) and secondary waves (s-waves) are two of the body waves which moves through the body of earth in different directions from the focus of the earthquake before reaching the surface. P-waves is the fastest of all waves and can travel through any medium while S-waves can only travel through solid materials and which is why beyond 105° from the epicentre of the earthquake the s-waves can't be felt. Surface waves are the generated due to body waves, but are more destructive than body waves. Love waves is the fastest surface wave while Rayleigh waves are the most destructive surface wave because when it rolls, it moves the ground up and down, and side-to-side in the same direction that the wave is moving.

10. Lester King was an English geomorphologist and geologist who worked upon slope development in the semi-arid climate of South Africa. He is the one who gave the slope replacement model of slope retreat in which steep slope is progressively replaced by lower slope deposits. The upper slope retreats parallel to itself while the lower slope gets replaced with deposits and forms what we called Pediplains.

11. Tectonic plate is a slab of rock, composed of continental and oceanic lithosphere. Plate tectonics is the movement of these plates leading to various geographical phenomena. On the basis of its nature, plats are named as oceanic and continental plate. Plate tectonic theory explains the formation of volcanoes, earthquakes, existence of ocean basin etc.

12. The term originally used by Chamberlin and Salisbury in 1904. It was used to include "all those processes which tend to bring the surface of lithosphere to a common level". They recognized that gradational processes belong to two categories- those which level down, degradation, and those which level up, aggradation.

13.

- Eliot Blackwelder has done the work "Exfoliation as a phase of rock weathering" in 1925.
- L.N Bowen is the author of the work " the reaction principle in petrogenesis" in 1922.
- T.C Chamberlin is the author of the work "geological process and their result" in 1904.
- R.W chapman and Greenfield M.A is the author of the work "Spheroidal weathering of igneous rocks" in 1949.

14. A rift valley is the result of two divergent late margins. When two plates are diverted by the tectonic activities forming a fault, in case of a rift valley, a piece of surface gets dropped between the other two blocks forming a graben. The rivers in India flowing through a rift valley are Narmada, Tapti, Mahi and River Damodar in Chota Nagpur plateau.

15.

- Volcano Huascaran is an extinct volcano of Peru.
- Kyushu-Palau Ridge is an extinct volcano in the Philippine sea.

- Mt. Buninyong is an extinct volcano in Australia
- Tamu Massif is an extinct volcano present in the northwest Pacific Ocean.

16. A tornado is a rapidly rotating column of air around a small area of intense low pressure with a circulation reaching the ground. It is actually a product of thunderstorm. It usually extends down from the base of a cumulonimbus cloud and can strike sporadically and violently.

17. Thornthwaite believed that temperature had an important role in the growth of vegetation. He, thus, devised an index of thermal efficiency which was expressed by the positive departure of mean monthly temperatures from the freezing point and proposed the following above formulae. T-E index is the sum of thermal efficiency ratios for 12 months. On the basis of the T-E index, he also divided the world into 6 temperature provinces which are A' Tropical, B' mesothermal, C' Microthermal, D' Taiga, E' Tundra, F' Frost.

32 climatic types were devised by Thornthwaite in 1931 on the basis of precipitation, thermal effectiveness and seasonal distribution.

18. Thornthwaite was an American climatologist. He gave climatic classification in 1933, which he modified in 1948. His climatic classification took precipitation efficiency and temperature effectiveness as parameters for delineation of climatic region. Precipitation efficiency ratio is calculated as monthly precipitation divided but monthly evaporation. Precipitation efficiency index is the sum total of precipitation efficiency index for the 12 months of the year. On the basis of precipitation efficiency index, Thornthwaite made 5 humidity zones which include A-wet, B-humid, C- Sub humid, D-Semiarid and E-Arid.

19. The heat wave is a period of prolonged high surface temperatures relative to those normally expected. In India, an increase of 5-6^0 C above the normal temperature is the norm for a heat wave. Exhaustion, sun stroke or heatstroke, dehydration can be some of the effects of heat waves. In 2015, a heat wave in India killed around 2500 people. As per World Meteorological Department, the heat wave is a rise of 5-6^0 F above the normal temperatures.

20. Albedo is the reflectance of solar energy from the earth's surface. The earth's average albedo called planetary albedo is 35%. Albedo of various surfaces: Fresh snow percentage is 80-85, old snow's percentage is 50-60, sand's percentage of albedo is 20-30 percent and grass's albedo are 20-25.

21. Koppen's system is strictly empirical. This is to say that each climate is defines according to the fixed values of temperatures and precipitation computed according to the averages of the year or of the individual month.

Aw – tropical savanna

Bs- steppe climate

Bw-desert climate

Cw- Temperate rainy climate with dry winter

Cf- Temperate rainy climate with moist all season

Cs- Temperate rainy climate with dry summer

DF- Cold snowy forest climate moist in seasons

Dw-Cold snowy forest climate with any winter

ET- Tundra Climate.

22. The fronts in the equatorial or tropical regions are called intertropical fronts which form at the meeting ground of north east and south east trade winds. It is also called intertropical convergence.

23. The ocean adjacent to Asia and north America being relatively low, high pressure cells develop over there. The high-pressure cells which develop over north pacific is called 'Pacific High' and the one which develop over North Atlantic is called 'Azores High'.

24. Cyclone is a large-scale air mass that rotates around a strong centre of low atmospheric pressure. They are inward spiral wind that rotate about a zone of low pressure.

The 2019 cyclone of region are-

Bangladesh had fani cyclone

Maldives had hikka cyclone

India had vayu cyclone

Pakistan had bulbul cyclone

25. The Sumatra Tsunami of 2004 hit several Indian coasts, but the Tamil Nadu coast was the most affected coastal state. Nagapattinam, Cuddalore as well as the Kanyakumari districts of Tamil Nadu suffered widespread damage from this Tsunami which toppled structures and assets as well as huge loss of life and property.

26. Tsunamis are also called seismic sea waves. Sudden vertical movements along the faults, landslides in the ocean bed all causes displacement in the volume of water and can generate tsunami waves which are shallow in nature but laden with high energy. Icebergs falling from glaciers can also causes tsunami.

27. When the tide is channeled between islands or into bays and estuaries are called tidal currents. The rise or fall in sea level as a tide crest approaches and passes will cause a tidal current of water to flow into or out of bays and harbors.

28. Ocean currents help in temperature and salinity redistribution over the oceans. The warm currents from the lower latitude moves towards the poles and the cold currents from the higher latitudes sinks down and moves underwater towards the low latitudes and in this way the energy redistribution in the form of temperature takes place. Shape of the ocean does have its impact on ocean circulation. The Indian Ocean witness seasonal reversal of ocean currents along with the seasonal reversal of atmospheric conditions called monsoons.

29. Offshore winds are the winds that blow from the coasts towards the sea. In this process, the winds at the surface also drag the water at the coast along its path and this displacement of surface water is replaced by the upwelling of cold water from below the sea surface. The isotherms are more regular and parallel to latitudes in the southern hemisphere vis-à-vis northern hemisphere because of vast surface of water and less continental area in southern hemisphere. The enclosed seas in the lower

latitudes – owing to the high temperature of the continents than the ocean – will have higher temperature as compared to the open seas.

30. • Nitrogen fixation means the conversion of atmospheric molecular nitrogen(N_2) into usable forms (such as ammonia and nitrate) in the soils which can be taken up by the plants through their roots. Lightning and biological activity are the two major pathways of nitrogen fixation.

• After the incorporation of inorganic nitrogen (NO_3) into an organic form via protein and nucleic acid synthesis, it is metabolized and returned to a major part of the cycle as waste products of that metabolism or as organized protoplasm in dead organisms. Many heterotrophic bacteria and fungi in soil and water use this organic nitrogen-rich substrate. In metabolizing organic nitrogen, they convert it to and release it in an inorganic form, ammonia. This is known as ammonification or mineralization.

• Although some autotrophic and many heterotrophic marine bacteria can use ammonia or ammonium salts to synthesize their own protoplasm, it is not generally accessible in this form and must be converted to nitrite or nitrate in a process known as nitrification.

• Denitrification means transformation of nitrates into gaseous nitrogen by denitrifying bacteria and fungi which operate in anaerobic conditions which goes back to the atmospheric storage pool and thus the nitrogen cycle is complete.

31. This is all a cyclic process. The organic elements are released through the decomposition of leaf falls from plants, parts of plants and dead animals by microbes. These are again converted to inorganic materials and join the soil pool. Another way is through the burning of vegetation covers which upon burning are released to the atmosphere and again fall down on the ground surface in soluble inorganic form and join the soil storage.

32. Forests, mainly tropical evergreen rainforests, temperate evergreen and deciduous forests and boreal forests are significant storages of biological carbon of the biosphere. The CO_2 assimilated by plants is stored in the woody tissues of plants.

33. Phosphorus is one of the most essential elements in the biosphere and is in short supply as it is only found in the phosphate rocks which are found in a few places. This element has a major sedimentary phase in the biogeochemical cycle.

34. Indian Environment Policy was introduced in the year 1992 by the Ministry of Environment and Forests, Govt. of India for the abatement of pollution. However, this policy stresses on a positive attitude in the society towards prevention of pollution; integration of environmental and ecological aspects; preventive aspects of pollution and introduction of technological aspects.

35. As the agricultural Europe was slowly becoming overpopulated during the 16th and 17th centuries, there was need for migration especially for the poorer countries. There has been a flow of migration from the time when the America was discovered. The rate of migration has never been uniform and what started as a slow tickle converted to tremendous proportions during the 19th century and early 20th century due to

rapid population expansion in Europe and poor living conditions. It was that during this time migration assumed international importance. The period from 1821 to 1910, more than 26 million European went to U.S.A. alone. The bulk of emigrants came from different countries at different times. The most significant factor in European migration in the 19th century was the improvement of transportation. Introduction of steamships at a less cost and less travel time made migration much easier. At the same time the development of railways eased the migrant's passage to the European ports and enabled the to spread across the American continent. However, European migration dominated the late 19th and early 20th century, as well as for the Asians due to the transportation efficiency.

36. The population structure is analyzed in terms of age and sex groupings and is represented by the population pyramids. By studying these, it is possible to get a clear knowledge of the population characteristics of any country. However, all the three statements above are correct and are all related to population composition and characteristics.

During the 20th century, the population structure that had emerged was totally different than the 19th century. The birth rates declined due to effects of the world war and the Depression of the 1920s. Children were no longer an economic asset. Slowly this trend was adopted by most of the families. Gradually, as the birth rates fell, the population pyramid acquired a narrow base and the broad bulge in the older age groups, implying the increase in the life expectancy due to various medical improvements. Britain therefore has an aging population.

Japan is one of the countries with the lowest death and infant mortality rates in the world today. During the early 1950s, the pyramid of Japan resembled any other Traditional developing country. With the impact of industrialization, urbanism and the high living standards, the birth rates declined. Still it took around 50 years to follow the pattern of the European countries.

Population characteristics are totally different on the Latin America and Africa countries. Though the death rates have declined markedly, there remains a big difference between the proportions of birth rates which remain high. This is due to lack of hygiene, nutrition, and traditional attitudes.

37. The reason why there is a huge gap between developed and developing countries are all given above. These all lead to low level of life expectancy in the less developed countries. In the developed countries, the primary causes of death are mainly environmental hazards and harmful lifestyles rather than the infectious diseases which spread in most of the developing countries. In the less developed countries only the urban areas received medicines. However, the governments are giving greater priority to basic health needs, improving sanitation and health supplies and much more. The importance of universalizing the availability of primary health care in less developed countries can also narrow down the gap as well as bring down the infant mortality.

38. The 1st type is common in areas which normally have less than 50cm of rainfall. They are found in the western Uttar Pradesh, Rajasthan, Punjab and parts of Maharashtra and Karnataka.

The 2nd type is most common in India. In areas of heavy rainfall, the sloping roof allows water to drain off. Throughout the Ganga and Brahmaputra plains, Orissa, Tamil Nadu, Kerala and along the Malabar Coast, rural dwellings have sloping roofs.

The 3rd type is restricted to certain tribal and caste areas of India and is not found elsewhere. The one-room huts of, Chenchus of Andhra Pradesh, Todas of Nilgiris are circular with conical roof. This type is not very common in western India.

39. Homer Hoyt's Sector theory was based on 25 widely distributed cities of the U.S.A. in the year 1939. From these he concluded that the rent areas in American cities tend to conform to the pattern of sector rather than of concentric circles. Hoyt presented a directional approach to the zonal model.

40. The rural-urban fringe may be in the form of a concentric circle or rectangular. Green belt or urban fringe surrounded the city and forms part of the rural-urban fringe. However, these fringe areas offer the greatest challenges when it comes to urban planning and development. Some of the major problems are the fringe areas suffer from concentration of land ownership, speculation on land and rapidly rising land values. All these need to be regulated. Secondly, the fringe zone has been used for the relocation of slums. Thirdly, Industries emitting polluted gases or generating chemical effluents are allowed to locate in the city's surrounding fringe areas.

41. Industries need to be located in an area where it is feasible and possible to get raw materials, labour and market for the goods produced. Along with that capital, climate, and insurance, which covers cost of damage, are necessary to be considered while selecting location of industries. Machine though are not included in the list of these factors.

42. The knowledge industry has grown after the scientific revolution. A modern capitalist economy developed which relied heavily on developing technology. Hence, we can see that knowledge industry has boosted capitalism. The various industries included in this industry are education, communication, and medical products industry, including pharmaceutical industry. The pharmaceutical companies require constant research and development of newer drugs and vaccines. Hence, they always employ highly educated people for the same.

43. The sector of Information Technology and Communication is a rapidly developing sector, playing an important role in the economy as well as day to day lives of people. Even study of geography is facilitated by the use of ICT. Any product that can store, retrieve, manipulate, receive, or transmit data in electronic format is a product of the ICT sector. The product though cannot exactly create of plan for data without substantial in-hand data.

44. The mid-Atlantic ridge representing the zone of divergent or constructive plate margins is the most striking relief feature which having 'S' shape extending from Iceland to Bouvet Island. This ridge is known as Dolphin rise (north of the equator) and Challenger rise (south of the equator).

45. All towns and cities are provided with nine industrial categories of workers. This classification of workers closely corresponds to the standard industrial classification of workers at the first digit level. These categories are cultivation, agricultural labour, forestry, household industry, manufacturing other than household industry, construction, trade and commerce, transport, storage and communication and services.

46. As given in the paragraph, an area in the surface of the earth, which is marked by homogeneity or the quality of being similar, is called as a region. Further we can see that the there are three main types of region, formal, functional, and vernacular region. Another important point to remember is that regions are marked by boundaries.

47. A region is an area in the earth with some homogeneous characteristics. The region is divided into three main types: - formal region, functional region, and vernacular region. The administrative region can be named as a sub-type of the functional region. But it is not a main type of region.

48. A functional region is one of the main types of region. It is also called as nodal region. The whole region, in the case of functional region, is tied to the central point or the node, through transportation, communication systems and economic or functional characteristics. The physical characteristics like climate are not considered in functional regions.

49. The North-East, South and North India are official vernacular region of the country. Although, some customs vary from place to place, these areas have homogeneity in terms of basic cultural identity. The Deccan plateau though is a part of the physical region of the peninsular India, a formal region rather than a vernacular region.

50. A climatic region is a type of formal region. It is so because a formal region can have homogeneity in any aspect, physical characteristic like climate or production of a crop or soil. Vernacular region are cultural regions and functional regions are based organized near or around a central point or node.

51. Commercial Plantation is carried out in parts of Latin America, Africa, and Asia. It developed during the European colonization. It is highly intensive capital framing. The crops grown are commercial tree crops and include tea, coffee, rubber, and oil palm.

52.

- Weaver's crop combination uses the formula in (iv). This formula is used for agricultural regionalization.

- Doi modified Weaver's formula which was converted into formula (iii). The crop combination with lowest value of d is considered to be true.

- Rafiullah had modified Weaver's method. He named it as Maximum Positive Deviation method. This formula is (i).

- M.G. Kendall gave the Ranking Coefficient method in formula (ii). In this method, any number of units growing the same range of crops is arranged in sequence.

53. Johann Heinrich von Thunen gave the land use model. He gave different zones in the forms of the rings of various activities. He updated his own model later. In centre is the city and later comes the river which is navigable that flows from the central city to the outside. The first zone is milk production which is followed by firewood and lumber production, crop farming without fallow

and livestock farming. The new model also has a sub-centre in the north east.

54. The first international organization of oceanography was created in 1902 as the International Council for the Exploration of the Sea. In 1921 Monaco formed the International Hydrographic Bureau (IHB).

Hence, the correct option is (A).

55. Mackinder used Mercator projection map, which created false picture of the unlimited expanse of the Arctic ice separating North America from Eurasia. North America and Heartland lie face to face across the narrow expanse of the Arctic.

Beyond the inner crescent, the world ocean and the widely separated lands of the insular crescent are located. Mackinder called this as the 2nd Heartland.

Events such as the rise of Germany as a major continental power in Europe, beginning of the war, advancing of the German armies into the region of the South Russian steppe and forcing Russia to come on a term led Mackinder to some new ideas and hence came up with the Heartland theory in his book Democratic Ideals and Realities.

56. The terms Environment and Human Health are interdependent because both are determined by the interplay and integration of two ecological factors – the internal environment and the external environment which surrounds humans. Any disease is due to the disturbance of the delicate balance between humans and environment. The more the environment is polluted, the more the public health will be disturbed. Pollution due to various activities of man contributed in various ways to the general deterioration of the environment. Direct threats to human health are the most obvious aspects of environmental fragmentation.

57. The Cultural ecology is the study of human adaptations to the physical and social environments. The process of human adaptation allows the population to survive and reproduce. These processes can be biological, cultural. Geographers have tried to adapt these processes of systems theory and ecology to the forms of human adaptations. Both are true, but (R) is not the correct explanation of (A).

58. The Munda Branch falls under the Austro-Asiatic Group of Languages. This group of languages lies in the mid-Indian region and extends from Maharashtra to West Bengal. There are various languages among the Munda branch of which the Kharia, Korku and Savara languages fall which extend over Bihar, Orissa, and Madhya Pradesh.

The Assam-Burmese branch among the other 3 branches fall under the Tibeto-Burman group of languages which is the most diverse. The Tripuri language falls under the Bodo group and has around 649,940 speakers altogether according to the enumeration of 1991. About 93% of Tripuri speakers lie in Tripura.

Gondi is classified as a language of the Central Dravidian branch and is a traditional dialect of the Gonds. Recent census studies reveal a decline in the numerical strength of the Gondi speakers. More than 90% of the Gondi speakers live in Madhya Pradesh and Maharashtra as well as Andhra Pradesh and Orissa.

Sindhi is language of the Indo-Aryan branch of the northwestern group and its domain lie in the Sind province of the neighbouring state of Pakistan. At the 1991 census, about 2/3rd of all the Sindhi speakers in India were enumerated in Gujarat and Maharashtra. A small proportion of Sindhi speakers is also found in Delhi and Uttar Pradesh.

59. Author of book social problems in India is Ahuja.

Author of book places and politics is Agnew

Author of book India-China war is Maxwell

Author of book Partition of Punjab is Satya Mehta Rai.

60. Geography has dualism regarding its views on keeping physical geography in centre or human geography in the centre. Human geography has been advocated by many foremost geographers like Carl Ritter, Strabo and Fredrick Ratzel. Ptolemy, on the other hand, was a supporter of physical geographer.

61.

- Alexander von Humboldt was a German geographer. He travelled extensively throughout the world, especially in South America. He put emphasis on studying geography general or systematic geography, wherein a concept is studied as it occurs throughout the world.

- Hartshorne was American and Hettner was a German geographer. They have supported the idea of regional geography.

- Ellen Semple was an American geographer. She has been one of the most leading propagators of Deterministic approach to geography. Determinism or environmental determinism says that physical environment affects human activities.

- Vida de la Balche was a French geographer. He supported possibilism, which states that culture, not the environment sets social conditions.

62. S. Thomas Kuhn, an American geographer was the first person to coin the term paradigm. He defined paradigm as universally recognized scientific achievements that for a time provide a model problems and solutions to a community of practitioners. He was of the opinion that science does not develop slowly, but has periodical revolutions which he called as paradigm shifts. As per Kuhn, the scientific knowledge develops like a plateau. It increases with sudden upheavals and rises abruptly and its smooth and slow at other times.

63. The space of geographical studies has been divided into four traditions, one of which is earth science. This tradition has requires study of earth, water, atmosphere, sun and the interaction of these things with earth. This tradition is well respected in scientific community as well as historians, sociologist. This is because of all the four traditions, only earth science has concrete objects that can be studied. So, both (A) and (R) are true and (R) is the correct explanation of (A).

64. Hecataeus was the first person to give two approaches to study of geography. These two approaches were Nomothetic and Ideographic. The Nomothetic approach was law seeking while the Ideographic approach was descriptive. He also wrote the book

Ges-periods which gave geographical information about Europe and Libya.

65. The Egyptians had developed several methods of measurement of land. This was for the collection of taxes. This measurement system was later used to identify the North-South line which was used to identify directions and preparing maps later by the Greeks. Thus, both (A) and (R) are true and (R) is the correct explanation of (A).

66. The National Atlas and Thematic Mapping Organization (NATMO) makes thematic maps. The Geological Survey of India and the Indian Meteorological Department are responsible for making geological and climatic maps respectively. The Naval Hydrographic Office on the other hand has more to do with coastal and oceanic amps rather than topographic maps.

67. CARTOSAT-2 was the successor of CARTOSAT-1. It was equipped with had a single high resolution panchromatic camera. It was developed for the advanced applications in agriculture. IRS-P6/ CARTSAT-2 is capable of providing scene-specific spot imagery. So, (A) is true and (R) is false.

68. Post-modernism is a very recent movement in the social sciences. The post-modernist philosophy emphasizes heterogeneity, uniqueness and particularity rather than generalization. The ideas of positivism, determinism, humanism and structuralism were all rejected before the emergence of post-modernism. It gives importance to political empowerment and openness in social and geographical enquiry.

69. Kirk was the first person to give a model based on the behavioral approach. In this model he explained that same information has different meaning for different people, which is shaped by socio-economic and cultural background of people. Every individual in the society reacts differently to information about resource, environment and space.

70.

- Arithmetic Mean of a set of observations is defined as their sum, divided by the number of observations. Hence, the computation of A.M. is easy. Even if all the observations are not known individually, this can be found, provided their sum and the number of observations known.

- As Mode of a given set of observations is that value which occurs with the maximum frequency, it has no significance unless many observations are available.

- Median is the real measure of central tendency as it gives the value of the most central observation. It is unaffected by the presence of extremely large or small observations. For instance, to find out the boy of average intelligence, the candidates may be ranked in order of intelligence and the median employed. Therefore, it is applicable in qualitative data.

- Given the product and the number of observations, G.M. can be calculated even if the magnitude of each observation is not known individually. Hence, G.M. is particularly suitable for averaging ratios, rates and percentages. It is therefore used in the construction of

index numbers. But it cannot be calculated if any of the observation is zero.

71. Bifurcation Ratio is defined as the dimensionless number denoting the ratio between the number of streams of one order and those of the next higher order in a drainage network. It may be a useful measure of proneness to flooding that is the higher the bifurcation ratio, the greater the probability of flooding .

72. Stream order is a measure of the relative size of the stream. The smallest tributaries are referred to as first order streams. The largest river Amazon is the twelfth order waterway. Over 80% of total length of Earth's waterways are headwater streams. Streams classified as fourth through sixth are considered medium streams.

73. Interpolation is a technique in which we find any value within the range of values we have based on the relationship between variables. In case of contour interpolation, we draw contours or isolines on the basis of known heights of neighbouring points. However in case of extrapolation, we try to find any data value based on the existing relationship between variables, but outside the given dataset or data range. In case of contour extrapolation, we keep in mind the angular position and the orientation of the contours.

74. A cartogram is a theme based map where in some form of statistical information commands over the size of the spatial unit. Such maps are most used to show population size, infant mortality in terms of absolute numbers in demography. The basic purpose of such maps is to draw the attention of the audience to the theme.

75. The average height indicates the mean height for a total of 4 individuals which is 170 cm. 170 cm is nothing but the sum of the height of all the four persons divided by 4. So we can understand that the total height would be the product of the mean height and the number of observation. Therefore 170 cm multiplied by 4 give 680cm. Thus 680 cm must also be the sum of the individual height of four person. Since we do not have the height of the fourth person, we can find it out by subtracting the sum of the height of three persons(525cm) from 680 cm. Hence, 680cm – 525 cm = 155 cm.

76. Drainage density, D, of an area A, is the total length of the streams draining that area, $\sum L$, divided by the area:

$$D = \frac{\sum L}{A}$$

The measurement of drainage density is a useful numerical measure of landscape direction and runoff potential.

77. Relief ratio is an indication of the intensity of erosional process operating on slope of the basin. Relief ratio is the maximum relief to the horizontal distance along the largest dimension of the basin parallel to the principal drainage line. Thus, it estimates the overall steepness of the drainage basin.

78. After the National Map Policy, 2005 , Government of India vis Survey of India came up with the concept of Open Series Maps for public use. But prior to it, the Survey of India used to publish topographic sheets which were drawn using polyconic projections. This projection is created by lining up an infinite number of cones along the central meridian.

79. Data in geography can be divided in two groups, i.e. spatial and non-spatial data. The spatial data is further divided into Raster Data, vector data and TIN data; whereas Non-spatial data are the attribute data which are not found as it is and rather it is assigned or attached with the spatial data to reach a comprehensive understanding. Point, Line and Polygon are example of vector data.

80. India has a monsoon climate and most of India's rainfall is convectional in nature. Convectional rainfall is mostly present in the equatorial region. Here the rising of warm air leads to its expansion which later cools and saturates. This leads to the formation of cumulous and cumulonimbus clouds. In such regions the rainfall occurs in the afternoon.

81. India is the second largest fish producer in the world with a total production of 13.7 million metric tonnes in 2018-19 of which 65 per cent was from inland sector.

82. The Sahyadris commence in Maharashtra. The Sahyadri starts from the border of Gujarat and Maharashtra, south of the Tapti River, and runs approximately 1,600 km through the states of Maharashtra, Goa, Karnataka, Kerala and Tamil Nadu ending at Kanyakumari, at the southern tip of India.

83. Infant mortality rate is the death of children under the age of 1. Its s calculated by taking out the number of children died per 1000 live births. As per 2016 report by the Sample Registration Survey (SRS):

- Arunachal Pradesh has 36 infant mortality rate.
- Andhra Pradesh has 34 infant mortality rate.
- Bihar has 38 infant mortality rate.
- Assam has 44 infant mortality rate.

84. There are 15 Agro climatic regions in India as prescribed by the planning commission of India. Rainfall witnessed in eastern climatic region is 200-400cm, Western Himalayan region witnesses rainfall of 75cm-150cm.

The lower Gangetic plains region witnesses rainfall 100cm-200cm and middle Gangetic plain region witnesses 100cm-200cm rainfall.

85. Department of promotion of industry and internal trade is a department coming under ministry of commerce and industry. It deals with the promotion of developmental measures for the industrial sector. It is not responsible for any individual policy like production, distribution etc. It is responsible for the overall industrial policy. It also facilitates foreign direct investment flows to the country.

86. In July of 1991 the Indian government devalued the rupee by between 18 and 19 percent. Dr. Man Mohan Singh introduced the new economic policy, Liberalisation, privatization and globalization(LPG) policy. It was a measure to deal with crisis India was dealing with then. The policy was made in 1991.

87. Kutch region of Gujarat comes under Very high damage risk earthquake zone. North-east states, Uttarakhand, Western Himachal Pradesh, Kashmir Valley, and the Kuchchh (Gujarat)are included in the Very High Damage Risk Zone. India divided into five earthquake zones:

(i) Very high damage risk zone

(ii) High damage risk zone

(iii) Moderate damage risk zone

(iv) Low damage risk zone

(v) Very low damage risk zone.

88. Owing to its Peninsular shape surrounded by the Bay of Bengal in the east and the Arabian Sea in the west, the tropical cyclones in India also originate in these two important locations. Though most of the cyclones originate between 10°-15° north latitudes during the monsoon season, yet in case of the Bay of Bengal, cyclones mostly develop during the months of October and November.

89. Todas is a pastoral tribe found in Tamil Nadu in the Nilgiri Hills. Garasia tribe is found in Rajasthan and Gujarat. Adis are found in Arunachal Pradesh. Gaddis are the nomadic tribal group found in Himachal Pradesh.

90. Among the Indian states the proportion of urban population is highest in Goa with 62.17 per cent. It is followed by Mizoram with 51.51 per cent. Both them are the only states with the share of urban population above 50 percent. However, Kerala has experienced the highest negative decadal growth in its rural population among the states with -25.96 percent since 2001 census. It is followed by Goa with -18.56 percent.

91. Himalayas are responsible for intercepting the summer monsoons and causing precipitation. Besides, Himalayas are also largely responsible for splitting the jet stream into two branches and these in turn play an extremely important role in bringing monsoons in India. The doons are important features of the Shiwaliks, also called the outer Himalayas. Siachen glacier is the largest non-polar glacier in located in the Karakoram Range. Bara Shigri glacier is located in the Pir Panjal range.

92. Arunachal Pradesh has the highest proportion of area under forest cover among these states around 80 per cent of its total area under forests. Arunachal Pradesh is second in the list of total area under forests following Madhya Pradesh.

93. Kanchenjunga National Park in Sikkim is the first site in India to get a mixed site status (Cultural and natural importance) under World Heritage Site by UNESCO. Gulf of Mannar and Panna Biosphere reserve are the largest and the smallest biosphere reserve respectively. The Forest policy of India which came in 1952 and was modified in 1988 aimed at bringing 33 per cent of its area under forest cover.

94. The Soil and Land Use Survey of India (SLUSI) under Ministry of Agriculture and Farmers Welfare has been conducting soil surveys since 1958. As per the agricultural census, during 2000-2011 there was a decline in the average size of operational landholdings in India. It came down from 1.33 hectares in 2001 to 1.15 hectares in 2011. However in case of the category of Large Holdings (10 hectares and above), the average size saw an increase from 17.12 hectares in 2001 to 17.38 hectares in 2011 but the total area under large holdings saw a decline from 13200 hectares in 2001 to 10600 hectares in 2011. Agricultural land covers more than 50 per cent of country's area while forest area covers more than 20 per cent.

95. The *rabi* is a cropping season in India which begins with the onset of winter in October-November and ends in March-April. *Zaid* is a short duration summer cropping season beginning after harvesting of rabi crops starting around the month of April and lasts till June. Kharif period starts from June and lasts till September. Such distinction of cropping seasons are not there in the southern region because of the tropical hot conditions and thus adequate sunshine round the year.

96. Gujarat is the largest producer of fertilizer in India followed by Tamil Nadu, Uttar Pradesh and Maharashtra. It accounts for more than one-fourth of the total production of nitrogenous as well as phosphatic fertilizers in the country.

97. India has a population of 1.2 billion. This population has increased the number of vehicles on the roads. The carrying capacity of our roads has not been able to keep up with the increasing population. Thus, there is a need to increase the road capacity of roads in India. Thus, both (A) and (R) are true, and (R) is the correct explanation of (A).

98. Iron and Steel plant was established in Rourkela as part of an industrial policy to develop backward tribal areas of the country. The first cotton textile mills were set up in Mumbai and Ahmedabad. Noida is a software technology park and Jamnagar in Gujarat is known for petrochemical industry.

99. The Great Bath is one of the best-known structures among the ruins of the ancient Indus Valley Civilization at Mohenjo-daro in Sindh, Pakistan. Archaeological evidence indicates that the Great Bath was built in the 3rd millennium BCE, soon after the raising of the "citadel" mound on which it is located.

100. The Social System of Harappans was fairly egalitarian (equality and equal rights). The archaeological record of the Indus civilization provides practically no evidence of armies, kings, slaves, social conflict, prisons, and other oft-negative traits that we traditionally associated with early civilizations. If there were neither slaves nor kings, a more egalitarian system of governance may have been practiced.

Mock Test 07

Q.1 Read the following statements given as pieces of evidence for the continental drift theory and select the correct answer using the code given below :

a) The similar fossils of Lystrosaurus found in Indian plate and African plate.

b) The age and type of rocks in the Appalachian Mountains and the Alps is similar

c) Similar glacial sediments found in East coast of South America, Southern Africa, India, Australia and Antarctica

d) Ocean basin contours of Western Africa and East coast of South America fit like two parts of the jigsaw puzzle

Code :

A. Only (a) is correct

B. (a) and (b) are correct

C. (a), (b) and (c) are correct

D. (a), (b) and (d) are correct

Q.2 Given below are two statements one is labelled as Assertion (A) and the other is labelled as Reason (R).

Assertion (A): The continent of Europe is the only continent which is not on cold part of the mantle or moving towards it.

Reason (R): Continents drift away from mantle hot zones.

Select the correct answer from options given below:

A. Both (A) and (R) are true and (R) is the correct explanation of (A)

B. Both (A) and (R) are true, but (R) is not the correct explanation of (A)

C. (A) is true, but (R) is false

D. (A) is false, but (R) is true

Q.3 Which of the following is a result of an endogenetic forces?

A. Weathering   **B.** Volcanism

C. Erosion   **D.** Deposition

Q.4 Which of the following is NOT a type of mechanical weathering?

A. Solution   **B.** Exfoliation

C. Frost Action   **D.** Salt Weathering

Q.5 Which of the following is NOT a factor that affects denudation?

A. Tectonic Activity   **B.** Geology

C. Ocean currents   **D.** climatic conditions

Q.6 Match List-I with the List-II and select the correct answer from the code given below:

List - I (Landform/ Surface)	List - II (Reference)
(a) Peneplain	(i) Crickmay
(b) Pediplain	(ii) Davis
(c) Panplain	(iii) Thomas
(d) Etchplain	(iv) Penck

Code:

A. (a)-(i), (b)-(iii), (c)-(iv), (d)-(ii)

B. (a)-(ii), (b)-(iv), (c)-(i), (d)-(iii)

C. (a)-(i), (b)-(iv), (c)-(iii), (d)-(ii)

D. (a)-(iv), (b)-(i), (c)-(ii), (d)-(iii)

Q.7 Which of the following statements relating to Penck's cycle of erosion are correct?

(a) Penck assumes that landscape development is time dependent.

(b) In the last stage of the model, a steep side conical hill called monadnock is formed.

(c) The upper part of the valley in the waning development is called as wash slope.

(d) The first phase of in the landform development is characterized by accelerated development.

Code:

A. (a) and (d)   **B.** (a) and (b)

C. (a), (c) and (d)   **D.** (b), (c) and (d)

Q.8 Which of the following is not an intrusion feature?

A. Lacolith   **B.** Batholith

C. Geysers   **D.** Dyke

Q.9 Differential heating and cooling of outer and lower rocks causes

A. Slaking   **B.** Flaking

C. Shattering   **D.** Shearing

Q.10 Which of the following statement(s) are correct about the earthquakes and volcanoes?

(a) The epicentre of the earthquake is the point wherefrom the energy is released in the form of waves.

(b) Both P-waves and S-waves have shadow zones between 105° and 145° from the epicentre of the earthquake.

(c) The intensity of any earthquake can be measured by Richter scale.

(d) Composite volcanoes are characterized with cold and less viscous lava flow.

Code:

A. Only (a)   **B.** Only (b)

C. (b) and (d)   **D.** (a), (b), (c) and (d)

Q.11 Read the passage and answer the questions that follow.

Over the last 30 years the theory of climate change must have been one of the most comprehensively tested in science. There are six main areas of evidence that should be considered. First, the rise of Greenhouse gases in the atmosphere and understand their role in past climate variations. Second, we know from laboratory and atmospheric measurements that these gases do indeed absorb heat when they are present in the atmosphere. Third, we have tracked significant changes in global temperatures and sea level rise over the last century. Fourth, we have analyzed the effects of natural changes on climate including sunspots and volcanic eruptions, and though these are essential to understanding the pattern of temperature changes over the last 150 years, they cannot explain the overall warming trends. Fifth, we have observed significant changes in the Earth climate system including the retreat of sea ice in the Arctic, retreating mountain glaciers on all continents, shrinking permafrost and increased depth of its active layer. So, we can conclude that temperature, precipitation, sea level and extreme weather events are some of the basic things that need to be examined as evidences for climate change.

Which of the following is a natural change that can lead to climate change?

A. Increased Greenhouse gases

B. Sunspots

C. Pollution

D. Increased CFCs

Q.12 Read the passage and answer the questions that follow.

Over the last 30 years the theory of climate change must have been one of the most comprehensively tested in science. There are six main areas of evidence that should be considered. First, the rise of Greenhouse gases in the atmosphere and understand their role in past climate variations. Second, we know from laboratory and atmospheric measurements that these gases do indeed absorb heat when they are present in the atmosphere. Third, we have tracked significant changes in global temperatures and sea level rise over the last century. Fourth, we have analyzed the effects of natural changes on climate including sunspots and volcanic eruptions, and though these are essential to understanding the pattern of temperature changes over the last 150 years, they cannot explain the overall warming trends. Fifth, we have observed significant changes in the Earth climate system including the retreat of sea ice in the Arctic, retreating mountain glaciers on all continents, shrinking permafrost and increased depth of its active layer. So, we can conclude that temperature, precipitation, sea level and extreme weather events are some of the basic things that need to be examined as evidences for climate change.

How many areas of evidence are there in support of climate change?

A. Three   **B.** Four   **C.** Five   **D.** Six

Q.13 Read the passage and answer the questions that follow.

Over the last 30 years the theory of climate change must have been one of the most comprehensively tested in science. There are six main areas of evidence that should be considered. First, the rise of Greenhouse gases in the atmosphere and understand their role in past climate variations. Second, we know from laboratory and atmospheric measurements that these gases do indeed absorb heat when they are present in the atmosphere. Third, we have tracked significant changes in global temperatures and sea level rise over the last century. Fourth, we have analyzed the effects of natural changes on climate including sunspots and volcanic eruptions, and though these are essential to understanding the pattern of temperature changes over the last 150 years, they cannot explain the overall warming trends. Fifth, we have observed significant changes in the Earth climate system including the retreat of sea ice in the

Arctic, retreating mountain glaciers on all continents, shrinking permafrost and increased depth of its active layer. So, we can conclude that temperature, precipitation, sea level and extreme weather events are some of the basic things that need to be examined as evidences for climate change.

Which of the following is NOT one of the evidences in support of climate change?

A. Rise in Greenhouse gases

B. Increased economic profits

C. Increase in global temperatures

D. Retreat of Arctic Sea

Q.14 Read the passage and answer the questions that follow.

Over the last 30 years the theory of climate change must have been one of the most comprehensively tested in science. There are six main areas of evidence that should be considered. First, the rise of Greenhouse gases in the atmosphere and understand their role in past climate variations. Second, we know from laboratory and atmospheric measurements that these gases do indeed absorb heat when they are present in the atmosphere. Third, we have tracked significant changes in global temperatures and sea level rise over the last century. Fourth, we have analyzed the effects of natural changes on climate including sunspots and volcanic eruptions, and though these are essential to understanding the pattern of temperature changes over the last 150 years, they cannot explain the overall warming trends. Fifth, we have observed significant changes in the Earth climate system including the retreat of sea ice in the Arctic, retreating mountain glaciers on all continents, shrinking permafrost and increased depth of its active layer. So, we can conclude that temperature, precipitation, sea level and extreme weather events are some of the basic things that need to be examined as evidences for climate change.

Which of the following is evidence in support of climate change?

A. Retreating mountain glaciers

B. Increased green cover

C. Increased economic activity

D. Increased mining

Q.15 Read the passage and answer the questions that follow.

Over the last 30 years the theory of climate change must have been one of the most comprehensively tested in science. There are six main areas of evidence that should be considered. First, the rise of Greenhouse gases in the atmosphere and understand their role in past climate variations. Second, we know from laboratory and atmospheric measurements that these gases do indeed absorb heat when they are present in the atmosphere. Third, we have tracked significant changes in global temperatures and sea level rise over the last century. Fourth, we have analyzed the effects of natural changes on climate including sunspots and volcanic eruptions, and though these are essential to understanding the pattern of temperature changes over the last 150 years, they cannot explain the overall warming trends. Fifth, we have observed significant changes in the Earth climate system including the retreat of sea ice in the Arctic, retreating mountain glaciers on all continents, shrinking permafrost and increased depth of its active layer. So, we can conclude that temperature, precipitation, sea level and extreme weather events are some of the basic things that need to be examined as evidences for climate change.

Which are the basic things that are to be examined as evidence of climate change?

A. rise in global temperatures
B. Sea level change
C. Extreme weather events
D. All of the above

Q.16 Match List-I with the List-II and select the correct answer from the code given below:

List - I (Layers of Atmosphere)	List-II (Characteristics)
(a) Stratosphere	(i) Less density of air
(b) Troposphere	(ii) Ozone layer
(c) Thermosphere	(iii) Presence of ions
(d) Exosphere	(iv) Dust particles & Water vapour

Code:

A. (a)-(i), (b)-(iii), (c)-(iv), (d)-(ii)
B. (a)-(ii), (b)-(iv), (c)-(iii), (d)-(i)
C. (a)-(i), (b)-(iv), (c)-(iii), (d)-(ii)
D. (a)-(iv), (b)-(i), (c)-(ii), (d)-(iii)

Q.17 When did Thornthwaite introduce the first climatic classification?

A. 1925　　B. 1929　　C. 1948　　D. 1931

Q.18 Consider the following statements

(i) La Nina causes draught in Ecuador and Peru. Low temperature, high pressure in Eastern Pacific.

(ii) La Nina causes heavy floods in Australia; High temperature in western Pacific, Indian Ocean, off coast Somalia and good rains in India.

Choose the correct answer:

A. Only (i)
B. Only (ii)
C. Both (i) and (ii)
D. Neither (i) nor (ii)

Q.19 Consider the following statements

(i). Deforestation is not the major human activity that causes drought.

(ii). Over-fishing and urbanization has much larger effect on environment causing drought.

Choose the correct answer:

A. Only (i) is true
B. Only (ii) is true
C. Both (i) and (ii) are true
D. Neither (i) nor (ii) is true

Q.20 What percent of carbon dioxide has increased in the atmosphere since preindustrial times?

A. About 10%
B. About 20%
C. About 30%
D. About 40%

Q.21 The Tsunami meters installed by the Pacific Tsunami warning system (PTWS) consist of which of the following components?

A. Deep sea pressure sensors
B. Floating buoys
C. Satellites
D. All of the above

Q.22 Match the following:-

List I (Types of tropical cyclones)	List -II (Explanation)
(a) Tropical depressions	(i) symmetrical and closed isobars
(b) Tropical disturbances	(ii) develop frequently in the Bay of Bengal
(c) Tropical storms	(iii) Wind velocity ranges form 40 - 50 km/hr
(d) Hurricanes	(iv) known as easterly waves

Choose the correct option:

A. a-3 b-4 c-2 d-1
B. a-4 b-3 c-2 d-1
C. a-1 b-3 c-4 d-2
D. a-1 b-2 c-3 d-4

Q.23 Which among the following is a precautionary measure taken as an immediate result of the tsunami in Hawaii?

A. Deep Ocean Assessment and Reporting of Tsunamis
B. Pacific Tsunami Warning Center
C. Japan Tsunami Warning Center
D. American Tsunami Warning Centre

Q.24 Which among the following is not a minor relief feature in the ocean?

A. Seamount
B. Trenches
C. Guyots
D. Submarine Canyons

Q.25 Which among the following statements is not true about Mid-Oceanic Ridges and Sea-floor Spreading?

A. Mid-Oceanic Ridge is exclusively found in Atlantic Ocean.
B. Seafloor spreading helps in acknowledging the concept of plate tectonics.
C. It is validated by the magnetic properties and age of adjacent rocks.
D. Sea-floor spreading is found far away from continental slopes near the abyssal plains.

Q.26 Given below are two statements. One is labelled as Assertion (A) and the other is labelled as Reason (R).

Assertion (A): The polar seas have much less salinity in comparison to other seas.

Reason (R): Melting of ice in polar areas yields fresh water.

Select the correct answer from options given below:

A. Both (A) and (R) are true and (R) is the correct explanation of (A)
B. Both (A) and (R) are true, but (R) is not the correct explanation of (A)
C. (A) is true, but (R) is false.
D. (A) is false, but (R) is true.

Q.27 Which among the following water bodies has the lowest salinity?

A. Red Sea   **B.** Dead Sea
C. North Sea   **D.** Baltic Sea

Q.28 Who is not connected with the concept of Human Ecology?
A. H.H. Barrows   **B.** A. Hawley
C. Robert Park   **D.** Neil Smith

Q.29 Which of the following statements are correct about ecosystem?
(a) Ecosystem comprises both biotic and abiotic components.
(b) Ecosystem is a closed system.
(c) Solar radiation is the main driving force of the ecosystem.
(d) Ecosystem does not have its own productivity
A. (a) and (b)   **B.** (b) and (c)
C. (a) and (c)   **D.** (c) and (d)

Q.30 In which year was the National Green Tribunal formed?
A. 2010   **B.** 2009   **C.** 2012   **D.** 2005

Q.31 Which of the following statements are correct relating to International conferences and Reports?
(a) The Stockholm Declaration contained 28 principles concerning the environment and development.
(b) Our Common Future was the report presented by the World Commission on Environment and Development.
(c) World Summit on Sustainable Development is also known as Rio +10.
(d) UN Conference on Sustainable Development produced its report named "The Future we Want"
A. (a) only   **B.** (b) only
C. (b), (c) and (d) only   **D.** (a), (b) and (d) only

Q.32 Match the List-I with List-II.

List-I (Author)	List-II (Work)
a) Colin J Burrows	i) Process of vegetation change
b) H.J Brown	ii) How the names are used for vegetation
c) Tian.G	ii) Foundation of Biogeography
d) Ebach M.L	iv) Origins of Biogeography

Code:
A. a-i b-iii c-ii d-iv   **B.** a-ii b-i c-iv d-iii
C. a-i b-ii c- ii d-iv   **D.** a-iii b-i c-iv d-ii

Q.33 Consider the following statements:-
a) The human ecology or the human-environment relation can be explained in terms of 3 traditional aspects- imperialistic, arcadian, and scientific.
b) The imperialistic tradition holds that humans as part of nature.
c) The basic truth is that Human Ecology is not different from other kinds of ecology.
d) Ernst Haeckel coined the term Human Ecology.
Which of the following statements are correct?
A. a and b   **B.** a and c
C. b and c   **D.** a, b, and c

Q.34 Consider the following statements:-

a) Food Chain is a non-linear relationship of food flow between producers and consumers.
b) In general, the number of links in a food web ranges from 20-40
c) Ecological pyramids are of 3 types and the energy transfer increases at each higher trophic level in a pyramid.
d) The energy pyramid gives an idea on the ecological productivity
Which of the following options are correct?
A. a and c   **B.** b and d
C. c and d   **D.** b, c, and d

Q.35 Which among the following will not contribute in carbon sequestration?
A. Soil Conservation
B. Zero Tillage
C. Sustainable Agriculture
D. Monoculture

Q.36 By whom was the origin of towns explained as the transformation of the Neolithic culture to an urban lifestyle?
A. Gordon Childe   **B.** Henri Pirenne
C. Lewis Mumford   **D.** Smith

Q.37 Consider the following statements:-
a) Christaller's Central Place Theory is concerned with the size and distribution of settlements within a rural setting and is only based on the principle of Centralization.
b) August Losch's study is based on the central places of South Germany while the Christaller's model is based on all over Germany.
c) One of the main assumptions of Losch's theory was that demand decrease with an increase in price and has also been criticized for overemphasizing it.
d) Losch's Theory had a hierarchical structure far less rigid than Christaller's.
Which of the following statements are correct?
A. a and b   **B.** c and d
C. a, b, and c   **D.** a and d

Q.38 Given below are two statements. One is labelled as Assertion (A) and the other is labelled as Reason (R).
Assertion (A)- The level of Urbanization refers to how much an urban area has developed.
Reason(R)- The factors leading to urbanization have never been the same.
Select the correct answer from options given below:
A. Both (A) and (R) are true and (R) is the correct explanation of (A)
B. Both (A) and (R) are true but (R) is not the correct explanation of (A)
C. (A) is true but (R) is false
D. (A) is false but (R) is true

Q.39 Read the following statements about National Population Policy (NPP) and select the correct answer from the code given below:

(a) As per NPP 2000, India had to reduce its infant mortality rate to 30 per thousand.

(b) As per NPP 2000, India had to achieve Total Fertility Rate of 2.1%

(c) As per NPP 2000, India had to achieve 100% registration of births, deaths, marriages and pregnancy.

(d) As per NPP 2000, India had to achieve population growth of 200 million.

Code:

A. (a) and (b) are true

B. (a), (b) and (d) are true

C. (a),(b) and (c) are true

D. Only (d) is true

Q.40 Read the following statements and select the correct answer from the code given below:

(a) World Population doubled in 37 years from 1950-1987

(b) World Population has been rising with a steady rate less than 1.1 percent.

(c) Life expectancy at birth for the world population is 72.6 years.

(d) World Population is expected to double by the year 2100.

Code:

A. (a) and (b) are true

B. Only (a) is true

C. (a), (b) and (d) are true

D. (a), (b) and (c) are true

Q.41 Which country has highest number of industries using wind power?

A. Germany   **B.** Canada

C. India   **D.** South Africa

Q.42 Which of the following statements is not correct about the ICT and Knowledge based industries in India?

A. India's IT services industry earns around USD 100 billion from exports

B. The size of India's IT sector is equally due to its growth in hardware and software services.

C. This potential in this sector has led to the creation of software parks in the country.

D. None of the above

Q.43 Which of the following pair of countries is the world's largest exporter and importer respectively?

A. China and USA   **B.** USA and China

C. US and UK   **D.** US and EU

Q.44 When and where was the World Trade Organization formed?

A. 1995, Washington   **B.** 2000, Munich

C. 1995, Geneva   **D.** 1995, Brussels

Q.45 Which of the following are the basic factors affecting interaction between regions as per Ulman's Flow theory??

(a) Accessibility

(b) Complementarity,

(c) Hierarchy

(d) Intervening Opportunity

Codes:

A. Only (a)   **B.** (b) and (d) only

C. (a), (b) and (d) only   **D.** (a), (b), (c) and (d)

Q.46 Which of the following work on spatial interaction was written by M.E . Hurst?

A. Transportation and the societal framework

B. Geography as Spatial Interaction

C. Locational Analysis in Human Geography

D. Network Analysis in Geography

Q.47 Which is the formula used by weaver?

A. $\frac{\Sigma d^2}{n}$ **B.** $\frac{d}{nx}$ **C.** $\frac{Dd}{n}$ **D.** $\frac{\Sigma f}{n}$

Q.48 Which among the following regions has Mediterranean agriculture system/region as per Whittlesey's classification of agricultural regions?

A. California   **B.** Kerala

C. Britain   **D.** Netherland

Q.49 Match List I with List II and select the correct answer from the code given below:

List - I (Zone)	List - II (Land use)
(a) Zone I	(i) Livestock Farming
(b) Zone II	(ii) Firewood and Lumber Production
(c) Zone III	(iii) Market gardening and milk production
(d) Zone VI	(iv) Crop Farming without Fallow

Code:

A. (a)-(ii), (b)-(i), (c)-(iii), (d)-(iv)

B. (a)-(ii), (b)-(iii), (c)-(iv), (d)-(i)

C. (a)-(iii), (b)-(ii), (c)-(iv), (d)-(i)

D. (a)-(iv), (b)-(ii), (c)-(iii), (d)-(i)

Q.50 Read the passage and answer the questions that follow.

The region is a common-sense notion, with regional categories being universally relied on as people classify spatial information. Regions are useful inasmuch as they provide pigeonholes into which spatial information may be sorted....The designation of region can be applied to any area larger than a point and smaller than the entire planet. A particular place can be included in more than one region depending on how the region is defined. Geographers identify three types of region – formal, functional and vernacular. A formal region is also called a uniform region which is an area within which everyone shares in common one or more distinctive characteristics. It can be a common language, an economic activity or an environmental property such as climate. Functional region is also called a nodal region. It is an area organized around a node or focal point. The characteristic chosen to define a functional region dominates at a central focus or node and diminishes in importance outward. Vernacular Region or perceptual region is a place that people believe exists as part of their cultural identity. Such regions emerge from people's informal sense of place rather than from scientific models developed through geographic thought....We can always conclude that a region is always homogeneous from the inside and heterogeneous from the outside.

The area showing the prevalence of a disease called Ebola is an example of :

A. Formal Region   **B.** Functional Region
C. Economic Region   **D.** Perceptual Region

Q.51 Read the passage and answer the questions that follow.

The region is a common-sense notion, with regional categories being universally relied on as people classify spatial information. Regions are useful inasmuch as they provide pigeonholes into which spatial information may be sorted....The designation of region can be applied to any area larger than a point and smaller than the entire planet. A particular place can be included in more than one region depending on how the region is defined. Geographers identify three types of region – formal, functional and vernacular. A formal region is also called a uniform region which is an area within which everyone shares in common one or more distinctive characteristics. It can be a common language, an economic activity or an environmental property such as climate. Functional region is also called a nodal region. It is an area organized around a node or focal point. The characteristic chosen to define a functional region dominates at a central focus or node and diminishes in importance outward. Vernacular Region or perceptual region is a place that people believe exists as part of their cultural identity. Such regions emerge from people's informal sense of place rather than from scientific models developed through geographic thought....We can always conclude that a region is always homogeneous from the inside and heterogeneous from the outside.

The extensive areas of support for the Bhartiya Janata Party in 2019 Lok Sabha elections represented through the map of parliamentary constituencies which were won by BJP is an example of :

A. Nodal Region
B. Uniform region
C. Vernacular Region
D. Cartographic Region

Q.52 Read the passage and answer the questions that follow.

The region is a common-sense notion, with regional categories being universally relied on as people classify spatial information. Regions are useful inasmuch as they provide pigeonholes into which spatial information may be sorted....The designation of region can be applied to any area larger than a point and smaller than the entire planet. A particular place can be included in more than one region depending on how the region is defined. Geographers identify three types of region – formal, functional and vernacular. A formal region is also called a uniform region which is an area within which everyone shares in common one or more distinctive characteristics. It can be a common language, an economic activity or an environmental property such as climate. Functional region is also called a nodal region. It is an area organized around a node or focal point. The characteristic chosen to define a functional region dominates at a central focus or node and diminishes in importance outward. Vernacular Region or perceptual region is a place that people believe exists as part of their cultural identity. Such regions emerge from people's informal sense of

place rather than from scientific models developed through geographic thought....We can always conclude that a region is always homogeneous from the inside and heterogeneous from the outside.

Match List I with List II and select the correct answer from the code given below:

List - I (Characteristic Examples)	List - II (Land use)
(a) Area under a map of "Akhand Bharat"	(i) Nodal Region
(b) Zone of distribution of a daily newspaper	(ii) Uniform Region
(c) Islamic countries of world	(iii) Economic Region
(d) Regions with 90% population in service sector	(iv) Perceptual Region

Code:

A. (a)-(ii), (b)-(i), (c)-(iii), (d)-(iv)
B. (a)-(iv), (b)-(iii), (c)-(i), (d)-(ii)
C. (a)-(iii), (b)-(ii), (c)-(iv), (d)-(i)
D. (a)-(iv), (b)-(i), (c)-(ii), (d)-(iii)

Q.53 Read the passage and answer the questions that follow.

The region is a common-sense notion, with regional categories being universally relied on as people classify spatial information. Regions are useful inasmuch as they provide pigeonholes into which spatial information may be sorted....The designation of region can be applied to any area larger than a point and smaller than the entire planet. A particular place can be included in more than one region depending on how the region is defined. Geographers identify three types of region – formal, functional and vernacular. A formal region is also called a uniform region which is an area within which everyone shares in common one or more distinctive characteristics. It can be a common language, an economic activity or an environmental property such as climate. Functional region is also called a nodal region. It is an area organized around a node or focal point. The characteristic chosen to define a functional region dominates at a central focus or node and diminishes in importance outward. Vernacular Region or perceptual region is a place that people believe exists as part of their cultural identity. Such regions emerge from people's informal sense of place rather than from scientific models developed through geographic thought....We can always conclude that a region is always homogeneous from the inside and heterogeneous from the outside.

Which of the following statements about region is not true?

A. Region is a common-place notion.
B. The scale of a region is dynamic and not fixed.
C. The Kurdish Nation is a uniform region
D. Biomes are natural regions.

Q.54 Read the passage and answer the questions that follow.

The region is a common-sense notion, with regional categories being universally relied on as people classify spatial information. Regions are useful inasmuch as they provide pigeonholes into which spatial information may be sorted....The designation of region can be applied to any area larger than a point and smaller than the entire planet. A particular place can be included in more than one region depending on how the region is defined. Geographers identify three types of region – formal, functional and vernacular. A formal region is also called a uniform region which is an area within which everyone shares in common one or more distinctive characteristics. It can be a common language, an economic activity or an environmental property such as climate. Functional region is also called a nodal region. It is an area organized around a node or focal point. The characteristic chosen to define a functional region dominates at a central focus or node and diminishes in importance outward. Vernacular Region or perceptual region is a place that people believe exists as part of their cultural identity. Such regions emerge from people's informal sense of place rather than from scientific models developed through geographic thought....We can always conclude that a region is always homogeneous from the inside and heterogeneous from the outside.

Christaller's Central Place Theory is at best an example of which kind of region:

A. Uniform Region   **B.** Functional Region
C. Formal Region   **D.** Perceptual region

Q.55 Which of the following scholar gave the theory of cumulative causation theory?

A. G. Myrdal   **B.** A.O. Hirschman
C. A.G. Frank   **D.** W. Rostow

Q.56 The disease generally occurs in the sugar mills and factory workers is-

A. Silicosis   **B.** Asbestosis
C. Anthracosis   **D.** Bagassosis

Q.57 The Heartland Theory was given by

A. Nicholas Spykman   **B.** HJ Mackinder
C. Richard Hartshorne   **D.** Reece Jones

Q.58 The sole purpose of this organization is to seek cooperation in the fields of telecommunication, shipping, infrastructure, agricultural sector. Which organization is it?

A. OAU   **B.** CENTO   **C.** SAARC   **D.** APEC

Q.59 "The geographical pivot of History" was published in which year?

A. 1904   **B.** 1905   **C.** 1903   **D.** 1906

Q.60 Which if the following is NOT a characteristic of the nomothetic approach?

A. Quantitative in nature
B. Qualitative in nature
C. Focuses on group averages
D. Establishes general laws

Q.61 Which parts of the world does the book 'Die Erdkunde' covers?

A. America and Asia
B. America and Europe
C. Asia and Africa
D. Africa and America

Q.62 Read the following statements and select the correct answer from the code given below:

(a) Space tradition was popularized by the spread of works of Immanuel Kant.

(b) Geographia by Strabo has locational details of Greece.

(c) Mapping has been an important part of spatial tradition in geography.

(d) Geometry and movement have been active interests of spatial geographers.

Code:

A. Only (a) is true
B. (a) and (b) are true
C. (a), (b) and (c) are true
D. (a), (c) and (d) are true

Q.63 Spatial analysis is based on

A. Positivism   **B.** Humanism
C. Feminism   **D.** Behaviouralism

Q.64 Which of the following are the characteristics of the humanistic approach in geography? Select your answer from the code given below:

(a) Humanism tries to extract meaning of life events.

(b) It is a statistical method.

(c) It has an expansive view of human abilities.

(d) It tries to identify individual's response to stimuli.

(e) It says that man doesn't interact much with the environment.

Code:

A. (a), (b), (c) and (d) are true
B. (a),(b) and (e) are true
C. (a), (c), (d) and(e) are true
D. (a), (c) and (d) are true

Q.65 Match List-I with List-II

List - I	List - II
(a) Geosophy	(i) Comte
(b) La utile	(ii) Reclus
(c) Structuralism	(iii) Wright
(d) Behaviouralism	(iv) Strauss

Select your answer from the code given below:

A. (a)-(iii),(b)-(i),(c)-(iv),(d)-(ii)
B. (a)-(ii),(b)-(i), (c)-(iv),(d)-(iii)
C. (a)-(iv),(b)-(iii),(c)-(ii), (d)-(i)
D. (a)-(ii),(b)-(iii),(c)-(iv), (d)-(i)

Q.66 The establishment of NATMO in 1956 led to development of

A. Cartography   **B.** Surveying
C. Climatic maps   **D.** Thematic maps

Q.67 Match the List-I with List-II

List - I (Books)	List - II (Geographers)
(a) Indian Cartographer	(i) L.R. singh
(b) Resource Atlas of Tamil Nadu	(ii) S.M. Alam
(c) Planning Atlas of Uttar Pradesh	(iii) B. K. Roy
(d) Census Atlas of India	(iv) A. Ramesh

Select the correct answer from the options given below:

A. (a)-(iv),(b)-(ii),(c)-(iii),(d)-(i)

B. (a)-(ii),(b)-(iv),(c)-(i),(d)-(iii)

C. (a)-(ii),(b)-(iii),(c)-(i),(d)-(iv)

D. (a)-(ii),(b)-(iii),(c)-(iv),(d)-(i)

Q.68 Read the following statements and select the correct answer from the code given below:

(a) The Greeks borrowed highly from Egyptian, Babylonian, Mesopotamian cultures and analyzed these concepts to development of geography and culture in the whole.

(b) Ptolemy described four winds coming from four directions in his book.

(c) Thales gave ten geometrical propositions.

(d) Anaximander introduced the Babylonian instrument Gnomon.

Code:

A. Only (a) is true

B. (a) and (b) are true

C. (a), (b) and (c) are true

D. (a) and (d) are true

Q.69 The sexagesimal system of dividing the year into 360 days was used first by

A. The Greek

B. The Romans

C. The Sumerians

D. The Mesopotamians

Q.70 Consider the following statements about reformative stage of Geography in India.

i. In the reformative stage departments of geography were grew up to 48.

ii. Concern with regards to the problems of planning and development.

iii. Lack of generalization in field of Geography.

Choose the correct option from below.

A. Only i

B. ii and iii

C. Only iii

D. i, ii and iii

Q.71 Match List-I with List-II and select the correct answer from the codes given below:

List - I (Spectral Range)	List - II (Wavelength)
(a) Microwave	(i) (0.7-3.0) micrometre
(b) Thermal Infrared	(ii) (0.1-0.4) micrometre
(c) Near Infrared	(iii) 1 millimetre (-) 1 metre
(d) Ultra-Violet	(iv) (8-12) micrometre

Code:

A. (a)-(iii), (b)-(ii), (c)-(iv), (d)-(i)

B. (a)-(iii), (b)-(iv), (c)-(ii), (d)-(i)

C. (a)-(iii), (b)-(iv), (c)-(i), (d)-(ii)

D. (a)-(ii), (b)-(i), (c)-(iv), (d)-(iii)

Q.72 Arrange the following maps in decreasing order of scale.

(a) Atlas maps

(b) Cadastral maps

(c) Topographical maps

(d) Wall maps

Codes:

A. (b), (c), (d), (a)

B. (a), (d), (c), (b)

C. (a), (b), (c), (d)

D. (d), (c), (b), (a)

Q.73 Which of the following depict relief?

A. Isochrones

B. Contour lines

C. Isobars

D. Isostades

Q.74 Match List-I with the List-II and select the correct answer from the code given below:

List - I (Measures of Mean)	List - II (Features)
(a) Harmonic Mean	(i) sum of the product of weight with the values divided by the sum of the weight.
(b) Geometric Mean	(ii) number of values divided by sum of the reciprocal of each values
(c) Quadratic Mean	(iii) nth root of product of (n) values
(d) Weighted Mean	(iv) square root of the average of the squares of each value

Code:

A. (a)-(iii), (b)-(i), (c)-(ii), (d)-(iv)

B. (a)-(iii), (b)-(iv), (c)-(ii), (d)-(i)

C. (a)-(ii), (b)-(iii), (c)-(iv), (d)-(i)

D. (a)-(ii), (b)-(i), (c)-(iv), (d)-(iii)

Q.75 The relation between vertical scale and horizontal scale in drawing of profiles is called

A. Scale Anomaly

B. Vertical Exaggeration

C. Horizontal Exaggeration

D. None of the above

Q.76 Given below are two statements. One is labelled as Assertion (A) and the other is labelled as Reason (R).

Assertion (A): Mode is useful as an approximate measure of central tendency.

Reason (R): Mode can be easily computed.

Select the correct answer from options given below:

A. Both (A) and (R) are true and (R) is the correct explanation of (A)

B. Both (A) and (R) are true, but (R) is not the correct explanation of (A)

C. (A) is true, but (R) is false

D. (A) is false, but (R) is true

Q.77 Read the following statements and choose the correct answer from the code given below:

(a) The Greek letter α (Alpha) is the symbol used to depict standard deviation.

(b) Standard deviation, interquartile range and variance are the common measures of dispersion.

(c) Variance is the square root of the standard deviation.

(d) Range is the value of the difference between the smallest and largest value.

Code:

A. (a) and (b) are true

B. (a), (b) and (d) are true

C. (b) and (d) are true

D. (c) and (d) are true

Q.78 Given below are two statements. One is labelled as Assertion (A) and the other is labelled as Reason (R).

Assertion (A): During sunrise and sunset, the sky appears to be red and orange.

Reason (R): Mie scattering occurs when the particles in atmosphere are smaller than the wavelength of the radiation.

Select the correct answer from options given below:

A. (A) is false, but (R) is true

B. (A) is true, but (R) is false

C. Both (A) and (R) are true, but (R) is not the correct explanation of (A)

D. Both (A) and (R) are true and (R) is the correct explanation of (A)

Q.79 The process of identifying and matching image co-ordinates to their true positions in ground co-ordinates is called as

A. Image registration

B. Geometric registration

C. Image enhancement

D. Ground positioning

Q.80 $Rb = \dfrac{Nu}{Nu+1}$ This is the formula for calculation of

A. Stream Order

B. Drainage density

C. Stream length

D. Bifurcation Ratio

Q.81 Consider the following statements:-

a) It was O.H.K. Spate who divided India into 7 major physiographic divisions.

b) The Vavul Mala, the Kudremukh are some of the important peaks of the Middle Sahyadris.

c) Geographically, the entire Himalayan region has been divided into the Shiwalik Range, the Middle Himalayas and the Central Himalayas.

d) The Kachchh Peninsula and the Kathiawar Peninsula lie on the West coastal plains.

Which of the following statements are correct?

A. a and d

B. b and c

C. a, b and c

D. b and d

Q.82 Match List I with the List II and select the correct answer from the code given below:-

List I (R.L. singh's Climatic Regions)	List II (Distribution)
a. Sub humid Littoral	i. Bihar, eastern part of UP
b. Semi-arid Tropical	ii. Odisha, West Bengal, Jharkhand
c. Humid South east	iii. Madhya Pradesh, Maharashtra
d. Sub humid Transition	iv. Tamil Nadu and coastal areas of Andhra Pradesh

A. (a)-(i), (b)-(iii), (c)-(iv), (d)-(ii)

B. (a)-(ii), (b)-(iii), (c)-(iv), (d)-(i)

C. (a)-(i), (b)-(iv), (c)-(iii), (d)-(ii)

D. (a)-(iv), (b)-(iii), (c)-(ii), (d)-(i)

Q.83 Who among the following explained the significance of the Tibet Plateau on the Indian monsoons?

A. P Koteshwaram

B. MT Yin

C. H Flohn

D. TN Krisnamurti

Q.84 Which of the following statements associated with Agricultural Productivity and Intensity are correct?

A. The level of agricultural productivity refers to the amount of the various inputs used to control the abiotic resources of the area and farming efficiency.

B. Cropping intensity is computed by the total cropped area and percentage of the net sown area.

C. Cropping intensity in states such as Punjab, Haryana and West Bengal are quite higher than the rest of the other states.

D. All of the above.

Q.85 What kind of agricultural practice is mostly observed in India?

A. Subsistence agriculture

B. Intensive agriculture

C. Plantation agriculture

D. Commercial farming

Q.86 Given below are two statements on one of the major industrial regions of India. One is labelled as Assertion (A) and the other is labelled as Reason (R).

Assertion(A)- Growth of the Hugli Industrial Region has declined as compared to other regions.

Reason(R)- One of the major causes of the decline is due to the silting of the Hugli Channel.

Select the correct answer from options given below:

A. Both (A) and (R) are true and (R) is the correct explanation of (A)

B. Both (A) and (R) are true, but (R) is not the correct explanation of (A)

C. (A) is true, but (R) is false

D. (A) is false, but (R) is true

Q.87 Which among the following year is declared the warmest year on record since 1901?

A. 2016 **B.** 2017 **C.** 2018 **D.** 2019

Q.88 Given below are two statements. One is labelled as Assertion (A) and the other is labelled as Reason (R).

Assertion (A): The Winter season experiences least tropical cyclone activity.

Reason (R): The sea surface temperature are low and ITCZ moves towards south.

Select the correct answer from options given below:

A. Both (A) and (R) are true and (R) is the correct explanation of (A)

B. Both (A) and (R) are true, but (R) is not the correct explanation of (A)

C. (A) is true, but (R) is false.

D. (A) is false, but (R) is true.

Q.89 Match the Rivers in List - I with specific characteristic features in List-II and select the correct answer from the codes given below:

List - I (Rivers)	List - II (Features)
(a) Ravi	(i) also known as Senge Khabbab

(b) Beas	(ii) formed by Chandra and Bhaga rivers
(c) Indus	(iii) flows through Kullu Valley
(d) Chenab	(iv) flows through Chamba Valley

A. (a)-(ii), (b)-(iv), (c)-(i), (d)-(iii)
B. (a)-(i), (b)-(iii), (c)-(iv), (d)-(ii)
C. (a)-(iv), (b)-(iii), (c)-(i), (d)-(ii)
D. (a)-(ii), (b)-(iv), (c)-(i), (d)-(iii)

Q.90 Which of the following is/are local storm of Hot weather or pre-monsoon season?

(a) Norwester

(b) Mango Shower

(c) Blossom Shower

(d) Guava Shower

A. (a) and (b) only
B. (a), (b) and (d) only
C. (a), (b) and (c) only
D. (a), (b), (c) and (d)

Q.91 Which among the following statements about the Himalayan cryosphere is incorrect?

A. Himalayan Cryosphere is the largest reserve of glaciers outside poles.

B. Lately most of the glaciers in the Himalayan cryosphere are retreating.

C. The number of glacial lakes in the Himalayan cryosphere is decreasing in recent times.

D. None of the above.

Q.92 As per the classification done by the Planning Commission of India, India was divided into how many zones?

A. 12   **B.** 15   **C.** 18   **D.** 20

Q.93 Match the methods of rice cultivation in List- I with the characteristic features in List – II and select the correct answer from the codes given below.

List - I (Methods)	List - II (Characteristics)
(a) Broadcasting	(i) Use of HYV seeds and fertilizers
(b) Drilling	(ii) minimum yields
(c) Transplantation	(iii) mainly in Peninsular India
(d) Japanese	(iv) practiced in fertile soil, abundant rainfall, and highest yields.

A. (a)-(ii), (b)-(iv), (c)-(i), (d)-(iii)
B. (a)-(ii), (b)-(iii), (c)-(iv), (d)-(i)
C. (a)-(iv), (b)-(iii), (c)-(i), (d)-(ii)
D. (a)-(ii), (b)-(i), (c)-(iv), (d)-(iii)

Q.94 Which among the following pairs is not matched?

A. Ankaleshwar: Petrochemical
B. Vishakapatnam: Shipbuilding
C. Alang Sosiya: Ship-Recycling
D. Koraput: Copper Smelting

Q.95 In which of the five-year plans, regional planning/development as a concept was incorporated explicitly by any means?

A. First Five Year Plan
B. Second Five Year Plan
C. Third five Year Plan
D. Fourth Five Year Plan

Q.96 Which among the following does not fall under Very High Damage Risk Zone category of the Earthquake zones in India?

A. Assam
B. Kutch of Gujarat
C. Arunachal Pradesh
D. Delhi

Q.97 Which among the following is/are factors influencing the location of industries in India?

A. Transport
B. State Policy
C. Climate
D. All of the above.

Q.98 Consider the following statements:-

a) In terms of the percentage of forest area to total area, Mizoram stands at the top.

b) Black soils are highly argillaceous in nature with about 62% clay factor.

c) West Bengal holds 2nd position in fish production in India.

Which of the following statements are correct?

A. a and b
B. b and c
C. only a
D. a, b, and c

Q.99 Which state observed a negative growth rate during the decade of 2001-2011?

A. Nagaland
B. Kerala
C. Manipur
D. Sikkim

Q.100 Consider the following statements:-

a) The five-year plans were failed to achieve its major objectives.

b) Regional planning concern with the well-being of the society of a concerned region.

The identification of the backward areas was carried out during the 1st decade of planning by the Planning Commission.

Which of the following statements are correct?

A. Only a
B. a and b
C. a and c
D. a, b, and c

// Smart Answer Sheet //

| Correct | Percentage of students who answered correctly. | Skipped | Percentage of students who skipped. |

Q.	Ans.	Correct / Skipped	Q.	Ans.	Correct / Skipped	Q.	Ans.	Correct / Skipped	Q.	Ans.	Correct / Skipped	Q.	Ans.	Correct / Skipped
1	D	40.0 % / 11.11 %	17	D	40.0 % / 28.89 %	33	B	6.67 % / 22.22 %	49	C	48.89 % / 28.89 %	65	A	13.33 % / 26.67 %
2	D	8.89 % / 28.89 %	18	C	42.22 % / 28.89 %	34	B	24.44 % / 28.89 %	50	A	22.22 % / 28.89 %	66	D	28.89 % / 28.89 %
3	B	46.67 % / 28.89 %	19	D	20.0 % / 20.0 %	35	D	24.44 % / 22.23 %	51	B	20.0 % / 28.89 %	67	B	26.67 % / 28.89 %
4	A	31.11 % / 28.89 %	20	C	35.56 % / 28.88 %	36	A	17.78 % / 28.89 %	52	D	33.33 % / 28.89 %	68	D	28.89 % / 28.89 %
5	C	28.89 % / 28.89 %	21	D	55.56 % / 26.66 %	37	B	17.78 % / 28.89 %	53	C	20.0 % / 28.89 %	69	C	15.56 % / 28.88 %
6	B	48.89 % / 28.89 %	22	A	15.56 % / 28.88 %	38	B	35.56 % / 28.88 %	54	B	37.78 % / 28.89 %	70	D	37.78 % / 28.89 %
7	A	6.67 % / 28.89 %	23	B	26.67 % / 22.22 %	39	C	35.56 % / 28.88 %	55	A	44.44 % / 28.89 %	71	C	31.11 % / 22.22 %
8	C	44.44 % / 28.89 %	24	B	28.89 % / 28.89 %	40	D	20.0 % / 28.89 %	56	D	20.0 % / 28.89 %	72	A	35.56 % / 28.88 %
9	B	20.0 % / 28.89 %	25	A	20.0 % / 28.89 %	41	A	24.44 % / 26.67 %	57	B	53.33 % / 28.89 %	73	B	48.89 % / 28.89 %
10	B	6.67 % / 28.89 %	26	A	46.67 % / 28.89 %	42	B	20.0 % / 28.89 %	58	C	26.67 % / 28.89 %	74	C	31.11 % / 28.89 %
11	B	33.33 % / 28.89 %	27	D	28.89 % / 24.44 %	43	A	40.0 % / 28.89 %	59	A	46.67 % / 28.89 %	75	B	11.11 % / 28.89 %
12	D	31.11 % / 28.89 %	28	D	13.33 % / 28.89 %	44	C	44.44 % / 28.89 %	60	B	26.67 % / 28.89 %	76	A	31.11 % / 28.89 %
13	B	51.11 % / 28.89 %	29	C	53.33 % / 26.67 %	45	B	8.89 % / 28.89 %	61	C	24.44 % / 28.89 %	77	C	6.67 % / 28.89 %
14	A	40.0 % / 28.89 %	30	A	28.89 % / 28.89 %	46	A	17.78 % / 28.89 %	62	D	33.33 % / 28.89 %	78	B	8.89 % / 28.89 %
15	D	51.11 % / 28.89 %	31	C	24.44 % / 28.89 %	47	A	53.33 % / 28.89 %	63	A	44.44 % / 28.89 %	79	B	13.33 % / 24.45 %
16	B	53.33 % / 28.89 %	32	A	6.67 % / 28.89 %	48	A	44.44 % / 28.89 %	64	D	33.33 % / 28.89 %	80	D	37.78 % / 28.89 %

Q.	Ans.	Correct		Q.	Ans.	Correct		Q.	Ans.	Correct		Q.	Ans.	Correct		Q.	Ans.	Correct
		Skipped				Skipped				Skipped				Skipped				Skipped
81	D	17.78 %		85	A	15.56 %		89	C	33.33 %		93	B	35.56 %		97	D	55.56 %
		26.66 %				28.88 %				28.89 %				28.88 %				28.88 %
82	D	15.56 %		86	A	44.44 %		90	C	33.33 %		94	D	15.56 %		98	D	35.56 %
		28.88 %				28.89 %				28.89 %				28.88 %				28.88 %
83	A	33.33 %		87	A	26.67 %		91	C	20.0 %		95	C	28.89 %		99	A	44.44 %
		28.89 %				28.89 %				28.89 %				28.89 %				28.89 %
84	D	51.11 %		88	A	44.44 %		92	B	42.22 %		96	D	35.56 %		100	B	13.33 %
		28.89 %				28.89 %				28.89 %				28.88 %				28.89 %

//Hints and Solutions//

1. The age and type of rocks found in the Appalachian Mountains of North America and the Caledonian Mountains in Norway, Ireland, Britain and Greenland are similar. As Wegner explained in that both these ranges were earlier a part of the same mountain system that got separated as the continents drifted away from each other.

2. When the continents move, they move towards and sometimes reach the cold part of the mantle. When they are stationary, they insulate the mantle underneath them, which keeps it warm. So, when they are moving or drifting away from each other, they eventually reach the cold parts. Most of the continents are thus in the cold part of the mantle. The only notable exception is of the continent of Africa, which is the stationary part of the supercontinent of Africa.

3. Endogenetic forces are the ones that take place inside the earth's surface. The other kind of processes is exogenetic forces are the ones that take place above the earth's surface. Examples of exogenetic process are weathering, and deposition. The examples of endogenetic processes include earthquakes and volcanoes.

4. Weathering is the process of mechanical disintegration and chemical decomposition of rocks. Various types of weathering include physical or mechanical weathering, chemical weathering and biological weathering. The various kinds of mechanical weathering include exfoliation or onion weathering, frost action, salt weathering, etc. Solution is a type of chemical weathering.

5. Denudation is the process of moving away materials on earth's surface by agents like winds, water, ice, etc. This leads to reduction in elevation and relief of landforms and landscapes. The agents of the denudation include biosphere, tectonic activity, geology, climatic conditions, etc. Ocean currents do not affect the process of denudation.

6. Davis gave the concept of peneplain in 1899. It is a surface with almost no relief and some residual hills (monadnocks). Penck gave the concept of Pediplain in 1924. It is a flat area at the foot of an elevated feature. The concept of Panplain was given by Crickmay in 1933 first. It is formed by lateral corrosion. It is a broad level surface. Etchplain was referenced in works of Thomas in 1989. It is a flattish surface in tropical and subtropical environments during the process of chemical weathering.

7. Walther Penck was a German scientist who gave a model of landform development. He assumed that the landscape development is also time dependent. The first stage is characterized by accelerated development. It is called as Aufsteigende Entwickelung. In the last stage, the valleys formed have two kinds of slopes- gravity slope and wash slope. The upper part of valley is called as gravity slope. The steep sided conical hill formed in this stage is called as inselberg.

8. The mobile and molten igneous rocks cool and solidify to form intrusion under the surface of the earth. Lacolith and batholiths are major intrusions while the dyke is a smaller one. Geysers on the other hand are natural fountains that throw up jets of hot water. Thus, they are extrusions, not intrusions.

9. Flaking is the process of detachment of think rock sheets from the rock mass due to differential expansion of rock shells caused by differential heating of outer and lower shells of a rock mass. Shattering is the breaking of outer shells of heated rocks into small fragments due to sudden light showers in hot climatic regions mainly in hot deserts. Slaking refers to disintegration of rocks due to alternate wetting and drying of rocks causing consequent expansion and contraction of rocks.

10. It is the focus or hypocenter of the earthquake which is the point of release of energy in the form of waves. Both the body waves (P and S waves) have shadow zones between 105° and 145° from the epicentre of the earthquake, beyond which only P-waves can travel. The intensity of any earthquake is measured with Mercalli scale. Richter scale is used to measure the magnitude of the earthquake. Composite volcanoes are characterized with cooler and more viscous lava when compared with shield volcanoes.

11. Climate change is the change in regional or global climatic patterns. There are various reasons for the reasons that lead to change in climatic patterns. The natural reasons include things like volcanic eruptions and sunspots. Human-induced reasons include pollution, increased CFCs, and greenhouse gases.

12. Climate change is one of the most important problems in the environment today. Scientists have been studying the increasing temperatures of the earth for the last 150 years now. They have come up with 6 evidences in support of climate change.

13. Climate change has affected the environment of the earth on a huge scale. The scientists have gathered six major evidences in support of climate change. They include rise in greenhouse gases, increase in global temperatures, retreat of Arctic sea, etc.

14. Climate change has been supported by scientists through 6 major evidences. These evidences include increase in global temperatures, retreating mountain glaciers, etc. Things such as increased green cover, economic activity and mining are not in these evidences.

15. The scientists have come up with six major evidences in support of climate change. These include rise in global temperatures, rise in greenhouse gases, retreating mountain glaciers, etc. These evidences indicate that the four major areas to concentrate on include temperature, sea level, extreme weather events and precipitation.

16. The atmosphere is made up of various layers. It is like a bubble of gases surrounding the earth's surface. Each of these layers has various characteristics. The first layer is troposphere. This layer is where most of the gases, water vapour and dust particles are present. The next is stratosphere, where the ozone layer or ozonosphere is found. The thermosphere is the fourth layer, after the third mesosphere. This layer has electronically charged particles or ions. The last is the exosphere, the outermost layer. This layer has the leas t density of air.

17. C.W Thornthwaite, an American climatologist, introduces two climatic classifications, one in 1931 and the other in 1948. He devised a complex and empirical classification which is very similar to Koppen's scheme.

18. La Nina is a climatic pattern that describes the cooling of surface ocean water along the tropical west coast of South America. La Nina is considered to be the counterpart to El Nino, which is characterized by usually warm ocean temperatures in equatorial region of the Pacific Ocean.

19. Drought is the condition where there is a prolonged shortage of water supply, whether atmospheric, surface water or ground water. It lasts for months in some cases or be of just 15 days. The main reason that triggers drought is deforestation.

20. The carbon dioxide in the atmosphere has increased about 30% since preindustrial times. It causes more heat to be trapped in the lower atmosphere. Human activities, industrialization and population growth are the main reason.

21. The Tsunami meters use these above components for detecting and measuring the magnitude of undersea earthquakes and tsunamis. The deep-sea sensors measure changes in water pressure of a tsunami wave and send the data to the buoys. The buoys capture wind speed, temperature, barometric pressure and after that these recorded data are being transmitted to the satellites which later relay the information to the Tsunami centres. These data are used for warnings against tsunamis.

22. • Tropical depressions are centers of low pressure surrounded by more than one closed isobar and are very small in size. The wind velocity around low pressure centre ranges between 40-50 km/hr. They are generally developed in the vicinity of the inter - tropical convergence but seldom develop in the trade wind belt.

• Tropical disturbances are migratory wave-like cyclones and are associated by easterly trade winds. They are characterized by heavy cumulus and cumulonimbus clouds which yield moderate to heavy rainfall with thunderstorms.

• Tropical storms are also low pressure centres and are surrounded by closed isobars where the velocity of winds is about 40 -120 km/hr. They develop in the Bay of Bengal and the Arabian sea during the summer season. These cyclones sometimes grow violent due to the heavy rainfall and therefore cause widespread flood.

• Hurricanes are represented by symmetrical closed circular isobars. Pressure increases sharply from the centre towards the outer margin resulting into steep pressure gradient. This is the reason for which the hurricanes move with great speed.

23. After the tsunami that struck Hawaii in 1946, it led to what is now known as Pacific Tsunami Warning System. As the name suggests, it is a tsunami warning system throughout Pacific Ocean. It coordinates information from 25 Pacific Rim countries and is headquartered in Ewa Beach near Honolulu in Hawaii. It uses seismic waves to forecast destructive tsunami.

24. Oceanic deeps or Trenches are major relief features in the ocean. They are the deepest parts of the ocean and are associated with active volcanoes and earthquakes. Seamounts, Guyots are under-water mountains while submarine canyons are deep valleys cutting across continental shelves and slopes. They often extend from the mouth of large rivers.

25. Mid oceanic ridges are the most extensive relief features, which is a chain of mountains running for a distance of more than 60000 km across Atlantic, Indian and Pacific Ocean. The mid oceanic ridges are associated with sea floor spreading which are indicative of divergent boundaries between two abyssal plains where continuous upwelling of lava takes place. It helps in the study of plate tectonics. The magmatic materials equidistant on either side of the volcanic vents are roughly of the same magnetic properties and their age is also studies.

26. The polar seas have much less salinity in comparison to other seas particularly of the ice melt and the process of freezing and thawing, which yields fresh water which is less in salinity. On the other hand, due to high evaporation, the salt content in the tropical oceans is very high.

27. Salinity is the measure of the total content of the dissolved salts in sea water, calculated as the grams of salt dissolved in 1000 grams of sea water. Dead sea and Red sea have very high salinity because of very high temperature and arid conditions. On the other hand, North Sea have relatively high salinity despite being in higher latitudes because the North Atlantic drift bring saline water into it. The Baltic sea has very low salinity because of influx of river waters in large quantity.

28. The concept of human ecology was introduced in geography by H.H. Barrows. He presented a case for Geography as Human Ecology. Amos Hawley was an American sociologist who worked extensively in the field of Human ecology. Robert Ezra Park was also an American urban sociologist who also coined the term for any academic discipline and did extensive work in that field. Neil Smith was a Scottish geographer in the field of economic geography and development.

29. Ecosystem is a dynamic system comprised of both biotic and abiotic components and the exchange of energy and matter among and between the components. Since it is a dynamic system, it is never a closed system. Also, the solar energy act as the primary source of energy which is used by the autotrophs for photosynthesis and producing food for themselves and other members of the ecosystem. Thus, ecosystem has its own productivity.

30. National Green Tribunal (NGT) was established in the year 2010 under National Green Tribunal Act for effective and expeditious disposal of cases relating to environmental protection and conservation of forests and other natural resources including enforcement of any legal right relating to environment and giving relief and compensation for damages to persons and property and for matters connected therewith or incidental thereto. It is a specialized body equipped with the necessary expertise to handle environmental disputes involving multi-disciplinary issues.

31. Stockholm Declaration was part of the Stockholm Conference of 1972 and it contained 26 principles. World Commission on Environment and Development is also known as Brundtland Commission and it presented a report in 1987 called "Our common future". Following the Rio Earth Summit also known as UN Conference on Environment and Development, after 10 years a world summit on Sustainable Development was held in Johannesburg in 2002 and was called Rio +10. UN Conference on Sustainable Development was held in 2012 in Rio and was called Rio +20 and in this conference, the report which was produced is called "The future we want".

32. * 'Process of vegetation' was work authored by Colin J Burrows.

* 'How the names are used for vegetation' is authored by Tian G.

* 'Foundation of Biogeography' was authored by H.J Brown.

* 'Origins of Biogeography' was authored by Ebach M.L.

33. No ecosystem is unaffected by other ecosystems and none is unaffected by humans, directly or indirectly; human ecology is not different from other kinds of ecology except to the degree to which humans affect their environment and an emphasis on application. The formal history of what can be called human ecology dates back to the 1921 as a sub discipline of social sciences.

Several diverse and distinct traditions have been recognized in the relationship between humans and the environment – imperialistic which holds that humans have dominion over nature; arcadian which holds humans as part of nature; scientific which holds that humankind is not independent of nature's ways and there is no distinction between humans and natural ecosystems.

34. The reviews that have been made on a number of natural food webs by Braind and Cohen(1987) have revealed that the actual number of links of all the chains in the webs ranged from 2 – 138, with the general range being 20-30 or 40.

Biomass pyramid gives only an idea of the biomass or the total weight of organic matter of each trophic level. The energy pyramid gives an idea on the ecological productivity and also helps in the comparison of the productivities of different ecosystems while the number pyramid helps in the comparative study of diversity of food chains and food webs.

35. Carbon sequestration is the process of removing carbon dioxide from the atmosphere and storing it in the form of solid or liquid. It helps in the goal of checking atmospheric CO_2 concentration. Soil Conservation, zero tillage and sustainable agriculture will reduce the chances of soil erosion and so limit the chance of the CO_2 trapped in the soil from being released into the atmosphere. Monoculture on the other hand is known to reduce the fertility of the soil, which requires the treatment through chemical fertilisers and pesticides and will eventually lead to soil degradation and soil erosion and release of carbon dioxide into air.

36. It was V. Gordon Childe whose theory was referred to as urban revolution and he termed urban revolution as the transformation of the Neolithic purely rural scenario into the one where cities and urban lifestyle emerged. During the beginning, there were only a few such cities. But wherever they did exist, the impact of man and land was remarkable.

37. August Losch's Theory of Market Centers gave major emphasis on demand. One of his main assumptions was that demand decreases with an increase in price. If this price increase was the result of an increase in transport costs, then the demand would decrease with distance from a production centre. The demand curve would be cone shaped and the market area circular. As more and more producer locate on the place, competition increases and the circular market areas become smaller as profits are competed away. Gradually, with each product, different market area importance, relative importance of transport costs, some of these patterns will coincide and form points of maximum demand. However, this assumption of his was criticized by many as it was overemphasized instead of other costs and benefits.

In Christaller's scheme, the hierarchy is composed of a series of discontinuous levels. This settlement system has a metropolitan city in its apex. The number of settlements increases at a level increases with the status in its hierarchy and produces the same kind of items at the same hierarchical level. However, Losch's theory was far less rigid. The less regular coincidence of centers of the same size may produce quite different combinations of goods. Losch's model incorporates other commercial functions.

38. Both statements are correct but none supports the other. Urbanization is what brought in refinement and culture. This idea emanated from the Romans, to whom civilized man was essentially a creature suited to living in the urbs. Villages normally had people who cultivated land or were artisan. But the urban areas were the centers of art, culture, leisure, and power. Urbanization was therefore a set of functions and functional relationships that were not found in the rural areas. Not only the occupations of people and their economic behavior, but also social and interpersonal relationships changed with transformation from rural to urban.

However, even though the urbanization process is the same, the factors affecting this have changed. In ancient times, cities rose due to the surplus agricultural production and the concentration of political powers. Manufacturing and technology were the new forces of the industrial age. Culture, finance, and recreation were the other factors. As these led to rural –urban migration this also led to urbanization.

39. As per goals given in National Population policy India needed to achieve Total Fertility Rate of 2.1%, infant mortality rate of 30 per thousand and 100% registration of births, deaths, marriages and pregnancy. The National Population Policy however was focused on reducing the growth rate and thus had no mention of population growth.

40. As given in the United Nations World Population Prospects 2019, the growth rate of world population has fallen below from 2.1 percent in 1950s to below 1.1 percent in 2019. The population of world was 2.5 billion in 1950 doubled to 5 billion in 1987, in just 37 years. Life expectancy of world population at birth was nearly 64 years in 1990. It has increased to 72.6 years as of 2019. The world population is projected to reach 10.1 billion by 2100, not double the current 7.7 billion at present.

41. Natural resources are classified as renewable and non-renewable resources. In renewable resource comes wind energy, water energy, solar energy, geothermal energy and biogas. Germany, Spain and USA are the leading countries of the world using wind power.

42. Within a very short span of time India's IT sector became one of the world's most profiteering sector. Every large MNC or TNC has its call centres and helpline services situated in India – is testimonial to that fact. Besides these outsourcing, software development in India has garnered huge admiration worldwide and this potential in India's IT sector led to the creation of software parks to facilitate this sector even further. However,

India's IT sector on the front of IT hardware's has not been impressive enough like that of the software industry.

43. Of the total exports, China holds the position of highest exports amounting upto USD 2.5 trillion. It is followed by US and Germany with USD 1.7 and USD 1.6 trillion. India's export is worth USD 326 billion. In terms of import, US is the biggest importer with USD 2.6 trillion followed by China with USD 2.1 trillion. India's import worth is USD 511 billion.

44. The world Trade Organization is international organization dealing with international trade rules. It was formed on 1st January 1995 in Geneva and currently 164 countries are signatories to it representing 98 per cent of world trade.

45. Ulman's flow theory is one of the major theoretical advancement in the field of spatial interaction. According to him the interaction between two regions is affected by complementarity (demand generated in Place B for goods in Place A), intervening opportunity (presence or absence of any other place in between Place A and B which could substitute the other's role) and transferability (the viability of the movement of the goods for the exchange or interaction to happen).

46. Michael Eliot Hurst is one of the pioneers of the spatial interaction paradigm long before transport geographers jumped into it. His famous work "Transportation and the societal framework" came in the year 1973, which gave a reasoned account of the development of the scholarship and literature in transport geography and also suggested new areas in the field of transport geography. Geography as Spatial Interaction was written by E. Ulman and the last two texts were written by Peter Haggett.

47. There are different methods applied for the delineation of crop combination regions, the first method for the crop combination is the arbitrary choice method, the second method is developed in terms of variable based on certain differences. Weaver pointed out , the relative , not absolute value being significant, square roots were not extracted. Thus, his formula is $\dfrac{\Sigma d^2}{n}$

48. The first scientific attempt for the delineation of agricultural region was carried out by D. Whittlesey in his paper "Major agricultural regions of the Earth" published in 1936 in the annals of Association of American geographers. He gave 13 types of agricultural region. Mediterranean region is specifically those regions around Mediterranean Sea and areas like California, Chile, Cape region, South African Coast, SW Australian coast which experiences wet winters and dry summers. This type of agriculture has been called distinctive and satisfactory in Whittlesey's words as there is the same old human and environment relation in the Old world.

49. The land use model propounded by Von Thunen suggests that the production of fresh milk, vegetables, fruits and flowers was concentrated in zone I, nearest to the city because of the perishable nature of these products. Zone II was used for production of wood, a bulky product in great demand in the city as fuel in the early part of 19th century. So this zone was called woods. Beyond the forest zones started the zones of cultivation with diminishing intensity away from the centre. The last zone,

that is zone VI was the farthest of all zones and was devoted to livestock farming, also known as ranching.

50. Ebola, a disease is chosen to be the distinctive characteristic to characterize a region. Hence, the areal units which are marked by the presence of Ebola is an example of formal region.

51. The extensive areas of support through won parliamentary seats is an example of the prevalence of the adherents/supporters of the Bhartiya Janata Party and thus such areas constitute a uniform region.

52. Formal or uniform region is the region which is characterized by one or more distinctive characteristics. Hence , religion suffices such criteria and the if we plot the Islamic countries in a world, the region will be created on the basis of a uniform criteria, religion. Zone of a distribution of a newspaper daily is representative of the fact that, the production of the newspaper from its head office or the printing press near the city centre has the maximum readership and farther we go from such node the function, and in this case readership keeps decreasing. Hence, it is a case of functional region. Economic region is also a subset of formal region, where economic criteria is the distinctive characteristic. Hence region with 90 per cent population engaged in service sector describes a dominance or prevalence of service sector. The map of Akhand Bharat is nothing but an imagination of geographical expanse of India which is not based on scientific facts, since it defies the theories of plate tectonics and Himalayan formation. Hence it is a perceptual region.

53. Region is a very commonly used concept to make it as medium to store or represent our information and its distribution or spatial organization. The scale of a region is very dynamic and can range from larger than a point to continents or even larger than continents. Biomes are the terrestrial ecosystems distinct from each other in terms of the vegetation and the wildlife found in different climatic zones. The idea of a Kurdish Nation is however a vernacular or Perceptual region as it has not been actualized on the ground and the Kurds, which are spread across few adjacent countries in the West Asia might have different imagination for the boundary of the same idea of Kurdish Nation.

54. Walter Christaller, who is known to have given the Central Place Theory, makes an assumption of isotropic surface. However, the central idea of his theory can be described using the concepts of hierarchy, threshold, range of goods, K principles. Hence they indicate the concept of functional regions in which centres or township or regions are drawn based on K principles and each has a zone of influence and also has boundaries between two adjacent regions each served by different centre. However, parts of two adjacent regions of same k principles can be part of a region of greater K principle.

55. It was Gunnar Myrdal who cave the theory of cumulative causation. It postulated that economic development once created in a region generates momentum for growth through cumulative causation and the same logic applies for the explanation of poorer regions through the concept of spread and backwash effects.

56. Workers in sugar mills generally suffer from this disease. Workers inhale dust from bagasse or sugarcane waste and causes acute respiratory problems. Due to this disease, workers suffer from headache, dry cough, chest pain, and loss of working power.

57. The Heartland theory can be explained using three simple statements, (i) One who controls Eastern Europe, controls Heartland, (ii) Who commands heartland command World Island and (iii) whoever commands World Island, controls the world. This theory was given by Halford John Mackinder.

58. SAARC or South Asian Association for Regional Cooperation was established in 1985 between Bangladesh, Bhutan, India, Nepal, Pakistan, Sri Lanka, Maldives. This Historic pact was signed at Dacca. The main purpose was to seek cooperation in the field of telecommunications, meteorology, shipping, infrastructure, agricultural rural sector, joint ventures, scientific and technical fields, market promotion in some selected commodities, educational, technical and cultural fields. It aims to provide a new impetus to the concept of a collective self-reliance in the region.

59. Alfred Mackinder's formulation for the heartland theory was set out in his article "The geographical pivot of History" was published in the year 1904. His concepts of geopolitics have significance of navies in world conflict.

60. Nomothetic approach is a precise and scientific method of logical reasoning applied to geography. It establishes laws based on scientific observation of large groups, taking averages into account, rather than focusing on a single individual. It is quantitative in nature, not qualitative.

61. The book 'Die Erdkunde' geography is a book written by Carl Ritter a German geographer. In this book Ritter has covered parts of Asia and Africa. He wanted to complete the geography of whole world, but sadly died in 1859 before he could complete the study of the remaining parts. The book is published in 21 volumes.

62. Immanuel Kant's works have helped in spreading the knowledge about spatial tradition in geography. Geometry and movement have been active interests of spatial geographers. Mapping has been important part of spatial geography. Geographia by Claudius Ptolemy contained information about location in Greece.

63. Spatial analysis is a quantitative tool for analysis. The goal is to build a general rule based on the behavior of individual members. Positivism was based on imperial evidence. It advocated the use of quantitative techniques. Thus, spatial analysis is based on positivism.

64. Man has a central position in humanistic approach. It states that man and the environment have constant interaction. The life events of man analyzed in order to understand their meanings. The aim of humanism is to identify individual's response to stimuli. It has a very expansive view of human abilities. This method is based on logical reasoning rather than statistics.

65. Wright gave the concept of Geosophy in 1947. He explained geographical systems as related to or based on the knowledge of people. It focused on how geography was related to how people conceived or imagined something. It was the beginning of the humanistic approach to geography.

La utile is one of the five principles of August Comte in 1830s. As per Comte, theories should be verified through empirical.

Theories thus proved should have some utility in social engineering.

Levi Strauss applied the model of structural linguistics to cultural anthropology. He put emphasis on exploring underlying pattern of human thought process that leads to development of a culture.

Reclus was a French geographer. He was a supporter of behavioral approach. He tried to explain that man is not passive. He plays and active and dynamic in nature.

66. The National Atlas and Thematic Mapping Organization (NATMO), as the name suggests has been established for creating thematic maps for the country. After its establishment in the year 1956, it has led to tremendous growth in the field of thematic mapping of India. The other organizations like Geological Survey of India and Indian Meteorological Department work for making geological and climatic maps respectively.

67. The book Indian Cartographer, Planning Atlas of Tamil Nadu was written by S.M. Alam in the year 1976.

The book Resource Atlas of Tamil Nadu by written by A. Ramesh in the year 1983.

L. R. Singh wrote the book Planning Atlas of Uttar Pradesh in the year 1987.

B.K. Roy wrote the book Census Atlas of India in the year 1981.

68. The Greek philosophers and thinkers used knowledge and ideas from different parts of the world like Egypt, Mesopotamia, etc and used these ideas for development of science, geography and culture. Homer is known to be one of the first of these thinkers, who, through his book Iliad gave four winds coming from four directions Boreas(north), Eurus(East), Notus (South) and Zephyrus(West). Thales gave 6 geometrical propositions which include ideas such as the circle is divided into 2 equal parts by the diameter which are taught to us in the high school. The Babylonian instrument Gnonmon was used to identify the location of celestial bodies. It was introduced to the Greeks by Anaximander.

69. The year was divided into 360 days in the sexagesimal system by the Sumerians. The Sumerians divide the year into 12 months each month with 30 days. They also divided the zodiac circle into 360 degrees from the idea of a circle to be divided into 360 degrees is taken.

70. In 1971, the field of geography got more developed and the number of departments grew to 48. In this stage 8 branches of geography have reached their development. These were economic geography, geography and planning, human geography, historical geography, political geography, regional geography, methodological review and research methods.

71. In the electromagnetic spectrum, energy of different characteristics or properties are arranged as per their wavelength. In one end of the spectrum are the energy wavelengths of the shortest size with highest frequency like Gamma rays followed by X-rays and ultra violet rays. The visible spectrum ranges between 0.4-0.7 micrometre. Infrared rays are larger in wavelength size than the visible spectrum. It is further divided into near infrared

(07-3.0 micrometre) and thermal infrared (8-12 micrometre). Microwave are the long wavelength rays with very low frequency.

72. Atlas maps, Wall maps are the maps displaying large part of the world or any country or state on a single material (paper). Thus any distance on the map represents very large distance on the actual ground and hence the scale is smaller. Atlas maps are even smaller than the wall maps. On the other hand cadastral maps are the maps used by the revenue officials for the land records of particular villages or revenue units and they have to be detailed. Thus any distance on the map would not be representing very large distance on the real ground unlike the previous two maps will be smaller. Thus the scale of cadastral maps will be highest. It will be followed by topographical maps. The world is divided into topographical zones assigned a particular number and they are done in order to give a fairly detailed view of the area concerned. The scale of topographical maps will be larger than that of atlas and cadastral maps.

73. Contour lines are isolines which depict points of equal altitude. Relief specifically means the difference between the maximum altitude and the minimum altitude of any area. Closely spaced contour lines will indicate steep slope and thus greater relief in a relatively smaller area and vice-versa.

74. The mean we calculate generally is called the arithmetic mean. There are instances when calculating the arithmetic mean don't give a true average and can be misleading. The most common is the weighted mean. It is used for calculating the average grade points for semester as the course taken may have different credits attached to them. Harmonic mean is used to calculate average speed for different speed on to and fro journey on the same route. Geometric mean is useful in finding the averages of percentages, ratios, growth rates and indexes. Quadratic mean is used in physical sciences such as voltage.

75. Vertical exaggeration is the ratio of vertical scale to horizontal scale. V.E. = V.Scale/Horizontal Scale. Generally the Vertical scale is chosen to be greater than the horizontal scale; otherwise the undulations would not be perceptible on the graph. One must always state the exaggeration below the profile. No exaggeration should be used for accurate geological sections.

76. Mode can be defined as the size of a variable which occurs most frequently. It is a value repeated maximum number of times. In case of ungrouped data, mode can be easily calculated by looking at the data. It is a crude and quick measure of central tendency.

77. Standard deviation, variance and interquartile range are common measures of dispersion. The range is the value of the difference between largest and smallest values. Standard deviation is the square root of the variance. Standard deviation is showed using the σ (sigma). It is also shown as SD.

78. During sunset and sunrise, the light from the sun has to travel far more distance trough the atmosphere than that at the time of midday. The scattering of shorter wavelengths is thus complete which leaves longer wavelengths of red and orange color to penetrate the atmosphere. This phenomenon, where the shortest available wavelength scatters is called as Rayleigh scattering. Thus, (A) is true and (R) is false.

79. The geometric registration process involves identifying the image coordinates(rows, columns)of several discernible points, called ground control points(or GCPs), in the distorted image(A-A1 to A4) and matching them to their true positions in ground coordinates (E.g. longitude and latitude) .

80. The bifurcation ratio is the ratio of number of streams of given order to number of streams of next higher order. The u stands for the number of stream order. Horton considered it to be index of relief and dissertation. Shumn gave the above formula for calculation of bifurcation ratio.

81. The Vavul Mala and the Kudremukh with a height of 2339m and 1892m respectively are some of the important peaks of the Middle Sahyadris. The Kachchh Peninsula and the Kathiawar Peninsula are some of the subdivisions of the west coastal plains based on relief and structure. The Kachchh Peninsula previously was an island which was surrounded by seas and lagoons. The Kathiawar Peninsula lies to the south of the Kachchh and the elevation ranges is below 200m.

82. Eastern Tamil Nadu and the coastal areas of Andhra Pradesh have a sub humid littoral climate. May is the hottest month when the temperature reaches to 38 degree C. Here summers are dry but winters are wet and the area receives 75-150cm of annual rainfall.

Large parts of Madhya Pradesh, Maharashtra, Gujarat, Chhattisgarh have semi arid tropical type of climate. Temperature varies from 13-29 degree C in January to 26-42 degree C in July. The average annual rainfall is about 50-100cm.

Humid South East includes Odisha, West Bengal, Jharkhand. Temperatures are 12-27 degree C and 26-34 degree C in January and July respectively. The average rainfall is 100-200 cm/yr.

The places with a sub humid transition type of climate are the eastern parts of Uttar Pradesh, Bihar and northern parts of Jharkhand. The temperatures are 9-24 degree C in January and 24-41 degree C in July. The average annual rainfall is 100-200 cm.

83. P. Koteshwaram tried to establish a relationship between the monsoons and the atmospheric conditions over the Tibet plateau. This plateau is surrounded by mountain ranges ranging from 6000-8000m above sea level. It gets heated during the summer. P. Koteswaram however, proposed that as the Tibet plateau is considered as a source of heat for the atmosphere, it generates an amount of rising air which spreads outwards and gradually sinks over the equatorial part of the Indian Ocean. During this stage, the ascending air is deflected to the right by the earth's rotational forces and moves in an anti-clockwise direction, thus leading to anticyclonic conditions in the upper troposphere over Tibet. Later on, it approaches the west coast of India as a return current from a South West direction. Hence, it picks up moisture from the Indian Ocean and leads to huge rainfall in India and the adjoining parts.

84. The Intensity of cropping is related to agricultural productivity. According to Singh, the level of agricultural productivity, as a concept, refers to the degree to which the economic, cultural, technical and organizational variables are able to exploit the abiotic resources of the area for agricultural production. Improvement in agricultural productivity is more of an efficient use of the factors of production such as environment, arable land, labour, etc.

Intensity of cropping refers to the number or amount of crops raised on a field during an agricultural year. The measure of cropping intensity is computed by calculating the total cropped area as percentage of the net sown area. The cropping intensity in India has changed a lot since Independence. This increase has been due to a variety of inputs such as fertilizers, irrigation and others. High intensity cropping in states like Punjab, Haryana, West Bengal, Manipur, and Lakshadweep varies from 100% to 190%.

85. Most parts of India still practice subsistence agriculture. The farmers own a small piece of land and grow crops just enough for his livelihood requirement with a little surplus to sell in the market. This type of agriculture has been practiced in India for the last several hundred of years and still continues even though the large changes in agriculture sector. This is due to number of reasons like small and fragmented land holdings, lack of mechanization, poor agricultural marketing practices, inadequate storage facilities, dependency on monsoon rainfall and many more.

86. The Hugli industrial region is still suffering due to the alarming rate of the silting problem. Dredging out of the silt that was rapidly filling up the water channel was very costly and just a temporary solution to save the Kolkata port. However, the construction of the Haldia port in the lower reaches of Hugli did ease a lot of pressure on the Kolkata port. But still, the industrial growth of this region has declined as compared to other regions. Moreover, the decline in jute industry after the partition of 1947 along with the silting problem are said to be the reasons behind this decline.

87. As per the 2019 annual climate summary published by IMD, 2019 was the seventh warmest year on record with an anomaly of +0.36°C of annual mean temperature above 1981-2010 average. However, it was also mentioned that the year 2016 was the warmest year on record with an anomaly of +0.71°C of annual mean temperature.

88. The winter season in India experiences least tropical cyclone activities because the sea surface temperature is quite low than what is required for the generation of tropical cyclone. Adding to this, in the winters, the Intra Tropical Convergence Zone also shifts farther south, which is why the storms generating during winters rarely reaches the Indian landmass. The ones generating in the Bay of Bengal sometimes touches Tamil Nadu.

89. Indus, Chenab, Ravi, Beas are part of the Indus River system., one of the largest river basins in the world. It originates near Mansarovar Lake in Tibet from a glacier near Bokhar Chu and is known as Senge Khabbab in the trans Himalayan region. Chenab is the largest tributary of Indus and is formed by two streams namely Chandra and Bhaga. Ravi rises west of the Rohtang pass in the Kullu hills of Himachal Pradesh and flow through the Chamba valley of the state whereas Beas river originates from Beas Kund near Rohtang Pass and flows through Kullu Valley.

90. Some of the famous local storms of the Hot Weather Season are namely loo, mango shower, blossom shower and norwester. Mango shower are pre monsoon showers occurring in the states of Kerala and Karnataka. Blossom shower is responsible for blossoming of the Coffee flowers in Kerala and nearby states. Norwesters are peculiar phenomena in West Bengal and Assam. Loo are hot, dry, and oppressing winds blowing in the northern plains from Punjab to Bihar.

91. All the regions on and beneath the earth and ocean where water is in solid form including snow cover, sea ice, lake ice, river ice, ice sheets and glaciers, frozen grounds (including permafrost) are termed as cryosphere. Himalayan cryosphere is also known as the third pole because of its sheer huge reserve of fresh water as ice and glaciers only next to the two poles. However, researches have showed that the huge proportion glaciers in the Himalayan cryosphere are retreating and in the process new glacial lakes are being formed and the existing ones growing in size. It has wide societal implications.

92. A country like India with unique and varied climatic conditions across its different parts makes the need of agriculture regionalization very imperative since the effect of climate on agriculture is profound. Many scholars had devised certain agricultural regionalization but the then Planning Commission of India, in 1989, came up with the concept of 15 agro-climatic zones.

93. In broadcasting method, seeds are sown broadcast by hand in areas comparatively dry and less fertile. It is also the easiest method but produce minimum yields as well. Drilling is predominantly carried out in Peninsular India where ploughing and sowing process is done by two persons. Transplantation is the method which is labour intensive, requires abundant rainfall and fertile soil and thus gives highest yields. Japanese method includes use of HYV seeds, chemical fertilizers and sowing seeds in a nursery and then transplanting in rows. It has been adopted lately by major rice producing regions.

94. Vishakhapatnam is known for its shipbuilding industry even before independence. Hindustan Shipyard Limited was set up in 1941 and the first ship launched was in 1948. Alang-Sosiya in Gujarat is the largest ship recycling yard in the world. Ankaleshwar in Gujarat is famous for its petrochemical industries. Koraput in Odisha is known for its Bauxite reserves and hence NALCO (National Alluminium Company limited) has its plants in Koraput.

95. In the first two five year plans, it was never mentioned about regional planning nor was it appreciated. It was in the third five year plan, that for the first time it was explicitly written about "balanced regional development" in Chapter 9 of the planning document. The philosophy of balanced regional development was thus appended to the era of five-year plans.

96. Based on an intensive analysis of more than 1,200 earthquakes that have occurred in India in different years in the past, and based on these, the National Institute of Disaster Management and Geological Survey of India has divided India into the following five earthquake zones. The zone named Very High Damage Risk Zone covers areas such as all of the north-eastern states, parts of Northern Bihar, Kutch district of Gujarat, parts of Himachal Pradesh (Dharamshala), parts of Uttarakhand and Kashmir Valley.

97. Transport and Climate are geographical factors influencing the location of industries. The development of railway network in India has strong correlation in the location of major industries in cities like Kolkata, Mumbai, Chennai. The extreme type of north-west India hinders the industrial development while the moderate climate of west coast of India is responsible for the clustering of Industries in the form of industrial regions and corridors. Government policy has a direct bearing on the industrial environment in the country. The five year plans are a good example to begin with. Also, the current Make in India and the concept of ease of doing business index reflects the influence of government policy in location of industries.

98. Andaman and Nicobar Islands, Arunachal Pradesh, Mizoram, Nagaland are those states which have 80% of their geographical area under forests. Percentage of forest area to total area serves as a better index of the forest cover. However, Madhya Pradesh has the largest area under forests in terms of India's total forest area.

Black soils are also called black cotton soils. These are highly retentive of moisture. As it has a high clay factor of more than 62%, it becomes sticky during the rainy season and under such conditions it becomes difficult to plough. Due to its high fertility and moisture retention capability, it is used for producing many crops. These soils are mainly found in Maharashtra, Andhra Pradesh, Gujarat and Tamil Nadu.

West Bengal is the 2nd largest producer of fish in India, with Andhra Pradesh being the largest fish producing state in India.

99. Around half of the states with a high population figure of about 10 million or more, have added less persons in the decade 2001-2011 compared to 1991-2001. However, this trend of low growth rate has been observed in a lot of states especially Nagaland, where there had been a steep fall in growth rate from 64.53% in 1991-2001 to a negative growth rate of -0.47%. This is the only state to have registered a negative trend in growth rate.

100. Even though the Five year plans were a partial success, it failed to achieve its major objectives such as providing a society free of exploitation, eradication of poverty, reducing hunger, malnutrition, unemployment, social injustice, gender discrimination, removal of economic, social and regional inequalities.

Regional planning is a specific type of planning, based on a specific planning structure, the primary aim of which is the well being of the society and improvement in living standards.

The identification of the backward areas was carried out during the second decade of planning.

Q.1 Who used the term inselberg in her/his theory of cycle of erosion?

A. Heald   **B.** Atwood   **C.** Hutton   **D.** Penck

Q.2 By which year the theory of plate tectonics widely accepted?

A. 1899   **B.** 1920   **C.** 1966   **D.** 1955

Q.3 Given below are two statements. One is labelled as Assertion (A) and the other is labelled as Reason (R).

Assertion (A): Secondary slopes are formed by processes tending to decrease relief.

Reason (R): Primary slopes evolve from the erosion and modification of secondary slopes.

Select the correct answer from options given below:

A. Both (A) and (R) are true and (R) is the correct explanation of (A)

B. Both (A) and (R) are true, but (R) is not the correct explanation of (A)

C. (A) is true, but (R) is false.

D. (A) is false, but (R) is true.

Q.4 What term refers to large pieces of ice-breaking off the front of a coastal glacier to form icebergs?

A. Ablation   **B.** Calving   **C.** Plucking   **D.** Surging

Q.5 Which of the following is not a cause for an earthquake?

A. Volcanic eruption   **B.** Mining

C. Tectonic activity   **D.** Deforestation

Q.6 Match List-I with the List-II and select the correct answer from the code given below:

List - I (Disaster)	List - II (Country)
(a) Maule Earthquake	(i) India
(b) Malin landslide	(ii) Afghanistan
(c) Krakatoa Volcanic eruption	(iii) Chile
(d) Salang Avalanche	(iv) Indonesia

code:

A. (a)-(i), (b)-(iii), (c)-(iv), (d)-(ii)

B. (a)-(ii), (b)-(iv), (c)-(i), (d)-(iii)

C. (a)-(i), (b)-(iv), (c)-(iii), (d)-(ii)

D. (a)-(iii), (b)-(i), (c)-(iv), (d)-(ii)

Q.7 Which of the following is an erosional landform made by the glacier?

A. Drumlins   **B.** Moraines

C. Cirque   **D.** Kettles

Q.8 Which of the following statements relating to folding and faulting are correct?

(a) Deformation must be slow in order to form folders.

(b) A fold where rock layers are warped downwards are called as anticline.

(c) A combination of a fault and a fold in one rock is called overthrust fault.

(d) Displacement of once connected blocks of rock along a fault plain is called as a fault.

Code:

A. (a) and (b) are true

B. (a) and (d) are true

C. (a), (b) and (d) are true

D. (a), (c) and (d) are true

Q.9 Cycles of pedimentation were envisioned by

A. L. C . King   **B.** Walther Penck

C. W. M. Davis   **D.** Crickmay

Q.10 Which of the following is NOT an assumption in Penck's geomorphic cycle?

A. The morphological characteristics on earth's surface are caused due to competition between denudational process and crustal movement.

B. Upliftment and erosion are always co-existent.

C. The slope is uniform in the first stage of geomorphic cycle.

D. Landscape development is time dependent.

Q.11 Which of the following gases is present in atmosphere in least amount?

A. Carbon dioxide   **B.** Nitrogen

C. Oxygen   **D.** Helium

Q.12 Given below are two statements One is labelled as Assertion (A) and the other is labelled as Reason (R).

Assertion (A): Clouds are formed due to dust particles.

Reason (R): Dust particles help in condensation of water vapour.

Select the correct answer from options given below:

A. Both (A) and (R) are true and (R) is the correct explanation of (A)

B. Both (A) and (R) are true, but (R) is not the correct explanation of (A)

C. (A) is true, but (R) is false

D. (A) is false, but (R) is true

Q.13 Which of the following statements relating to the cyclones in India are correct?

(a) Cyclones in India occur in two phases.

(b) Cyclones can cause some partial benefits like relieving drought conditions.

(c) May is the primary peak for cyclone in India.

(d) National Cyclone Risk Mitigation Project (NCRMP) is implemented on a state to state basis.

Code:

A. (b) and (c)   **B.** (a) and (c)

C. (a), (c) anc (d)   **D.** (a), (b) and (d)

Q.14 Which of the following is NOT a characteristic of an air mass?

A. Continental Polar air masses are cold and dry.

B. Monsoon air masses are dry and stable.

C. Equatorial air masses occur over the lower latitudes.

D. Polar air masses are the most stable.

Q.15 Match List-I with the List-II and select the correct answer from the code given below:

List-I (Name of cyclone)	List-II (Major affected country)
(a) Cyclone Nargis	(i) Myanmar
(b) Typhoon Haiyan	(ii) USA
(c) Cyclone Fani	(iii) Philippines
(d) Hurricane Katrina	(iv) India

Code:

A. (a)-(i), (b)-(iii), (c)-(iv), (d)-(ii)

B. (a)-(ii), (b)-(iv), (c)-(iii), (d)-(i)

C. (a)-(iii), (b)-(ii), (c)-(iv), (d)-(i)

D. (a)-(iv), (b)-(i), (c)-(ii), (d)-(iii)

Q.16 Which of the following statements relating to the cloudburst are true?

(a) Cloudburst is caused due to orographic lift.

(b) Rainfall rate in a cloudburst is 10 mm per hour.

(c) Cloudbursts can cause flash floods.

(d) Cloudburst occurs only when a cloud clashes with a solid body like a mountain.

Code:

A. (b) and (c)   **B.** (a) and (c)

C. (a), (c) anc (d)   **D.** (a), (b) and (d)

Q.17 Given below are two statements on Koppen's climatic classification. One is labelled as Assertion (A) and the other is labelled as Reason (R).

Assertion (A): Areas with BW climate has higher rainfall than in areas with BS climate.

Reason (R): Areas with BS climate experience mid-tropical cyclones & inter-tropical convergence.

Select the correct answer from options given below:

A. Both (A) and (R) are true and (R) is the correct explanation of (A)

B. Both (A) and (R) are true, but (R) is not the correct explanation of (A)

C. (A) is true, but (R) is false

D. (A) is false, but (R) is true

Q.18 Which of the following statements relating to Thornwaite's climatic classification are true?

(a) Thornwaite's climatic classification divides the world into 32 climatic types.

(b) A A'r climate is tropical wet climate.

(c) B A'w is a tropical humid climate with rainfall deficient in winter.

Code:

A. Only (a)   **B.** (a) and (c)

C. (b) and (c)   **D.** (a), (b) and (c)

Q.19 The La-Nina is characterized by

A. Warm ocean   **B.** Cold ocean

C. Monsoon wave   **D.** Cyclone

Q.20 How much of the total insolation is absorbed by the land and ocean?

A. 50%   **B.** 55%   **C.** 47%   **D.** 23%

Q.21 Match List-I with List-II and select the correct answer from the codes given below:

List - I (Relief Features)	List - II (Characteristics)
(a) Continental slopes	(i) most extensive terrain on earth
(b) Abyssal Plains	(ii) minimal to no oceanic deposits
(c) Continental Shelves	(iii) photic ecosystem
(d) Continental rise	(iv) formed when few deep-sea fans coalesce

code:

A. (a)-(ii), (b)-(i), (c)-(iii), (d)-(iv)

B. (a)-(i), (b)-(iv), (c)-(ii), (d)-(iii)

C. (a)-(ii), (b)-(iv), (c)-(i), (d)-(iii)

D. (a)-(iii), (b)-(ii), (c)-(i), (d)-(iv)

Q.22 Which among the following is not a technique of measuring negative reliefs?

A. Precision Depth Recorder

B. Sea MARC

C. GLORIA

D. Clinometer

Q.23 Which of the following waves best characterizes Tsunami?

A. shallow-water waves

B. deep-water waves

C. transitional waves

D. none of the above

Q.24 Which of the following regions is most likely to have experienced tsunamis?

A. The Circum pacific belt

B. Indian Ocean

C. Mid-Atlantic Ridges

D. Seas in the Antarctic

Ques (25-30):Direction: Read the passage and answer the following questions that follow.

"The interaction between man and environment therefore has two aspects: with environment influencing man and man influencing environment. This might be seen as a simple two-way system, but reality is not so simple and consequences of this interaction are inevitable. Mismanagement of the environment by bad farming practices on the High Plains of the USA were compounded by a period of drought in the years 1933-38, and this produced disastrous consequences for man as strong winds blew away the exhausted topsoil in a series of 'black blizzards' to produce the notorious 'Dust Bowl' which covered 6-5 million hectares. In this area, the direct effect of human activity on the environment produced feedbacks, which are described as positive when they operate to amplify change and negative when they operate to reduce change. Large areas were made useless for agriculture by bad farming practice but the national emergency caused by soil erosion had some beneficial effect on man's ability to manage the environment by the establishment of the US Soil Conservation Bureau and the National Resource Board, whose conservation practices provided negative feedback to reduce the damage. There was of course a time-lag between the occurrence of the damage and the effect of the policies and this type of change is also described as lagged' feedback. On the other hand, the disaster had a harmful effect in causing mass migration to California, where good agricultural lands became overcrowded. Thus the positive feedback from events in Oklahoma and Texas was transferred to California and such feedbacks in which one area pays for the actions of another are described as 'staggered'. Far from being a simple two-way system, man's impact on the environment may be direct, but it is much more likely to result in feedbacks, which can be positive or negative and lagged and/or staggered, depending on circumstance. As a result, the simple interaction model becomes a complicated system".

Q.25 Which among the following factors influence the ocean currents?

(a) Rotation of the earth

(b) Air Pressure and Wind

(c) Revolution of the Earth

(d) Density of Ocean Water

A. (a), (b) and (d) only

B. (b) only

C. (a) and (b)

D. (a), (b), (c) and (d)

Q.26 Which one of the following is NOT described in the above paragraph?

A. Human influences on environment.

B. Disastrous consequences of farming practices.

C. Methods of conservation.

D. 'Staggered' feedback

Q.27 Human-environment relationship is described in terms of

A. Simple two-way system

B. Complex three-way system

C. Realistic four-way system

D. Simple two-way system with complex consequences.

Q.28 Which one of the following comprises 'positive feedback'?

A. When human activity operates to intensity change.

B. Causes mass migration

C. One area pays for the actions in another area

D. When human activity on the environment reduce change.

Q.29 Which ONE of the following defines 'staggered' feedback?

A. Staggered feedback is a subset of positive feedback

B. It is a subset of negative feedback

C. It can be described as 'lagged' feedback

D. Feedback in which one area pays for the actions in another area

Q.30 Which of the following statements can be inferred from the above paragraph?

(a) Human is no longer a passive agent but an active modifier of the environment by triggering feedbacks.

(b) The author has used the concept of system analysis in the above paragraph.

(c) The increasing number extreme climatic events can be understood as the result of the feedback mechanism of earth.

(d) Overcrowding in the cities is always a staggered feedback.

A. (a), (b) and (c) only

B. (a) and (c) only

C. (b) and (c) only

D. (a), (b), (c) and (d)

Q.31 Match the major Grassland ecosystems (List-I) with the Regions (List-II) they are mainly found:

List - I (Grasslands)	List - II (Areas in the World)
(a) Velds	(i) North America
(b) Prairies	(ii) South America
(c) Pampas	(iii) Africa
(d) Steppes	(iv) Europe

A. (a)-(iii), (b)-(i), (c)-(ii), (d)-(iv)

B. (a)-(iii), (b)-(iv), (c)-(ii), (d)-(i)

C. (a)-(i), (b)-(ii), (c)-(iii), (d)-(iv)

D. (a)-(iv), (b)-(iii), (c)-(ii), (d)-(i)

Q.32 Which environmental policy was set up prior to the Stockholm period i.e., prior to 1972?

A. OEPC (Office of the Environment Planning and Coordination)

B. Tiwari Committee

C. Ministry of Environment and Forests

D. None of the above

Q.33 Match List I with List II and select the correct answer from the code given below:

List - I (Demographic Data Sources)	List - II (Organization/Agency)
(a) CENSUS	(i) Registrar General
(b) NFHS	(ii) University of Maryland; NCAER
(c) National Sample Survey	(iii) IIPS
(d) IHDS	(lv) NSSO

A. (a)-(i), (b)-(ii), (c)-(iv), (d)-(iii)

B. (a)-(ii), (b)-(iii), (c)-(iv), (d)-(i)

C. (a)-(i), (b)-(iii), (c)-(iv), (d)-(ii)

D. (a)-(iv), (b)-(ii), (c)-(iii), (d)-(i)

Q.34 Given below are two statements. One is labelled as Assertion (A) and the other is labelled as Reason (R).

Assertion (A): The Demographic Transition Theory tries to establish a causal relationship between modernization and natural change in population.

Reason (R): Low Birth and Death Rate shifts towards toward high birth and death rates.

Select the correct answer from options given below:

A. Both (A) and (R) are true and (R) is the correct explanation of (A)

B. Both (A) and (R) are true, but (R) is not the correct explanation of (A)

C. (A) is true, but (R) is false.

D. (A) is false, but (R) is true.

Q.35 Match List – I with list – II and select the correct answer from the codes given below.

List - I (Theories)	List - II (Propounders)
(a) Optimum Population	(D) Thompson-Notestein
(b) Demographic Transition	(ii) Ravenstein
(c) Migration Theory	(iii) Cannon-Saunders
(d) Intervening Opportunities	(iv) S. Stouffer

A. (a)-(iii), (b)-(i), (c)-(ii), (d)-(iv)

B. (a)-(ii), (b)-(iii), (c)-(iv), (d)-(i)

C. (a)-(iv), (b)-(i), (c)-(ii), (d)-(iii)

D. (a)-(iv), (b)-(ii), (c)-(iii), (d)-(i)

Q.36 Which of the following statements related to India's National Population Policy, 2000 are correct?

(a) The immediate objective was to address the unmet needs of contraception, health care infrastructure, and health personnel and to provide integrated service delivery for basic reproductive and child health care.

(b) The medium term objective was to bring the TFR to replacement levels by 2010.

(c) The long term objective was to achieve a stable population by 2045.

(d) In pursuance of these objectives, National Socio-Demographic Goals were set up.

A. (d) only

B. (c) and (d) only

C. (a), (b) and (c) only

D. (a), (b), (c) and (d)

Q.37 Which among the following Rn values indicates a uniform or regular distribution of settlements?

A. 2.15   **B.** 1.5   **C.** 3.15   **D.** 0

Q.38 In which famous book of Lewis Mumford, did he explain the growth of towns and cities?

A. Culture of Cities

B. The City in History

C. City Development

D. The Story of Utopias

Q.39 Given below are the two statements, one labelled as Assertion (A) and the other labelled as Reason (R). Select your answer from the code given below:

Assertion (A) : According to Malthus' theory, the population outruns food supply.

Reason (R) : According to Malthus' theory, the food supply increases in geometric progression.

Code :

A. Both (A) and (R) are true and (R) is the correct explanation of (A).

B. Both (A) and (R) are true but (R) is not the correct explanation of (A).

C. (A) is true but (R) is false.

D. (A) is false but (R) is true.

Q.40 Which among the following is the correct sequence of land use from periphery to the centre in the urban land use model of Burgess?

A. Commuters' Zone, Zone of Better Residence, Zone of Workers' home and the Central Business District

B. Zone of Workers Home, Commuters' Zone, Zone of Better Residences and the Central Business District

C. Zone of Better Residence, Commuters' Zone, Zone of Workers' home and the Central Business District

D. Commuters Zone, Zone of Workers' Home, Zone of Better Residences and the Central Business District

Q.41 Which among the following industries is not a knowledge-based industry explicitly?

A. Software Industry   **B.** Education Industry

C. Medical Industry   **D.** None of the above

Q.42 Which of the following statements is not correct about world trade?

A. WTO replaced the earlier General Agreement on Tariff and Trade.

B. The North in general has emerges to be the global core and the south in general acts as periphery to the North in terms of Global trade.

C. Over the years Global South-South trade has outperformed both world trade and North-South trade.

D. India and China are the largest exporters in world trade.

Q.43 Which of the following statements best describes Pi Index relating to Graph theory?

A. The relationship between the total length of the graph(network) and the distance along its diameter.

B. It is the value of circumference of the transport network.

C. The number of nodes divided by number of edges in a network.

D. The number of links divided by beta index.

Q.44 The oceanic resources upto 200 nautical miles from the maritime boundary of a country is called:

A. Special Exclusive Zone

B. Special Economic Zone

C. Exclusive Economic Zone

D. Marine Economic Zone

Q.45 Given below are two statements. One is labelled as Assertion (A) and the other is labelled as Reason (R).

Assertion (A): All Natural Resources are non-renewable resources.

Reason (R) : Nonrenewable resources exhausts at a much faster rate than its replenishment.

Select the correct answer from options given below:

A. Both (A) and (R) are true and (R) is the correct explanation of (A)

B. Both (A) and (R) are true, but (R) is not the correct explanation of (A)

C. (A) is true, but (R) is false.

D. (A) is false, but (R) is true.

Q.46 Which of the following factors plays a major role in the spatial organization of agriculture?

(a) Relief, Climate and Soil

(b) Irrigation Facility

(c) Landholding size

(d) Availability of Technological inputs

Choose the correct option from below:

A. Only (a)

B. (a), (b) and (c)

C. (a) and (b)

D. (a), (b), (c) and (d)

Q.47 Which of the following is not a factor of industrial location?

A. Cost of Raw Materials

B. Cost of Distribution of Production

C. Presence of agglomeration economies

D. Religious makeover of the working population

Q.48 Match List I with List II and select the correct answer from the code given below:

ListI(Enterprise)	List II(Industry)
a. SAIL	i. Joint Sector
b.TISCO	ii. Private Sector
c.AMUL	iii. Public Sector
d.Mahanagar Gas limited	iv.Cooperative Sector

Code:

A. (a)-(ii), (b)-(i), (c)-(iii), (d)-(iv)

B. (a)-(ii), (b)-(iii), (c)-(iv), (d)-(i)

C. (a)-(iii), (b)-(ii), (c)-(iv), (d)-(i)

D. (a)-(iv), (b)-(ii), (c)-(iii), (d)-(i)

Q.49 Given below are two statements. One is labelled as Assertion (A) and the other is labelled as Reason (R).

Assertion (A): On the basis of ownership, industries can be classified as Basic/Key Industries and Consumer Industries.

Reason (R) : BHEL is an enterprise under public sector industries.

Select the correct answer from options given below:

A. Both (A) and (R) are true and (R) is the correct explanation of (A)

B. Both (A) and (R) are true, but (R) is not the correct explanation of (A)

C. (A) is true, but (R) is false.

D. (A) is false, but (R) is true.

Q.50 Which among the following is the most suitable reason for the Japan's high production of steel despite very low reserves of raw material?

A. Availability of technology

B. Cheap labour

C. Labor Unionism

D. Climate

Q.51 Which of the following statements about the concept of growth poles/growth centres is/are correct?

(a) The concept of growth poles was used in geography by Perroux.

(b) Lower order growth centres are located quite far away as compared to higher order growth centres.

(c) Higher order Growth centres are located far away while lower order growth centres are located closer to one and another.

(d) Growth foci is the modified version of the growth pole theory in Indian context by VLS Prakasha Rao.

Codes:

A. (a) and (b) only

B. (b) and (c) only

C. (a) and (c) only

D. (a), (c) and (d) only

Q.52 Which among the following method is not a measure of soil conservation?

A. Terrace Farming

B. Contour Ploughing

C. Strip Farming

D. Deep Tillage

Q.53 Which among the following regions has the highest productivity of wheat in the world?

A. South America

B. Asia

C. western Europe

D. North America

Q.54 Given below are two statements. One is labelled as Assertion (A) and the other is labelled as Reason (R).

Assertion (A): The dairy and the perishable products are located near the centre as per Von Thunen's model of agricultural location.

Reason (R) : The locational rent of milk will fall steeply compared to wheat as the distance from the city centre increases.

Select the correct answer from options given below:

A. Both (A) and (R) are true and (R) is the correct explanation of (A)

B. Both (A) and (R) are true, but (R) is not the correct explanation of (A)

C. (A) is true, but (R) is false.

D. (A) is false, but (R) is true.

Q.55 Which among the following best describes J.C Weaver's method of crop combination?

A. Mean Positive Deviation Method

B. Minimum Deviation Method

C. Modified minimum deviation

D. Maximum positive deviation method

Q.56 Match List-I with the List-II and select the correct answer from the code given below:

List - I (Organization)	List-II (Headquarters)
(a) SAARC	(i) Brussels
(b) ASEAN	(ii) Vienna
(c) OPEC	(iii) Kathmandu
(d) EU	(iv) Jakarta

Code:

A. (a)-(i), (b)-(iii), (c)-(iv), (d)-(ii)
B. (a)-(iii), (b)-(iv), (c)-(ii), (d)-(i)
C. (a)-(iii), (b)-(iv), (c)-(i), (d)-(ii)
D. (a)-(iv), (b)-(i), (c)-(ii), (d)-(iii)

Q.57 Given below are two statements One is labelled as Assertion (A) and the other is labelled as Reason (R).

Assertion (A): The Schengen Area is an area of countries which have abolished border control at mutual borders.

Reason (R): European Union is a customs Union between the nations of European continent.

Select the correct answer from options given below:

A. Both (A) and (R) are true and (R) is the correct explanation of (A)
B. Both (A) and (R) are true, but (R) is not the correct explanation of (A)
C. (A) is true, but (R) is false
D. (A) is false, but (R) is true

Q.58 Which of the following statements relating to the geopolitics in Indian Ocean are correct?

(a) India has maritime dispute with Pakistan regarding the demarcation of boundary along Sir Creek.

(b) India has no maritime issues with Sri Lanka.

(c) Indian Ocean is important for oil trade due to presence of Malacca Strait providing the sea passage from Persian Gulf to open sea.

(d) India has maritime issue with Bangladesh regarding the ownership of New Moore Island.

Code:

A. (b) and (c)
B. (a) and (d)
C. (a), (c) and (d)
D. (b), (c) and (d)

Q.59 Which of the following statements relating Heartland theory are correct?

(a) North America, South America, Africa south of Sahara and Oceania are part of outer crescent.

(b) The Midland area would control the world as per the modifications of the 1943.

(c) Mackinder has been criticized for constantly modifying his own theory.

(d) In 1943, Mackinder modified his theory to include the whole outer crescent of land.

Code:

A. (a), (b) and (c)
B. (a) and (d)
C. (a), (c) and (d)
D. (b), (c) and (d)

Q.60 Given below are two statements one is labeled as Assertion (A) and the other is labeled as Reason (R).

Assertion (A): Feminists geography is not considered while studying cultural geography.

Reason (R): Political geography studies ways in which political processes are themselves affected by spatial structure.

Select the correct answer from options given below:

A. Both (A) and (R) are true and (R) is the correct explanation of (A)
B. Both (A) and (R) are true, but (R) is not the correct explanation of (A)
C. (A) is true, but (R) is false
D. (A) is false, but (R) is true

Q.61 Which of the following statements relating to Chinese geographer is correct?

(a) Fan Chengda belonged to Song dynasty.

(b) Fan Chengda's work dealt with peasants' life.

(c) He has authored important geographical treaties known as Gui Hai Yu Heng Zhi.

Code:

A. (b) and (c)
B. (a) and (c)
C. Only (c)
D. (a),(b) and (c)

Q.62 Who is known as the father of Indian geography?

A. James Rennell
B. Marthus Augustus
C. Majid Hussain
D. Arya Bhatta

Q.63 Match List-I with the List-II and select the correct answer from the code given below:

List - I (German Geographers)	List - II (Birth Years)
(a) Bernhardus Verenius	(i) 1724
(b) Immanuel Kant	(ii) 1622
(c) Alexander von Humbolt	(iii) 1779
(d) Carl Ritter	(iv) 1769

Code:

A. (a)-(i), (b)-(iii), (c)-(iv), (d)-(ii)
B. (a)-(ii), (b)-(i), (c)-(iv), (d)-(iii)
C. (a)-(i), (b)-(iv), (c)-(iii), (d)-(ii)
D. (a)-(iv), (b)-(i), (c)-(ii), (d)-(iii)

Q.64 Given below are two statements about a major geographic work of Humboldt. One is labelled as Assertion (A) and the other is labelled as Reason (R).

Assertion (A): Cosmos written by Humboldt has 5 volumes.

Reason (R): The first volume focused on the human aspects on earth.

Select the correct answer from options given below:

A. Both (A) and (R) are true and (R) is the correct explanation of (A)
B. Both (A) and (R) are true, but (R) is not the correct explanation of (A)
C. (A) is true, but (R) is false
D. (A) is false, but (R) is true

Q.65 Given below are two statements on man-land tradition. One is labelled as Assertion (A) and the other is labelled as Reason (R).

Assertion (A): Human Health is influenced by external conditions like nature .

Reason (R): Environment conditions partially depend on the actions of human beings.

Select the correct answer from options given below:

A. Both (A) and (R) are true and (R) is the correct explanation of (A)

B. Both (A) and (R) are true, but (R) is not the correct explanation of (A)

C. (A) is true, but (R) is false

D. (A) is false, but (R) is true

Q.66 According to Pattison which tradition of geography focuses on the Earth as the home to human survival?

A. Earth Science tradition

B. Man-land tradition

C. Area studies tradition

D. Spatial tradition

Q.67 Which of the following statements relating to physical and human geography is correct?

(a) Human groups can be generalized on the basis of probability.

(b) Varenius's work Geographia generalis was published in 1650 .

(c) Physical geography can be concluded by certainty.

(d) Hecataeus emphasized more on physical geography.

Code:

A. (b) and (c)   **B.** (a) and (d)

C. (a), (c) and (d)   **D.** (a),(b), (c) and (d)

Q.68 Who defined Kuhn's "paradigm of science" as super model?

A. Hagget   **B.** Ritter

C. Hartshorne   **D.** Haushofer

Q.69 In which period did behaviourlism became prominent in geography?

A. 1920-1930   **B.** 1960-1970

C. 1910-1920   **D.** 1940-1950

Q.70 Who is the author of "companion to feminist geography"?

A. Seager and Johnson   **B.** W.M Smith

C. Keval Aggarval   **D.** Edward Honds

Q.71 Which form of data gives information about a feature that is geographically referenced?

A. Spatial Data   **B.** Non-Spatial Data

C. Metadata   **D.** None of the above

Q.72 Match List I with the List II and select the correct answer from the codes given below:-

List I	List II
a. Simple line Diagram	i. Land use of a district
b. Vertical Bar	ii. Rural and urban population of some

Diagram	states
c. Multiple Bar Diagram	iii. Growth of population in India from (1901- 2011)
d. Pie Diagram	iv. Mean monthly temperature of a city

code:

A. (a)-(i), (b)-(iii), (c)-(iv), (d)-(ii)

B. (a)-(ii), (b)-(iii), (c)-(iv), (d)-(i)

C. (a)-(i), (b)-(iv), (c)-(iii), (d)-(ii)

D. (a)-(iv), (b)-(iii), (c)-(ii), (d)-(i)

Q.73 Consider the following statements:-

a) Isopleth maps are a form of qualitative maps and generally use ordinal data.

b) Dot maps are most useful when values are unevenly distributed.

c) The basic principle of Choropleth maps is that the intensity of shading is directly proportional to the density of elements.

d) The greatest advantage of chorochromatic maps is that many elements can be shown together on a single map.

Which of the following statements are correct?

A. a, b and c   **B.** b and c

C. a and c   **D.** b, c and d

Q.74 Given below are two statements on GIS. One is labelled as Assertion(A) and the other is labelled as Reason(R).

Assertion(A)- Spatial Information Systems are designed for data pertaining to real world features.

Reason(R)- Not all spatial information systems can be termed as GIS.

Select the correct answer from options given below:-

A. Both A and R are true, and R is the correct explanation of A

B. Both A and R are true, but R is not the correct explanation of A

C. A is true but R is false

D. A is false but R is true

Q.75 Consider the following statements:-

a) Geometric corrections include correcting sensor irregularities, and unwanted sensor or atmospheric noise.

b) Linear contrast stretch involves identifying upper and lower bounds from the histogram and applying a transformation to stretch this range to fill the full range.

c) Low pass filters are used to sharpen the appearance of fine detail in an image.

d) In a supervised classification, the analyst identifies in the imagery homogenous samples of different surface cover types.

Which of the following statements are correct?

A. b and d   **B.** a, b and d

C. a and c   **D.** b and c

Q.76 Which of the following option is correct for the measures of central tendency?

A. Median can calculated from a frequency distribution with open-end intervals.

B. During the calculation of mean, the values of all items are taken into consideration.

C. Median is more affected by sampling fluctuations than the

Arithmetic Mean.

D. All of the above.

Q.77 Consider the following statements:-

a) Random Sampling is sampling in a haphazard manner.

b) The larger the sample in random sampling, the smaller is the standard error of the sample mean.

c) The parameter value remains constant as it doesn't have a sampling distribution or a standard error.

d) Standard error of mean refers to the absolute mean deviation in the sampling distribution of mean.

Which of the following statements are correct?

A. a and b

B. b and c

C. a, b and c

D. c and d

Q.78 In the river basin morphology, the ratio of average length of segment of order 'u' to the mean or average length of order 'u-1' is known as

A. Bifurcation Ratio

B. Stream Length ratio

C. Elongation Ratio

D. Circularity Ratio

Q.79 What does the Hypsometric curve describe?

A. Mean monthly values of selected climatic elements of a particular station

B. Flow rate of streams as a function of time at a specified location

C. Relationship between cropping patterns and the rhythm of climatic elements

D. the area-height relation of a drainage basin.

Q.80 Match List I with the List II and select the correct answer from the codes given below:-

List I	List II
a. Strahler	i. the stream orders of 2 streams are added and provide the rank number of the stream
b. Horton	ii. Stream ordering that allocates '1' to the river with its mouth at the sea
c.Gravelius	iii. Stream order number increase by one at every confluence
d. Shreve	iv. Top-down system where two 1ˢᵗ order streams unite to form a 2ⁿᵈ order stream and so on

Codes

A. (a)-(i), (b)-(iii), (c)-(iv), (d)-(ii)

B. (a)-(ii), (b)-(iii), (c)-(iv), (d)-(i)

C. (a)-(i), (b)-(iv), (c)-(iii), (d)-(ii)

D. (a)-(iv), (b)-(iii), (c)-(ii), (d)-(i)

Q.81 Match List I with List II:-

List I(Major Rivers)	List II(Origin)
a. Godavari	i. Dandakaranya near Sihawa in Raipur district
b.Satluj	ii. Trimbak Plateau near Nashik
c.Ghaghara	iii. Manasarovar-Rakas Lakes
d.Mahanadi	iv. Near Gurla Mandhota peak

code:

A. a-1 b-2 c-3 d-4

B. a-4 b-3 c-1 d-2

C. a-2 b-3 c-4 d-1

D. a-2 b-1 c-4 d-3

Q.82 In which of the following years was the National Disaster Management Act framed in India?

A. 2006   **B.** 2005   **C.** 2004   **D.** 2003

Q.83 Which one of the following natural disaster is not associated with Himalayan Region?

A. GLOF

B. Landslides

C. Avalanches

D. Drought

Q.84 Given below are two statements. One is labelled as Assertion (A) and the other is labelled as Reason (R).

Assertion (A): In the first five year plan, the emphasis was on constructing new heavy industries.

Reason (R): In the first five year plan industrial output grew by 40 per cent while agricultural output grew by 30 per cent.

Select the correct answer from options given below:

A. Both (A) and (R) are true and (R) is the correct explanation of (A)

B. Both (A) and (R) are true, but (R) is not the correct explanation of (A)

C. (A) is true, but (R) is false.

D. (A) is false, but (R) is true.

Q.85 Which among the following statements relating to Agro-Climatic Regions is not correct?

A. East Himalaya is the region with lowest net sown area.

B. A modified version of agro-climatic region came to be known as agro-ecological region.

C. Agro-Ecological Region was different from agro climatic region in the way that land carved out of agro-climatic was region super-imposed on landforms and soil condition to form agro ecological regions.

D. None of the above.

Q.86 Which of the following are the limitations associated with the Green Revolution?

(a) Increased regional disparity

(b) Use of High Yielding Variety (HYV) of seeds

(c) Homogeneity of crops and their varieties in a region.

(d) Increased inter-personal inequalities

A. (b) only

B. (a) and (b) only

C. (a), (c) and (d) only

D. (a), (b) and (d) only

Q.87 Which among the following states has the lowest proportion of its total irrigated area under all crops?

A. Assam

B. West Bengal

C. Bihar

D. Jharkhand

Q.88 Which among the following states has the largest average size of the operational landholdings?

A. Punjab

B. Rajasthan

C. Bihar

D. Uttar Pradesh

Q.89 Given below are two statements. One is labelled as Assertion (A) and the other is labelled as Reason (R).

Assertion (A): Tamil Nadu mainly receives rainfall due to the south west monsoon.

Reason (R): It falls in the rain shadow area of the Arabian Sea branch of S.W. Monsoon

Select the correct answer from options given below:

A. Both (A) and (R) are true and (R) is the correct explanation of (A)

B. Both (A) and (R) are true, but (R) is not the correct explanation of (A)

C. (A) is true, but (R) is false.

D. (A) is false, but (R) is true.

Q.90 Arrange the following tributaries of river Indus from North to South :

(a) Chenab

(b) Jhelum

(c) Ravi

(d) Sutlej

Select the correct answer using the code given below :

A. (d)-(c)-(a)-(b)

B. (b)-(c)-(a)-(d)

C. (a)-(b)-(c)-(d)

D. (b)-(a)-(c)-(d)

Q.91 Which among the following statements regarding the Himalayan rivers and peninsular rivers are correct?

(a) All Peninsular rivers flows from west to east direction.

(b) The peninsular rivers are characterized by fixed course, absence of meanders, and seasonal flow of water.

(c) Himalayan drainage system is younger than the peninsular drainage system.

(d) Many of the Himalayan rivers are examples of antecedent drainage.

A. (b) only

B. (b), (c) and (d) only

C. (a), (b) and (d) only

D. (a), (b), (c) and (d)

Q.92 Which of the following options associated with horizontal seismic coefficient isolines are correct?

A. Horizontal seismic coefficient isolines are lines indicating limits of seismic zones.

B. The areas of high seismic coefficient zones are situated in Jammu and Kashmir, Himachal Pradesh

C. The Zones having medium horizontal seismic coefficients are spread over some parts of Maharashtra and Gujarat.

D. All of the above

Q.93 Which of the following schemes under IRDP primarily aimed at providing additional employment benefits and living standards of the rural areas?

A. TRYSEM

B. Jawahar Rojgar Yojana

C. Indira Aawas Yojana

D. National Rural Livelihood Mission(NRLM)

Q.94 Match List I with the List II and select the correct answer from the code given below:-

List I (Industries)	List II (Highest Distribution)
a) Jute Textiles	i. Maharashtra
b) Silk Industry	ii. Andhra Pradesh
c) Ship Building	iii. Karnataka
d) Automobile Industry	iv. West Bengal

A. (a)-(i), (b)-(iii), (c)-(iv), (d)-(ii)

B. (a)-(ii), (b)-(iii), (c)-(iv), (d)-(i)

C. (a)-(i), (b)-(iv), (c)-(iii), (d)-(ii)

D. (a)-(iv), (b)-(iii), (c)-(ii), (d)-(i)

Q.95 Match the seasons in List - I with specific months in these seasons in List-II as per IMD's classification and select the correct answer from the codes given below:

List - I (Seasons)	List - II (Months)
(a) Pre-Monsoon	(i) January to February
(b) Post Monsoon	(ii) March to May
(c) Winter	(iii) June to September
(d) Monsoon	(iv) October to December

A. (a)-(iii), (b)-(iv), (c)-(i), (d)-(ii)

B. (a)-(i), (b)-(iii), (c)-(iv), (d)-(ii)

C. (a)-(iv), (b)-(iii), (c)-(ii), (d)-(i)

D. (a)-(ii), (b)-(iv), (c)-(i), (d)-(iii)

Ques (96-100):Read the passage carefully and answer the questions that follows:-

The Agriculture of India is determined by various numbers of factors such as Environmental, Institutional and Technological. These factors affect the agricultural development and intensity to a great extent. However there are a variety of environmental factors like relief, climate and soil. Relief refers to the difference in height between highest and lowest points. There are variety of relief features like plains, plateaus and mountains depending on which agriculture operations and various crops are identified. Plains are the most preferred areas for agriculture than the other two features. Next comes Climate which is the biggest determinant of agriculture and patterns of cropping. There are a number of elements such as Temperature, Frost, winds, snow, Rainfall, Moisture or Humidity, etc. Then comes soil which constitutes the physical base for any agricultural practice. The physical and chemical compositions of the soils are the basis on which the agricultural productivity depends. Each soil type has its own specific characteristics and is suitable to a particular group of crops. The next determinant is the Institutional which includes land tenures, size of holdings and land reforms. Abolition of intermediaries, tenancy reforms, ceiling of land holdings, organization of cooperative farms, and land records system were some of the scope of land reforms. Last is the technological determinant which includes the HYV seeds, fertilizers, and insecticides.

Q.96 Which of the following are the institutional factor that affect Agriculture of India?

A. land tenures

B. size of holdings

C. land reforms

D. all of the above

Q.97 Which of the following element is mainly responsible for the shifting of sugarcane industry from north to South India?

A. Temperature and Humidity

B. Winds

C. Rainfall

D. Cheap labour

Q.98 Which soil is mostly suitable for growing oil seeds, tobacco, potatoes and fruits?

A. Laterite soils

B. Black soils

C. Sandy loam soils

D. Red soils

Q.99 What kinds of land tenure systems were established before Independence?

A. Permanent System
B. Ryotwari
C. Mahalwari
D. All of the above

Q.100 Which of the following are the merits of application of HYV seeds?

A. Shorter Life Cycle
B. Suitable for the use of fertilizers
C. Both A and B
D. None of the above

// Smart Answer Sheet //

Correct Percentage of students who answered correctly. **Skipped** Percentage of students who skipped.

Q.	Ans.	Correct / Skipped	Q.	Ans.	Correct / Skipped	Q.	Ans.	Correct / Skipped	Q.	Ans.	Correct / Skipped	Q.	Ans.	Correct / Skipped
1	D	45.95 % / 8.1 %	17	D	18.92 % / 32.43 %	33	C	29.73 % / 27.03 %	49	D	13.51 % / 32.44 %	65	B	10.81 % / 32.43 %
2	C	48.65 % / 32.43 %	18	D	56.76 % / 32.43 %	34	C	29.73 % / 32.43 %	50	A	59.46 % / 32.43 %	66	A	27.03 % / 32.43 %
3	C	24.32 % / 32.44 %	19	B	48.65 % / 27.03 %	35	A	51.35 % / 27.03 %	51	C	16.22 % / 32.43 %	67	D	40.54 % / 32.43 %
4	B	27.03 % / 32.43 %	20	C	21.62 % / 32.43 %	36	D	37.84 % / 32.43 %	52	D	51.35 % / 32.43 %	68	A	35.14 % / 32.43 %
5	D	59.46 % / 32.43 %	21	A	43.24 % / 27.03 %	37	A	40.54 % / 32.43 %	53	C	21.62 % / 32.43 %	69	B	59.46 % / 32.43 %
6	D	40.54 % / 32.43 %	22	D	16.22 % / 32.43 %	38	B	27.03 % / 32.43 %	54	B	10.81 % / 32.43 %	70	A	40.54 % / 32.43 %
7	C	45.95 % / 32.43 %	23	A	29.73 % / 27.03 %	39	C	35.14 % / 32.43 %	55	B	32.43 % / 32.43 %	71	B	10.81 % / 29.73 %
8	D	24.32 % / 32.44 %	24	A	48.65 % / 32.43 %	40	A	43.24 % / 32.44 %	56	B	51.35 % / 32.43 %	72	D	51.35 % / 32.43 %
9	A	37.84 % / 32.43 %	25	A	32.43 % / 32.43 %	41	D	45.95 % / 29.73 %	57	C	2.7 % / 32.44 %	73	B	5.41 % / 32.43 %
10	C	16.22 % / 32.43 %	26	C	32.43 % / 32.43 %	42	D	32.43 % / 32.43 %	58	B	18.92 % / 32.43 %	74	A	10.81 % / 32.43 %
11	D	62.16 % / 32.43 %	27	D	27.03 % / 32.43 %	43	A	29.73 % / 32.43 %	59	A	5.41 % / 32.43 %	75	A	2.7 % / 32.44 %
12	A	51.35 % / 32.43 %	28	A	27.03 % / 32.43 %	44	C	40.54 % / 32.43 %	60	D	29.73 % / 32.43 %	76	D	59.46 % / 32.43 %
13	D	43.24 % / 29.73 %	29	D	27.03 % / 32.43 %	45	D	45.95 % / 29.73 %	61	D	45.95 % / 32.43 %	77	B	8.11 % / 32.43 %
14	B	48.65 % / 32.43 %	30	A	13.51 % / 32.44 %	46	D	59.46 % / 32.43 %	62	A	27.03 % / 32.43 %	78	B	24.32 % / 32.44 %
15	A	51.35 % / 32.43 %	31	A	51.35 % / 32.43 %	47	D	64.86 % / 32.44 %	63	B	48.65 % / 32.43 %	79	D	43.24 % / 29.73 %
16	B	10.81 % / 35.14 %	32	A	37.84 % / 32.43 %	48	C	48.65 % / 32.43 %	64	C	16.22 % / 32.43 %	80	D	21.62 % / 32.43 %

Q.	Ans.	Correct / Skipped
81	C	54.05 % / 29.73 %
82	B	45.95 % / 32.43 %
83	D	56.76 % / 32.43 %
84	D	24.32 % / 32.44 %

Q.	Ans.	Correct / Skipped
85	A	10.81 % / 32.43 %
86	C	45.95 % / 32.43 %
87	A	18.92 % / 32.43 %
88	A	48.65 % / 32.43 %

Q.	Ans.	Correct / Skipped
89	D	35.14 % / 32.43 %
90	D	35.14 % / 32.43 %
91	B	40.54 % / 32.43 %
92	D	56.76 % / 32.43 %

Q.	Ans.	Correct / Skipped
93	B	21.62 % / 29.73 %
94	D	59.46 % / 32.43 %
95	D	62.16 % / 32.43 %
96	D	56.76 % / 32.43 %

Q.	Ans.	Correct / Skipped
97	A	51.35 % / 32.43 %
98	D	5.41 % / 32.43 %
99	D	59.46 % / 32.43 %
100	C	48.65 % / 32.43 %

//Hints and Solutions//

1. Inselberg is the last hill remained after the land around it has eroded away. It is a hill of volcanic rock that has resisted wind and weather and has remained strong. Eventually it also consumes the total area dominated by a series of concave wash. The surface produces at the of this cycle is called Endrumpf.

Thus, the Correct answer is D.

2. Most scientists, researchers and geophysicists started to accept plate tectonics theory in 1966. The theory was originated from the continental drift theory which explains the drifting apart of continents from a single big continent called Pangea. This theory of continental drift was in controversy all through 1050s after which the theory of plate tectonics was postulated giving a reason to various geographic phenomena.

Thus, the Correct answer is C.

3. Genetically slopes can be divided into two types: primary and secondary slopes. Primary slopes are formed by processes that tend to promote relief. (Relief generally means the variation in altitude or the range among the landforms in terms of their height. Greater the relief, larger is the variation between highest and the lowest landform.) The primary slope can originate due to tectonic origin like fault scarps or by other factors like volcanoes, glacial activities etc. However, processes that work upon primary slopes, so that the primary slopes are eroded or modified and the general relief is decreases leads to the formation of secondary slopes.

4. Icebergs are the masses of ice that have broken free from glaciers terminating in the ocean or from floating ice shelves. And this process of breaking-off of ice masses from the terminus or the edge of glacier is called calving. Icebergs float very low in water as they are only slightly less dense than water.

5. The earthquakes are violent tremors of the earth's crust. They can be caused due to volcanic eruptions, mining activities, tectonic activity. But deforestation is not directly responsible for earthquakes. India is a major host spot for earthquakes due to presence of fault lines.

6. The Maule earthquake was one of the deadliest earthquakes in the world. It occurs in Chile in the February 2010. It was of the magnitude 8.8 on the Richter scale. The Malin landslide took place in Ambegaon tehsil of Maharashtra in India in the year 2014. The Krakatoa volcanic eruption of Indonesia is still one the most violent volcanic eruptions of all times. It occurred in the year 1883. The Salang avalanche was a series of 17 avalanches that occurred in the Salang pass of Hindu Kush mountains in Afghanistan in the year 2010.

7. The erosion of a glacier form the amphitheater-like valley called as cirque. The drumlins, moraines and kettles are depositional landforms made by a glacier. The examples of cirque include Chandratal lake in Himachal Pradesh, Blue Lake Cirque in Australia, etc.

8. Folding occurs when rocks bend due to intense compressional forces. One of the major requirements for folding to occur is that the resultant deformation must occur over a large period of time and must be very slow. A combination of a fold and a fault is called as an overthrust fault. Faulting is defined as displacement of once connected blocks of rock along a fault plain. A fold where the rock layers are warped downwards is called as a syncline, not an anticline.

9. Penck's model of geomorphic cycle was adopted and developed by Lester King Charles. He envisioned the cycle of pedimentation. The cycle starts with cymatogenic diastrophism. It passes into a period of diastrophic quiescence. The relief to a pediplain reduces due to subaerial processes during its quiescence.

10. Walther Penck's geomorphic cycle was called as morphological system. His assumptions include that upliftment and erosion are always co-existent, landscape development is time dependent and morphological characteristics on earth's surface are caused due to competition between denudational process and crustal movement. The uniformity of slope is not an assumption in Penck's model.

11. The amount of carbon dioxide, nitrogen and oxygen in the atmosphere is 0.04%, 78% and 21%. Helium is present in 0.0005 % in the atmosphere. The other gases in atmosphere are present in traces which include Neon, Argon, Ozone, etc.

Thus, the correct answer is D.

12. The atmosphere is made up of various gases, water vapour and dust particles. The dust particles are found in higher amount in the temperate and tropical regions. They come in the form of soot, oceanic salt, smoke, ash, etc. they help in condensation of water. Water gets condensed around these dust particles leading to formation of clouds.

Thus, the correct answer is A.

13. Nearly 40% of India's population lives in coastal areas. This population is vulnerable to cyclones. The cyclones in India occur in 2 phases. The month of November is the primary peak and May is the secondary peak. Sometimes, cyclones are helpful like they help in relieving effects of drought and help in maintaining the overall temperature of the earth. The National Cyclone Risk Mitigation Project (NCRMP) is the project under which state to state management of cyclones is done.

14. An air mass is a large parcel of air that is defined by its temperature and moisture. They adapt to characteristics of the surface below them. The continental polar air masses originate from the land area in polar areas. They are cold & dry. Equatorial air masses form over land areas in lower latitudes. Polar air masses are formed in cold areas and most stable. The monsoon air masses are moist & most unstable.

15. The cyclone Nargis occurred in Bay of Bengal. It affected the country of Myanmar considerably. It is the second most deadly named cyclone. It occurred in 2008. Typhoon Haiyan occurred in the Philippines. It happened in the year 2013. Cyclone Fani occurred in India in the year 2019. Hurricane Katrina in occurred in Aug 23-Aug 30, 2005. It was a tropical cyclone in Gulf of Coast of the United States.

16. A cloudburst is when an extreme amount of precipitation occurs over a short period of time. They occur via orographic lift when a cloud clashes with a solid body like a mountain. But they can also be caused when a warm air parcel meets a cooler air

parcel. During a cloudburst, rainfall rate is either 100 mm per hour or more. Cloudburst can cause flash floods.

17. In Koppen's climatic classification, BS climate is a semi-arid climate and BW is dry climate. The areas with BW climate have lesser rainfall than the areas with BS climate. The areas with BS climate have mid-tropical cyclones and inter-tropical convergence which leads to rainfall in these areas. Thus, (R) is true and (A) is false.

18. Thornthwaite divided the world into 32 climate types. The A A'r climate is tropical wet climate and B A'w is a tropical humid climate with rainfall deficient in winter

Thornthwaite used two factors, e.g. precipitation effectiveness and temperature effectiveness, for the delimitation of boundaries of different climatic regions.

19. La-Nina means *The Little girl* in Spanish language. They are sometimes called *El Viejo* or *anti- El-Nino*. It is characterized by cold ocean. When the *La-Nina* occurs, winter temperatures are warmer than usual in Southeast and cooler than usual in Northwest. It has opposite effect than *El-Nino*.

20. Heat budget is the balance of incoming and outgoing solar radiation. Out of the total insolation coming, 23% is absorbed by the atmosphere, 30% is reflected by the clouds or land or scattered into the space. 47% of the insolation is absorbed by the land and ocean. Thus, the correct answer is C.

21. Continental shelves are the landmass extending from the continental coast towards the sea with gentle slope. They are also the zone of photic ecosystem as continental shelves are never beyond the depth of 200 metres. Following a shelf break, the slope gets steeper and the landmass extending further beyond are called continental slopes which has the lowest of all oceanic deposits - because of its slope, almost everything is washed down the slope At the base of the continental slopes, deep sea fans are formed of the deposits flowing down the slope; when few such fans coalesce, they form sea rise. Beyond continental slopes, are the flat and the most extensive features on the earth – the abyssal plains.

22. Measurement of negative reliefs essentially means bathymetry or the measurements of ocean depths. Clinometer is a hypsometric instrument which measures the slope of the relief features above the sea surface. Sea MARC (Sea Mapping and Remote Characterization), Precision Depth Recorders and GLORIA (Geological Long Range Inclined Accoustical Instrument) are advanced methods and techniques of bathymetry.

23. Tsunamis are generated in the oceans due to events which causes displacement in the volume of sea water, for example earthquake. The tsunami waves are huge in its wavelength (exceeding 200 kilometers in the open sea) but the wave height is extremely low (less than 1 km in the open sea) and since the maximum part of its journey is takes place in the ocean, it is called shallow-water lakes.

24. The circum pacific belt, also known as the Pacific Ring of Fire is a the boundary zone (subduction zone) between Pacific plates and other plates where Pacific plate being heavier in mass

subsides beneath the lighter mass creating subduction zones and potential conditions for generating tsunamis. Of all the major tsunamis, barring a few in Indian ocean, most of the tsunamis have generated near this belt and island arcs.

25. Rotation of the earth creates two conspicuous current systems – a clockwise movement of water in the Northern hemisphere and a counter-clockwise movement of water in the southern hemisphere. Air Pressure and winds certainly exerts a drag on the ocean waters and thus the pressure gradient causing the wind movement also influences the ocean current movement. Density of ocean water affects the vertical mobility of currents as the denser water tends to sink down and relatively lighter water tends to rise.

26. Although there has been a mention about conservation, but methods of conservation has not been discussed in the paragraph. Human influences on the environment is discussed in the paragraph which is believed to have caused disastrous consequences of farming practices which in other words are also called feedbacks which can be positive or negative. When positive feedback induces the response on the part of individuals and the actions humans take and if causes burden over a new place, it is called staggered feedback.

27. The interaction between man and environment therefore has two aspects: with environment influencing man and man influencing environment. This might be seen as a simple two-way system, but reality is not so simple and consequences of this interaction are inevitable. Thus, it is a two-way system but with complicated interrelations and consequences resulting into positive, negative, and staggered feedbacks.

28. Positive feedback in system analysis refers to the action in which the flow (of energy) amplifies the changes which are a major deviation from their normal state. Similarly, when human activity operates to intensify change it is called positive feedback.

29. When positive feedback creates inevitable conditions for the elements in the system to move to a new place or find a new source (component) for survival, the new source (component) gets over burdened and this phenomena is called staggered feedback when the feedback in which one area pays for the actions in another.

30. The concept of feedbacks is an intrinsic part of the system analysis. And if the earth is considered to be a system, humans, with the number of more than 7 billion cannot be a passive agent. Overcrowding in the cities is not always a staggered feedback because it is not triggered by a positive feedback and thus not always causing from bad farming practices. It is rather a more complex process which can be best described by the social and economic processes at play.

31. Ecosystems can be divided into terrestrial and aquatic ecosystems. Terrestrial ecosystems are also called biomes. Biogeographers recognize five principal biomes: forest, grassland, savanna, desert, and tundra. They are further divided into formation classes. Velds are the grasslands predominantly found in South Africa. Prairies are the grasslands found in the North America. The grasslands of Argentina are called Pampas while the grasslands in Australia is called Downs.

32. Office of the Environment Planning and Coordination was set up by the National Committee on Environmental Planning and Coordination (NCEPC) in February 1972 under the direction of the chairman Dr. Pitambar Pant of the committee. It was the apex advisory body in all the matters related to environmental protection. This was created after the 24th United Nations General Assembly.

33. The Census of India is the largest data collection exercise in the world wherein the whole population is enumerated. It is conducted every ten years and is under the office of Registrar General of India. The National Sample Surveys are the second best reliable source of demographic data pertaining to the large samples and its reliance on multiple techniques of sampling to minimize error and bias. It works under the National Sample Survey Organization under the Ministry of Statistics and Programme Implementation. International Institute of Population Sciences(IIPS) is the nodal agency for conducting demographic health surveys like NFHS and DLHS-RCH. Besides, University of Maryland is the organization which carries out the India Human Development Survey (IHDS), a household survey on demography, education, economic status with the help of NCAER, New Delhi.

34. The origin of Demographic Transition Theory is traced to the work of Warren Thompson and F. Notestein. Demographic Transition Theory states that societies which experience modernization progress from a pre-modern regime of high fertility and high mortality to a post-modern one in which both are low.

35. Optimum Population Theory was given by Carr Saunders and later popularized by Edwin Cannon. Demographic Transition Theory is a seminal work in the field of Demography developed by Warren Thompson and Frank Notestein. Ravenstein is known for his laws of migration and S. Stouffer, an American sociologist gave the theory of Intervening opportunities which was later used by E. Ulman in his flow theory of spatial interaction.

36. The NPP 2000 provides a policy framework for advancing goals and prioritizing strategies during the next decade, to meet the reproductive and child health needs of the people of India, and to achieve net replacement levels (TFR) by 2010. It is based upon the need to simultaneously address issues of child survival, maternal health, and contraception, while increasing outreach and coverage of a comprehensive package of reproductive and child health services by government, industry and the voluntary non-government sector, working in partnership. The immediate objective of the NPP 2000 is to address the unmet needs for contraception, health care infrastructure, and health personnel, and to provide integrated service delivery for basic reproductive and child health care. The medium-term objective is to bring the TFR to replacement levels by 2010, through vigorous implementation of inter-sectoral operational strategies. The long-term objective is to achieve a stable population by 2045, at a level consistent with the requirements of sustainable economic growth, social development, and environmental protection. And for the pursuance of the same objectives, National Socio-demographic Goals were set up to be achieved in each case by 2010.

37. Rn Values are associated with the concept of Nearest Neighbour Analysis. It is a technique which is used to tell about the nature of spread of any phenomena over space, in this case it is about the pattern of distribution of the settlements over a fixed/specified space. The Rn Values obtained ranges from 0 to 2.15. A value closer to 0 indicates the quality of being clustered or concentrated in terms of distribution, while a value closer to 2.15 indicates a uniform or regular spaced distribution. The nature/pattern of the distribution progresses from clustered (Rn=0) to Random (Rn=1) towards Uniform (2.15)

38. The famous historian Lewis Mumford is one of the most widely read scholar in the field of urban and town planning. He was a historian and in 1961 his book named *The City in History* came as an alternative theory of origin of towns and cities to what Gordon Childe had floated his concept of urban revolution. In that book, apart from the technical and economic factors Mumford talks about the spatial implosion of multiple cultures and identities within the confines of a walled city, which was made possible more so with the cultural factors.

39. Thomas Robert Malthus was an economist who published his theory about increasing population in 1798. He believed the supply of food increases in arithmetic progression and the population increases in geometric progression. Thus, the increase in population exceeds the food supply. This leads to miserable situation in world. So, (A) is true and (R) is false.

Thus, the Correct answer is C.

40. E. W. Burgess is known to have given the concentric zone model of urban land use. By virtue of its categorizations, it is also called as the ecological theory of city structure. Burgess' model was based on the idea that the growth of a city takes place outwards from its central area to form a series of concentric zone. He was doing his research on finding the determinants of urban social problems such as vice and crime and the mapping of those characteristics manifested in a concentric zonal pattern. CBD, the high rental valued space was at the centre of any city followed by a zone where independent workers' home are located. The CBD keeps expanding via its business and hence there was also a zone of transition between the first two zones. The next zone was that of the Zone of Better Residences where the middle and the upper middle classes lived of various professions. The outer most zone was the area of the dormitory towns and the area of comparatively low rental value and was mostly occupied by the population who could choose to commute to the city everyday for work.

41. Knowledge based industries are the industries which employ knowledge as an input to the production process and by the same logic the output in the form of knowledge product is also traded. It is a fact that, no industries can be said to have no use of knowledge in the production process, but the line of distinction here rather than the bulk of raw materials or finished products, the ideas are deciding factors. Thus, KPOs, BPOs, Consultancy services, Law Firms, IT industry, Education and Education service industry, medical industries are all examples of knowledge-based industries.

42. GATT which stands for General Agreement on Tariffs and Trade. It came into being in 1948 and was replaced by WTO in 1995. Over the years the pattern of World Trade can be understood through core-periphery model. Barring China's recent advancement, the North has emerged to be the global core especially due to the concentration of capital in those countries

and South acts as periphery where concentration of capital is less and the productive workforce is drawn to the core region for the sake opportunities. But recently, since 21st century the global South-South trade has crossed North-South Trade. India is not among the top exporters.

43. Graph Theory is a method used in transport geography to measure the accessibility and the connectivity of the transport network. Beta Index is the ratio of number of links to the number of nodes. Pi Index also measures the connectivity of the network in the same way of the value of Pi in a circle. It is calculated as the total length of the network divided by the length of the diameter (distance between the two farthest point)

44. Exclusive Economic Zone (EEZ) is the region beyond 200 nautical miles from the coast of a country which belongs to economic use for that country and resources can be extracted within this region by the very country. Beyond this EEZ, it is considered open sea and international institutions have to considered before carrying out any operation.

45. The macro level division of resources gives in two types of resources: Natural and Human Resources. Natural Resources can be both renewable and Non-renewable. Water in general is a renewable resource along with wind and solar energy. Non-renewable resources are generally the mineral and energy resources from fossil fuels.

46. Relief, climate (temperature and precipitation) and soil are the physical factors which play the most important role in the spatial organization of agriculture. Irrigation facility will determine the kind of crops the farmer can choose from. Landholding size would decide the scale of operation which can be afforded by the farmers and lastly the availability of technological inputs like soil testing facility, HYV seeds, fertilizers would also influence the spatial organization of agriculture in a region.

47. Religious Composition of the working population is never a decisive factor influencing the industrial location as long as the population available as workers possess the required skills. Cost of raw materials at site, cost of distribution of production, i.e. transportation costs and the presence or absence of agglomeration economies have a great impact on the location of industries as they will eventually have a bearing on the total cost of setting up a production unit.

48. Private, public, joint and cooperative sector are the type of industries classified on the basis of ownership. SAIL stands for Steel Authority of India Limited and is a public sector enterprise since its inception. It functions under Ministry of Steel. TISCO stands for Tata Iron and Steel Company and is a private sector enterprise. AMUL stands for Anand Milk Union Limited and is a cooperative sector enterprise which is owned by 3.6 million milk producers. Mahanagar Gas Limited is a joint sector enterprise which is one of the largest City Gas Distribution companies in India which is promoted by the GAIL India Limited.

49. On the basis of ownership industries can be classified as private sector, public sector, Joint Sector, Cooperative Sector Industries. Basic/key industries and Consumer industries is the classification of industries on the basis of their main role. The same industries can be classified into many ways depending upon the basis of the classification. TISCO is a heavy industry, Key/Basic Industry, Large scale industry, Heavy Industry, and a private sector industry at the same time.

50. In terms of crude steel production, Japan sits in the top three countries despite very low reserves of raw material. However, because of the level of technology Japan possesses because of R&D, they import raw materials and then manufacture steel. Availability of technology thus play a very important role in manufacturing output.

51. Growth Pole Theory is the brainchild of Francios Perroux. It was based on the Schumpeterian model of development. The theory suggested that growth can occur in certain specific region and these were called propulsive units and were capable of generating and disseminating growth. Lower order growth centres would always be larger in number and in close proximity to one another as they would cater to the local populace and higher order growth centres would cater to large population, city for instance. The modified form of growth pole theory was given by R.P. Mishra in Indian context.

52. Soil, which is the most important renewable resource supports the plant growth directly and indirectly the life of every other terrestrial animals including humans. And it is a living system as it is formed with its depth increasing over a very long period of time but the soil cover is denuded and washed down in a very short span called soil erosion. Terrace farming, Contour Ploughing and Strip farming are techniques to prevent soil erosion. Contour ploughing employs ploughing along the contours which decelerate the flow of water. Terrace farming is farming done on slopes cut out as steps called terraces. Strip Farming is allowing long grass to grown between crops to break up the force of wind. Deep tillage enhances soil erosion.

53. EU or more generally the northern and western Europe has had the advantage of higher productivity of wheat from rest of the world. In 1961, the wheat yield for India stood at 0.85 tonnes per hectare, while for the EU it stood 1.96 tonnes per hectare and for North America, it stood at 1.33 tonnes per hectare. After the impact of Green Revolution all over the world all the down reaching 2005, India's wheat yield stands at 2.74 tonnes per hectare while for North America and EU stands at 2.75 and 5.74 tonnes per hectare, respectively.

54. Johann Heinrich Von Thunen developed a crop theory in 1826 in which he took various assumptions like an isolated estate, isotropic surface, uniform price for a crop in the market and there would be only one market for one agricultural area where the surplus of the agricultural area will be sold. The concept of locational rent takes is the net profit after working out the production cost and the transportation cost. The perishable goods without preservation technology would be very costly to transport and thus would find its location near the centre.

55. J.C. Weaver gave this formula $\sqrt{\dfrac{\Sigma d^2}{n}}$ for delineating crop combination region, when he studied crop combination for the Middle-East countries. He gave this method in 1954 and it was called minimum deviation method. Before him, L.L. Pownall, a Kiwi geographer, in 1953 gave his mean positive deviation method of delineating crop combination regions. Modifying Weaver's method Doi and Rafiullah gave their modified minimum deviation method and maximum positive deviation method, respectively.

56. SAARC is the South Asia Organization for Regional Cooperation. It consists of 8 countries of Southeast Asia. It has its headquarters at Kathmandu in Nepal. ASEA is the Association of Southeast Asian Nation. It has 10 member states and headquarters at Jakarta, Indonesia. Organization of the Petroleum Exploiting Countries is consists of 13 states and has headquarters in Vienna. The European Union is the trade block of 27 nations in the continent of Europe. It has headquarters in Brussels, Belgium.

57. 22 member nations of European Union signed an agreement to abolish the entire passport and other border control protocols for each other in 1985 under the Schengen Agreement. 4 nations which are not the part of the EU are also included in this area. The European Union is a single market, not a customs union. Thus, (A) is true and (R) is false.

58. India has maritime disputes with Sri Lanka., Bangladesh and Pakistan. With Pakistan, the issue is regarding boundary along Sir Creek and with Bangladesh is regarding the ownership of New Moore Island. The Indian Ocean is important for oil trade due to the presence of Strait of Hormuz which provides the only way from Persian Gulf to open sea.

59. The Heartland theory was propounded by Mackinder. He arranged the land in world into three parts. These were Heartland, Inner crescent and outer crescent. The outer crescent consists of North America, South America, Africa south of Sahara and Oceania are considered to be the outer circle. As per Mackinder, the midland area would control the world as per the modifications given by 1943. As per this prediction, the Midland consists of outer parts of the outer crescent. Mackinder has bee criticized of constantly modifying his own theory, diluting his own theory.

60. Political geography is the study of uneven outcomes of political processes in spatial terms and the ways I which political processes are themselves affected by spatial structure. The various areas with political geography include feminist geography, queer theory, youth studies, environmental justice, etc. Thus, (A) is false, but (R) is true.

61. China began the study of Geography in 5th century B.C. Since then, there have been various Chinese geographers and philosophers in the field to put forth their contribution. One of them was Fan Chengda who belonged to a poor peasant family belonging to song dynasty. He acquired his degree in the subject in 1154 A.D. He has written many books in geography and one of his prominent work is Gui Hai Ye Hung.

Thus, the correct answer is D.

62. James Rennell is known as the Father of Indian geography. He was born in the year 1742 and dies in1830. He primarily produced first accurate map of Bengal. He later produced an accurate outline map of India. He was an English geographer and was a pioneer in Oceanography. Thus, he is also called the father of Oceanography.

Thus, the correct answer is A.

63. Berhardus Verenius was born in 1622 and died in 1650. He was a German geographer.

Immanuel Kant was born in 1724 and dies in 1804. He was a German geographer and being a philosopher he had great contribution in geography like one of them the concept of space.

Alexander Von Humboldt was born in 1769 was a German biologist and geographer. The main work done by him which has significance even today is Cosmos.

Carl Ritter was born in 1779 and died in 1859. He is considered one of the founders of modern geography. One of his work is " Erdkunde"

Thus, the correct answer is B.

64. Alexander Von Humboldt was a German geographer who is known as one of the founding fathers of modern geography. Cosmos was lecture series started by him which later got written and published in the following years. The work cosmos has five volumes and the first volume focused on the physical aspects inside and outside the Earth. The second volume describes about the history of science.

Thus, the correct answer is C .

65. The man-land tradition focused on the study of relationship between human beings and the environment they are living in. The human body has lot of dependency on the environment that is even the basic human process like breathing is dependent on the environment similarly, environmental. Along with population geography, political and cultural geography is also taken into account by them.

Thus, the correct answer is B.

66. Earth-Science tradition focuses on the study of planet Earth as the home to human, its systems and its survival. It focuses on the physical aspects of the geography or the earth and concepts like solar system and space. It emphasizes on the earth's location in the solar system and how it effects the earth's all he spheres like the hydrosphere, atmosphere, biosphere etc.

Thus, the correct answer is A.

67. The dualism in geography between physical geography and human geography deals with the focus of both the subject which are poles apart and yet it confines and makes it under one umbrella. Hecataeus focused on the physical geography whereas Herodotus emphasized on human geography. Physical geography can be dependent on certainty but human geography needs more probable answers to come to a conclusion.

Thus, the correct answer is D.

68. According to Kuhn any theory in science is not a regulated concept. Thus, he provided a set of problems and solutions and termed it as the "paradigm of science" which can be used by a set of practitioners. The moment new problem occurs the whole process witnesses a paradigm shift. The model prepared by Kuhn was called super model by Peter Hagget.

Thus, the correct answer is A.

69. Behaviouralism is an approach in human geography that dealt with close analysis of the behaviors of human and animals and the result was observed which was further taken as a data. The spatial behavior was taken into account in the case of

behvaiouralism n geography. It became a prominent part of human geography in the years 1960s-1970s.

Thus, the correct answer is B.

70. Feminist geography is a branch of human geography which deals with involvement of feministic theories to study the spatial aspects involving human environment and society. It majorly focused on the involvement of race, class, ability and sexuality to the subject of geography and to treat them equally. The role of gender was considered a very narrow concept by feminist geographers in the subject. The book companion to feminist geography was authored by Seager and Johnson

Thus, the correct answer is A.

71. The data which gives information about the spatial data or some data that has locational feature or is geographically referenced can be termed as Non-spatial data. It defines the various attributes of the spatial data. For example, if a map shows an administrative unit such as a block, then all information regarding the block will be non-spatial data.

72. This is a simple graph in which the statistical data are shown with the help of a line. It is generally used for showing the temperature or production of a commodity. Since there is only one curve in this diagram and shows only one element such as changes in temperature, pressure, population, export, import, etc. with reference to time, a simple line graph is useful in this case.

Vertical bar diagrams are drawn when the data are to be shown with reference to time. Such as, vertical bar diagrams are more suitable when we want to show the population of India from 1901-2011 or rainfall distribution in 12 months of the year. It is easy to draw comparisons of quantities conveniently and quickly by vertical bar diagrams.

Multiple bar diagrams are useful for showing the rural and urban population of some states as these are used to show two or more data of the same category. These data are shown by a set of bars drawn adjacent to each other. For example, data concerning rural and urban population, males and females, literate and illiterate, production of different agricultural crops can be shown.

Pie diagram is a 2-dimensional diagram in which the quantities are shown by the area of the circle. Then the circle is divided into various sectors whose areas are proportional to the quantities represented by them. Land use categories of a district, reserves of important minerals in India are some items that can be perfectly shown with the help of Pie-diagrams.

73. Dots maps are useful especially when the values are unevenly distributed and sporadic in character. In this kind, quantities or values are represented by dots of uniform sizes, each dot having a specific value. The dots are inserted within the particular administrative units for which data is available.

The basic principle of Choropleth maps is that the intensity of shading is directly proportional to the density of elements. This is quite true as the choropleth maps are technically quantitative areal maps that show the spatial distribution of the intensity or density of an element with the help of a system of graded shading or colour, drawn following the boundaries of the administrative units.

74. The reason totally supports the assertive statement. The reason is that GIS is a special class of information system. Spatial information systems are those designed for processing data pertaining to real-world features or features that are described in terms of locations. Based on the history, many consider GIS as only a spatial information system but that is not correct. It is important to note that not all spatial information system can be termed as GIS. Computer-assisted drafting and manufacturing (CAD and CAM) are typical examples of spatial information systems that are not GIS. These systems use spatial data, but they are totally different from GIS in purpose and data-processing requirements. Logically, only those spatial information systems that are used for processing and analyzing geospatial data or geographically referenced data can be termed as GIS. Thus, not all spatial information systems can be labeled as GIS.

75. Geometric distortions take place from the earth's curvature, platform movements such as altitude, orientation and velocity, perspective of the sensor optics, relief displacement and non-linearities in scanning motion. Radiometric corrections include correcting the data from atmospheric noise or irregularities of the sensor.

The simple type of enhancement process is the linear contrast stretch. Suppose, the minimum value in the image histogram is 84 and maximum value is 153. These 70 levels occupy less than 1/3rd of the full 256 levels available. A linear stretch uniformly expands this small range to cover the full range of values from 0 to 255. This enhances the contrast in the image with lightened areas appearing lighter and dark areas appearing darker, making visual interpretation much easier. However, this technique is applied to a single band, grayscale image, where the image data is mapped to the fullest range of the display device.

In a supervised classification, there are 3 stages which are training, supervision and classification. Firstly, the analyst identifies the homogenous representative samples from the different surface cover types of interest which are called training areas. Then these are selected by the analyst based on his knowledge with the geographical features of the area.

76. The greatest advantage of median is that it can be calculated without any difficulty from grouped frequency distributions with classes of unequal width or with open-end classes. Median is more affected by sampling fluctuations than the A.M. and is less reliable. The A.M. is stable as regards sampling fluctuations. If many samples are drawn from the same population and each time several measures of central tendency calculated, it will be found that A.M. fluctuates less from sample to sample.

The computation of mean is easy. Even if all the observations are not known are not known individually, A.M. can be found, provided their sum and the number of observations is known.

77. Random Sampling is sampling with equal probability. The standard deviation calculated from the sampling distribution of a statistic is called its Standard Error. The standard error gives a measure of dispersion of the concerned statistic. It depends on the sample size n and goes on diminishing as the sample size increases.

Hence, as n increases, $SE\left(\overline{x}\right)$ increases. Thus, the standard errors of the sample mean $\left(\overline{X}\right)$ and sample

proportion (p) are used to find the confidence limits for the population and the population proportion(P) respectively.
The parameter has no sampling fluctuation. Usually parameters are unknown and statistics are used as estimates of parameters. Any statistical measure based on all units in the population is called a parameter,
e.g., population mean, population s.d. and others. However, since the parameter is constant it has neither a sampling distribution nor a standard error.

78. The Stream Length Ratio is a linear aspect of the basin morphology. The Stream Length Ratio(RL) refers to the ratio of mean or average length of segment of order 'u' to the mean or average length of order 'u-1'.

79. A Hypsometric curve describes the area-height relationship of a drainage basin. In this, x is the ratio between area and area of the whole drainage basin and y is the ratio of the height between the mouth of the basin and the contour which defines the lower limit of the basin, and the relative relief of the basin.

80. In the Strahler method, 1st order streams are the longest upstream channels that have no tributaries. When 2 1st order streams unite, they form a 2nd order stream. In the same way, when two 2nd order streams unite, a third order stream is created and so on. When 2 streams of different order join, the combined stream retains the order of the higher order stream contributing to it.

In Horton's method, a 1st order stream is an un-branched tributary, a 2nd order stream is a tributary formed by two or more 1st order streams. A 3rd order stream is a tributary formed by two or more 2nd order streams and so on. Hence, stream order number increases by one at every confluence.

The method of Gravelius' stream ordering is that it calculates main streams of the main catchment and every sub catchments. The main stream of every catchment is set to 1and all of its tributaries receive order 2. Their tributaries receive order 3 and so on.

In the Shreve method, the stream order of the two streams contributing to a junction is added and provides the rank number of the stream below the junction. The rank of a stream represents the total number of the 1st order streams contributing to it.

81. The Godavari is the largest river system of the Peninsular India and is also known as Dakshina Ganga. Its source is in the Trimbak plateau of the North Sahyadri near Nashik in Maharashtra which is only 80 km. from the shore of the Arabian Sea.

The Satluj is a major river of the Indus Drainage system and rises from the Manasarovar-Rakas Lakes near Darma Pass in western Tibet within 80 km. of the source of the Indus. The river has formed deep gorges where it pierces the Great Himalayas and the other Himalayan ranges.

The Ghaghara river has its source near the Gurla Mandhata peak, south of the Manasarovar Lake in Tibet and is of trans-Hiamalayan origin, it is known as the Karnaili in western Nepal. The river has a high flood frequency and has changed its course several times.

The Mahanadi is an important river of the Peninsular India and originates from the northern foothills of the Dandakaranya near Sihawa in Raipur district of Chhattisgarh at an elevation of 442 m. The Mahanadi finally empties itself in the Bay of Bengal.

82. National Disaster management Act was passed by the Parliament and received the assent of the President at the end of 2005. It allowed for the formation of a National disaster Management Authority which became the apex body to plan policies and rules for disaster management in India. It covers both natural and man-made disasters under its purview.

83. Landslides, Avalanches are very common in the high altitude Himalayan environment. They can be triggered by tectonic movements and simply because of chemical weathering aided by mass movement. GLOF stands for Glacial lake Outburst Floods and are evident in the regions of retreating glaciers due to changing climate and subsequent warming of atmospheric conditions.

84. In the first five year plan (1951-56), just four years after the independence, the thrust area of planning led development was put upon agriculture and emphasis was given on expanding the existing industries and not venturing into creation of new heavy industries. However, by the end of the plan, industrial production saw a growth of 40 percent while agriculture experienced 30 per cent growth. This potential in industries in India set the basis of future progress of industries.

85. Agro climatic regions are fifteen in number. It is the Islands region and not the East Himalayan region with lowest share of net sown area out of its total geographic area. Islands has 4.2% of its total area under net sown area. It is followed by Western Himalayas. When agro climatic region was modified based on soil condition and landforms, it became agro-ecological regions. There are 20 agro-ecological regions and 60 ago-ecological sub regions.

86. The very premise of Green revolution was based upon the genetically superior seeds, i.e. High yielding variety of seeds. Its use took pace in India in the mid 1960s when the yield of wheat increased many folds using the new seeds. The biggest criticism of Green revolution is that it increased regional disparity. It affected only 40 per cent of the total area. States like UP, Haryana and Punjab in the North and Andhra Pradesh and Tamil Nadu in the south were the ones which benefitted solely from this programme. This regional disparity manifested in the form of increasing inter-personal disparity, as the big farmers were the ones who could mobilize resource to buy the inputs whereas the small and marginal farmers and agricultural labour could not reap the benefits and thus the gaps increased. Also, the homogeneity of crops and their varieties in a region under this programme posed the risk of being susceptible to infections and thus reduced the genetic biodiversity of crops.

87. As per the Agricultural Statistics, 2019, Assam is the lowest of all states in terms of total cropped area under irrigation with less than percent of area under all crops being irrigated. Punjab on the other hand has its largest share of total irrigated area under all crops. Jharkhand (13 per cent) , West Bengal (64 per cent) and Bihar (69.3 per cent) are other states with irrigated area under all crops higher than Assam.

88. All land which is used wholly or partly for agricultural production and is operated as one technical unit by one person alone or with others without regard to the title, legal form, size or location is an operational landholding and it is the unit for the collection of agricultural data. As per the Agricultural Statistics, 2013, the average size of the landholdings is largest in case of Nagaland with 5.99 hectares. Punjab has the average landholdings size of 3.77 hectares followed by Rajasthan (3.07 hectares). Both Bihar and Uttar Pradesh have average landholdings size below 1 hectare.

89. Tamil Nadu receives its share of rainfall in the retreating monsoon and not in the south west monsoon. This is so because it lies in the rain shadow area or at the leeward side of the Western Ghats and the predominant Arabian Sea Branch of South West monsoon can't reach Tamil Nadu because of the orographic control. The Bay of Bengal Branch of Southwest monsoon also rushes towards Bengal and Assam leaving Tamil Nadu with very low moisture.

90. The Indus River originates near the Mansarovar Lake in the Tibetan plateau, on the northern slopes of the Kailash Mountain Range. Given below are the main tributaries of the Indus River from north to south: Jhelum, Chenab, Ravi, Sutlej.

91. Himalayan rivers are young, perennial rivers while Peninsular rivers are old and seasonal rivers. This is mainly due to the evolutionary history of these landforms. The deep gorges of Indus, Staluj, Beas, Brahmaputra, Alaknanda rivers are evident of the fact that these rivers were present even before the formation of the mountains, hence they are also called antecedent rivers. But the peninsular rivers are mature rivers which have reached the base level for most parts of the peninsular drainage network and hence the flow of water in the broad shallow valleys are is lower than that of Himalayan rivers. Narmada, Tapi are the examples of western flowing peninsular rivers.

92. The horizontal seismic coefficient isolines are lines indicating limits of seismic zones. The medium coefficient areas are spread over the Satluj-Ganga Plain, Godavari basin of Andhra Pradesh, Ratnagiri and Raigad districts of Maharashtra and some parts of Gujarat. The areas that come under the high seismic coefficient zones are situated in Jammu and Kashmir, Himachal Pradesh, Uttarakhand, northern parts of Bihar. These are highly susceptible to earthquakes.

93. The primary objective of the Jawahar Rojgar Yojana is to provide additional employment opportunities to unemployed and under-employed men and women and to increase their assets. Moreover, this scheme aims at improving the living conditions of the villagers and to provide sustainable employment. This scheme was further strengthened during the 9th Five Year Plan.

94. West Bengal has the largest concentration of jute mills. Most of which are along the banks of the Hugli river.

Karnataka is the biggest silk producing state in India. It accounts for 50% of the mulberry silk of the country.

Hindustan Shipyard Pvt. Ltd. in Vishakhapatnam (Andhra Pradesh) is the first shipbuilding industry of the country established in the year 1941.

The Automobile industry is one of the largest industries and is a key driver of economy. This industry has made a considerable progress in the recent decades. Mumbai, Pune in Maharashtra are major centres producing automobiles.

95. Indian Meteorological department has classified the climate of India into 4 distinct seasons. They are namely Winter, Pre-Monsoon, South-West Monsoon, and Post Monsoon. Winter season comprises the month of January to February. Following this is the Pre monsoon season which comprises the months of March to May, and is also called the Summer Season. Southwest Monsoon or simply the monsoon season comprises the months of June to September and is also called Rainy season. The final season is the Post Monsoon season which covers the months of October to December.

96. The Agriculture of India is determined by various Institutional factors such as land tenures, size of holdings and land reforms. Land tenure and tenancy is a system under which the type of and ownership can be determined. Small Land holdings are a great cause that affects the method of agriculture. Moreover, the owners of the land are not economically strong enough to support the various inputs to increase yields. Land reform refers to a number of laws that were implemented for the smooth agricultural production.

97. Sugarcane is grown in both South and North India but due to much congenial temperature conditions the sugarcane industry is shifting towards the South India. Temperature regulates all chemical and physical processes of plant metabolism.

98. Red soils are mostly suitable for growing these kinds of crops and are available on almost the whole of Tamil Nadu, parts of Karnataka, Andhra Pradesh, Madhya Pradesh and Odisha. The soil texture varies from sandy to clay, mostly loams. The color of these soils is red due to the high percentage of iron content.

99. All of these systems were a form or means of collecting revenues. Zamindari system was prevalent in most of North India and which included Uttar Pradesh, Bihar, West Bengal and most of Odisha and Rajasthan. Ryotwari system, also known as batai, was prevalent over most of South India consisting of present day Maharashtra, Karnataka, Tamil Nadu. Mahalwari was present in the parts of the present day Madhya Pradesh, and Odisha. These systems had ill effects on land tenure and led to low productivity in Indian agriculture.

100. HYV seeds are suitable for the use of fertilizers. It has been observed that new seeds give much higher yields than the old seeds for the same amount of fertilizers. Moreover, HYV seeds have a shorter life cycle. These seeds give early maturing crops and greater benefits to a farer for carrying out various cropping patterns. Thus, new seeds help in increasing the farm production.

Q.1 Small sheared fragments of continents are called as

A. Plates   **B.** Mini continents

C. Terranes   **D.** Minor plates

Q.2 Which of the following statements relating to the endogenetic and exogenetic processes are correct?

(a) Diastrophism is large-scale deformation of earth's crust.

(b) Orogenic process is an example of exogenetic process.

(c) Epirogenic processes are mechanisms of mountain building.

(d) Horizontal movements of plate tectonics are an example of diastrophism.

Code:

A. (b) and (d)   **B.** (a) and (d)

C. (a), (c) and (d)   **D.** (b), (c) and (d)

Q.3 Given below are two statements one is labelled as Assertion (A) and the other is labelled as Reason (R).

Assertion (A): Constant freeze and thaw of water occurs in some rocks.

Reason (R): Water seeps through cracks of rocks.

Select the correct answer from options given below:

A. Both (A) and (R) are true and (R) is the correct explanation of (A)

B. Both (A) and (R) are true, but (R) is not the correct explanation of (A)

C. (A) is true, but (R) is false

D. (A) is false, but (R) is true

Q.4 Given below are two statements one is labelled as Assertion (A) and the other is labelled as Reason (R).

Assertion (A): In mature stage of the river, landforms such as meanders, oxbow lakes, flood plains, etc. are formed.

Reason (R): The river in its youthful stage flows along an uneven surface and there is intensive bottom erosion.

Select the correct answer from options given below:

A. Both (A) and (R) are true and (R) is the correct explanation of (A)

B. Both (A) and (R) are true, but (R) is not the correct explanation of (A)

C. (A) is true, but (R) is false

D. (A) is false, but (R) is true

Q.5 A plain formed of floodplains joined by their own growth is

A. Monadnock   **B.** Etchplain

C. Panplain   **D.** Pediplain

Q.6 Match List-I with the List-II and select the correct answer from the code given below:

List - I (Landform)	List - IIT(Method of formation)
(a) Gorge	(i) River
(b) Drumlins	(ii) Air
(c) Wave-cut platforms	(iii) Glacier
(d) Inselbergs	(iv) Sea/Ocean

Code:

A. (a)-(i), (b)-(iii), (c)-(iv), (d)-(ii)

B. (a)-(ii), (b)-(iv), (c)-(i), (d)-(iii)

C. (a)-(i), (b)-(iv), (c)-(iii), (d)-(ii)

D. (a)-(iv), (b)-(i), (c)-(ii), (d)-(iii)

Q.7 A rift valley is the large scale feature of the

A. Reverse fault   **B.** Horst fault

C. Graben fault   **D.** Normal fault

Q.8 Which of the following statements relating to earthquake and volcanic eruptions are correct?

(a) The only active volcano of India, Barren Island erupted last in 1945.

(b) Mt Agung in Bali erupted in 2017.

(c) A violent earthquake in Latur occurred in 1993.

(d) An earthquake occurred in Andaman Islands of India on 11 Aug 2009.

Code:

A. (a) and (b) are true

B. (a) and (d) are true

C. (b), (c) and (d) are true

D. (a), (c) and (d) are true

Q.9 Who is the author of the book "the continental drift controversy" ?

A. Wegener   **B.** Frankel

C. Smith   **D.** Thornbury

Q.10 Match List-I with List-II:

List-I (Mountain)	List-II (Highest peak's height)
(a) Rockies	(i) 6962
(b)Atlas	(ii) 4401
(c) Alps	(iii) 4167
(d) Andes	(iv) 4809

A. a- iii b-ii c-i d-iv   **B.** a-ii b-iii c-iv d-i

C. a-i b-ii c-iii d-iv   **D.** a-iii b-i c-iv d-ii

Q.11 A swirling wind forming on the edge of the severe thunderstorm is knows as:

A. Blizzard   **B.** Tornado

C. Gustnado   **D.** Eye

Q.12 Given below are two statements one is labelled as Assertion (A) and the other is labelled as Reason (R).

Assertion (A): Kalbaishakhi rains occurs in coastal Orissa and Andhra Pradesh.

Reason (R): Rains occurs due to convergence of sea winds in Tamil Nadu knows as mango showers.

Select the correct answer from options given below:

A. Both (A) and (R) are true and (R) is the correct explanation of (A)

B. Both (A) and (R) are true, but (R) is not the correct explanation of (A)

C. (A) is true, but (R) is false

D. (A) is false, but (R) is true

Q.13 Which of the following statements relating to solar insolation are true?

(a) Transparency of atmosphere does not affect insolation.

(b) Insolation is counted as the amount of solar energy received per square centimeter.

(c) Solar constant is one of the reasons for increase in insolation.

(d) Insolation is strongest at sunset.

Code:

A. (b) and (c)

B. (a) and (c)

C. (a), (c) and (d)

D. (a), (b) and (d)

Q.14 The Mediterranean climate is denoted by ___ in Koppen's climatic classification?

A. Cfa

B. BW

C. Dw

D. Cs

Q.15 Which among the following is/are natural causes of climate change?

A. Sunspots activity

B. Changes in obliquity of earth's orbit

C. Variation in eccentricity and precession of earth's orbit

D. All of the above

Q.16 Which among the following climatic events is best characterized with conditions good for fishing in the eastern pacific and heavy rainfall in the western Pacific?

A. El Niño

B. La Niña

C. Negative SOI

D. Walker Circulation

Q.17 Given below are two statements. One is labelled as Assertion (A) and the other is labelled as Reason (R).

Assertion (A): La Niña refers to colder-than normal sea-surface temperatures along the coastline of Ecuador and Peru

Reason (R): This event is dominated by strong anti trade winds and a strong equatorial current.

Select the correct answer from options given below:

A. Both (A) and (R) are true and (R) is the correct explanation of (A)

B. Both (A) and (R) are true, but (R) is not the correct explanation of (A)

C. (A) is true, but (R) is false.

D. (A) is false, but (R) is true.

Q.18 Match List-I with the List-II and select the correct answer from the code given below:

List - I (Pressure Systems)	List - II (Direction of wind)
(a) Cyclonic in Northern Hemisphere	(i) clockwise with high in centre
(b) Anti-cyclonic in Northern Hemisphere	(ii) clockwise with low in centre
(c) Cyclonic in Southern Hemisphere	(iii) anticlockwise with high in centre
(d) Anti-cyclonic in Southern Hemisphere	(iv) anti-clockwise with low in centre

Code:

A. (a)-(i), (b)-(iii), (c)-(iv), (d)-(iii)

B. (a)-(iv), (b)-(iii), (c)-(ii), (d)-(i)

C. (a)-(iv), (b)-(ii), (c)-(i), (d)-(iii)

D. (a)-(iv), (b)-(i), (c)-(ii), (d)-(iii)

Q.19 During which period of the day would the relative humidity of air be highest and lowest respectively?

A. just before sunset, just before sunrise

B. at twelve noon, just before sunset

C. in mid-afternoon, just before dawn

D. just before dawn, in mid-afternoon

Q.20 What is the value of -40°C expressed in the Fahrenheit scale?

A. 0°F

B. -20°F

C. -40°F

D. -58°F

Q.21 Which of the following statements is correct?

A. Open seas in the low latitudes record relatively higher temperature than the enclosed seas.

B. Enclosed seas in the higher latitudes have lower temperature than the open seas.

C. Oceans in the southern hemisphere record higher temperature than in the northern hemisphere.

D. Ocean's surface temperature is always less than the surrounding atmospheric temperature.

Q.22 Given below are two statements. One is labelled as Assertion (A) and the other is labelled as Reason (R).

Assertion (A): The diurnal range of oceanic temperature is more than that of land.

Reason (R): The specific heat of water is more than that of land.

Select the correct answer from options given below:

A. Both (A) and (R) are true and (R) is the correct explanation of (A)

B. Both (A) and (R) are true, but (R) is not the correct explanation of (A)

C. (A) is true, but (R) is false.

D. (A) is false, but (R) is true.

Q.23 Match List-I with List-II and select the correct answer from the codes given below:

List - I (Tides)	List - II (Characteristics)
(a) Spring	(i) two high and two low tides in a day
(b) Neap	(ii) one high and one low tide in a day
(c) Diurnal	(iii) during 1st & 3rd quarter of the moon
(d) Semi-diurnal	(iv) highest tides

A. (a)-(iii), (b)-(iv), (c)-(i), (d)-(ii)

B. (a)-(iv), (b)-(iii), (c)-(i), (d)-(ii)

C. (a)-(iv), (b)-(iii), (c)-(ii), (d)-(i)

D. (a)-(ii), (b)-(i), (c)-(iv), (d)-(iii)

Q.24 Which among the following statements about Tsunami is not true?

A. They are known as seismic sea waves.

B. Tsunamis are affected by the ocean bottom relief features.

C. Tsunamis are always shallow water waves.

D. There is a single surge and hence a single tsunami wave which hits the coast and causes destruction.

Q.25 Average salinity of the oceanic water is

A. 45 grams/1000 gm   **B.** 35 grams/1000 gm

C. 38 grams/1000 gm   **D.** 32 grams/1000 gm

Q.26 Given below are two statements. One is labelled as Assertion (A) and the other is labelled as Reason (R).

Assertion (A): The pyramid of biomass in a lake or pond ecosystem is upright.

Reason (R) : The biomass of the consumers at subsequent trophic levels keeps increasing in a lake/pond ecosystem.

Select the correct answer from options given below:

A. Both (A) and (R) are true and (R) is the correct explanation of (A)

B. Both (A) and (R) are true, but (R) is not the correct explanation of (A)

C. (A) is true, but (R) is false.

D. (A) is false, but (R) is true.

Q.27 In which of the following conventions was the "Agenda 21" adopted?

A. Stockholm Convention

B. Paris Conference

C. Rotterdam Convention

D. Rio-Earth Summit

Q.28 Match the major National legislations with respect to environment in List-I with the year in which they were enacted in List – II.

List - I (Legislations/Policies/Project)	List - II (Year)
(a) Environmental Protection Act	(i) 1972
(b) Wildlife Protection Act	(ii) 1973
(c) National water Policy	(iii) 1986
(d) Project Tiger	(iv) 1987

A. (a)-(ii), (b)-(i), (c)-(iv), (d)-(iii)

B. (a)-(iii), (b)-(iv), (c)-(i), (d)-(ii)

C. (a)-(iv), (b)-(ii), (c)-(iii), (d)-(i)

D. (a)-(iii), (b)-(i), (c)-(iv), (d)-(ii)

Q.29 The concentration of which among the following gases or atmospheric particles is the cause of acid rain?

A. SO_2 and NO_2 **B.** CO_2 and CO

C. SO_2 and CO **D.** Ozone and Dust

Q.30 Which among the following materials can cause environmental hazards?

A. Global Warming

B. Lead

C. Polychlorinated biphenyls

D. All of the above.

Q.31 Which among the following task of data collection is done by the office of Registrar General and Census Commissioner in India?

(a) Decennial Census and its publication

(b) Annual Land use Data

(c) Publication of Annual Health and Education Data

(d) Publication of Annual Vital statistics based on sample registration system

A. (a) only   **B.** (a) and (b) only

C. (a) and (d) only   **D.** (a), (c) and (d) only

Q.32 In which year was Ravenstein's paper titled "The Laws of Migration" came up for the first time?

A. 1880   **B.** 1885   **C.** 1890   **D.** 1895

Q.33 Match List – I with list – II and select the correct answer from the codes given below.

List - I (Type of Mortality)	List - II (Propounders)
(a) Infant Mortality	(i) Death before 5 years of age
(b)Child Mortality	(ii) Death before first birthday
(c)Post neonatal Mortality	(iii)Death between 1st month and1st birthday
(d) Neonatal Mortality	(iv) Death before 28 days

A. (a)-(iii), (b)-(ii), (c)-(i), (d)-(iv)

B. (a)-(ii), (b)-(iii), (c)-(iv), (d)-(i)

C. (a)-(iv), (b)-(i), (c)-(ii), (d)-(iii)

D. (a)-(ii), (b)-(i), (c)-(iii), (d)-(iv)

Q.34 Given below are two statements. One is labelled as Assertion (A) and the other is labelled as Reason (R).

Assertion (A): Rural Settlements differ drastically from urban settlements in social and economic structure.

Reason (R): The rural society depends mostly on agriculture and it is again -marked with social boundaries.

Select the correct answer from options given below:

A. Both (A) and (R) are true and (R) is the correct explanation of (A)

B. Both (A) and (R) are true, but (R) is not the correct explanation of (A)

C. (A) is true, but (R) is false.

D. (A) is false, but (R) is true.

Q.35 Who among the following used the term "urban revolution" while explaining the origin of town and cities?

A. Lewis Mumford   **B.** Gordon Childe

C. Henry Pienne   **D.** GK Zipf

Q.36 Which of the following is a factor of industrial location?

A. Consumer Behavior

B. Buying capacity of people

C. Labour

D. Emotions of consumer

Q.37 Given below are two statements on cotton textile industry in India. One is labelled as Assertion (A) and the other is labelled as Reason (R).

Assertion (A): Cotton textile mills are established in part of Gujarat and Mahrashtra.

Reason (R): Maharashtra and Gujarat have favorable climate and water availability for development of the cotton industry.

Select the correct answer from options given below:

A. Both (A) and (R) are true and (R) is the correct explanation of (A)

B. Both (A) and (R) are true, but (R) is not the correct explanation of (A)

C. (A) is true, but (R) is false

D. (A) is false, but (R) is true

Q.38 Which of the following is NOT an incentive provided by the Government in order to encourage industries in backward areas?

A. Human resource
B. Subsidized Power
C. Lower Transport Cost
D. Infrastructural facilities

Q.39 Match List-I with the List-II and select the correct answer from the code given below:

List - I (Natural Resource)	List - II (major source country)
(a)Oil	(i) Russia
(b) Thorium	(ii) Brazil
(c) Iron Ore	(iii) India
(d) Natural Gas	(iv) Venezuela

Code:

A. (a)-(i), (b)-(iii), (c)-(iv), (d)-(ii)
B. (a)-(iv), (b)-(iii), (c)-(ii), (d)-(i)
C. (a)-(i), (b)-(iv), (c)-(iii), (d)-(ii)
D. (a)-(iv), (b)-(i), (c)-(ii), (d)-(iii)

Q.40 Which of the following countries is the largest leather producing industry in the world?

A. Brazil   **B.** India   **C.** USA   **D.** China

Q.41 Which of the following factors is the most important for the tertiary and quaternary activities which are situated in the centre of any city or urban system?

A. Climate   **B.** Government policy
C. Land Rent   **D.** Foreign Investment

Q.42 Given below are two statements about World Trade Organization. One is labelled as Assertion (A) and the other is labelled as Reason (R).

Assertion (A): The WTO replaced GATT under the Tokyo Agreement.

Reason (R): The Marrakesh Agreement was signed by 123 nations on 15th April 1994.

Select the correct answer from options given below:

A. Both (A) and (R) are true and (R) is the correct explanation of (A)
B. Both (A) and (R) are true, but (R) is not the correct explanation of (A)
C. (A) is true, but (R) is false
D. (A) is false, but (R) is true

Q.43 The spatial interaction model that measures interactions between all the possible location pairs is

A. Retail Model   **B.** Potential Model
C. Gravity Model   **D.** Hefty Model

Q.44 Which of the following statements relating to the world distribution of industries are correct?

(a) The oldest iron & steel industry in India was located at Jamshedpur.

(b) Osaka in Japan is one of the major centers of iron & steel industry in world.

(c) Pittsburgh in United States of America has developed due to availability of coal.

(d) Bengaluru is the hub of IT industry in India.

Code:

A. (b) and (c)   **B.** (a) and (c)
C. (a), (c) and (d)   **D.** (b), (c) and (d)

Q.45 Which of the following is NOT an element of natural resource management in the world?

A. Biodiversity Conservation
B. Land management
C. Oil Extraction
D. Precautionary Biodiversity Management

Q.46 In Java (Indonesia), shifting cultivation is called as

A. Jhum   **B.** Roka   **C.** Kumari   **D.** Ladang

Q.47 The Farmers, as per the Von Thunen's model work in order to

A. Maintain their land
B. Satisfy their family's needs
C. Maximise their profits
D. Benefit of the state

Q.48 The maximum positive deviation method was given by

A. Rafiullah   **B.** Dou
C. Weaver   **D.** Von Thunen

Q.49 The following formula for crop combination was given by $d = \frac{\Sigma d^2}{n}$

A. Weaver   **B.** Doi
C. Rafiullah   **D.** Von Thunen

Q.50 Given below are two statements about Stages of Economic Growth by Walt Whitman Rostow. One is labelled as Assertion (A) and the other is labelled as Reason (R).

Assertion (A): Rostow gave five stages for economic development.

Reason (R): Rostow modeled his theory after the socialist countries.

Select the correct answer from options given below:

A. Both (A) and (R) are true and (R) is the correct explanation of (A)
B. Both (A) and (R) are true, but (R) is not the correct explanation of (A)
C. (A) is true, but (R) is false
D. (A) is false, but (R) is true

Q.51 India does not share maritime boundary with

A. Pakistan   **B.** Maldives
C. Indonesia   **D.** China

Q.52 Which of the following statements are correct?

(a) Culture is the process by which patterns develop.

(b) Culture blends the people of different backgrounds together.

(c) Culture is a way of life.

(d) Culture is a pattern used for differentiation of people.

Code:

A. (b) and (c)

B. (a) and (d)

C. (a), (c) and (d)

D. (b), (c) and (d)

Q.53 Which of the following is NOT included in studies of political geography?

A. Study of behavior of people

B. The relationship between people and their government

C. Study of electoral results

D. The functions, demarcations and policing of boundaries

Q.54 Which of the following is NOT a part of Spykman's division of world?

A. Landlocked states

B. Inner Crescent

C. Island states

D. States that have both land and sea frontiers

Q.55 Match List-I with the List-II and select the correct answer from the code given below:

List - I(Country)	List - II (Direction in which they lie with reference to India)
(a)Pakistan	(i)North East
(b) Sri Lanka	(ii) West
(c) Nepal	(iii)East
(d) Myanmar	(iv) South

Code:

A. (a)-(i), (b)-(iii), (c)-(iv), (d)-(ii)

B. (a)-(iii), (b)-(iv), (c)-(ii), (d)-(i)

C. (a)-(iii), (b)-(iv), (c)-(i), (d)-(ii)

D. (a)-(ii), (b)-(iv), (c)-(i), (d)-(iii)

Q.56 Read the passage and answer the following questions that follow.

At the bottom of the social ladder are Nirvasita meaning 'excluded' or the exterior castes, so called casteless, officially 'scheduled castes'. Since the Government of India Act of 1935, they have been listed in special official schedules for administrative and representational purposes. Article 341 of the Constitution provides that the President may, with respect to any State or Union territory, specify the castes, races or tribes or parts of groups within castes, races or tribes which shall for the purposes of the Constitution be deemed to be Schedules Castes in relation to that State/ Union territory and are valid only within the jurisdiction of that State or Union territory and not outside.

It is important to mention here that under the Constitution (Scheduled Castes) Order, 1950, no person who professed a religion different from Hinduism was deemed to be a member of a Scheduled Caste in addition to every member of the Ramdasi, Kabirpanthi, Mahjabi or Siraligar caste resident in Punjab or Patiala and east Punjab States Union (PESPU) were in relation to that State whether they professed the Hindu or Sikh religion.

The people in the bottom of the social ladder. Those of the exterior castes are called as

A. Scheduled tribes

B. National Tribes

C. National Castes

D. Scheduled Castes

Q.57 Read the passage and answer the following questions that follow.

At the bottom of the social ladder are Nirvasita meaning 'excluded' or the exterior castes, so called casteless, officially 'scheduled castes'. Since the Government of India Act of 1935, they have been listed in special official schedules for administrative and representational purposes. Article 341 of the Constitution provides that the President may, with respect to any State or Union territory, specify the castes, races or tribes or parts of groups within castes, races or tribes which shall for the purposes of the Constitution be deemed to be Schedules Castes in relation to that State/ Union territory and are valid only within the jurisdiction of that State or Union territory and not outside.

It is important to mention here that under the Constitution (Scheduled Castes) Order, 1950, no person who professed a religion different from Hinduism was deemed to be a member of a Scheduled Caste in addition to every member of the Ramdasi, Kabirpanthi, Mahjabi or Siraligar caste resident in Punjab or Patiala and east Punjab States Union (PESPU) were in relation to that State whether they professed the Hindu or Sikh religion.

As per the Article 341 of the Constitution, who may specify castes, races, or tribes?

A. Prime Minister

B. Chief Minister

C. President

D. Home Minister

Q.58 Read the passage and answer the following questions that follow.

At the bottom of the social ladder are Nirvasita meaning 'excluded' or the exterior castes, so called casteless, officially 'scheduled castes'. Since the Government of India Act of 1935, they have been listed in special official schedules for administrative and representational purposes. Article 341 of the Constitution provides that the President may, with respect to any State or Union territory, specify the castes, races or tribes or parts of groups within castes, races or tribes which shall for the purposes of the Constitution be deemed to be Schedules Castes in relation to that State/ Union territory and are valid only within the jurisdiction of that State or Union territory and not outside.

It is important to mention here that under the Constitution (Scheduled Castes) Order, 1950, no person who professed a religion different from Hinduism was deemed to be a member of a Scheduled Caste in addition to every member of the Ramdasi, Kabirpanthi, Mahjabi or Siraligar caste resident in Punjab or Patiala and east Punjab States Union (PESPU) were in relation to that State whether they professed the Hindu or Sikh religion.

Any caste, tribe or race under the Act 341 of the Constitution are valid only in

A. The country

B. The continent

C. The State/ Union Territory

D. The administrative

Q.59 Read the passage and answer the following questions that follow.

At the bottom of the social ladder are Nirvasita meaning 'excluded' or the exterior castes, so called casteless, officially 'scheduled castes'. Since the Government of India Act of 1935, they have been listed in special official schedules for administrative and representational purposes. Article 341 of the Constitution provides that the President may, with respect to any State or Union territory, specify the castes, races or tribes or parts of groups within castes, races or tribes which shall for the purposes of the Constitution be deemed to be Schedules Castes in relation to that State/ Union territory and are valid only within the jurisdiction of that State or Union territory and not outside.

It is important to mention here that under the Constitution (Scheduled Castes) Order, 1950, no person who professed a religion different from Hinduism was deemed to be a member of a Scheduled Caste in addition to every member of the Ramdasi, Kabirpanthi, Mahjabi or Siraligar caste resident in Punjab or Patiala and east Punjab States Union (PESPU) were in relation to that State whether they professed the Hindu or Sikh religion.

A person from which religion can be deemed as a member of Scheduled Castes?

A. Christianity   **B.** Hinduism
C. Jainism   **D.** Judaism

Q.60 Read the passage and answer the following questions that follow.

At the bottom of the social ladder are Nirvasita meaning 'excluded' or the exterior castes, so called casteless, officially 'scheduled castes'. Since the Government of India Act of 1935, they have been listed in special official schedules for administrative and representational purposes. Article 341 of the Constitution provides that the President may, with respect to any State or Union territory, specify the castes, races or tribes or parts of groups within castes, races or tribes which shall for the purposes of the Constitution be deemed to be Schedules Castes in relation to that State/ Union territory and are valid only within the jurisdiction of that State or Union territory and not outside.

It is important to mention here that under the Constitution (Scheduled Castes) Order, 1950, no person who professed a religion different from Hinduism was deemed to be a member of a Scheduled Caste in addition to every member of the Ramdasi, Kabirpanthi, Mahjabi or Siraligar caste resident in Punjab or Patiala and east Punjab States Union (PESPU) were in relation to that State whether they professed the Hindu or Sikh religion.

Which of the following caste resident of Punjab in Hindu or Sikh religion is considered as Scheduled caste?

A. Ramdasi   **B.** Gond   **C.** Kumari   **D.** Naga

Q.61 Match List-I with the List-II and select the correct answer from the code given below:

List-I (Greek Geographer)	List - II (Books)
(a)Plato	(i) Corpus aristotilum
(b) Aristotle	(ii) symposium
(c)Ptolemy	(iii) Geographic
(d) Strabo	(iv) Geography

Code:
A. (a)-(i), (b)-(iii), (c)-(iv), (d)-(ii)
B. (a)-(ii), (b)-(i), (c)-(iv), (d)-(iii)
C. (a)-(i), (b)-(iv), (c)-(iii), (d)-(ii)
D. (a)-(iv), (b)-(i), (c)-(ii), (d)-(iii)

Q.62 Assertion (A): Ibn Fadlan was a 10th century Muslim traveler.

Reason (R): Some of his works is present in Ridawiya Library.

Select the correct answer from options given below:

A. Both (A) and (R) are true and (R) is the correct explanation of (A)
B. Both (A) and (R) are true, but (R) is not the correct explanation of (A)
C. (A) is true, but (R) is false
D. (A) is false, but (R) is true

Q.63 Ritter's work "**Vorhalle der europaischen Volkergeschichte vor Herodotus um den Kaukasus und um die Gestade des Pontus, eine Abhandlung zur Altertumskunde**" showed his interest in which country?

A. Australia   **B.** Britain   **C.** Brazil   **D.** India

Q.64 Which of the following statements relating to Karl Haushofer's system Autarky is correct?

(a) Autarky is the other name of self sufficiency.
(b) The system supports international trade
(c) Autarky is a system which exists in political states and economies.
(d) Economies having this kind of system is known as closed economies.

Code:
A. (b) and (d)   **B.** (a) and (c)
C. (a), (c) and (d)   **D.** (a),(b), and (d)

Q.65 Given below are two statements on the radical geography. One is labelled as Assertion (A) and the other is labelled as Reason (R).

Assertion(A)- Radicalism is entirely based on quantification.

Reason(R)- The elucidation of social issues is the core of radicalism.

Select the correct answer from options given below:

A. Both (A) and (R) are true and (R) is the correct explanation of (A)
B. Both (A) and (R) are true, but (R) is not the correct explanation of (A)
C. (A) is true, but (R) is false
D. (A) is false, but (R) is true

Q.66 Match List I with the List II and select the correct answer from the code given below:-

List I Geographical themes/ Perspectives	List II Features
(a)Positivism	(i) Imperfected reality and fallibilistic

	views of knowledge
(b)Behaviouralism	(ii) Participant observation, livelihood and economies, human interaction
(c)Humanism	(iii) Dynamic interrelation between man and environment
(d)Pragmatism	(iv) Anti-idealist and supports the exclusion of normative questions

Codes:

A. (a)-(i), (b)-(iii), (c)-(iv), (d)-(ii)

B. (a)-(ii), (b)-(iii), (c)-(iv), (d)-(i)

C. (a)-(i), (b)-(iv), (c)-(iii), (d)-(ii)

D. (a)-(iv), (b)-(iii), (c)-(ii), (d)-(i)

Q.67 What kind of paradigm shift was being initiated by Schaefer in order to explain geography?

A. Possibilist-regional paradigm

B. Spatial Organisation paradigm

C. Entropy-maximizing paradigm

D. None of the above

Q.68 Consider the following statements:-

1) Systematic Geography can also be termed as 'nomothetical approach'

2) Systematic Geography is the whole world as an unit while special geography deals with unique situations and peculiarities

3) Vidal de la Blache, Ratzel were some of the supporters of the human geography

4) The dichotomy of physical versus human geography has been considered logical and realistic.

Which of the following options are correct?

A. a and b

B. b and c

C. a, b and c

D. a, b and d

Q.69 Given below are two statements on the Concept of Dualisms. One is labelled as Assertion (A) and the other is labelled as Reason (R).

Assertion(A)- Formulation of scientific laws is not possible in the field of special geography.

Reason(R)- The sole concept of regional geography is the description and interpretation of complex items in unique units.

Select the correct answer from options given below:

A. Both (A) and (R) are true and (R) is the correct explanation of (A)

B. Both (A) and (R) are true, but (R) is not the correct explanation of (A)

C. (A) is true, but (R) is false

D. (A) is false, but (R) is true

Q.70 Which of the following option is correct regarding the traditions of Geography?

A. The first person to consider the influence the human-environment tradition was George Perkins Marsh.

B. The regional tradition was eliminated in the mid-1950s due to its unscientific nature.

C. Earth Science tradition can be explained as the study of the earth as the home of humanity.

D. All of the above

Q.71 Which of the following map is used for demarcating boundaries or is useful for revenue collection purposes?

A. Cadastral Maps

B. Topographical Maps

C. Wall Maps

D. Atlas Maps

Q.72 Which of the following statements are correct regarding diagrammatic maps?

A. In a line graph, the X axis shows months, years, countries while the Y-axis represents the changes with reference to elements of the X-axis.

B. Bar diagrams fail to show elements having continuity.

C. In a bar diagram, all the bars must be equi-spaced and figures shown must be rounded off.

D. All of the above.

Q.73 The distance measured between 2 points on a map is 2cm. The corresponding distance on an aerial photograph is 4cm. What would be the scale of the aerial photo when the scale of the map is 1:10000?

A. 1: 200000

B. 1:5000

C. 1:150000

D. 1:100000

Q.74 Given below are two statements on Absorption, reflectivity and spectral response. One is labeled as Assertion(A) and the other is labeled as Reason(R).

Assertion(A)- The proportions of energy reflected, absorbed, or transmitted on an object certainly vary at the same wavelength, thus leading to a spectral response.

Reason(R)- Leaves appear green due to its chlorophyll content and water appears typically blue or blue green.

Select the correct answer from options given below:-

A. Both A and R are true, and R is the correct explanation of A

B. Both A and R are true, but R is not the correct explanation of A

C. A is true but R is false

D. A is false but R is true

Q.75 What is meant by Azimuth?

A. Across-track dimension perpendicular to the flight direction

B. Along-track dimension parallel to flight direction

C. Angle between the radar beam and ground surface

D. Area imaged on the surface

Q.76 In a moderately skewed distribution, if the Mean and Median are given, which formula is employed for the calculation of Mode?

A. Mean-Mode= 3(Mean –Median)

B. Mode= Mean + Median

C. Mean-Mode= Mean-Median

D. Mean-Mode= 3(Mean + Median)

Q.77 What would be the type of correlation if the pattern of points on the scatter diagram shows a linear path from the upper-left hand corner to the bottom-right on a graph?

A. Positive

B. Negative

C. Zero

D. None of the above

Q.78 Match List I with the List II and select the correct answer from the codes given below:-

List I (Components of time series)	List II(Examples)
(a)Secular trend	(i) Flood, Earthquakes
(b)Seasonal variation	(ii) A recession
(c)Cyclical fluctuation	(iii)Passenger traffic during 24 hours of a day
(d)Irregular movements	(iv) Decline in death rate due to medical advancements

Codes:

A.   (a)-(i), (b)-(iii), (c)-(iv), (d)-(ii)
B.   (a)-(ii), (b)-(iii), (c)-(iv), (d)-(i)
C.   (a)-(i), (b)-(iv), (c)-(iii), (d)-(ii)
D.   (a)-(iv), (b)-(iii), (c)-(ii), (d)-(i)

Q.79 Given below are two statements on Sampling. One is labeled as Assertion(A) and the other is labeled as Reason(R).

Assertion(A)- One cannot afford to examine every single grain of rice or dig out a whole mine to examine its quality.

Reason(R)- Sampling is a necessity under certain conditions.

Select the correct answer from options given below:-

A.   Both A and R are true, and R is the correct explanation of A
B.   Both A and R are true, but R is not the correct explanation of A
C.   A is true but R is false
D.   A is false but R is true

Q.80 Which one of the following are the areal aspects of a river basin?

A. Drainage Texture   B. Basin Relief
C. Stream Order   D. Relief Ratio

Q.81 Which river is also known as 'Yarlung Zangbo Jiangin'?

A. Brahmaputra   B. Ganga
C. Indus   D. Mahanadi

Q.82 Which of the following statements are correct regarding the seasons of the Indian Climate?

A.   The major features of the cold weather season are low temperature, cool and slow northern winds and pressure of around 1015-1020 mb.
B.   Accordingly, the highest temperatures are recorded in May but in certain areas, June is the month of highest temperature and is mostly observed in North India.
C.   The normal date of the onset of south-west monsoons over Kerala is 1st June.
D.   All of the above

Q.83 Given below are two statements on Monsoon Characteristics of India. One is labelled as Assertion (A) and the other is labelled as Reason (R).

Assertion(A)- Rainfall over India is mainly orographic in nature

Reason(R)- Cherrapunji receives the highest annual rainfall of about 1102 cm.

Select the correct answer from options given below:

A.   Both (A) and (R) are true and (R) is the correct explanation of (A)

B.   Both (A) and (R) are true, but (R) is not the correct explanation of (A)
C.   (A) is true, but (R) is false
D.   (A) is false, but (R) is true

Q.84 To which of the following mode of transport is the Bharatmala Pariyojana related?

A. Roadways   B. Railways
C. Waterways   D. Airways

Q.85 Which of the following is the oldest public sector undertaking in fertilizer industry?

A.   Fertilizer Corporation of India (FCI)
B.   National Fertilizers Limited (NFL)
C.   Rashtriya Chemicals and Fertilizers Limited (RCF)
D.   Hindustan Fertilizer Corporation Limited

Q.86 Which among the following is not a mega cluster in handloom sector?

A. Sivasagar (Assam)   B. Varanasi (UP)
C. Murshidabad (WB)   D. None of the above.

Q.87 Which among the following river basins cover the largest basin area?

A. Brahmaputra   B. Narmada
C. Tapti   D. Krishna

Q.88 Which among the following rivers is the Dhuandhar Falls part of?

A. Godavari   B. Narmada
C. Krishna   D. Tapi

Q.89 Given below are two statements. One is labelled as Assertion (A) and the other is labelled as Reason (R).

Assertion (A): The number of agro ecological zones is greater than that of agro-climatic regions of India.

Reason (R): The soil map is superimposed on the agro-climatic region map.

Select the correct answer from options given below:

A.   Both (A) and (R) are true and (R) is the correct explanation of (A)

B.   Both (A) and (R) are true, but (R) is not the correct explanation of (A)
C.   (A) is true, but (R) is false.
D.   (A) is false, but (R) is true.

Q.90 Match List-I with the List-II and select the correct answer from the code given below:

List - I (Characteristics)	List - II (Natural Hazards)
(a) Water-Spout	(i) Tropical Cyclone
(b) Cumulonimbus Convection condition	(ii) Tropical Cyclone
(c)Storm Surge	(iii)Floods
(d) GLOFs	(iv) Cloudbursts

Code:

A.   (a)-(iv), (b)-(ii), (c)-(i), (d)-(iii)
B.   (a)-(ii), (b)-(iii), (c)-(iv), (d)-(i)
C.   (a)-(ii), (b)-(iii), (c)-(i), (d)-(iv)

D. (a)-(ii), (b)-(iv), (c)-(i), (d)-(iii)

Q.91 In which among the following pair of months India has experienced most number of tropical cyclones during the last 100 years?

A. December-January **B.** February-March
C. July-August **D.** October-November

Q.92 Which among the following states has large parts of its area characterized by red soils?

A. Chhattisgarh **B.** Bihar
C. Assam **D.** Gujarat

Q.93 What is the minimum desirable area under forest cover as per the National Forest Policy in terms of proportion to total area?

A. 25 per cent **B.** 35 per cent
C. 33 per cent **D.** 30 per cent

Q.94 Given below are two statements. One is labelled as Assertion (A) and the other is labelled as Reason (R).

Assertion (A): During Summer season, the westerly jet stream withdraws from the Indian region.

Reason (R): ITCZ shifts northwards and it leads to the maritime tropical airmass to come towards the Indian region.

Select the correct answer from options given below:

A. Both (A) and (R) are true and (R) is the correct explanation of (A)

B. Both (A) and (R) are true, but (R) is not the correct explanation of (A)

C. (A) is true, but (R) is false.

D. (A) is false, but (R) is true.

Q.95 *Malnad* and *Maidan* topography are the characteristic features of which among the physiographic divisions?

A. Maharashtra Plateau

B. Karnataka Plateau

C. Telangana Plateau

D. Chotanagpur Plateau

Q.96 Read the passage and answer the following questions that follow.

The foundation of planning in India was laid much before Independence during the heat of India's freedom struggle by the stalwarts of Indian thought and freedom movement like Mahatma Gandhi, Subash Chandra Bose and Jawaharlal Nehru...... The National Institution for Transforming India (NITI Aayog) came into existence in 2015 replacing the Planning Commission which was established in 1950. The NITI Aayog is the successor to the Planning Commission. The Planning Commission was set up in March, 1951 in pursuance of declared objectives of the Government to promote a rapid rise in the standard of living of the people by efficient exploitation of the resources of the country, increasing production and offering opportunities to all for employment in the service of the community.... Keeping in view the large-scale import of food grains in 1951 and inflationary pressures on the economy, the First Plan (1951-56) accorded the highest priority to agriculture including irrigation and power projects. Second five-year plan was devoted to the development of industries as the crisis of foods shortage was dealt with in the previous plans. Heavy industrialization characterized the second FYP. The Third Plan (1961-62 to 1965-66) aimed at securing a marked advance towards self-sustaining growth. Between 1966 and 1969, three Annual Plans were formulated within the framework of the draft outline of the Fourth Plan. The Fourth Plan (1969-74) aimed at accelerating the tempo of development of reducing fluctuations in agricultural production as well as the impact of uncertainties of foreign aid. It sought to raise the standard of living through programmes designed to promote equality and social justice....It was these plans and the later ones which introduce the planning measures via policies like Integrated Rural Development Project, Hill Area Development programme, Desert area development programme, Command Area Development to bridge the regional disparities in the country.

Which of the following institution was replaced by the NITI Aayog as a successor institution?

A. National Planning Committee

B. Planning Commission

C. National development Council

D. National Committee for Planning and Regional development

Q.97 Read the passage and answer the following questions that follow.

The foundation of planning in India was laid much before Independence during the heat of India's freedom struggle by the stalwarts of Indian thought and freedom movement like Mahatma Gandhi, Subash Chandra Bose and Jawaharlal Nehru...... The National Institution for Transforming India (NITI Aayog) came into existence in 2015 replacing the Planning Commission which was established in 1950. The NITI Aayog is the successor to the Planning Commission. The Planning Commission was set up in March, 1951 in pursuance of declared objectives of the Government to promote a rapid rise in the standard of living of the people by efficient exploitation of the resources of the country, increasing production and offering opportunities to all for employment in the service of the community.... Keeping in view the large-scale import of food grains in 1951 and inflationary pressures on the economy, the First Plan (1951-56) accorded the highest priority to agriculture including irrigation and power projects. Second five-year plan was devoted to the development of industries as the crisis of foods shortage was dealt with in the previous plans. Heavy industrialization characterized the second FYP. The Third Plan (1961-62 to 1965-66) aimed at securing a marked advance towards self-sustaining growth. Between 1966 and 1969, three Annual Plans were formulated within the framework of the draft outline of the Fourth Plan. The Fourth Plan (1969-74) aimed at accelerating the tempo of development of reducing fluctuations in agricultural production as well as the impact of uncertainties of foreign aid. It sought to raise the standard of living through programmes designed to promote equality and social justice....It was these plans and the later ones which introduce the planning measures via policies like Integrated Rural Development Project, Hill Area Development programme, Desert area development programme, Command Area Development to bridge the regional disparities in the country.

In which five-year plan was the Command Area Development programme was launched?

A. Third Five Year Plan
B. Fourth Five-year Plan
C. Fifth Five Year Plan
D. Sixth five Year Plan

Q.98 Read the passage and answer the following questions that follow.

The foundation of planning in India was laid much before Independence during the heat of India's freedom struggle by the stalwarts of Indian thought and freedom movement like Mahatma Gandhi, Subash Chandra Bose and Jawaharlal Nehru...... The National Institution for Transforming India (NITI Aayog) came into existence in 2015 replacing the Planning Commission which was established in 1950. The NITI Aayog is the successor to the Planning Commission. The Planning Commission was set up in March, 1951 in pursuance of declared objectives of the Government to promote a rapid rise in the standard of living of the people by efficient exploitation of the resources of the country, increasing production and offering opportunities to all for employment in the service of the community.... Keeping in view the large-scale import of food grains in 1951 and inflationary pressures on the economy, the First Plan (1951-56) accorded the highest priority to agriculture including irrigation and power projects. Second five-year plan was devoted to the development of industries as the crisis of foods shortage was dealt with in the previous plans. Heavy industrialization characterized the second FYP. The Third Plan (1961-62 to 1965-66) aimed at securing a marked advance towards self-sustaining growth. Between 1966 and 1969, three Annual Plans were formulated within the framework of the draft outline of the Fourth Plan. The Fourth Plan (1969-74) aimed at accelerating the tempo of development of reducing fluctuations in agricultural production as well as the impact of uncertainties of foreign aid. It sought to raise the standard of living through programmes designed to promote equality and social justice....It was these plans and the later ones which introduce the planning measures via policies like Integrated Rural Development Project, Hill Area Development programme, Desert area development programme, Command Area Development to bridge the regional disparities in the country.

In which of the five-year plans was the new industries like Iron and steel and the fertilizer industries were set up on a broad scale for the first time?

A. First Five-Year Plan
B. Second Five-Year Plan
C. Fourth Five Year Plan
D. Sixth Five Year Plan

Q.99 Read the passage and answer the following questions that follow.

The foundation of planning in India was laid much before Independence during the heat of India's freedom struggle by the stalwarts of Indian thought and freedom movement like Mahatma Gandhi, Subash Chandra Bose and Jawaharlal Nehru...... The National Institution for Transforming India (NITI Aayog) came into existence in 2015 replacing the Planning Commission which was established in 1950. The NITI Aayog is

the successor to the Planning Commission. The Planning Commission was set up in March, 1951 in pursuance of declared objectives of the Government to promote a rapid rise in the standard of living of the people by efficient exploitation of the resources of the country, increasing production and offering opportunities to all for employment in the service of the community.... Keeping in view the large-scale import of food grains in 1951 and inflationary pressures on the economy, the First Plan (1951-56) accorded the highest priority to agriculture including irrigation and power projects. Second five-year plan was devoted to the development of industries as the crisis of foods shortage was dealt with in the previous plans. Heavy industrialization characterized the second FYP. The Third Plan (1961-62 to 1965-66) aimed at securing a marked advance towards self-sustaining growth. Between 1966 and 1969, three Annual Plans were formulated within the framework of the draft outline of the Fourth Plan. The Fourth Plan (1969-74) aimed at accelerating the tempo of development of reducing fluctuations in agricultural production as well as the impact of uncertainties of foreign aid. It sought to raise the standard of living through programmes designed to promote equality and social justice....It was these plans and the later ones which introduce the planning measures via policies like Integrated Rural Development Project, Hill Area Development programme, Desert area development programme, Command Area Development to bridge the regional disparities in the country.

Which among the following statements is incorrect?

A. The NITI Aayog replaced the former Planning Commission
B. The Prime Minister is the Chairperson of the NITI Aayog.
C. The foundation of Indian Planning was laid out before Independence only.
D. It was the Ninth five-year plan which was launched after the Structural Adjustment policies.

Q.100 Read the passage and answer the following questions that follow.

The foundation of planning in India was laid much before Independence during the heat of India's freedom struggle by the stalwarts of Indian thought and freedom movement like Mahatma Gandhi, Subash Chandra Bose and Jawaharlal Nehru...... The National Institution for Transforming India (NITI Aayog) came into existence in 2015 replacing the Planning Commission which was established in 1950. The NITI Aayog is the successor to the Planning Commission. The Planning Commission was set up in March, 1951 in pursuance of declared objectives of the Government to promote a rapid rise in the standard of living of the people by efficient exploitation of the resources of the country, increasing production and offering opportunities to all for employment in the service of the community.... Keeping in view the large-scale import of food grains in 1951 and inflationary pressures on the economy, the First Plan (1951-56) accorded the highest priority to agriculture including irrigation and power projects. Second five-year plan was devoted to the development of industries as the crisis of foods shortage was dealt with in the previous plans. Heavy industrialization characterized the second FYP. The Third Plan (1961-62 to 1965-66) aimed at securing a marked advance towards self-sustaining growth. Between 1966 and 1969, three Annual Plans were formulated within the framework

of the draft outline of the Fourth Plan. The Fourth Plan (1969-74) aimed at accelerating the tempo of development of reducing fluctuations in agricultural production as well as the impact of uncertainties of foreign aid. It sought to raise the standard of living through programmes designed to promote equality and social justice....It was these plans and the later ones which introduce the planning measures via policies like Integrated Rural Development Project, Hill Area Development programme, Desert area development programme, Command Area Development to bridge the regional disparities in the country.

Which among the following committee created by the Planning Commission looked after the financial and fiscal incentives for starting industries in backward areas?

A. Wanchoo Committee

B. Pande Committee

C. Chakravarti Committee

D. Ashok Mehta Committee

// Smart Answer Sheet //

Correct — Percentage of students who answered correctly.   **Skipped** — Percentage of students who skipped.

Q.	Ans.	Correct / Skipped
1	C	20.0 % / 16.67 %
2	B	40.0 % / 40.0 %
3	B	16.67 % / 33.33 %
4	B	30.0 % / 40.0 %
5	C	26.67 % / 40.0 %
6	A	53.33 % / 40.0 %
7	C	33.33 % / 40.0 %
8	C	23.33 % / 40.0 %
9	B	46.67 % / 43.33 %
10	B	33.33 % / 40.0 %
11	C	13.33 % / 40.0 %
12	B	13.33 % / 40.0 %
13	A	46.67 % / 30.0 %
14	D	53.33 % / 40.0 %
15	D	56.67 % / 40.0 %
16	B	50.0 % / 40.0 %

Q.	Ans.	Correct / Skipped
17	C	20.0 % / 40.0 %
18	D	40.0 % / 40.0 %
19	D	16.67 % / 23.33 %
20	C	36.67 % / 30.0 %
21	B	23.33 % / 30.0 %
22	D	40.0 % / 40.0 %
23	C	30.0 % / 23.33 %
24	D	26.67 % / 40.0 %
25	B	60.0 % / 40.0 %
26	D	23.33 % / 40.0 %
27	D	53.33 % / 30.0 %
28	D	46.67 % / 40.0 %
29	A	60.0 % / 33.33 %
30	D	53.33 % / 40.0 %
31	C	26.67 % / 40.0 %
32	B	40.0 % / 36.67 %

Q.	Ans.	Correct / Skipped
33	D	30.0 % / 33.33 %
34	A	56.67 % / 40.0 %
35	B	46.67 % / 33.33 %
36	C	56.67 % / 40.0 %
37	A	60.0 % / 40.0 %
38	A	40.0 % / 40.0 %
39	B	50.0 % / 40.0 %
40	D	40.0 % / 40.0 %
41	C	16.67 % / 33.33 %
42	D	30.0 % / 40.0 %
43	C	36.67 % / 33.33 %
44	C	36.67 % / 40.0 %
45	C	56.67 % / 30.0 %
46	D	53.33 % / 40.0 %
47	C	50.0 % / 40.0 %
48	A	43.33 % / 40.0 %

Q.	Ans.	Correct / Skipped
49	B	6.67 % / 40.0 %
50	C	16.67 % / 40.0 %
51	D	53.33 % / 33.34 %
52	C	30.0 % / 30.0 %
53	A	46.67 % / 40.0 %
54	B	10.0 % / 40.0 %
55	D	60.0 % / 40.0 %
56	D	43.33 % / 40.0 %
57	C	53.33 % / 40.0 %
58	C	43.33 % / 40.0 %
59	B	50.0 % / 40.0 %
60	A	63.33 % / 30.0 %
61	B	30.0 % / 40.0 %
62	B	36.67 % / 40.0 %
63	D	16.67 % / 40.0 %
64	C	43.33 % / 40.0 %

Q.	Ans.	Correct / Skipped
65	D	26.67 % / 40.0 %
66	D	26.67 % / 40.0 %
67	B	33.33 % / 40.0 %
68	C	36.67 % / 40.0 %
69	A	36.67 % / 40.0 %
70	D	50.0 % / 40.0 %
71	A	56.67 % / 30.0 %
72	D	66.67 % / 30.0 %
73	B	40.0 % / 43.33 %
74	D	3.33 % / 40.0 %
75	B	23.33 % / 40.0 %
76	A	30.0 % / 40.0 %
77	B	36.67 % / 40.0 %
78	D	36.67 % / 40.0 %
79	A	36.67 % / 30.0 %
80	A	16.67 % / 33.33 %

Q.	Ans.	Correct / Skipped		Q.	Ans.	Correct / Skipped		Q.	Ans.	Correct / Skipped		Q.	Ans.	Correct / Skipped		Q.	Ans.	Correct / Skipped
81	A	53.33 %		85	A	20.0 %		89	A	23.33 %		93	C	53.33 %		97	C	6.67 %
		30.0 %				40.0 %				43.34 %				30.0 %				43.33 %
82	D	60.0 %		86	D	30.0 %		90	D	36.67 %		94	A	46.67 %		98	B	50.0 %
		40.0 %				40.0 %				40.0 %				40.0 %				40.0 %
83	B	26.67 %		87	D	16.67 %		91	D	43.33 %		95	B	40.0 %		99	D	16.67 %
		40.0 %				40.0 %				40.0 %				40.0 %				40.0 %
84	A	46.67 %		88	B	50.0 %		92	A	43.33 %		96	B	53.33 %		100	A	16.67 %
		40.0 %				40.0 %				40.0 %				40.0 %				40.0 %

EDUGORILLA
PUBLICATION

//Hints and Solutions//

1. Sometimes the continents break into small fragments due internal movements. These smaller continents are called as terranes. These terranes float around on mantle, until they meet another continent and attach themselves to it. Because they come from different continent than the one, they were attached to, they are called as exotic or suspect terranes.

2. The endogenetic movements are that operate beneath crust of the earth. The slow movement of mountain building is an orogenic movement. They are endogenetic movements. Diastrophism is a large-scale deformation of earth's crust. The horizontal movement of plate tectonics is an example of diastrophism.

3. Rocks develop cracks and many times, water seeps through these cracks. Due to constant change of temperature, the freeze and thaw of water occurs leading to disintegration of rocks. This is called as physical weathering. Thus, both (A) and (R) are true, but (R) is not the correct explanation of (A).

4. The river, in its youthful stage, flows along an uneven surface and intensive erosion occurs. In the mature stage, river attains a profile of equilibrium. It drainage system is fully developed by this stage. Thus, landforms such as oxbow lakes, flood plains, meanders, cuestas, mesa, etc. are formed in this stage. Thus, both (A) and (R) are true, both (R) is not the correct explanation of (A).

5. Crickmay in 1933 gave the concept of panplain. A panplain is formed by floodplains joined by their own growth. It is formed due to lateral erosion. A panplain is formed due to eventual joining of valley flats. A panplain is much flatter than the pediplain.

6. Gorge is a valley caused by erosional work of the river. Drumlins are tear-shaped hills of rock, soil, ice under the glacier. It is a depositional landform. Wave-cut platforms are formed due to erosional work of a sea/ocean. Inselbergs are small hills formed due to erosional work of the air in the desert.

7. Fault is defined as displacement of once connected rocks along a fault plain. A graben fault occurs when there is subsidence of a block of rock due to tensional stress from both the sides. The extended, large scale feature of this fault is called as rift valley. Examples of rift valleys include The Great Rift Valley of Africa and the Narmada Rift Valley.

8. Barren island is the only active volcano in India. It erupted last in 2017, though it was a minor activity. The volcanic eruption of Mt Agung in Bali in 2017 occurred after a series of volcanic earthquakes. The Latur earthquake in 1993 was of the magnitude 6.6 on Richter scale. The earthquake of Andaman Islands on 11 Aug 2009 was of the magnitude 7.5 on Richter scale.

9. As the name suggests, continental drift theory is the study of continents' nature of shifting their places on the surface of the earth. It was firstly stated by a geophysicist Alfred Wegener who also explained how this is a reason for the similar nature of fossils, vegetation etc in the places that are far away. Whereas, Henry Frankel stated objection claiming to continental drift accepted as a response to plate tectonics, and according to him plate tectonics had no mechanism .

Thus, the Correct answer is B.

10. * Highest peak of Rockies ranges is Mt. Elbert, and its height is 4401 meters.

* Highest peak of Atlas Mountain Ranges is Mt. Toubkal which has a height of 4167meters.

* Highest peak of Alps is Mt. Blanc which has a height of 4809 meters.

* The highest peak of Andes is Mt. Aconcagua having a height of 6962 meters.

Thus, the Correct answer is B.

11. Gustnado is a swirling wind that occurs on the edge of a severe thunderstorm that occurs for a short time. It occurs on the leading edge of the thunderstorm. They may be accompanied by rain, dust, and small debris. It is not connected to the base of a cloud.

12. The Loo wind from Rajasthan reaches West Bengal, Bihar, Assam, and Bangladesh. These winds cause cyclonic turbulence and yield rains called as Kalbaishakhi in coastal parts of Andhra Pradesh and Orissa. Sea winds converge in Tamil Nadu and form low pressure zone in Tamil Nadu. This leads to huge & powerful winds in the area in March & April. It leads to mangoes falling due to these winds. That is why these winds

13. Insolation is the incoming solar radiation. It is counted as the amount of solar energy received by the earth per square centimeter. Solar constant, the angle of incidence, duration of the day, transparency of atmosphere is factors that affect insolation. It is most strong at noon.

14. The Mediterranean climatic zone is the zone when a rainfall is highest during the winters. This occurs due to mid-latitude cyclones. Hardly any rainfall occurs in summer. Examples for this type of climate include Oregon, Portland, California, etc. It is denoted by Cs.

15. Changes in obliquity (changes in the angle that the axis makes with the plane of Earth's orbit), Change in eccentricity (shape of the Earth's orbit) and The wobbling of earth's axis (precession) like a top are explained through the concept of Milankovitch Theory of climate change. Using these factors, Milankovitch calculated variations in the receipt of solar energy and the corresponding surface temperature of Earth back into time, in an attempt to correlate these changes with the climate fluctuations of the Ice Age. It should be noted that these factors cause little or no variation in the total solar energy reaching the ground. Instead, their impact is felt because they change the degree of contrast between the seasons. Somewhat milder winters in the middle to high latitudes mean greater snowfall totals, whereas cooler summers bring a reduction in snowmelt. Thus, the theory explained that the orbital geometry of the earth is largely responsible for the succession of the Quaternary ice ages or the natural climate variability in terms of glacial and inter-glacial periods throughout history. Several proposals for climate change, based on a variable Sun, relate to sunspot cycles. Sunspots are huge magnetic storms that extend from the Sun's surface deep into the interior. There appears to be close correlation between sunspots and temperature and sunspots and droughts.

16. La Niña is characterized with strong trade winds system and accompanied strong westward moving equatorial current. The pressure conditions are low in the western pacific and high in the eastern pacific. The warm water off the western pacific coast induces convective currents and cloud formation and hence heavy rainfall. On the other hand, on the eastern Pacific coast, to make up for the displaced water along the equator, the cold Peruvian current moves northward towards equator and it causes upwelling of cold water which eventually is beneficial for fishing grounds.

17. El Nino broadly refers to the gradual warming of waters in the eastern Pacific in December or January. La Niña is the opposite of El Niño and refers to colder than normal sea-surface temperatures along the coastline of Peru and Ecuador. This phenomenon is characterized by strong trade winds which generate strong equatorial current that flows westward from South America toward Australia and Indonesia. In addition, a cold ocean current is observed flowing equatorward along the coast of Ecuador and Peru. The latter flow, called the Peru Current, encourages upwelling of cold, nutrient-filled waters that serve as the primary food source for millions of small feeder fish, particularly anchovies. Every few years, however, the circulation associated with La Niña is replaced by an El Niño event.

18. A cyclonic pressure system is the one characterized by rings of isobars and not straight lines with the isobars with lower values at the centre or *low*. Contrary to this, an anti-cyclonic pressure system is the one characterized by rings of isobars with higher values at the centre or *high*. However, the difference between the direction of wind in both pressure systems in northern and southern hemisphere is due to the impact of Coriolis force. As Coriolis force deflects wind to its right in northern hemisphere, the anti-cyclonic circulation in northern hemisphere is characterized by outward moving wind continuously deflected towards its right and hence a clockwise direction. In the same way, the cyclonic circulation has a low pressure system in both hemisphere but the direction is anti-clockwise in northern hemisphere and clockwise in southern hemisphere. Anti-cyclonic circulation in southern hemisphere has an anti-clockwise direction.

19. Relative humidity is a measure of humidity which tells about the amount and the rate of evaporation. It is calculated as the absolute humidity of air divided by the humidity capacity of the air at the particular temperature times 100 (in terms of percentage). The denominator value which refers to the humidity capacity is a function of temperature as increase or decrease in temperature can influence humidity capacity and thus relative humidity. Just before dawn, earth's temperature is the lowest due to outgoing terrestrial radiation and thus it implies higher relative humidity and as the day progresses, with temperature rising, the value of humidity capacity also increases leading to lower relative humidity.

20. The Fahrenheit scale was developed in the early 1700s by the physicist G. Daniel Fahrenheit. In this scale freezing point or 0°C is equivalent to 32°F and the boiling point or 100°C is equivalent to 212°F. And Fahrenheit made 180 equal divisions between the freezing point and the boiling point. By simple unitary method we can guess that 1°C increase is equal to an increase of 1.8°F

and a value of -40°C = 32 – (1.8 × 40) which is nothing but 32-72=-40°F.

The formula for conversion is °C= $\frac{5}{9}(- 32)$. The answer can also be found from this formula.

21. Open sea in the low latitudes record relatively lower temperature than the enclosed seas. This is mainly due to the effect of continentality. Land have lower specific heat than the oceans. Thus enclosed seas in the higher latitudes have lower temperature than the open seas. Oceans in the northern hemisphere record higher temperature than that of southern hemisphere. And ocean's surface temperature may be less or more than the surrounding atmospheric temperature.

22. The diurnal range of oceanic temperature is lower than that of the land because of the high specific heat of water vis-à-vis land. Also, the water in the oceans are constantly in motion, both horizontal and vertical, this also constantly redistributes heat.

23. Semi diurnal tides are the most common of all having two high tides and two low tides in a day while diurnal tides have a high tide and a low tide each day. Spring tides are the highest tides which occur when the sun, moon and the earth are in alignment. Neap tides occur generally after a gap of 7 days from spring tides, during 1st and 3rd quarter of the moon.

24. Tsunamis are shallow water waves because they are generated in the oceans with wavelength exceeding 200 kilometers while the wave height is less than 1 km in the open sea. The mechanisms that trigger tsunamis are generally seismic in nature and thus tsunamis are also called seismic sea waves. Tsunamis are surely affected by the bottom ocean relief features and are commonly refracted. The most interesting feature of the tsunami waves which makes it different than other sea waves is that its wavelength gets shortened and its wave height increases and it does not break all of a sudden and thus when it hits a coast, there are multiple surges or multiple tsunami waves which follows the first wave before the water recedes.

25. On an average, the salinity of oceanic waters is 35 grams per 1000 gm at 25^0 C, the flow of fresh water, wind, oceanic currents, rate of evaporation are some of the factors affecting salinity of ocean waters. Salinity is generally low in equatorial areas.

Thus, the correct answer is B.

26. Biomass is nothing but the amount of the living matter (plant or animal) in a given habitat. Thus in a lake or pond ecosystem, the amount of biomass at the trophic level of producers or autotrophs is less than that of the primary producers (small fish) which is again less than that of the biomass at secondary consumers (relatively large fish). Hence, the pyramid of biomass is not upright, rather inverted in a pond or lake ecosystem.

27. Agenda 21 refers to the action plan which was adopted in the Rio earth Summit in 1992. It is non-binding in nature. The Rio Earth Summit is also known as UN Conference on Environment and Development. Agenda 21 basically refers to the development goals at various levels (global, national, regional, and local) which the parties hoped to achieve by 2021.

28. The Wildlife Protection Act was enacted in 1972 followed by the Project Tiger in 1973. The Environmental Protection Act came

in 1986. It was followed by the National water Policy of India which was framed in 1987. The National Water Policy was reviewed and updated in 2002 and later in 2012.

29. Burning of fossil fuels or smelting of mineral ores which contain Sulphur produces Sulphur dioxides. Nitrogen oxides (NO_x) are the oxides of nitrogen like Nitrogen dioxide (NO_2), Nitric Oxide (NO) which are released by burning of fossil fuels or fuel combustion. Sulphur Dioxides(SO_2) and Nitrogen Dioxides (NO_2) when dissolved with rainwater (H_2O) forms Sulphuric acid (H_2SO_4) and Nitric Acid (HNO_3) respectively and higher concentration of these acid in rainwater is called acid rain.

30. An environmental hazard is any condition, process or state that adversely affects the environment. Environmental hazards have potential for widespread harm to humans and the physical environment and appear to be increasing in number and extent. Today, global warming appears to be emerging as possibly the most dire and pervasive future environmental hazard. Polychlorinated biphenyls (PCBs) are emitted from the burning of plastics and causes air pollution. Lead is a significant industrial waste which is capable of soil degradation, water pollution. It also tends to accumulate in the environment and has high acute and chronic effects on plants, animals and microorganisms. In case of human it can cause lead poisoning.

31. The Registrar General of India under the Ministry of Home Affairs is responsible for the census operation and for vital statistics in India. The office of the Registrar General of India was created in 1951 and the vital statistics department was transferred to this office from the Director of Health Services in 1960. In the absence of reliable data from the civil registration system (CRS), the Government of India in late 1960s, initiated the Sample Registration System that is based on a Dual Recording System. In this, regular registration of births and death is carried out in the sample areas that keep changing every 10 years or so. It was done in 1983, 1993 and 2003. The Sample registration System (SRS) provides reliable annual data on fertility and mortality at the state and national levels for rural and urban areas separately.

32. Although E.G. Ravenstein had written about migration in context of the British population for the first time in the Geographical Magazine in 1876, he published a paper with the title "The Laws of Migration" in the Journal of the Statistical Society of London in 1885 where he mentioned the general laws of migration. His second paper with the same name came in 1889 in the Royal Statistical Society.

33. These are the measures of the early childhood mortality estimation. The neonatal mortality rate is the probability of a child exposed in a specific period dying before reaching the age of 1 month. The post-neonatal mortality rate is the probability of a child exposed in a specific period on or after the age of 1 month but before reaching the age of 1 year, calculated as the difference between the infant mortality rate and the neonatal mortality rate. The infant mortality rate is the probability of a child exposed in a specific period dying before reaching their first birthday. The child mortality rate is the probability of a child exposed in a specific period dying on or after their first birthday but before reaching the age of five years.

34. The rural settlements, leaving aside the difference in the built-forms and shape of the settlements, differ from urban settlements in size, and socio-economic structure. The size of the rural settlements is relatively small compared to the few but large urban settlements. On the economic front, the rural settlements are closely related to primary activities mostly to do with subsistence while urban settlements engage in secondary and tertiary from economic activities. Also, the rural settlements in India is characterized by its social norms as in intimate social relations owing to their low mobility unlike the urban settlements.

35. For the first time, in his book *Man Makes Himself* in 1939, Gordon Childe used the term Urban Revolution to explain the origin of towns and cities. By revolution, he indicated the sheer number of population coming together at a large scale for the first time which was unprecedented. Also, he held technical and economic factors largely responsible for that Urban Revolution.

36. Industrial location is based on a lot of factors, almost crucial for the development of an industry. These factors include the raw material, climate, capital availability, labour, etc. The emotions of a consumer, his behavior and buying capacity affect the market rather than the location of an industry.

37. Cotton industries are located in areas where cotton is grown. Maharashtra and Gujarat have favorable climate and water availability for development of the cotton industry. They too are centers for cotton industries, too. Cotton is a market-oriented industry. 80 % of the cotton industries are located near to the cotton growing tracts.

38. The government provides several concessions to large scale industries in order to encourage them to build their factories in backward areas. These include availability of subsidized power, lower transport cost, infrastructural facilities, etc. The human resource is a perk for these industries as these areas already have huge population present in these backward areas.

39. Venezuela has the largest deposits of oil in the world. India has the lead in the deposits of thorium in the world. The Cajaras mine in Brazil is the largest mine of iron ore in the world. The largest deposits of natural gas in the world are found in Russia.

40. China is the largest of the producer of leather in the world. it produces about 2364 million sq. feet of leather. The countries of Brazil, India and USA rank second, fifth and eighth in the list. China's production of leather is almost double than that of Brazil.

41. For any economic activity to be situated at the centre of an urban system, the most important factor to be considered is the land rent also sometimes referred to as economic rent. This is so because of the cut-throat competition for the same space between competing firms and only those firms could survive which can make profit even after paying the hiked price of the land caused due to the demand of the location.

42. The World Trade Organization is an international unit for promotion of trade. It replaced the General Agreement on Tariff and Trade under the Marrakesh agreement. The Marrakesh Agreement was signed by 123 nations on 15th April 1994.

43. The gravity model measures the interaction between all the possible location pairs. It is the most common model used for spatial interaction. It is very similar to the formulation of the Newton's law of gravity. As per gravity model, the spatial interaction model location of origin and destination are proportional to their respective importance divided by their distance.

44. Jamshedpur, formerly known as Sakchi, was the place where Tata Iron and Steel Company Limited(TISCO) was started in the year 1097. It is the oldest iron & steel industry in India. Osaka in Japan is famous for the textile industry. Pittsburgh in USA has developed iron & steel industry. The coal available locally is useful for the development of this industry. Bengaluru, on Deccan plateau is the hub for Information Technology in India.

45. Natural Resource management is necessary due to increasing population of world and subsequent burden on the resources. The items that are included in natural resource management are biodiversity conservation, land management and precautionary biodiversity management. Oil extraction is not included in management of natural resources.

46. Shifting cultivation is a primitive form of agriculture. It is the practice of burning trees on a part of land in order to cultivate new crops. It is not very productive, but it provides for needs of the cultivators. It has different names in different parts of the world. It is called as Ladang in Java and Indonesia, Jhum in North-Eastern India, Roka in Brazil and Kumari in western Ghats.

47. One of the many assumptions of Von Thunen's model of agricultural land use is that the farmers work in order to maximize their profits. This assumption has been criticized a lot. The other assumption include that the land is flat, there are no rivers or mountains or rivers, etc.

48. Rafiullah improved on Weaver's crop combination method on the year 1965 and introduced a new method. He called this method as the maximum positive deviation method. This method he calculated deviation with the help of positive differences and negative differences from the medial value.

49. D is the deviation. This formula was given by Doi. As per Doi, all those crops are included in the combination whose cumulative percentage is less than 50 or the critical value for all the crops at different ranks against 50 in zero.

50. Walt Whitman Rostow gave the Stages of Economic Growth. He was a member of John. F. Kennedy's administration. He was against communism. He based his theory on the western capitalist economies. As per Rostow, there are five stages of economic growth.

51. India does not share maritime boundary with China. India shares its maritime boundary with 7 countries (Pakistan, Maldives, Sri Lanka, Bangladesh, Myanmar, Thailand, Indonesia). India has a long coastline of nearly 7500 km and Exclusive Economic Zones (EEZ) of nearly 23 lakh square kilometers.

52. Culture can be called as a way of life. It is the opposite of nature, what makes us human and keeps us apart from other animals. It is the process by which patters develop. It is a set of markers that sets people apart from each other. Thus, culture is a pattern used for differentiation of people.

53. The cotemporary political geography studies various areas like feminist geography, youth studies, etc. Along with that the

study of political geography include things like study of the functions, demarcations and policing of boundaries, the relationship between government and its people, study of electoral results and sometimes voters. But the study of behavior of people is considered under behavioural geography, not political geography.

54. Nicholas Spykman was a Dutch-American political geographer. He gave the Rimland theory in 1942. As per Spykman's division of the world, there are three divisions of the world. They include landlocked states, island states and states that have both land and sea frontiers. Inner crescent is a part of the heartland theory.

55. The country of Pakistan lies to the West of India. Nepal lies to Northeast. Sri Lanka lies to the South of the country in the Indian Ocean. The country of Myanmar lies to the east of the India. The other countries that share border with are China, Bangladesh, etc.

56. The people at the bottom of social ladder, the exterior, the Nirvasita are the scheduled castes. The specific state or union territory decide that the scheduled castes of the specific area. They are listed in special official schedules for administrative and representative purposes.

57. The Article 341 of the Constitution has the special provisions for the schedules castes. The President may specify the castes, races or tribes or parts of groups within castes, races or tribes which shall for the purposes of the Constitution be deemed to be Schedules Castes in relation to that State/ Union territory and are valid only within the jurisdiction of that State or Union territory and not outside.

58. The President may specify the caste, races or tribes or part of groups within castes, but this is applicable only within the jurisdiction of the particular state.

59. According to the Constitution (Scheduled Castes) Order, 1950, a person from the Scheduled caste should be from the Hindu religion. The only exception for this is the members of the Ramdasi, Kabirpanthi, Mahjabi or Siraligar castes who are the residents of Punjab. They are considered scheduled castes even if they are Hindu or Sikh.

60. The various castes which, if resident of Punjab or Patiala States Union (PESPU) in Hindu or Sikh religion are called as scheduled castes include the Ramdasi, Kabirpanthi, Mahjabi or Siraligar castes. The other scheduled caste members have to be Hindu in religion.

61. Some of the most eminent scholars in Greek were Herodotus, Plato, Ptolemy etc.

Plato wrote the book Symposium.

Book Corpus Aristotlicum was written by Aristotle.

Ptolemy wrote the book Geography.

Strabo Authored the book Geographica.

Thus, the correct answer is B.

62. Ibn Fadlan was an 10th century Arabic Muslim traveler. He has some of the major contribution in the subject of geography. Most of his works were based on ethnographic researches. Some

of the works were acquires in the Ridawiya Library MS 5229. His work was published in 1923 by Christian Martin Frahn.

He was born in 879 Baghdad, Abbasid Caliphate which is now Iraq.

Thus, the correct answer is B.

63. Ritter's Erdkunde is a very extensive part of German literature which a high significance in it. The first two volumes of Erdkunde were published in 1817 and 1818, respectively. "Vorhalle der europaischen Volkergeschichte vor Herodotus um den Kaukasus und um die Gestade des Pontus, eine Abhandlung zur Altertumskunde" marked his interest in India.

Thus, the correct answer is D.

64. Autarky was a political system put forth by Karl Haushofer in Germany which mean self-dependency. It had various guidelines under which included independent economy, no export, military etc. The system majorly exists in political sates and economies. Economies having autarky s called closed economy where the economy is self sufficient and refuses to conduct any form of foreign trade.

Thus, the correct answer is C.

65. The 1st statement is wrong as radicalism was born as a reaction against quantitative revolutionary concepts and positivism that tried to make geography as a spatial science. During that period there was no emphasis on social issues on the pages of geography. According to radicalists, inequality is inherent in the capitalist mode of production.

The followers of radicalism stressed on issues of great social relevance like inequality, racism, crime, delinquency, discrimination against black and exploitation of environment resources. It was surrounded around domestic issues.

66. Positivism refers to a philosophical movement and viewpoint which is anti-idealist in character and since this theme cannot investigate and test moral norms and values, people should keep away from normative questions.

Behaviouralism is an approach or a theme of geographical thought adopted by the psychologists and philosophers to analyze the man-environment relationship and to develop models for humanity.

Humanism developed against the theory of positivism and quantitative revolution. It stressed more on human world and human issues such as social attitudes, institutions, morals, customs, etc.

The most important feature of pragmatism is that geographic space is a collection of error and knowledge and because of the changing world status; one cannot guarantee a specified result from a specific experiment that had been done in the past. Pragmatism is a modified version of positivism.

67. Schaefer was the one who introduced the spatial organization paradigm. He claimed that geography must be conceived as the science which is concerned with the preparation of the laws governing the spatial distribution of certain features on the Earth's surface. He assigned the nomothetic approach to geography as a spatial and social science.

68. Systematic Geography has also been termed as nomothetical approach because the significant theme of this form of geography is the application of variable phenomena and tracing it systematically over the whole of the Earth's surface. However, it is termed so as it requires the development and testing of theories and models in order to develop geographical laws.

Systematic geography deals with the whole world as a unit. For instance, if we take the patterns of distribution of temperature, rainfall, vegetation, minerals, etc. and examine them at the world level or continent, it would be a case of systematic geography while regional geography deals with unique situations. For instance, if one studies landforms, climatic variables, soils, etc. and superimpose these physical factors on the cultural landscape, then it would be termed as regional geography.

Friedrich Ratzel, Vidal de la Blache, are some of the scholars to support the human geography. They considered man as agent who brought change in the physical landscape. Vidal de la Blache was the one who founded the school of human geography. He gave less importance to physical environmental factors.

69. The reason supports the assertive statement and both the statements are perfectly correct. In Regional geography, it is viewed as the study of areal differentiation and it seeks to describe and interpret the variable character from place to place of the Earth as the home of man. Formulation of scientific laws cannot be done in regional geography as we know that it deals with the description and elaboration of unique individual but interrelated forms of areal phenomena with distinct areal expression and the integration of all interrelated features at individual, homogenous units of places. Hence, scientific laws can be established in laboratory experiments which only allow less independent variable to vary and suggest some kind of determinism.

70. George Perkins Marsh was the 1st person to consider and take into account the influence of human activity in shaping the character of the landscape. This was presented in his book Man and Nature or Physical Geography as Modified by Human Action. This book stated an analysis of how humans can be a force or a cause in shaping landscapes.

71. Cadastral Maps are of immense importance to the local government as they allow for revenue collection purposes. As these maps are drawn on a very large scale, it shows all possible details of an area. These cadastral maps are especially made to demarcate the boundaries of fields, buildings, etc., for better town planning along with the registration of the ownership of the properties. Because of these reasons, Cadastral maps are considered to be highly effective.

72. All the above statements are correct. The line graph is drawn with the help of two coordinates. One is in the horizontal direction and is called X axis while the other, the vertical one is the Y-axis. The X-axis shows months, years, states, countries, etc., while the Y-axis represents the changes with reference to the elements shown on the X-axis. Thus the Y-axis shows normally temperature, population, production according to the elements on the X-axis.

One of the demerits of Bar diagrams is that it fails to show elements having continuity like temperature, pressure, etc. Bar diagrams are however useful for showing data concerning areas, time, etc., Hence, they are used for showing production, consumption, import, export, or rainfall in 12 months of the year, etc.

The bars should be equi-spaced and figures shown by the bars should be rounded off. These are some of the rules that must be maintained while drawing it. The spaces separating the bars should not be more than the width of the bars. Sometimes, the bars are placed adjacent to each other without leaving a gap between them.

73. Scale of an aerial photograph can be calculated if the distances between two given points on a reliable map as well as on the aerial photograph are known. The relationship between the two distances may be expressed as:

Photo Scale: Map scale= Photo distance: Map distance

Hence, from this relation, we get,

Photo Scale(Sp)= Photo distance(Dp): Map distance(Dm) ✕Map scale factor(msf)

Thus,

Sp= Dp:Dm ✕msf

= 4 cm: 2 cm ✕10000

= 4cm : 20000 = 1cm: 20000/4= 1cm: 5000cm

= 1 unit represents 5000 units => Sp= 1:5000

74. Due to the presence of chlorophyll, leaves appear green or yellow according to its chlorophyll content. This compound strongly absorbs radiation in red and blue wavelengths but reflects green wavelengths. Thus, leaves appear green during the summer due to high chlorophyll content. In autumn there is less chlorophyll in the leaves, so there is less absorption and proportionately more reflection of the red wavelengths, making the leaves appear red or yellow. The internal structure of healthy leaves act as excellent diffuse reflectors of near-infrared wavelengths and are used for monitoring the vegetation quality. Similarly, longer wavelength visible and NIR radiation is absorbed more by water than shorter visible wavelengths giving water a blue or bluish-green colour due to stronger reflectance at these shorter wavelengths and darker if viewed at red or NIR wavelengths.

If the wavelength remains the same we won't be able to differentiate between the different features. Water and vegetation may reflect somewhat similar in the visible wavelengths but are almost separable in the infrared. Hence, depending on the complex make up of the target that is being looked at, and the wavelengths of radiation involved, one can observe very different responses to the mechanisms of absorption, transmission, reflection. From this, a spectral response can be drawn for those objects.

75. Azimuth means the along-track dimension parallel to the flight direction or path. This term is usually related to the imaging geometry of the radar. This side-looking viewing geometry is typical of imaging radar systems such as airborne and spaceborne. However, azimuth resolution is determined by the angular width of the radiated microwave beam and the slant range distance. Better azimuth resolution can be achieved by increasing the antenna length.

76. For unimodal distribution of moderate skewness, the formula; Mean- Mode= 3(Mean-Median) has been used to approximate the relation between the mean, median and mode. Sometimes this relation may be utilized for the calculation of mode. When the distribution is symmetrical, mean, median and mode coincide. In particular, for the normal distribution, mean, median and mode are all equal. In most frequency distributions, it has been observed that the 3 measures of central tendency, viz. mean, median and mode, obey the approximate relation given above, provided the distribution is not very skew. Thus, this is applied to estimate one of them when the values of the other two are known.

77. If the pattern of dots be such as to indicate a straight line path from the upper-left hand corner to the bottom right, correlation is negative, which means, the association is indirect, high values of one variable being associated with low values of the other.

78. Secular trend is the smooth, regular, and long-term movement of time series exhibiting the basic tendency to growth, decline over a period of time. Here sudden or frequent changes do not exist in the trend. The decline in death rate due to medical advancements for quite a number of year, and from that it may be noticed that the figures on a whole show a decrease in the death rate as time passed by.

Seasonal variations are comparatively short-range in nature, whose period does not exceed one year. The fluctuations are found to maintain a definite periodicity, and reappear almost unerringly at regular intervals of time. Examples of seasonal variations are best explained by the passenger traffic during 24 hours of a day or the number of books issued from a library during the 7 days of week, the quarterly production of a factory, etc.

Cyclical fluctuations are a type of periodic movement where the period is more than a year and these fluctuations exist in most business and economic conditions. Recession or depression is a type of business state that can be explained as cyclical fluctuation.

Irregular or Random movements are such variations which are caused by factors due to an erratic nature and are unpredictable or caused by unforeseen events such as war, flood, earthquakes, lockout, etc.

79. There are some situations where sampling does not turn out to be an alternative to census, but is a must; because census is either impossible or useless. There are statements which support this statement. A rice merchant cannot afford to examine every single grain of rice he purchases. He has to depend only on a sample based on which he forms an idea about the quality of rice. Here, sampling is the only option. Similarly, it is impossible to dig out the whole mine. Hence, sampling also is the only method since only a few ounces of ore by digging is sufficient for chemical analysis.

80. Areal aspects deal with 2-dimensional parameters such as Drainage Density, Stream Length, Stream Length Ratio, Drainage

Texture, Stream Frequency and some others. However, Drainage Texture may be defined as the total number of stream segments of all order in a basin per perimeter of the basin. Drainage Texture depends on the underlying lithology, infiltration capacity, and relief aspect of the terrain and on several natural factors.

81. Also known as Tsangpo in Tibet, the Brahmaputra River is called as 'Yarlung Zangbo Jiangin' in Chinese language. This river is one of the most remarkable navigable waterways of the world. The Brahmaputra river, with a total length of 2900km, passes through Tibet, India, and Bangladesh.

82. All of the above statements given are correct. The northern parts of India have mean temperature below 21 degree C but in the southern parts the temperatures are generally above 20-degree C. This is because of the isotherm of 20-degree C. High pressure of around 1019mb prevails around the north west while pressure of around 1013 mb remains around the southeastern side.

The Rainfall that occurs during this monsoon season all over the country is due to the SW monsoons from the Indian Ocean. As the rainfall first hits the southern tip of the peninsula, Kerala receives rainfall during 1st of June which is the first place of entry into the mainland of India.

83. The effect of the Himalayas and the Western Ghats has a huge impact on the distribution and amount of rainfall. This gives us an idea that the rainfall is mainly orographic in nature.

Moreover, as the first stream of the Bay of Bengal branch of the SW monsoon winds reach Meghalaya, it is here that the orographic effect and the continuous rainfall is mostly observed. Cherrapunji, located at an elevation of 1313m above mean sea level receives an annual rainfall of 1102 cm. Most of the rainfall is received during June to August. Such is the case for Mawsynram which receives a huge amount of rainfall. Both these stations are located on the southern slopes of the Khasi hills at the northern end of a deep valley running from south to north.

84. Bharatmala Pariyojana is a flagship scheme of the Ministry of Road Transport and Highways and all the important and new works under the National Highway Development programme (NHDP) are subsumed within this programme. The Ministry has taken up detailed review of National Highways (NHs) network with a view to develop the road connectivity to border areas, development of coastal roads including road connectivity for non-major ports, improvement in the efficiency of national corridors, development of economic corridors, inter corridors and feeder routes along with integration with Sagarmala, etc., under Bharatmala Pariyojana. The Bharatmala Pariyojana envisages development of about 26,000 km length of economic corridors, which along with Golden Quadrilateral (GQ) and North-South and East-West (NS-EW) Corridors are expected to carry majority of the freight traffic on roads.

85. Out of all these public sector undertakings, The Fertilizer Corporation of India is the first to be incorporated as a PSU in January 1961. It has 4 units: one at Sindri (Jharkhand), Gorakhpur (UP), Talcher (Odisha) and Ramagundam (Telangana). Sindri was in fact the first state owned fertilizer plant.

86. Handloom is one of the sectors in the textile industry; it symbolizes rich heritage and ethos of the Indian culture. Also, the handloom sector provides a large number of employments within the textile industry next only to the powerloom sector. Europe and USA accounts for about two-third of the exports of the Indian Handloom and handicraft products. Thus, the concept of mega cluster as a kind of recognition is brought in so that more benefits can be availed by the handloom sector. Sivasagar in Assam, Varanasi in UP, Murshidabad in West Bengal and Virudhanagar in Tamil Nadu are examples of handloom sector.

87. River basin is the area drained by the main river and its tributaries and is interchangeably used with the term catchment area. Out of the following rivers Krishna river has the largest basin area covering 7.9 per cent of the total area of the country and is closely followed by Brahmaputra with 7.8 per cent of area under its river basin. Interestingly, Brahmaputra despite being 5th in terms of size of river basin and highest in terms of annual water yield and rate of flow, the storage capacity is one of the lowest of all the major rivers.

88. It is the Narmada river, which after travelling around 400 km from its source (western flanks of Amarkantak plateau), when it slopes down Jabalpur it is there when the river cascades into a 15 meter gorge to form the famous Dhuan Dhar Falls.

89. The concept of agro-ecological region is the modified version of agro-climatic region and FAO in 1983 brought out the difference between the two. As agro climatic region is based on the length of growing period of various crops and the bio climatic characteristics, agro-ecological regions is obtained by imposing the soil map over the bio climatic map and on the resultant map, the length of growing period map is incorporated using GIS. Thus, an agro climatic region can have a few agro ecological region.

90. One of the peculiar characteristics of the tropical cyclone which is having a very high damage potential is storm surges. Storm surges are an abnormal rise of sea water due to tropical cyclone and are greatly amplifies where the coastal water is shallow. Water spout is related with tornadoes. Tornadoes occurring over sea suck water up to the base of the mother cloud. The cloud becomes linked with water body and this phenomena is called water spout. Cumulonimbus convection condition refers to the process of the rapid uplifting of clouds by the steep orography of the region leading to the formation of convective clouds extending up to 15 kilometers and hence cumulonimbus clouds. This process is the cause behind cloudbursts. GLOFs are special kind of flood occurring due to the outbursts of the glacial lakes in the upstream region of Himalayas.

91. As per the record of IMD from 1897-2014, the months of October and November jointly has the highest frequency of occurrence of cyclonic storms as well as severe cyclonic storms. Besides, May and June months are also period of higher frequencies of tropical cyclones. January February and March has very low frequency of occurrence of these cyclonic storms.

92. Red soil are the soils which are formed due to the weathering of ancient crystalline and metamorphic rocks. They are mainly found in large parts of Tamil Nadu, Chhattisgarh, Telangana, south-east Maharashtra, parts of Madhya Pradesh, among others. Bihar and Gujarat have the riverine alluvial soils while Assam has both alluvial and lateritic soils.

93. According to the National Forest policy, the minimum desired area which is considered safe for a tropical country like India is 33 per cent where in reality we have currently 21.67 per cent area under forest cover as reported by the State of Forest Report in 2019.

94. Western Disturbances are caused by the westerly jet streams during the winters in the northern hemisphere when there is a high pressure over the Indian region. However in the summers, the ITCZ (low pressure zone) shifts northwards roughly parallel to the 20° - 25° N latitude and following this the moist maritime Tropical air mass rushes in towards ITCZ and subsequently the effect of western disturbance becomes minimal.

95. The largest unit of the Peninsular Plateau region is the Deccan plateau with an expanse of more than 5 lakh sq. km. Karnataka Plateau is a sub-division of the Deccan Plateau, made up of Archaean formations with an average elevation of 600-900 m dissected by numerous rivers originating from Western Ghats. The plateau is further subdivided into Malnad and Maidan which means hill country and rolling plains, respectively.

96. NITI in NITI Aayog stands for National Institute for Transforming India. It was set up in the year 2015 replacing the erstwhile Planning Commission. The Planning Commission was set up by a resolution of the government of India in March 1951.

97. An area reserved by canals, wells, tube wells, tanks etc. for irrigation is known as command area. The irrigation potential created could not be used to its optimum level due to reasons like lack of proper infrastructure for carrying the water from its source to the agricultural fields, lack of proper agricultural system ecologically, lack of awareness, lack of proper maintenance of canal and over irrigation and shortage of water in different parts due to mismanagement. Keeping in view the above problems, the Union Government started Command Area Development programme in 1974-75. This period coincides with the Fifth five-year plan.

98. It was the second five-year plan (1956-196) after having seen the potential I the performance of the manufacturing industries in the first FYP that government announced a comprehensive Industrial Policy resolution on 20th April 1956. Iron and Steel, heavy engineering, lignite projects and fertilizer industries formed the basis of this industrial planning.

99. It was the Eighth Five Year Plan. The Eighth Five-Year Plan (1992-97) was launched immediately after the initiation of structural adjustment policies and macro stabilization policies, which were necessitated by the worsening Balance of Payments positions and the position of inflation during 1990-91.

100. In the year 1968, the Planning Commission set up two Working Groups for studying the regional imbalances. One group was for recommending the criteria for the identification of backward area and the other for recommending the fiscal and financial incentives for starting industries in the backward areas. The committee for specifying the criteria for identification of backward areas was set up under the chairmanship of B.D. Pande and is popularly known as Pande Committee. The other committee for recommending fiscal and financial incentives in the backward areas was set up under the chairmanship of N. Wanchoo and is popularly known as Wanchoo Committee.

Q.1 Which of the following is the consequence or is a resultant action of the divergent movement of the plates?

A. Formation of folded mountains and island arcs

B. No creation of ridge and valley

C. Shallow focus earthquakes

D. No volcanic activity

Q.2 Given below are two statements one is labeled as Assertion (A) and the other is labeled as Reason (R).

Assertion(A)- Continents and ocean basins are in constant motion.

Reason(R)- Harry Hess propounded that there is continuous creation of new crust along the mid-oceanic ridges.

Select the correct answer from options given below:

A. Both (A) and (R) are true and (R) is the correct explanation of (A)

B. Both (A) and (R) are true, but (R) is not the correct explanation of (A)

C. (A) is true, but (R) is false

D. (A) is false, but (R) is true

Q.3 Consider the following statements:-

a) Epeirogenetic movements are also known as tangential forces and these affect larger parts of the continents while orogenetic movements include emergence and submergence.

b) Anticlinorium includes numerous anticlines and synclines and within one anticline while synclinorium includes numerous anticlines and synclines within one syncline.

c) Wave-like bends formed due to horizontal movements are called folds while fault refers to fracture in the crustal rocks.

d) The sudden forces and diastrophic forces are both the same and are also known as destructive forces.

Which of the following options are correct?

A. a and b

B. b and c

C. a and d

D. a, b and c

Q.4 Which of the following climatic conditions are suitable for all types of chemical weathering processes?

A. High temperature and humidity

B. Low temperature and dry conditions

C. High temperature and dry conditions

D. Low temperature and humidity

Q.5 Which of the following theory fall under the historical type of geomorphic theories?

A. Theory of uniformitarianism by James Hutton

B. Geographical cycle by WM Davis

C. Gully erosion and management by Savindra Singh

D. Theories by AE Scheidegger and GH Dury

Q.6 Which of the following theory is formed on the basic premise that the form of hillslope is not directly controlled by slope processes?

A. Slope replacement theory by Penck

B. Slope decline theory of WM Davis

C. Slope evolution theory of A Wood

D. Hillslope cycle theory by LC King

Q.7 Volcanoes such as Virunga, Meru, Stromboli, Etna are found in which of the following volcanic belts?

A. Circum-Pacific Belt

B. Mid-continental belt

C. Mid- Atlantic belt

D. Intra-plate volcanic belt

Q.8 Flat and rolling marshy lands developed in the coastal areas of humid tropics are known as

A. Spit and Hook

B. Tombola

C. Sabkha or salt flats

D. Coastal Wetlands

Q.9 Which of the following options are correct?

A. Earthquakes are caused due to folding and faulting, isostatic equilibrium.

B. Nuee ardente is a glowing cloud of hot gases and ash erupted from a volcano.

C. Pahoehoe lava has high fluidity while aa lava flow has less fluidity.

D. All of the above

Q.10 Match List-I with List-II:

List - I(Earthquakes)	List - II (Year)
a) Valdivia Earthquake	i)1964
b) Alaska Earthquake	ii)1960
c) Indian Ocean earthquake	iii)2011
d)Tohoku Earthquake	iv)2004

A. a- iii b-ii c-i d-iv

B. a-ii b-i c-iv d-iii

C. a-i b-ii c-iii d-iv

D. a-iii b-i c-iv d-ii

Q.11 Match List-I with the List-II and select the correct answer from the code given below:

List - I(Gases)	List - II (Volume)
a) Argon	i) 0.039%
b) CO_2	ii) 0.93%
c) CH_4	iii) 0 - 4%
d) Water Vapour	iv)0.00017%

Code:

A. (a)-(i), (b)-(iii), (c)-(iv), (d)-(iii)

B. (a)-(ii), (b)-(iii), (c)-(iv), (d)-(i)

C. (a)-(ii), (b)-(i), (c)-(iv), (d)-(iii)

D. (a)-(iv), (b)-(iii), (c)-(ii), (d)-(i)

Q.12 Which among the following statements about the temperature and insolation are correct?

(a) Sun's energy is not evenly distributed over the earth.

(b) The temperature of air is the measure of the average potential energy of the atoms and molecules in the air.

(c) Higher temperature means faster average speeds of the atoms and molecules

Codes:

A. (a) only

B. (a) and (b)

C. (b) and (c)

D. (a) and (c)

Q.13 Which among the following statements about heat transfer and atmospheric pressure are correct?

(a) Condensation is a cooling process as it cool downs the area around.

(b) Air pressure drops more rapidly with altitude in a column of cold air.

(c) Warm air aloft tends to exhibit higher pressure than cold air at the same

Altitude

(d) Higher concentration of water vapour increases the density of air column and thus increase the air pressure.

Code:

A. (a) and (b) only

B. (b) and (c) only

C. (a), (b) and (c) only

D. (a), (b), (c) and (d)

Q.14 Which among the following is the resultant wind aloft when Coriolis force is equal in strength and opposite in direction to pressure gradient force?

A. Gradient Wind

B. Geostrophic wind

C. Ekman Spiral

D. Cyclonic wind

Q.15 Given below are two statements. One is labelled as Assertion (A) and the other is labelled as Reason (R).

Assertion (A): For a curved path of wind aloft in a cyclonic system, the pressure gradient force must be greater than Coriolis force.

Reason (R): For a curved path of wind aloft in a high-pressure system, the Coriolis force must be greater than pressure gradient force.

Select the correct answer from options given below:

A. Both (A) and (R) are true and (R) is the correct explanation of (A)

B. Both (A) and (R) are true, but (R) is not the correct explanation of (A)

C. (A) is true, but (R) is false.

D. (A) is false, but (R) is true.

Q.16 Which among the following principal climate groups by Vladimir Koppen was not based on the primary criterion of temperature?

A. B type   **B.** C type   **C.** E type   **D.** A type

Q.17 Read the passage and answer the following questions that follow.

Tropical cyclones are violent storms that originate over oceans in tropical areas and move over to the coastal areas bringing about large scale destruction caused by violent winds, very heavy rainfall and storm surges. This is one of the most devastating natural calamities. They are known as Cyclones in the Indian Ocean, Hurricanes in the Atlantic, Typhoons in the Western Pacific and South China Sea, and Willy-willies in the Western Australia. Tropical cyclones originate and intensify over warm tropical oceAnswer ||| The conditions favourable for

the formation and intensification of tropical storms are: (i) Large sea surface with temperature higher than 27° C; (ii) Presence of the Coriolis force; (iii) Small variations in the vertical wind speed; (iv) A pre-existing weak low-pressure area or low-level-cyclonic circulation; (v) Upper divergence above the sea level system. The energy that intensifies the storm, comes from the condensation process in the towering cumulonimbus clouds, surrounding the centre of the storm. With continuous supply of moisture from the sea, the storm is further strengthened.....The systems developing in the mid and high latitude, beyond the tropics are called the middle latitude or extra tropical cyclones. The passage of front causes abrupt changes in the weather conditions over the area in the middle and high latitudes. Extra tropical cyclones form along the polar front. Initially, the front is stationary. In the northern hemisphere, warm air blows from the south and cold air from the north of the front. When the pressure drops along the front, the warm air moves northwards and the cold air move towards, south setting in motion an anticlockwise cyclonic circulation. The cyclonic circulation leads to a well developed extra tropical cyclone, with a warm front and a cold front There are pockets of warm air or warm sector wedged between the forward and the rear cold air or cold sector. The warm air glides over the cold air and a sequence of clouds appear over the sky ahead of the warm front and cause precipitation.

Which among the following scale of atmospheric phenomena does the mid-latitude cyclone represents?

A. Micro-scale

B. Meso-scale

C. Synoptic Scale

D. Planetary Scale

Q.18 Read the passage and answer the following questions that follow.

Tropical cyclones are violent storms that originate over oceans in tropical areas and move over to the coastal areas bringing about large scale destruction caused by violent winds, very heavy rainfall and storm surges. This is one of the most devastating natural calamities. They are known as Cyclones in the Indian Ocean, Hurricanes in the Atlantic, Typhoons in the Western Pacific and South China Sea, and Willy-willies in the Western Australia. Tropical cyclones originate and intensify over warm tropical oceAnswer ||| The conditions favourable for the formation and intensification of tropical storms are: (i) Large sea surface with temperature higher than 27° C; (ii) Presence of the Coriolis force; (iii) Small variations in the vertical wind speed; (iv) A pre-existing weak low-pressure area or low-level-cyclonic circulation; (v) Upper divergence above the sea level system. The energy that intensifies the storm, comes from the condensation process in the towering cumulonimbus clouds, surrounding the centre of the storm. With continuous supply of moisture from the sea, the storm is further strengthened.....The systems developing in the mid and high latitude, beyond the tropics are called the middle latitude or extra tropical cyclones. The passage of front causes abrupt changes in the weather conditions over the area in the middle and high latitudes. Extra tropical cyclones form along the polar front. Initially, the front is stationary. In the northern hemisphere, warm air blows from the south and cold air from the north of the front. When the pressure drops along the front, the warm air moves northwards and the cold air move towards, south setting in motion an anticlockwise cyclonic

circulation. The cyclonic circulation leads to a well developed extra tropical cyclone, with a warm front and a cold front There are pockets of warm air or warm sector wedged between the forward and the rear cold air or cold sector. The warm air glides over the cold air and a sequence of clouds appear over the sky ahead of the warm front and cause precipitation.

In which of the following latitudes can the extra-tropical cyclones be found generally?

A. 5°N – 5°S   **B.** 15°N – 15°S
C. 35°N – 55°N   **D.** 60°N – 90°N

Q.19 Read the passage and answer the following questions that follow.

Tropical cyclones are violent storms that originate over oceans in tropical areas and move over to the coastal areas bringing about large scale destruction caused by violent winds, very heavy rainfall and storm surges. This is one of the most devastating natural calamities. They are known as Cyclones in the Indian Ocean, Hurricanes in the Atlantic, Typhoons in the Western Pacific and South China Sea, and Willy-willies in the Western Australia. Tropical cyclones originate and intensify over warm tropical oceAnswer ||| The conditions favourable for the formation and intensification of tropical storms are: (i) Large sea surface with temperature higher than 27° C; (ii) Presence of the Coriolis force; (iii) Small variations in the vertical wind speed; (iv) A pre-existing weak low-pressure area or low-level-cyclonic circulation; (v) Upper divergence above the sea level system. The energy that intensifies the storm, comes from the condensation process in the towering cumulonimbus clouds, surrounding the centre of the storm. With continuous supply of moisture from the sea, the storm is further strengthened.....The systems developing in the mid and high latitude, beyond the tropics are called the middle latitude or extra tropical cyclones. The passage of front causes abrupt changes in the weather conditions over the area in the middle and high latitudes. Extra tropical cyclones form along the polar front. Initially, the front is stationary. In the northern hemisphere, warm air blows from the south and cold air from the north of the front. When the pressure drops along the front, the warm air moves northwards and the cold air move towards, south setting in motion an anticlockwise cyclonic circulation. The cyclonic circulation leads to a well developed extra tropical cyclone, with a warm front and a cold front There are pockets of warm air or warm sector wedged between the forward and the rear cold air or cold sector. The warm air glides over the cold air and a sequence of clouds appear over the sky ahead of the warm front and cause precipitation.

Which among the following statements about cyclones is not correct?

A. The temperate cyclone has an anti-clockwise movement of wind in the northern hemisphere.

B. The tropical cyclone in the southern hemisphere has a clockwise movement of wind.

C. Both temperate cyclones and tropical cyclones are large scale atmospheric phenomena originating out of collision of different air mass.

D. The tropical cyclone does not originate close to equator.

Q.20 Read the passage and answer the following questions that follow.

Tropical cyclones are violent storms that originate over oceans in tropical areas and move over to the coastal areas bringing about large scale destruction caused by violent winds, very heavy rainfall and storm surges. This is one of the most devastating natural calamities. They are known as Cyclones in the Indian Ocean, Hurricanes in the Atlantic, Typhoons in the Western Pacific and South China Sea, and Willy-willies in the Western Australia. Tropical cyclones originate and intensify over warm tropical oceAnswer ||| The conditions favourable for the formation and intensification of tropical storms are: (i) Large sea surface with temperature higher than 27° C; (ii) Presence of the Coriolis force; (iii) Small variations in the vertical wind speed; (iv) A pre-existing weak low-pressure area or low-level-cyclonic circulation; (v) Upper divergence above the sea level system. The energy that intensifies the storm, comes from the condensation process in the towering cumulonimbus clouds, surrounding the centre of the storm. With continuous supply of moisture from the sea, the storm is further strengthened.....The systems developing in the mid and high latitude, beyond the tropics are called the middle latitude or extra tropical cyclones. The passage of front causes abrupt changes in the weather conditions over the area in the middle and high latitudes. Extra tropical cyclones form along the polar front. Initially, the front is stationary. In the northern hemisphere, warm air blows from the south and cold air from the north of the front. When the pressure drops along the front, the warm air moves northwards and the cold air move towards, south setting in motion an anticlockwise cyclonic circulation. The cyclonic circulation leads to a well developed extra tropical cyclone, with a warm front and a cold front There are pockets of warm air or warm sector wedged between the forward and the rear cold air or cold sector. The warm air glides over the cold air and a sequence of clouds appear over the sky ahead of the warm front and cause precipitation.

Match List-I with the List-II and select the correct answer from the code given below:

List - I(Stages)	List - II (Characteristics of Temperate Cyclone)
a) Stage 1	i) development of cyclonic flow
b) Stage 2	ii) cyclogenesis
c) Stage 3	iii) Mature stage where pressure around low keeps Dropping down
d) Stage 4	iv) Occlusion

Code:

A. (a)-(i), (b)-(ii), (c)-(iii), (d)-(iv)
B. (a)-(ii), (b)-(i), (c)-(iii), (d)-(iv)
C. (a)-(ii), (b)-(i), (c)-(iv), (d)-(iii)
D. (a)-(iv), (b)-(iii), (c)-(ii), (d)-(i)

Q.21 Read the passage and answer the following questions that follow.

Tropical cyclones are violent storms that originate over oceans in tropical areas and move over to the coastal areas bringing about large scale destruction caused by violent winds, very heavy rainfall and storm surges. This is one of the most devastating natural calamities. They are known as Cyclones in the Indian Ocean, Hurricanes in the Atlantic, Typhoons in the Western Pacific and South China Sea, and Willy-willies in the

Western Australia. Tropical cyclones originate and intensify over warm tropical oceAnswer ||| The conditions favourable for the formation and intensification of tropical storms are: (i) Large sea surface with temperature higher than 27° C; (ii) Presence of the Coriolis force; (iii) Small variations in the vertical wind speed; (iv) A pre-existing weak low-pressure area or low-level-cyclonic circulation; (v) Upper divergence above the sea level system. The energy that intensifies the storm, comes from the condensation process in the towering cumulonimbus clouds, surrounding the centre of the storm. With continuous supply of moisture from the sea, the storm is further strengthened.....The systems developing in the mid and high latitude, beyond the tropics are called the middle latitude or extra tropical cyclones. The passage of front causes abrupt changes in the weather conditions over the area in the middle and high latitudes. Extra tropical cyclones form along the polar front. Initially, the front is stationary. In the northern hemisphere, warm air blows from the south and cold air from the north of the front. When the pressure drops along the front, the warm air moves northwards and the cold air move towards, south setting in motion an anticlockwise cyclonic circulation. The cyclonic circulation leads to a well developed extra tropical cyclone, with a warm front and a cold front There are pockets of warm air or warm sector wedged between the forward and the rear cold air or cold sector. The warm air glides over the cold air and a sequence of clouds appear over the sky ahead of the warm front and cause precipitation.

Which of the following names refer to tropical cyclones in the Atlantic?

A. Hurricane
B. Willy – Willies
C. Typhoons
D. Thunderstorms

Q.22 Match the List-I with List-II

List- I(Landforms)	List- II (Location)
a) Aden ridge	(i) coast of the Pacific Northwest region of North America.
b) Explorer ridge	(ii) southeastern coastline of Arabian Sea
c) Gorda ridge	(iii) Near Vancouver Island
d) Juan de Fuca ridge	(iv) coast of Oregon and north California

A. (a)-(ii) (b)-(iii) (c)-(iv) (d)-(i)
B. (a)-(iii) (b)-(ii) (c)-(i) (d)-(iv)
C. (a)-(i) (b)-(ii) (c)-(iii) (d)-(iv)
D. (a)-(iv) (b)-(iii) (c)-(ii) (d)-(i)

Q.23 Which of the following statements relating to ocean salinity is correct?

(a) Red sea has 10% salinity.
(b) Ocean salinity varies from ocean to ocean.
(c) When the sedimentation amount is less and the ocean water mixes with fresh water the salinity will be less.
(d) Salts comprise 1% of the ocean mass.

A. (b) and (c)
B. (a) and (c)
C. (a), (c) and (d)
D. (a),(b), (c) and (d)

Q.24 Which ocean current is the fastest in the world?

A. Oyashio current
B. Kuroshio current
C. Aghullas current
D. Gulf stream

Q.25 Waves in the water is generated due to?

A. Gravitational energy
B. Chemical energy
C. Physical energy
D. Biological energy

Q.26 Consider the following statement about Tides:

1) Tidal flows are helpful in navigation.
2) Tides are helpful in desilting the sediments.
3) Tides are used to generate electrical power.

A. Only 1
B. 1 and 2
C. 2 and 3
D. 1, 2 and 3

Q.27 Given below are two statements. One is labelled as Assertion (A) and the other is labelled as Reason (R).

Assertion (A): Nitrobacter is a nitrifying bacteria.

Reason (R): It helps in converting nitrates in soil to free nitrogen in the atmosphere.

Select the correct answer from options given below:

A. Both (A) and (R) are true and (R) is the correct explanation of (A)
B. Both (A) and (R) are true, but (R) is not the correct explanation of (A)
C. (A) is true, but (R) is false.
D. (A) is false, but (R) is true.

Q.28 Match the Conventions/Treaties/Agreement (List-I) with the characteristic features (List-II)

List- I(Treaty/convention)	List- II (Key Features/Themes)
a) Stockholm Conference	(i) Talanoa Dialogue
b) Stockholm Convention	(ii) Against Persistent Organic Pollutants
c) Kyoto Protocol	(iii) Reduce greenhouse gas emissions
d) COP-23	(iv) creation of UNEP

A. (a)-(ii), (b)-(i), (c)-(iv), (d)-(iii)
B. (a)-(iii), (b)-(iv), (c)-(ii), (d)-(i)
C. (a)-(iv), (b)-(ii), (c)-(iii), (d)-(i)
D. (a)-(iv), (b)-(iii), (c)-(ii), (d)-(i)

Q.29 Which among the following statements relating to the National Environment Policy of India is not correct?

A. It was adopted in the year 2006.
B. The National Environment Policy is a response to India's national commitment to a clean environment.
C. Environmental Impact Assessment (EIA) continues to be the principal methodology for appraising and reviewing new projects.
D. None of the above.

Q.30 Which among the following statements best describes BOD?

A. The amount of O_2 utilized by organisms in water
B. The total amount of O_3 present in water
C. The amount of O_2 utilized by micro-organisms for decomposition

D. All of the above.

Q.31 During the 20th century which nation contributed maximum in the CO_2 emissions?

A. USA **B.** China **C.** India **D.** Russia

Q.32 COMPREHENSION

Read the passage and answer the following questions that follow.

Urbanization is a defining phenomenon of the century and the developing countries are at the focus of this transformation. Cities today are home to more than half of the world's population and the population share is expected to reach 68 per cent till 2050. However the urban shift has happened in the last few decades largely due to rapid mega cities growth in developing countries. The characteristics and the process of urbanization are very different for developed and developing countries....In the developed countries, rural-urban contrasts have all but vanished; around 90 per cent of their people now live in urban areas and the remaining about 10 per cent live in isolated farm houses and hamlets. The majority of those who live in these rural habitations are not engaged in agriculture, for the labour force engaged in farming is only about 5 per cent of the total labour force. Moreover, even the isolated farm houses have all the modern amenities such as piped water supply, telephones, electricity etc. In contrast, the absence of these facilities is common to both urban and rural areas in developing countries like India, Pakistan and Bangladesh...Unplanned expansion of relatively low density urban land use into rural areas, usually alongside the roads is called urban sprawl and is a characteristic feature of mainly cities of developing countries. Slums and squatter settlements are a part of everyday geographies for an urban resident.

As per the 2011 Census, what is the proportion of population who lives in urban areas in India?

A. 26 **B.** 31 **C.** 35 **D.** 41

Q.33 COMPREHENSION

Read the passage and answer the following questions that follow.

Urbanization is a defining phenomenon of the century and the developing countries are at the focus of this transformation. Cities today are home to more than half of the world's population and the population share is expected to reach 68 per cent till 2050. However the urban shift has happened in the last few decades largely due to rapid mega cities growth in developing countries. The characteristics and the process of urbanization are very different for developed and developing countries....In the developed countries, rural-urban contrasts have all but vanished; around 90 per cent of their people now live in urban areas and the remaining about 10 per cent live in isolated farm houses and hamlets. The majority of those who live in these rural habitations are not engaged in agriculture, for the labour force engaged in farming is only about 5 per cent of the total labour force. Moreover, even the isolated farm houses have all the modern amenities such as piped water supply, telephones, electricity etc. In contrast, the absence of these facilities is common to both urban and rural areas in developing countries like India, Pakistan and Bangladesh...Unplanned expansion of relatively low density

urban land use into rural areas, usually alongside the roads is called urban sprawl and is a characteristic feature of mainly cities of developing countries. Slums and squatter settlements are a part of everyday geographies for an urban resident.

Which among the following South Asian countries has the lowest urbanization?

A. India **B.** Sri Lanka
C. Bangladesh **D.** Nepal

Q.34 COMPREHENSION

Read the passage and answer the following questions that follow.

Urbanization is a defining phenomenon of the century and the developing countries are at the focus of this transformation. Cities today are home to more than half of the world's population and the population share is expected to reach 68 per cent till 2050. However the urban shift has happened in the last few decades largely due to rapid mega cities growth in developing countries. The characteristics and the process of urbanization are very different for developed and developing countries....In the developed countries, rural-urban contrasts have all but vanished; around 90 per cent of their people now live in urban areas and the remaining about 10 per cent live in isolated farm houses and hamlets. The majority of those who live in these rural habitations are not engaged in agriculture, for the labour force engaged in farming is only about 5 per cent of the total labour force. Moreover, even the isolated farm houses have all the modern amenities such as piped water supply, telephones, electricity etc. In contrast, the absence of these facilities is common to both urban and rural areas in developing countries like India, Pakistan and Bangladesh...Unplanned expansion of relatively low density urban land use into rural areas, usually alongside the roads is called urban sprawl and is a characteristic feature of mainly cities of developing countries. Slums and squatter settlements are a part of everyday geographies for an urban resident.

What is the term that can be used to substitute the gradation of the ways of life between the rural and urban society, especially in the developed countries?

A. Urbanism
B. Globalization
C. Rural-Urban Continuum
D. Rural-Urban Fringe

Q.35 COMPREHENSION

Read the passage and answer the following questions that follow.

Urbanization is a defining phenomenon of the century and the developing countries are at the focus of this transformation. Cities today are home to more than half of the world's population and the population share is expected to reach 68 per cent till 2050. However the urban shift has happened in the last few decades largely due to rapid mega cities growth in developing countries. The characteristics and the process of urbanization are very different for developed and developing countries....In the developed countries, rural-urban contrasts have all but vanished; around 90 per cent of their people now live in urban areas and the remaining about 10 per cent live in isolated farm houses and hamlets. The majority of those who live in these rural habitations are not engaged in agriculture, for the labour force engaged in farming is only about 5 per cent of the total labour force. Moreover, even the isolated farm houses have all the modern amenities such as piped water supply, telephones, electricity etc. In contrast, the absence of these facilities is common to both urban and rural areas in developing countries like India, Pakistan and Bangladesh...Unplanned expansion of relatively low density urban land use into rural areas, usually alongside the roads is called urban sprawl and is a characteristic feature of mainly cities of developing countries. Slums and squatter settlements are a part of everyday geographies for an urban resident.

Which among the following statements about the urbanization is incorrect?

A. The rate, nature and the process of urbanization in developed countries is different than that of developing countries.

B. The difference between the rural and urban way of life in developed countries, has over the years increased.

C. Urban sprawl, Slums and squatter settlements are generally characteristic features of cities of developing countries.

D. Unplanned cities, exploding population, unemployment and informal nature of urban economy have been the reason behind difference in urban areas of developed and developing countries.

Q.36 COMPREHENSION

Read the passage and answer the following questions that follow.

Urbanization is a defining phenomenon of the century and the developing countries are at the focus of this transformation. Cities today are home to more than half of the world's population and the population share is expected to reach 68 per cent till 2050. However the urban shift has happened in the last few decades largely due to rapid mega cities growth in developing countries. The characteristics and the process of urbanization are very different for developed and developing countries....In the developed countries, rural-urban contrasts have all but vanished; around 90 per cent of their people now live in urban areas and the remaining about 10 per cent live in isolated farm houses and hamlets. The majority of those who live in these rural habitations are not engaged in agriculture, for the labour force engaged in farming is only about 5 per cent of the total labour force. Moreover, even the isolated farm houses have all the modern amenities such as piped water supply, telephones, electricity etc. In contrast, the absence of these facilities is common to both urban and rural areas in developing countries like India, Pakistan and Bangladesh...Unplanned expansion of relatively low density urban land use into rural areas, usually alongside the roads is called urban sprawl and is a characteristic feature of mainly cities of developing countries. Slums and squatter settlements are a part of everyday geographies for an urban resident.

Which among the following statements can be inferred from the passage above as incorrect?

A. A Ghetto is always a slum area found only in developing countries.

B. Slums and squatter settlements are very common in developing countries.

C. Complex and formal economies of the West has managed to bridge the fundamental gap between rural and urban way of life

D. The future of the urbanization depends on the developing countries.

Q.37 Given below are two statements on the factor of industrial location. One is labelled as Assertion (A) and the other is labelled as Reason (R).

Assertion(A)- A Green Belt zone around towns is created in order to control urban sprawl and encourage spread of industries.

Reason(R)- The influence of government policy is very important in some types of industries and in some areas.

Select the correct answer from options given below:

A. Both (A) and (R) are true and (R) is the correct explanation of (A)

B. Both (A) and (R) are true, but (R) is not the correct explanation of (A)

C. (A) is true, but (R) is false

D. (A) is false, but (R) is true

Q.38 People engaged in primary activities can be termed as 'red collar workers' because

A. Outdoor work nature

B. Processing and construction purposes

C. Data interpretation and use of new technologies

D. Not tied to resources or market

Q.39 Match List I with the List II and select the correct answer from the code given below:-

List- I(Resoucres)	List- II (Major Source)
a) Coal	(i) China
b) Petroleum	(ii) South Africa
c) Manganese	(iii) Venezuela
d) Tungsten	(iv) USA

A. (a)-(i), (b)-(iii), (c)-(iv), (d)-(ii)

B. (a)-(ii), (b)-(iii), (c)-(iv), (d)-(i)

C. (a)-(i), (b)-(iv), (c)-(iii), (d)-(ii)

D. (a)-(iv), (b)-(iii), (c)-(ii), (d)-(i)

Q.40 Which of the following region of Britain has heavy engineering and metallurgical industries?

A. The Lancashire Region

B. The Belfast Region

C. North-East England

D. Great London Industrial Region

Q.41 Consider the following statements:-

a) Complementarity refers to the presence of goods that can be used in case of another good.

b) Friction of distance depends on the transport and the price of energy and has decreased over time.

c) No interaction will occur if the friction of distance is high.

d) Intervening opportunities tend to be created even if interaction between two locations is present.

Which of the statements are correct?

A. a and c
C. b and c
B. b and d
D. a, b and d

Q.42 In which year, the spatial interaction theory was introduced by Edward Ullman?
A. 1950   **B.** 1952   **C.** 1954   **D.** 1956

Q.43 Which of the following options are correct regarding the functions and activities of WTO?
A. Forum for trade negotiations
B. Managing trade disputes
C. Checking national trade policies and technical assistance to developing countries
D. All of the above

Q.44 Which of the following statements relating to the industrial location are correct?
(a) Industrial location is not dependent upon the government policies.
(b) Many industries are located near water due to their requirement of huge quantities of water.
(c) Harsh climate often discourages establishment of industries.
(d) Availability of labour is important factor for industrial location.
Code:
A. (b) and (c)
C. (a), (c) and (d)
B. (a) and (c)
D. (b), (c) and (d)

Q.45 $T_{ij} = f\left(V_i, W_j, S_{ij}\right)$ is the general formulation for?
A. Transportation Model
B. Behavioral Model
C. Spatial Interaction Model
D. Land Use Model

Q.46 Match List I with the List II and select the correct answer from the code given below:-

List- I(Major industrial regions)	List- II (Core function)
a) Detroit Industrial Region	(i) Iron and steel, food processing
b) Urals industrial Region	(ii) Texoles and light industries
c) Thanjin and Beijing	(iii) Heavy and metalluryical industries
d) Xi Jiang Industrial Region	(iv) Automobile industry

A. (a)-(i), (b)-(iii), (c)-(iv), (d)-(ii)
B. (a)-(ii), (b)-(iii), (c)-(iv), (d)-(i)
C. (a)-(i), (b)-(iv), (c)-(iii), (d)-(ii)
D. (a)-(iv), (b)-(iii), (c)-(ii), (d)-(i)

Q.47 Consider the following statements:-
a) Weaver calculated deviation of the real percentage of crops for all the possible combinations.
b) According to Weaver, for the determination of minimum deviation, the S.D. method used was $\dfrac{\sqrt{\sum d2}}{n}$

c) Doi's technique was a modification of the weaver's and the formula used calculating crop combination pattern is $(\sum d)3$.
d) Rafiullah's maximum positive deviation method is more accurate, objective and scientific.
Which of the following options is correct?
A. a and c
C. a, b and c
B. b and c
D. a, b and d

Q.48 Which of the following option represent correct sequence of the Von Thunen's agricultural land use model?
A. Central Market, Market Gardening, Livestock farming, Crop farming with fallow
B. Central Market, Market Gardening, Crop farming with fallow, Livestock farming
C. Crop farming with fallow, Central Market, Livestock farming, Market Gardening
D. Crop farming with fallow, Livestock farming, Central Market, Market Gardening

Q.49 Given below are two statements on agricultural systems. One is labeled as Assertion (A) and the other is labeled as Reason (R).
Assertion(A)- Intensive subsistence agriculture is dominated by paddy and practiced in the monsoon lands of Asia.
Reason(R)- Much hand labour is entailed in paddy cultivation.
Select the correct answer from options given below:
A. Both (A) and (R) are true and (R) is the correct explanation of (A)
B. Both (A) and (R) are true, but (R) is not the correct explanation of (A)
C. (A) is true, but (R) is false
D. (A) is false, but (R) is true

Q.50 Truck Farming is another name for
A. Mixed Farming
B. Market gardening and Horticulture
C. Commercial Diary Agriculture
D. Intensive Subsidence Agriculture

Q.51 Which of the following statement is incorrect regarding the Perrouxian view of regional imbalance?
A. Growth appear everywhere at the same time
B. It grows in points or poles of growth with a variable levels
C. It spreads by different channels and affects the economy as a whole.
D. None of the above

Q.52 Who among the following coined the term cultural ecology?
A. Julian Steward
C. H.H. Barrows
B. Eric Wolf
D. Richard Hartshorne

Q.53 Given below are two statements. One is labelled as Assertion (A) and the other is labelled as Reason (R).
Assertion (A): The subfield of political ecology came up as a response to the growing criticism of cultural ecology.
Reason (R): Cultural ecology fell short of tools in 1990s to provide political contextualization in its explanation for the larger processes of change in the marginalized societies.

Select the correct answer from options given below:

A. Both (A) and (R) are true and (R) is the correct explanation of (A)

B. Both (A) and (R) are true, but (R) is not the correct explanation of (A)

C. (A) is true, but (R) is false.

D. (A) is false, but (R) is true.

Q.54 Who among the following is associated with the Rimland Theory?

A. Spykman

B. Mackinder

C. Raiz

D. Smith

Q.55 Which among the following control the Diego Garcia Island in the Indian Ocean Region?

A. France

B. Germany

C. Australia

D. United Kingdom

Q.56 Who among the following has written the famous book "Political Geography: World-Economy, Nation-State and Locality"?

A. Colin Flint

B. R.J. Johnston

C. Martin Ira Glassner

D. John Agnew

Q.57 Which among the following countries is not a member-state of ASEAN?

A. Philippines

B. China

C. Indonesia

D. Thailand

Q.58 Which among the following type of political boundaries best characterize the boundary between India and Pakistan?

A. Geometric Political Boundary

B. Natural Political Boundary

C. Cultural Political Boundary

D. Superimposed Political boundary

Q.59 Which of the following is NOT a type of cultural heritage?

A. Built Environment

B. Natural Environment

C. Technological development

D. Artifacts

Q.60 Which is the country that shares the most length of common border with India?

A. Pakistan

B. China

C. Bangladesh

D. Nepal

Q.61 Consider the following statements:-

1) It was Thales who considered water to be the prime substance on the Earth.

2) In order to observe the various positions of the planets, Anaximander invented a device known as the astrolabe.

3) Plato is regarded as the father of ethnography.

4) Aristotle was the one to give the concept of a perfect state in the field of political geography.

Which of the following statements are correct?

A. a and c

B. b and d

C. a, b and c

D. a and d

Q.62 Match List I with the List II and select the correct answer from the code given below:-

List I Scholars	List II Contributions
a) Al-Maqdisi	(i) Invention of the term 'chorology"
b) Ibn sina	(ii) Differential coefficient and calculus
c) Bhaskara	(iii) Concept of landscape erosion
d) Strabo	(iv) Division of world in 14 climatic regions

Codes:

A. (a)-(i), (b)-(iii), (c)-(iv), (d)-(ii)

B. (a)-(ii), (b)-(iii), (c)-(iv), (d)-(i)

C. (a)-(i), (b)-(iv), (c)-(iii), (d)-(ii)

D. (a)-(iv), (b)-(iii), (c)-(ii), (d)-(i)

Q.63 Who among the following developed and put forward the concept of mountain sicknesses?

A. Humboldt

B. Ritter

C. Elisee Reclus

D. Miss Semple

Q.64 Which of the following is considered as Ritter's monumental work and explains the Earth as the home of man?

A. Erdkunde

B. Kosmos

C. Geographia Generalis

D. La Terre

Q.65 Which of the following consider as a technique to help in concept of Spatial Tradition?

A. Geology

B. Natural Hazards

C. Geographic Information Systems

D. Paleontology

Q.66 What kinds of assumptions were made in order to achieve the core objectives of quantitative revolution?

A. Man is a rational being

B. Place for normative questions

C. Non-promotion of capitalism

D. Use of language of literature for understanding

Q.67 Among these scholars, who first formalized humanistic approach in Geography?

A. Kirk

B. Yi-Fu Tuan

C. Peet

D. Soja

Q.68 Who described regional geography as the 'study of all the features of a two-dimensional area of interest'?

A. Ritter

B. Varenius

C. Hartshorne

D. Humboldt

Q.69 When was logical positivism further developed by 'Vienna Circle'?

A. 1910

B. 1920

C. 1930

D. 1940

Q.70 Idiographic approach focuses mainly on ?

A. Individual and qualitative data

B. general and quantitative data

C. Both A and B

D. None of the above

Q.71 Bifurcation ratio is

A. Ratio of number of stream segments of the given order to number of segments of next higher order

B. Ratio of number of streams of highest order to the number of streams of lowest order

C. Ratio of number of streams of highest order to the number of streams of the given order

D. Ratio of total number of streams to number of streams of given order

Q.72 Which of the following statements relating to the ordering of streams are correct?

(a) The number of streams increases as per the increasing stream order.

(b) The count of stream channel in given order is termed as stream number.

(c) Stream frequency is the sum of all stream segments of all orders per unit area.

(d) When the bed rock is permeable, more number of smaller length streams are produced.

Code:

A. (a) and (c)
B. (b) and (c)
C. (a), (c) and (d)
D. (b), (c) and (d)

Q.73 Time series analysis deals with

A. Time series data
B. Discrete data
C. Continuous Data
D. Stratified Data

Q.74 Which of the following test is a non-parametric test for hypothesis testing?

A. T-test
B. F-test
C. Chi-square test
D. ANOVA

Q.75 Match List-I with the List-II and select the correct answer from the code given below:

List - I (Type of Aerial Photograph)	List -11 (Characteristics)
a) Vertical	(i) Covers Trapezoidal area
b) Low Oblique	(ii) the scale is smaller than 1: 30000
c) Large-scale	(iii) Covers square area
d) Small-scale	(iv) The larger than 1: 15000

Code:

A. (a)-(i), (b)-(iii), (c)-(iv), (d)-(ii)
B. (a)-(iii), (b)-(i), (c)-(iv), (d)-(ii)
C. (a)-(i), (b)-(iv), (c)-(iii), (d)-(ii)
D. (a)-(ii) (b)-(i), (c)-(iv), (d)-(iii)

Q.76 Which of the following is NOT a basic component of GPS?

A. GPS satellites
B. GPS receivers
C. Telescope
D. Computer software

Q.77 Which of the following statements relating to the aerial photographs are correct?

(a) Aerial photographs use central projection.

(b) The scale of the aerial photographs is uniform.

(c) Enlargement/ reduction of aerial photographs is easily possible.

(d) Aerial photographs transformed to be used for map view are called as orthophotos.

Code:

A. (a) and (c)
B. (b) and (c)
C. (a), (c) and (d)
D. (b), (c) and (d)

Q.78 The term Choropleth map was introduced by-

A. John Wright
B. John Synder
C. Mark Newman
D. Jess Miller

Q.79 Which of the following statements relating to the Dasymetric maps are correct?

(a) Dasymetric maps were created for representation of population data.

(b) A Dasymetric map is modified version of an Isarithmic map.

(c) A wide range of Dasymetric procedures are still under researched.

(d) Zonal boundaries in Dasymetric maps are established for general purposes.

Code:

A. (a) and (c)
B. (b) and (c)
C. (a), (c) and (d)
D. (b), (c) and (d)

Q.80 What kind of river basin shape would exist if the elongation ratio is 0.7-0.8?

A. Elongated
B. Less Elongated
C. Circular
D. Oval

Q.81 Match List-I with the List-II and select the correct answer from the code given below:

List - I (Features)	List - II (Physiographic regions)
a) Karewas	(i) Himachal and Uttarakhand Himalayas
b) Duars	(ii) Kashmir Himalayas
c) Duns	(iii) Darjeeling and Sikkim Himalayas
d) Jhumming	(iv) Arunachal Himalayas

Code:

A. (a)-(iv), (b)-(ii), (c)-(i), (d)-(iii)
B. (a)-(ii), (b)-(iii), (c)-(iv), (d)-(i)
C. (a)-(ii), (b)-(iii), (c)-(i), (d)-(iv)
D. (a)-(iv), (b)-(i), (c)-(ii), (d)-(iii)

Q.82 Who among the following used the 18°C isotherm as a reference line following the Tropic of Cancer roughly for the climatic classification of India?

A. Koppen
B. Thornthwaite
C. L.D. Stamp
D. R.L. Singh

Q.83 Based on the Climatic classification of India by Koppen, Match List-I with the List-II and select the correct answer from the code given below:

List - I (Climate types)	List - II (Regions)
a) Cwg	(i) Arunachal Pradesh
b) Amw	(ii) Kerala

c) E	(iii) Himanchal Pradesh
d) Dfc	(iv) Bihar

Code:
A. (a)-(iv), (b)-(ii), (c)-(iii), (d)-(i)
B. (a)-(ii), (b)-(iii), (c)-(iv), (d)-(i)
C. (a)-(ii), (b)-(iii), (c)-(i), (d)-(iv)
D. (a)-(iv), (b)-(i), (c)-(ii), (d)-(iii)

Q.84 Which among the following statements are correct about the Indian Monsoons?

(a) The monsoon approaches the landmass through Arabian Sea Branch and retreats through Bay of Bengal Branch.

(b) Tamil Nadu remains dry in this season.

(c) The Himalayas also deflect the incoming branch of monsoon into two direction, one towards west up to Punjab Plains and one towards Brahmaputra Valley.

(d) The rainfall in the western coast is mainly frontal rainfall.

Code:
A. (a) and (b) only
B. (b) and (c) only
C. (b), (c) and (d) only
D. (a), (b), (c) and (d)

Q.85 Which among the following statements are correct regarding the state of natural vegetation in India?

(a) The montane forest of India hosts a unique floral community named Sundari

(b) Madhya Pradesh is the state with largest absolute area under forest cover among all states.

(c) Arunachal Pradesh is the state with largest forest cover of all the 8 north-eastern states.

(d) The coniferous forests and the broad-leaved forests are distributed in the country in a proportion of 40 and 60 per cent of total area, respectively.

Code:
A. (a) and (b) only
B. (b) and (c) only
C. (a), (b) and (c) only
D. (b), (c) and (d) only

Q.86 Which among the following statements are correct about the mountain passes of the Himalayan physiography?

(a) Khardung La Pass is the highest motorable pass in the world

(b) Zoji La Pass connects Srinagar and Kargil-Leh region.

(c) Niti Pass is in Himachal Pradesh

(d) Shipki La Pass is in Uttarakhand.

Code:
A. (a) and (b) only
B. (a), (b) and (d) only
C. (a), (b) and (c) only
D. (a), (b), (c) and (d)

Q.87 Where was the first office of Allcargo Logistics located in India?
A. Mumbai
B. Bhubaneshwar
C. Kolkata
D. Noida

Q.88 Which among the following plan came into light after India's independence?
A. Bombay Plan
B. Congress Plan
C. Mahalanobolis Plan
D. Visveswaraya Plan

Q.89 Which among the following districts was not selected for the Hill Area Development programme in its inception?
A. Nilgiri of Tamil Nadu
B. Darjeeling of West Bengal
C. Hilly districts of Arunachal Pradesh
D. Hilly districts of undivided Uttar Pradesh

Q.90 Which among the following major states has the lowest yield in case of food grains in India?
A. Uttar Pradesh
B. Karnataka
C. Maharashtra
D. Haryana

Q.91 Which of the following is the correct sequence of states in terms of HDI ranking from highest to lowest according to the year of 2011?
A. Kerala, Himachal Pradesh, Punjab, Maharashtra
B. Himachal Pradesh, Madhya Pradesh, Uttarakhand, Kerala
C. Kerala, Tamil Nadu, Punjab, Gujarat
D. Maharashtra, Rajasthan, Gujarat, Chhattisgarh.

Q.92 Match List I with the List II and select the correct answer from the code given below:-

List - I (Minerals)	List II (Major Distribution and Production)
a) Magnetite ore	(i) Andra Pradesh
b) Manganese	(ii) Madhya Pradesh
c) Copper	(iii) Maharashtra
d)Mica	(iv) Karnataka

A. (a)-(i), (b)-(iii), (c)-(iv), (d)-(ii)
B. (a)-(ii), (b)-(iii), (c)-(iv), (d)-(i)
C. (a)-(i), (b)-(iv), (c)-(iii), (d)-(ii)
D. (a)-(iv), (b)-(iii), (c)-(ii), (d)-(i)

Q.93 Badland Topography is quite observable near-
A. Chambal river
B. Gandak
C. Godavari
D. Kosi

Q.94 Which among the following port is not situated on the west coast of India?
A. Deen Dayal Port
B. Jawaharlal Nehru Port
C. V.O. Chidambaranar Port
D. New Mangalore Port

Q.95 Under which of the following plan/scheme does the private companies are invited to build roadways and bridges and allowed to collect toll tax?
A. Nagpur Plan
B. Twenty Year Plan
C. The Rural Development Plan
D. Build Operate Transfer (BOT)

Q.96 Which among the following statements are correct about the growth of manufacturing industries in India?

(a) In the first five-year plan, emphasis was given to the agriculture over industries.

(b) Despite this the growth of industrial output was higher than that of the agricultural output.

(c) It led to the emphasis on creation of heavy industries in the second five-year plan.

(d) This is the reason why the share of manufacturing industries to the GDP is the higher than agriculture and service sector.

Code:

A. (a) and (c) only

B. (a) and (b) only

C. (a), (b) and (c) only

D. (a), (b), (c) and (d)

Q.97 In the regimes of the following rivers, which one has the lowest range n variation between the maximum discharge and minimum discharge?

A. Ganga River

B. Brahmaputra River

C. Jhelum River

D. Godavari River

Q.98 Which among the following state is the largest producer of wheat?

A. Madhya Pradesh

B. Haryana

C. Rajasthan

D. Bihar

Q.99 Which among the following states has the lowest cropping intensity?

A. Himachal Pradesh

B. Arunachal Pradesh

C. Sikkim

D. Chhattisgarh

Q.100 Given below are two statements. One is labelled as Assertion (A) and the other is labelled as Reason (R).

Assertion (A): Geologically the khadar soil is the newer alluvium and bhabar soil is the older alluvium.

Reason (R): Khadar soils are found in the lower areas in the valleys closer to the river.

Select the correct answer from options given below:

A. Both (A) and (R) are true and (R) is the correct explanation of (A)

B. Both (A) and (R) are true, but (R) is not the correct explanation of (A)

C. (A) is true, but (R) is false.

D. (A) is false, but (R) is true.

// Smart Answer Sheet //

Correct Percentage of students who answered correctly. **Skipped** Percentage of students who skipped.

Q.	Ans.	Correct / Skipped	Q.	Ans.	Correct / Skipped	Q.	Ans.	Correct / Skipped	Q.	Ans.	Correct / Skipped	Q.	Ans.	Correct / Skipped
1	C	38.24 % / 23.52 %	17	C	14.71 % / 52.94 %	33	B	2.94 % / 41.18 %	49	B	5.88 % / 52.94 %	65	C	35.29 % / 52.95 %
2	A	26.47 % / 50.0 %	18	C	29.41 % / 50.0 %	34	C	17.65 % / 52.94 %	50	B	38.24 % / 52.94 %	66	A	29.41 % / 50.0 %
3	B	17.65 % / 47.06 %	19	C	29.41 % / 29.41 %	35	B	29.41 % / 38.24 %	51	A	38.24 % / 47.05 %	67	B	38.24 % / 52.94 %
4	A	38.24 % / 52.94 %	20	B	29.41 % / 47.06 %	36	A	23.53 % / 50.0 %	52	A	29.41 % / 47.06 %	68	C	23.53 % / 52.94 %
5	B	17.65 % / 50.0 %	21	A	47.06 % / 41.18 %	37	B	5.88 % / 52.94 %	53	A	32.35 % / 52.94 %	69	B	20.59 % / 50.0 %
6	A	20.59 % / 52.94 %	22	A	35.29 % / 52.95 %	38	A	32.35 % / 52.94 %	54	A	44.12 % / 52.94 %	70	A	14.71 % / 52.94 %
7	B	23.53 % / 52.94 %	23	A	35.29 % / 38.24 %	39	D	26.47 % / 52.94 %	55	D	29.41 % / 50.0 %	71	A	32.35 % / 41.18 %
8	D	23.53 % / 50.0 %	24	D	32.35 % / 52.94 %	40	C	2.94 % / 52.94 %	56	A	17.65 % / 52.94 %	72	B	8.82 % / 47.06 %
9	D	44.12 % / 52.94 %	25	A	35.29 % / 52.95 %	41	C	2.94 % / 41.18 %	57	B	38.24 % / 52.94 %	73	A	17.65 % / 50.0 %
10	B	29.41 % / 52.94 %	26	D	44.12 % / 52.94 %	42	D	11.76 % / 50.0 %	58	C	29.41 % / 50.0 %	74	C	29.41 % / 52.94 %
11	C	41.18 % / 50.0 %	27	C	5.88 % / 41.18 %	43	D	52.94 % / 47.06 %	59	C	41.18 % / 52.94 %	75	B	29.41 % / 52.94 %
12	D	29.41 % / 50.0 %	28	C	38.24 % / 52.94 %	44	D	44.12 % / 52.94 %	60	C	41.18 % / 47.06 %	76	C	32.35 % / 52.94 %
13	B	5.88 % / 47.06 %	29	D	20.59 % / 41.17 %	45	C	23.53 % / 47.06 %	61	D	8.82 % / 50.0 %	77	C	23.53 % / 50.0 %
14	B	26.47 % / 50.0 %	30	C	14.71 % / 52.94 %	46	D	44.12 % / 50.0 %	62	D	32.35 % / 52.94 %	78	A	26.47 % / 50.0 %
15	B	14.71 % / 50.0 %	31	A	29.41 % / 50.0 %	47	D	32.35 % / 50.0 %	63	A	29.41 % / 52.94 %	79	A	11.76 % / 41.18 %
16	A	26.47 % / 50.0 %	32	B	32.35 % / 50.0 %	48	B	38.24 % / 52.94 %	64	A	47.06 % / 52.94 %	80	B	8.82 % / 50.0 %

Q.	Ans.	Correct / Skipped
81	C	50.0 %
		44.12 %
82	C	17.65 %
		50.0 %
83	A	47.06 %
		52.94 %
84	B	23.53 %
		52.94 %

Q.	Ans.	Correct / Skipped
85	B	20.59 %
		50.0 %
86	A	26.47 %
		50.0 %
87	A	26.47 %
		52.94 %
88	C	35.29 %
		52.95 %

Q.	Ans.	Correct / Skipped
89	C	14.71 %
		52.94 %
90	C	20.59 %
		52.94 %
91	A	14.71 %
		52.94 %
92	D	38.24 %
		52.94 %

Q.	Ans.	Correct / Skipped
93	A	35.29 %
		47.06 %
94	C	38.24 %
		52.94 %
95	D	35.29 %
		52.95 %
96	C	14.71 %
		52.94 %

Q.	Ans.	Correct / Skipped
97	C	8.82 %
		52.94 %
98	A	14.71 %
		50.0 %
99	D	5.88 %
		52.94 %
100	D	5.88 %
		50.0 %

//Hints and Solutions//

1. Divergent movement of plates, which is movement of two plates in opposite directions, is constructive plate margins. They are constructive because there is continuous formation of new crust along the margins because of magma coming up from the rifting of plates along the mid-oceanic plates. However, this type of movement leads to the occurrence of shallow focus earthquakes as there is no collision. Moreover, this results in the creation of new oceanic crusts, formation of submarine mountain ridges and rises, etc.

2. Both the statements are true and the 2nd statement supports the 1st statement. During a survey on the Pacific Ocean's sea floor, Harry Hess propounded that the mid oceanic ridges were situated on the rising thermal convection currents coming up from the mantle. The oceanic crust moves in opposite horizontal directions from the mid oceanic ridges and hence there is continuous upwelling of molten materials along the mid oceanic ridges. Later, these molten lavas cool down and solidify to form new crust along the ends of the divergent plates. Hence, there is continuous creation of new crust along the mid oceanic ridges. In this way, sea floor spreads along the mid oceanic ridges and expanding plate are destroyed. This fact states that the continents and ocean basins are in constant motion.

3. Anticlinorium and synclinorium refer to those folded structures where the numerous anticlines and synclines are within one extensive anticline and syncline respectively. Anticlinorium is formed when the horizontal compressive forces do not work regularly while synclinorium is formed when due to irregular folding consequent upon irregular compressive forces.

Folds are wave-like bends formed in the crustal rocks due to compressive tangential forces due to horizontal movements caused by the endogenetic force originating deep within the earth. Faults are those structures which are created when the crustal rocks are displaced, due to tensional movement that are also caused by endogenetic forces, along a plane.

Epeirogenetic movement includes emergence and submergence of continental landmasses and these vertical movements affect larger parts of the continents while orogenetic movements or horizontal forces and movements are tangential forces which work in two ways which are in opposite directions and towards each other.

Diastrophic forces and sudden forces are called constructive forces. Sudden forces create certain relief features on the earth's surface such as volcanic cones and mountains and extensive lava plateaus due to volcanic eruptions while diastrophic forces affect larger areas of the globe and produce reliefs such as mountains, plateaus, plains, etc. These are the vertical and horizontal movements which are caused due to forces deep within the earth.

4. Chemical changes in the rocks through formation of new compounds, solution or formation of new substances due to change in their weight and volume, is called chemical weathering. Water vapour and water are the media which activate several types of chemical reactions within the rocks. Hence, the rate and intensity of chemical weathering is rapid in areas of high temperature and humidity since the conditions help in the activation of several chemical reactions.

5. Historical theories are generally based on the 'law of evolution' or the 'law of historical succession'. Models of cycle of erosion, denudation chronology, and tectonic theory fall under this category. These theories are not considered as scientific as they are based on singular events. Davis's geographical cycle is considered to be the first attempt for the formulation of theoretical model in geomorphology. This model aimed at the genetic classification and description of landforms on the basis of regional spatial and temporal scales. Hence, this theory stands as a prime example of historical theory.

6. The slope replacement theory by W. Penck is based on the premise that the form of hillslope is dependent on the relative rates of vertical erosion by streams at the slope base and denudation and moreover, the form of hillslope is not directly controlled by slope processes because those act as agents of removal of weathered slope debris downslope. The major role of denudational processes is to expose bare rock slope surface for weathering processes.

7. The volcanoes such as Virunga, Meru , Stromboli and Etna are found in this mid-continental belt. This belt extends from the volcanoes of Alpine mountain chains and the Mediterranean Sea and the volcanoes of the fault zone of Eastern Africa. Here the eruptions are caused due to the collision of Eurasian, African and Indian plates.

8. Flat and marshy lands developed in the coastal areas of humid tropics are known as coastal wetlands. These are depositional landforms produced by wave erosion. No reliefs are present and sea water remains stagnant in these wetlands. Deposited sediments are fine and water is of saline type. Such wetlands are extensively found in the coastal zones of Paschim Banga.

9. Folding and faulting are related to compressional and tensional forces in the rocks and thus cause earthquakes. Examples of this type of earthquakes are the Bihar earthquake of 1934 and the Assam earthquakes of 1950. Moreover, earthquakes are also caused due to isostatic equilibrium. The upper sial of the earth's crust is lighter and floats on the denser sima and whenever this balance is destroyed, earthquakes are formed.

Nuee ardente is a turbulent and fast moving cloud of hot gas and ash erupted from a volcano. They are formed during explosive eruptions and are also known as pyroclastic flows. The term glowing cloud refers to the red and orange colour of lava sometimes visible during an eruption.

Pahoehoe and aa lava flow are Hawaiian terms of lava flow. Pahoehoe lava is less viscous and spreads like thin sheets while aa lava flow is much more viscous. Pahoehoe lava when gets cooled is called as pillow lava.

10. * The earthquake Valdivia happened in May 22nd , 1960 had the highest magnitude.

* The earthquake Alaska earthquake took place on March 27th, 1964 had second highest magnitude.

* The Indian Ocean earthquake occurred on 26th December 2004 ranks third in worlds biggest earthquakes.

* The Tohoku Earthquake took place on 11th March 2011, ranks fourth.

Thus, the Correct answer is B.

11. Amongst these four gases only argon is a permanent gas and the rest of the three gases Methane (CH_4), Carbon dioxide (CO_2) and water vapour (H_2O) are variable gases. Argon is the highest in concentration after Nitrogen and Oxygen in pure dry air with 0.93% by volume. Carbon dioxide though increasing throughout recorded history especially after Industrial revolution is currently 0.039% of the atmosphere by volume and water vapour varies from anything above 0 to 4% of the atmosphere by volume depending upon weather. Methane is present in a very small but significant amount.

12. Sun's energy (incoming solar radiation) is not distributed evenly over the earth, as tropical regions receive more energy than the polar regions and it is this energy imbalance that drives our atmosphere into the dynamic patterns we experience as wind and weather. The temperature of the air is a measure of its average kinetic energy or the average speed (or motion) of the atoms and molecules, where higher temperature corresponds to faster average speeds.

13. Evaporation is a cooling process and condensation is a warming process. During the process of evaporation, the higher-temperature (faster-moving) molecules escape the surface. As a result, the average molecular motion (temperature) of the remaining water is lowered—hence the expression "Evaporation is a cooling process. Condensation, the reverse process, occurs when water vapor changes to the liquid state. During condensation, water-vapor molecules release energy (latent heat of condensation) in an amount equivalent to what was absorbed during evaporation. Cold air invariably indicates dense air and by dense it means more less inter-molecular space and concentration of the molecules near the surface under the influence of gravity. On the other hand a warm, less dense column of air indicates higher average motion of air molecules and thus less concentration of air molecules near the surface. Thus the drop in pressure is steeper for cold air and at higher altitude the cold air has low pressure due to low concentration of air molecules vis-à-vis warm air at the same altitude. And contrary to popular belief higher water vapour content in the atmosphere actually reduces the air density and hence reduces air pressure. It is because the molecular weight of Nitrogen and oxygen are greater than that of water vapour and higher amount of water vapour in the air means the lesser amount of nitrogen and oxygen (displaced by water vapour) and it means humid air having low pressure than dry air.

14. When winds moves horizontally aloft under the influence of Pressure Gradient Force (from high pressure to low pressure), the Coriolis force is the only balancing force. As the wind gains speed, so does the intensity of Coriolis force (right to the direction of the wind) deflecting the wind. Higher the speed, higher is the deflection. This carries on until the pressure gradient force is equal to the Coriolis force and the resultant wind is blowing parallel to the isobars.

15. Occasionally the isobars connect to form roughly circular cells of either high or low pressure. Thus, unlike geostrophic winds that flow along relatively straight paths, winds around cells of high or low pressure follow curved paths in order to parallel the isobars. For curved path of winds aloft in a cyclonic or low-pressure system the Pressure Gradient Force (PGF) has to be greater than Coriolis Force (CF) to balance the Coriolis force and also provide for the centripetal acceleration. Similarly, in case of high-pressure system, the CF has to be greater than the PGF for the inward-directed CF to be able to provide inward acceleration to the outgoing wind. The centripetal acceleration is nothing but the change in direction which is caused by the imbalance between PGF and CF.

16. Vladimir Koppen, a German climatologist gave a scheme for world climate classification. As a tool for presenting the general world pattern of climates, the Köppen classification has been the best-known and most-used system for decades. Köppen believed that the distribution of natural vegetation was the best expression of overall climate. Consequently, the boundaries he chose were largely based on the limits of certain plant associations. Four of these major groups (A, C, D, and E) are defined on the basis of temperature. The fifth, the B group, has precipitation as its primary criterion.

17. The atmospheric phenomena can be categorized into three categories on the basis of the life span and size of the phenomena. They are microscale, mesoscale and macroscale phenomena. The smallest scale of air motion is referred to as microscale circulation. These small, often chaotic winds normally last for seconds or at most minutes. Examples include simple gusts, which hurl debris into the air, downdrafts, and small, well-developed vortices such as dust devils. Mesoscale winds generally last for several minutes and may exist for hours. These middle-size phenomena are usually less than 100 kilometers (62 miles) across. Further, some mesoscale winds. Examples are thunderstorm, tornadoes, local winds and land and sea breeze etc. The macro scale phenomena are divided into synoptic scale and planetary scale. Planetary scale phenomena are the largest in size and include trade winds and westerlies. Synoptic scale phenomena include mid-latitude cyclone, anticyclones, tropical cyclones.

18. The extra tropical cyclones are also known as the mid-latitude cyclones. Owing to its name, the mid-latitude region corresponds to 30° - 60° latitudes on both the hemispheres. Hence the latitudes 35°N - 55°N falls in this latitudinal zone. They are also called temperate cyclones. Below 30° latitudes it is considered low latitudes and above 60° latitudes are termed as higher latitudes.

19. It is the temperate or the extra-tropical cyclone which originates under the influence of creation of fronts between two large air masses of different physical properties. The source region of these air masses are sub-polar and sub-tropical and the mid-latitude area are the zone where both these airmass meet and forms cyclone. Cyclones in northern hemisphere has an anticlockwise movement of wind whereas in the southern hemisphere wind in cyclone moves in clockwise direction. Tropical cyclone originates in the tropical region away from the equator where it gets enough moisture and large pressure variation for a rapid movement of air from high pressure to low pressure. The moisture gives it the energy for the updraft following the convergence after continuously being deflected by Coriolis force.

20. Midlatitude cyclones are low-pressure systems with diameters that often exceed 1000 kilometers (600 miles) and travel from west to east across the middle latitudes in both hemispheres. Lasting from a few days to more than a week, a midlatitude cyclone in the Northern Hemisphere has a counterclockwise circulation pattern with airflow directed inward toward its center. Most midlatitude cyclones have a cold front and a warm front extending from the central area of low pressure. Surface convergence and ascending air initiate cloud development that frequently produces precipitation. The life cycle of a mid latitude cyclone is understood in terms of five or six stages – the first of which is called cyclogenesis, i.e. cyclone formation. In this stage, two air masses of different densities (temperatures) are moving roughly parallel to a front but in opposite directions. Under suitable conditions the frontal surface that separates these two contrasting air masses becomes wave shaped and is usually several hundred kilometers long. In the second stage named development of cyclonic flow/circulation, as a wave evolves, warm air advances poleward to form a warm front, while cold air moves equatorward to form a cold front. This change in the direction of the surface flow is accompanied by a readjustment in the pressure pattern and results in somewhat circular isobars and setting off cyclonic circulation. During the third stage, i.e. mature stage of a midlatitude cyclone, the pressure surrounding the low continues to drop, causing winds to strengthen and frontal weather to develop. Usually, a cold front advances more rapidly than the warm front. In the next stage, as it moves, a cold front begins to overtake (lift) the warm front, as shown in. This process forms an occluded front, which grows in length as the warm sector is displaced aloft. Thus, the horizontal temperature (density) difference that existed between the two contracting air masses is largely eliminated. In the last or fifth stage the cyclone dissipates.

21. Tropical cyclones are violent storms that originate over oceans in tropical areas and move over to the coastal areas bringing about large scale destruction caused by violent winds, very heavy rainfall and storm surges. This is one of the most devastating natural calamities. They are known as Cyclones in the Indian Ocean, Hurricanes in the Atlantic, Typhoons in the Western Pacific and South China Sea, and Willy-willies in the Western Australia.

22. Ridge is that point below the ocean which is the boundary between two diverging plates. It is a chain of mountain ranges below the water having a rift valley formed due to tectonic activities.

Aden Ridge is located in the western coastline of Arabian sea. Explorer ridge is located 150 km west of Vancouver Island. Gorda ridge is located in coast of Oregon and northern California north of Cape Mendocino. Juan de Fuca Ridge is located in coast of the Pacific Northwest region of North America.

Thus, the Correct answer is A.

23. Salinity comprise 3.5% of the total ocean sediments. It is formed by the sediments the water carries while flowing before it gets mixed with water in the ocean. Salinity varies from ocean to ocean. When the sedimentation amount is less and the ocean water mixes with fresh water the salinity will be less. Red sea has 30% salinity, which is the maximum of the average salinity of ocean water.

Thus, the correct answer is A.

24. Gulf stream is the fastest ocean current in the world flowing at a velocity of 2m/s. It is a warm current in the Western North Atlantic Ocean. It Flows through the coast of Florida and then turns eastward off of North Carolina. It is very important current in moderating the temperatures on neighboring countries of north America and Western Europe and northwestern Africa.

Thus, the Correct answer is D

25. The waves in water is generated by gravitational energy. The gravitational wave is a form of wave generated in fluid. Waves of different wavelengths travel at different speed. The waves are created on the surface of the water bodies due to gravity and surface tension. The process of the water due to gravitational forces is called dispersion.

Thus, the Correct answer is A.

26. Tidal flows are of great importance in navigation. Tidal heights are very important, especially harbours near rivers and within estuaries having shallow 'bars' at the entrance, which prevent ships and boats from entering into the harbour. Tides are also helpful in desilting the sediments and in removing polluted water from river estuaries. Tides are used to generate electrical power.

27. Nitrification is the process where the ammonia (after it is converted from nitrogen by nitrogen fixing bacteria) is oxidized into nitrites and nitrates by the nitrifying bacteria. Nitrobacter is a nitrifying bacteria which helps in converting the nitrites into nitrates.

28. The Stockholm conference held in 1972 is one of the first global consensus on the issue of environment. It is officially known as the United Nations Conference on the Human Environment, the result of which the creation of the United Nation Environment Programme (UNEP). In the Earth Summit of 1992 in Rio de Janeiro, an international environment treaty for convention on climate change (UNFCCC) was held and Kyoto Protocol was an extension of the treaty to address the issue of climate change by reducing greenhouse emissions. Stockholm Convention is an international environmental treaty signed in 2001 which aims to eliminate or restrict the use of Persistent Organic Pollutants (POPs). COP-23, or the 23rd Conference of the Parties to the UNFCCC was held in 2017 in Bonn. It was presided by FIJI to discuss ways to make the Paris Agreement operation. It resulted into Talanoa Dialogue.

29. India's National Environment Policy, 2006 seeks to extend the coverage, and fill in gaps that still exist among the environmental management policies like National Forest Policy(1988), National Conservation Strategy and Policy Statement on Environment and Development (1992), Policy Statement on Abatement of Pollution(1992), National Agriculture Policy (2000), National Population Policy (2000) and National Water Policy (2002). It does not displace, but builds on the earlier policies. The National Environment Policy (NEP) is also intended to be a statement of India's commitment to making a positive contribution to international efforts. The is a response to our national commitment to a clean environment, mandated in the Constitution in Articles 48 A and 51 A (g), strengthened by judicial interpretation of Article 21. Environmental Impact

Assessment (EIA) continues to be the principal methodology for appraising and reviewing new projects, and the assessment process are to be made in line with the Govindarajan Committee Recommendations.

30. BOD refers to Biological Oxygen Demand, a concept used to assess the level of pollution in aquatic ecosystem. It essentially means the requirement of dissolved oxygen in the aquatic ecosystem for the bacteria to be able to decompose the organic wastes. Hence, higher BOD refers to low amount of Dissolved Oxygen (DO) in the water.

31. During the 1950s, U.S.A. contributed about 42% of the total world emissions of CO2 and Russia stood 2nd. The situation changed by 1986, as the relative percentage of the contribution of CO2 for the developing countries had increased due the rapid rate of industrialization. But the data from the emissions of CO2 from the burning of fossil fuels revealed that U.S.A. and Russia still were the top contributors of CO2. The per capita emission of CO2 is highest in the U.S.A., but the pattern is changing as total emissions are increasing in China, most of Asia.

32. As per the Census of India 2011, the urban population of India was at 31.16 per cent while in 2001 Census, close to 28 per cent of India's population resided in urban areas. However, this absolute increase of around 90 million urban population in a decade owes much to the migration from rural areas to especially Class I towns and cities.

33. Sri Lanka is one of the least urbanized countries of South Asia as well as the whole world with its urban population amounting to over 18 per cent of the country's total population while in case of Nepal it is around 21 per cent and for India it is around 31 per cent as per Census 2011. Urbanization in Bangladesh is around 35 per cent and is one of the highest in South Asia.

34. Rural Urban Continuum is the concept that explains the phenomenon of the increasing disappearance of the rural urban contrasts in the developed countries. The concept of rural-urban continuum was given by R.E.Pahl in 1966.

35. The difference between the rural and urban way of life among the rural and urban societies in the developed countries has over the years bridged and not increased. It is this continuous gradation of ways of life is called the rural – urban continuum. In general, the phases of urbanization the developing countries go through, to some extent have been experienced by the developed countries as well , but the intensities and the consequences thereof has been very different in developing countries. Thus, today urban sprawl and slums and squatter settlements are generally characteristic features of urban areas of developing countries.

36. A ghetto is not necessarily a slum area; it is a part of the city which is generally populated with the people of a minority group, be it religion, ethnicity or social group, whereas slum is the area where people, in most of the cases do not own or rent up the land they occupy. Despite the fact, the urban economy of the developing countries is supported to a large extent by the services provided by the population living in slums. Every other large towns or cities in India have slum population. However, the formal nature and the complex economy of the West has led to the dissemination of the urban amenities even to the rural

regions and increasingly urbanism as a way of life has gained ground. On the other hand, the developing countries, who were earlier the colonies of the developed West were disadvantageous in terms of resource, planning and technology since their independence. Adding to the woes, the Western model of market, the terms of which were set by the institutions like IMF, WB – product of Bretton Woods Agreement – are the macro level framework which kept the developing countries remain serving as the periphery to the West and thus in the absence of education, the rising population led to unemployment and informal nature of economy; and only available work for the mass led to the flooding of cities with migrants.

37. The reason supports the statement. The government overrules policies to encourage industrial development in certain areas to provide jobs or to open up underdeveloped parts of the country. Similarly the government may use their powers to discourage industrial development in certain areas. They may preserve certain areas as National Parks; keep a Green Belt round towns. A Green Belt zone is often designated around towns so that the town dwellers can reach pleasant countryside and urban sprawl does not engulf the amenity areas. However, these are created by the government whenever the industrial expansion has reached an expansion stage. Here the spread of industries are taken into consideration.

38. People engaged in primary activities are called 'red collar workers' due to the outdoor nature of work. This means that the primary activities are directly dependent on environment and refer to the utilization of Earth's resources such as land, water, vegetation, minerals, etc. It includes hunting and gathering, pastoral activities, fishing, forestry, agriculture, mining, and quarrying.

39. The amount of coal deposited in U.S.A. has been estimated at 1723.4 million tonnes or 34.4 percent of world coal reserves. Anthracite, bituminous and sub-bituminous coal accounts for 1303.1 billion metric tonnes or about 76% of the country's coal reserves.

Venezuela has the largest petroleum reserves of any other country in the world with more than 300 billion barrels of proven reserves.

South Africa is the world's largest producer of manganese, accounting for 33.5% of the world's production. The country has an annual manganese production of 6.2 million tonnes and the major mining centres include the Postmasburg and Kimberly regions.

China accounts for 22% of the world's total tungsten production and is the highest producer.

40. The North-East Region of Britain has heavy engineering and a wide range of metallurgical industries. By virtue of its location on the Northumberland and Durham coalfield, and its proximity to the iron ore of the Cleveland hills, it developed an iron and steel industry, with related marine, mechanical and constructional engineering, shipbuilding, chemical and glass industries. Newcastle on the River Tyne has shipbuilding and transport equipment industries.

41. The Friction of Distance depends on the existing transportation and the price of energy resources. If the

transportation exists in a particular region, the spatial interaction between two regions exists. It is measured in real economic terms such as travel costs and time.

If the friction of distance is great, interaction will not occur even with a complementarity relationship. With distance, the interaction tends to fall. If the friction or some form of obstacle is there, one does not go much far from a spatial distance. However, there is an inverse relation between number of interaction and the distance. Thus, less is the number of interactions with increasing distance.

42. The development of a modern spatial interaction theory was first recognized by Edward Ullman in the year 1956. He proposed a theory on the various forms of interdependence between cities. Ullman identified 3 different parameters for spatial nitration which were complementary, transferability, and intervening opportunity.

43. The functions of WTO that help trade flow in a smooth way and freely comprise all the above activities. However, WTO negotiates any reduction or elimination of obstacles in a trade like import taxes and other barriers. It settles the disputes between the member countries about the application and interpretation of the agreements. It also helps build the capacity of a developing nation and its government officials in the matters of international trade.

44. Water is important in industries like iron and steel, textile, and chemicals. That is why it is important factor in deciding industrial location. Availability of labour is also important for industry to function and is thus a factor of industrial location. Harsh climate is not suitable for many industries and thus a push factor for industries. Government policies are important in order to determine permissions, taxes, and other legal formalities. Thus, it is a factor affecting location if industries.

45. This is the basic formulation of a spatial interaction model. T_{ij} is the interaction between location and origin. V_i are the attributes of location of i. W_j is the attribute of location of j and S_{ij} is the attribute of separation between location of origin(i) and location of destination(j).

46. Located at the western end of Lake Erie is the greatest automobile manufacturing region of U.S.A., centred at Detroit. The city was first a centre of wagon and carriage making which later led to the assembly of the automobiles in the region. It houses several giant motor corporations including Ford, Chrysler, General Motors, etc.

The Urals Industrial Region is well-endowed for heavy and metallurgical industries with many mineral resources at hand. There are rich reserve of copper, iron ore, chromium, nickel, cobalt, manganese, vanadium, lead and zinc.

Tianjin and Beijing industrial region of China has always been a major industrial region. The light industries, textiles and machine making in the Beijing or Peking region, the national capital are important in this region. The presence of coalfields in Shanxi and Hebei has contributed to this development.

The Xi Jiang industrial region of China has a few important industries among which the iron and steel, shipbuilding,

chemicals, brewing, handicrafts, and food processing are the most important.

47. Weaver calculated deviation of the real percentages of crops for all the possible combinations in the component areal units against a theoretical standard. However, the theoretical curve for the standard measurement was like this:- for monoculture- 100% of the total harvested crop land in one crop, then 2 crop combination- 50% in each of the two crops and so on.

For the calculation of minimum deviation, the standard deviation method was used which is S.D.= $\dfrac{\sqrt{\sum d2}}{n}$. Where d is the difference between the actual crop percentages in a given country and the appropriate percentage in the theoretical curve and n is the number of crops in a given combination. The crop combination with the lowest deviation is considered as the optimum combination to be practiced.

In the maximum positive deviation, unlike the standard deviation method, the differences of actual values are calculated from the middle value of the theoretical standard and thus this method also gives the desired critical combination. This method includes lesser number of crops in combination and thus avoids the inclusion of insignificant crops from the combination and has the capacity to handle the highly diversified cropping structures. That is why it is much accurate and provides a sound base for agricultural development and planning.

48. In zone 1, the land near the central market would be used to produce perishable items, principally milk and vegetables i.e., market gardening. These activities would be concentrated in the inner zone due to slowness of transportation and absence of food preserving techniques. Then, the inhabitant of the second zone would specialize in the producing wood, with firewood in much greater demand than lumber. The zones 3,4 and 5 would tend to be devoted mainly to grains and other crops. The distinction among these zones need not be spelled out, except to note that with distance from the city the intensity of cultivation would decrease. This is indicated by the proportion of fallow land- 0 in zone 3, 14% in zone 4 and 33% in zone 5. Lastly, the zone 6 would be the region of livestock faming.

49. Intensive subsistence agriculture is highly developed in and confined to the monsoon lands of Asia. It is found in China, Japan, India, Pakistan, Sri Lanka, etc. There are two types of intensive subsistence agriculture, one is wet paddy cultivation.

However, paddy cultivation required a huge amount of hand labour. Farm implements are often very simple. Animal farming is less developed and farming is very intensive.

50. Truck farming is another name for market gardening and horticulture. The vegetables, fruits and flowers are solely grown for the urban market. It is developed in North-eastern USA and industrial districts of North-western Europe.

51. French economist Perroux to understand the modern process of economic development developed a theory of regional imbalance where he explained that growth does not appear everywhere at the same time. Perroux relied heavily on Schumpeter's theory of economic development. Perroux proposed that once growth emerges in a particular place, it becomes centre of growing economic activities and in their turn

induces growth in the dependent regions. He also explained that process of economic development is unbalanced.

52. The term "cultural ecology" was coined by Julian Steward and popularized in his book *Theory of Culture Change* (1955). He did not provide a concise definition but emphasized that the field was concerned with cultural adaptations to environment and the range of choices available to cultural groups—as opposed to environmental determinism, which he rejected, and which attempts to come up with universal laws of human ecology which did not interest him as much as local adaptations did.

53. Cultural ecology is the study of the relationships between culture and environment. Its goal is to understand the range of cultural adaptations and to offer solutions to a number of important contemporary problems, such as deforestation, loss of species, food scarcity, and climate change etc. Although it is presumed that cultural geography was apolitical, although it was not, it was so because Cultural ecology focused on the process and the material culture per se, and to do so, the research methods employed were empirical-field based and not much on theory like political ecology that dominated the field later. However it fell short of tools to explaining the human-environment interaction in the third world marginalized world serving as periphery to the global cores in the neoliberal era, to which the post-structuralist and post-modernist tools could explain the larger process of change and then came political ecology which whole heartedly embraced social theory and rose to dominance.

54. Nicholas J Spykman, a Dutch-American Political geographer and a Yale Professor gave his theory of Rimland in 1942 in response to Mackinder's Heartland Theory. Spykman accused Heartland of overrating the Heartland to be of immense strategic importance. As per Spykman, landlocked states usually faced security challenges from their immediate neighbours. Island states normally faced potential pressure from other naval powers, but if they are offshore island states (Great Britain and Japan) they could also face security challenges from nearby coastal powers. Offshore island states often approached the latter security challenge by conquering or colonising coastal areas, maintaining coastal buffer states and/or supporting a balance of power between continental powers. States with both land and sea frontiers determined their principal security orientation, which among others include the extent of their sea and land frontiers, and the power potential of their immediate or nearby neighbours.

55. Diego Garcia Island is the largest Island of the Chagos archipelago in the Western Indian Ocean and is currently under the control of United Kingdom. It, along with the whole of Chagos archipelago is considered as the British Indian Ocean Region (BIOR) and is disputed with Mauritius's claim for the whole of the archipelago as theirs.

56. The famous book "Political Geography: World-Economy, Nation-State and Locality" is currently in its 7th edition and is written by Colin J Flint and Peter J Taylor. However, it was first written in 1985 alone by Peter J Taylor and is a sought-after book in the field of Political Geography.

57. ASEAN stands for the Association of South-East Asian Nations and comprises of 10 south-east Asian countries for better

regional, economic, and socio-cultural cooperation and integration and China is not a part of the ASEAN.

58. The boundary between India and Pakistan is best characterized by cultural political boundary as cultural political boundaries mark changes in the cultural landscape, such as boundaries that divide territories according to religion or language. The borders carved modern-day Pakistan were created to give Muslims a territory. The creation of Israel is an example of superimposed boundary while boundary between France and Spain is an example of Natural political boundary as they are divided by Pyrenees Mountains. The boundary between North Korea and South Korea is an example of geometric boundary.

59. Cultural Heritage is an expression of the ways of living developed by a community and passed on from generation to generation, including customs, practices, places, objects, artistic expressions, and values. Cultural Heritage is often expressed as either Intangible or Tangible Cultural Heritage as defined by the ICOMOS, 2002. Built environment, natural environment and artifacts are the three types of cultural heritage.

60. The country of Bangladesh shares most length of common border-4096.7 km. The states that share border with Bangladesh are West Bengal, Assam, Meghalaya, Tripura, and Mizoram. The countries of China, Pakistan and Nepal share the lengths of 3488, 3323 and 1751 km, respectively.

61. Thales of Miletus held the view that water in various states formed the prime substance or material from which all observable features of the Earth were made and also conceived that the Earth was a flat disc floating in water. His most important contribution was that the solution of practical problems of measurement was less of an intellectual success than the rational generalization of specific solutions.

Anaximander invented a Babylonian instrument known as the gnomon which was basically used for the observations regarding the relative positions of the celestial bodies on various seasons and it also was possible to identify the solstice and equinox.

Herodotus is known as the father of ethnography because of his vivid portrayal of the cultural traits of the people strange to the Greeks. He was considered to have brought in the literary tradition.

Aristotle's contribution in the field of political geography is noteworthy. He presented a model of the ideal or perfect state and introduced many ideas such as notions of ideal sizes of population, the locational and morphological problems of the capital city, etc.

62. Al-Maqdisi is known for his preparation of a new climatic map of the world that consisted of 14 climatic regions. He stated that climate varied not only in terms of latitude but also in terms of longitudinal positions.

Avicenna or Ibn Sina contributed the idea of landscape erosion. He put forward a hypothesis on the basis of an observation which explained that mountains were being constantly worn down by streams and other agents and the highest peaks occurred where the rocks were resistant to erosional factors.

Bhaskara or Bhaskaracharya is particularly known for his discovery of the principles of differential coefficient and calculus and its application to astronomical problems and computations.

Strabo, the Roman geographer, was the first who brought in the word 'chorology'. However, the term chorology refers to the description of the visible characteristics of an area. Strabo placed divisions based on natural boundaries such as mountains, rivers, etc. and artificially drew political units. Hence, he was the first to declare geography as a chorological science.

63. Humboldt, during his expedition to the Andes Mountain, observed the influence of altitude on the human body and it was he who explained the feeling of dizziness that resulted from low air pressure. He pointed out that this disease is due to scarcity of oxygen at high altitudes.

64. Erdkunde is Carl Ritter's monumental work which stands for the science of earth in relation to nature and history. In this book he remarks that the earth and its inhabitants share a relationship and one cannot survive without the other. Thus, history and geography are inseparable. Erdkunde, however, gave the core concept of regional geography.

65. The concept behind the Spatial Tradition relates to the in-depth analysis of the particulars of a place such as the distribution of one aspect over an area using various quantitative techniques and tools that might include things like geographic information systems, GPS, Remote Sensing, spatial patterns and analysis, densities, movement and transportation. This tradition encourages the kind of specialization that can help someone to get to research category in a particular topic.

66. The quantitative revolution assumed that man is a rational or economic being who always tries to optimize his profits. This assumption, according to the preachers of quantitative techniques, would help in achieving this subject as a scientific discipline and in the formulation of models and theories. Later this assumption was criticized as in the real world decisions are rarely optimal in the case of maximizing profits. In most of the cases, a man takes decision about the utilization in order to satisfy his desires.

67. The term 'humanistic approach' was used for the 1st time by Yi-Fu Tuan in the year 1976. For him, humanistic geography was a viewpoint that disclosed the complexity and ambiguity of relations between people and place which is man and environment. It was Tuan who argued for humanistic geography.

68. Hartshorne termed the distinction in geography as systematic geography and regional geography. In regional geography he took a two dimensional region and focused on the study of the region. The study involved knowing the world in the region and the region itself. In the systematic approach the study is conducted in a more generalized manner, by case studies of a region but the study is conducted of a phenomenon which is universal.

Thus, the correct answer is C.

69. Positivism is a set of philosophical approach where scientific and logical approaches are applied to social phenomena in order to explain. Positivism is derived by observation, calculation and verification. The concept of positivism was further divided into logical positivism and critical rationalism. Logical positivism was further developed in 1920 by 'Vienna circle'. Critical rationalism was developed by Karl Popper in response to logical positivism.

Thus, the correct answer is B.

70. Idiographic approach focuses mainly on individual person and is majorly qualitative in nature. It's a type of data collection where the data collected id more specific in nature. On the other hand nomothetic approach uses general and quantitative data. The type of data collected in nomothetic approach or method is more general in nature.

Thus, the correct answer is A.

71. The bifurcation ratio is the ratio of the number of stream segments of the given order to the number of segments of next higher order. Horton in the year 1945 considered it as index of relief and dissertation. In areas with reasonable homogeneous geology and no structural disturbances, the mean bifurcation ratio is between 3.0 and 5.0.

72. The count of stream channel in given order is stream number. When the bed rock for the streams is permeable, the longer streams are formed. Less permeable bed rock leads to formation of smaller length streams. The stream frequency is the sum of all streams of all order per the unit area. It is, sometimes a tool used for initiation of erosional processes in an area. The number of streams decreases as per the increasing stream order.

73. Time series data means that data is in a series of particular time periods or intervals. The time series analysis is a statistical technique which deals with time series data. The time series data are of three types. These are time-series data, pooled data, and cross-sectional data.

74. The non-parametric tests are distribution free tests. The t-test, f-test and ANOVA are all parametric tests. But the chi-square test is a non-parametric test. Other examples of non-parametric tests include Kruskal-Wallis test, spearman's rank correlation, sign test, etc.

75. In a vertical aerial photograph, the area captured is square in shape. The trapezoidal area is covered in low or high oblique aerial photographs. The large-scale photograph has a scale larger than 1:15000 and small-scale one has smaller than 1:30000

76. Global Positioning System is a used for determining geographical location. It was first developed for defense use but then later distributed to civilians, too. The three main components of GPS are the GPS satellites, GPS receivers and computer software required to decode the signals. Computer hardware is not one of the three basic components of GPS.

77. The aerial photographs use central projection and do not have uniform scale. It is easily possible to reduce or enlarge them without damaging their quality. Aerial photographs need to be transformed into planimetric view in order to be used for map view. These transformed photographs are called as orthophotos.

78. In his book "Problems in Population Mapping", John Kirtland Wright introduced the term choropleth map. The earliest known Choropleth map was created by Baron Pierre Dupin in the year 1826.

79. The Dasymetric maps are a modified version of a Choropleth map, although they lie somewhere between Choropleth and Isarithmic map. They were primarily created to show population data. A wide range of procedures used for creation of Dasymetric maps are still under researched. The zonal boundaries in Dasymetric maps are based on sharp changes in statistical surface.

80. The Shape of the basin would be less elongated if the elongation ratio is 0.7-0.8. Elongation ratio (Re) refers to as the ratio of diameter of a circle of the same area as the basin to the maximum basin length. The value of Re varies from 0 to unity or 1.0. Thus, higher the value of elongation ratio, more circular will be the shape of the basin.

81. Karewas are the thick glacial deposits of clay and other materials which moves with moraines and are very helpful in cultivation of Saffron in the Kashmir Himalayas. Duns and Duars are the lacustrine plains in the valley area of between two Himalayan ranges; They are called Duns in the Western Himalayas like Dehradun, Kotli Dun etc. and they are called Duar in the eastern Himalayas especially in the Darjeeling and Sikkim Himalayas, for instance Alipurduar. Jhumming is the practice of shifting cultivation in the region of Arunachal Himalayas and the Eastern hills and Mountains as the mode of cultivation.

82. Lawrence Dudley Stamp, a British regional geographer prepared a climatic classification of India based on 18°C isotherm roughly following the Tropic of Cancer for the month of January. The north of this isotherm, according him had a continental climate while the south of this isotherm represents tropical climate.

83. Koppen has suggested five major types of climate which correspond with five principal vegetation groups namely A (Tropical wet), B (Dry climate where there is excess of evaporation over precipitation), C (Mid-Latitude rainy climate with mild winters), D (Mid-Latitude rainy climate with severe winters) and E (Polar Climate). Small letters w and s represented dry season in summer and winters respectively, f represented no dry season, m represented monsoon type climate having short dry season, c represented cool summers and g represented Ganges type climate (hottest month before summer solstice and summer rainy season). Thus, Bihar falls in Cwg category. Arunachal Pradesh have Rainy climate with no dry season and has cool summers. Himachal Pradesh gets placed under E type i.e. Polar climate and Kerala has Amw type climate with Tropical wet monsoon type climate with short dry season, that too in winter.

84. The monsoon approaching the Indian landmass comes from two distinct branches, i.e. the Arabian Sea Branch and the Bay of Bengal Branch. The Arabian Sea Branch or the S.W. Monsoon hits the Western Ghats and causes orographic rainfall and not frontal rainfall. The Bay of Bengal Branch monsoon after being deflected towards the Indian landmass by the Arakan mountains strikes the Himalayas after crossing West Bengal and gets deflected towards both east and west. In the whole process, Tamil Nadu, being a rain-shadow region does not receive rainfall.

85. The plant species of Sundari are endemic to the Sundarbans and Sundarbans is also named after this species. Madhya Pradesh is the state with largest forest cover followed by Arunachal Pradesh. On the basis of composition, the natural vegetation in India can be divided into two categories: broad leaved and coniferous. The coniferous forests are restricted to the Himalayan region and accounts for around 5 per cent of the total forest area while broad leaved forests comprises 95 per cent of the forest cover.

86. Khardung La Pass is situated at an altitude of 5602 m near Leh in the Union Territory of Ladakh. It is also the highest motorable pass/road in the world. Zoji La Pass connects Srinagar on one side and Leh and Kargil on the other side. Niti Pass is situated across Greater Himalayas in Uttarakhand and provides a link to join Uttarakhand and Tibet while Shipki La Pass provides a road connection between Himachal Pradesh and Tibet.

87. Allcargo logistics was found in the year 1993 and its very first office was located in Mumbai. It offers multimodal transportation services making itself one of the top 10 logistics company. It offers various range of multi modal transport services. It includes less container loads, non vessel operating common carrier and full load container.

Thus, the Correct answer is A.

88. The second five year plan is also known as the Mahalanobolis Plan. It emphasized on heavy industrialization. Visvesvraya Plan came in 1934 and stressed on 10-year plan. Bombay plan was drawn by few influential business persons and industrialists as the roadmap to Indian planning and development in 1944. Congress Plan is also known as National Planning Committee which was drawn as early as 1938.

89. The Hill Area Development Programme was initiated in the Fifth Five Year Plan and that time chose 15 districts as the target area. It included all the hilly districts of Uttar Pradesh (now Uttarakhand), Mikir Hill and North Cachar Hills of Assam, Darjeeling district of West Bengal and Nilgiri district of Tamil Nadu.

90. Yield is the concept to determine the productivity of a region in terms of any crop. It is computed by the total production divided by total area cropped. As per the latest Agricultural Statistics of all the major states in India, Punjab (4656 kg/hectare) has the highest yield closely followed by Haryana (3979 kg/hectare). Maharashtra has the lowest yield of food grains in India among the major states with 1136 kg/hectare.

91. According to the Economic Survey 2011-12, Kerala is the most prosperous state of India with respect to HDI and ranks 1st among the other states. This state can compete with some of the advanced countries of the world in terms of human development. Himachal Pradesh ranks 3rd, Punjab with a rank of 5th and Maharashtra with a rank of 7th in terms of HDI. HDI depends on certain indicators such as life expectancy at birth, general literacy rate, real GDP per capita and Purchasing power parity.

92. Magnetite ore, the 2nd best ore right after Hematite ore, is found in most of the reserves of Karnataka. It has a metallic content varying from 60-70%.

Manganese is an important mineral which is used for making iron and steel. However, among the major manganese producing states, Maharashtra stood 1st.

Copper is produced by a number of states. During 2011-12 and onwards, Madhya Pradesh has become the largest producer of copper surpassing Karnataka, Rajasthan, and other states.

Andhra Pradesh is the largest mica producing state, followed by Rajasthan and Jharkhand.

93. Badland Topography can be observed near the Chambal river valley as the river flows below its banks because of severe erosion. This is caused by very poor rainfall and hence numerous deep ravines form on the Chambal Valley leading to Badland topography. This kind of topography generally develops in arid to semi arid areas where the bedrock is poorly cemented. The Chambal river is a part of the Ganga River system.

94. V.O. Chidambaranar Port is the name of the Tuticorin Port in the south-eastern part of India in the Gulf of Mannar region. Deendayal Port is the other name of the erstwhile Kandla Port in Gujarat. Jawaharlal Nehru port is also known as the Nava Sheva Port in Mumbai. New Mangalore Port is in Karnataka which is also the deepest inner harbor on the west coast.

95. Build Operate Transfer (BOT) is a scheme under which the private players are invited to construct roads and bridges and are thus allowed to collect toll tax from the vehicles using those facilities for a specific period of time. After that period, the constructions are transferred to the government for public use. The National Highways Act has been amended to facilitate private investment in real construction under BOT scheme.

96. In the first five year, the main thrust area was on agriculture as the country was facing shortage of food grains. Hence the first five-year plan gave special emphasis on agriculture. No new industries were developed and existing ones were maintained and operated efficiently. Still the growth in manufacturing sector was more than that of growth in agriculture bringing into light the potential of the manufacturing sector and thus it led to the second FYP emphasizing heavily on industrialization. But before the country could thrive on the manufacturing sector, India jumped towards the service sector with the advent of IT revolution.

97. River regime is the seasonal fluctuation in the volume of water in a river. The regimes of the Himalayan rivers are both monsoonal as well as glacial, while that of the peninsular rivers has monsoonal regime. The mean maximum discharge of the Ganga at the Farakka Barrage is about 45000 cubic feets per second while the mean minimum is only 1300 cusecs making it one of the major rivers with such great range in variation of discharge/flow. On the other hand, river Jhelum has overall a less voluminous discharge with its mean maximum flow being 600 cusecs and the mean minimum being 50 cusecs.

98. As per the agricultural statistics of 2019, Madhya Pradesh is the third largest wheat producing state after Uttar Pradesh and Punjab. It's share to all India production of wheat is over 15 per cent whereas Uttar Pradesh and Punjab contributes roughly 32 and 18 per cent of the country's wheat production, respectively. Haryana, Rajasthan, and Bihar systematically follow the order after Madhya Pradesh.

99. The intensity of cropping refers to the number of crops raised on field during an agricultural year. It is calculated by dividing the total cropped area divided by net sown area in terms of per centage. As per the agricultural statistics, Chhattisgarh is one of the major states with cropping intensity of 118.7%. Himachal Pradesh and Arunachal Pradesh has 130% and 179% respectively. Foe Sikkim , the cropping intensity is close to 186%.

100. Geologically the alluvial soil can be divided into khadar and bhangar, Khadar being the newer alluvium and the bhangar being the older alluvium. Khadar soils are found in the lower region of the valley which is flooded frequently. Bhabar is the pebbly soils found along the foothills of the Shiwaliks which are part of the alluvial fans formed there.

// Notes //

// Notes //